Trinitarian Theology after Barth

Princeton Theological Monograph Series

K. C. Hanson, Charles M. Collier, D. Christopher Spinks,
and Robin Parry, Series Editors

Recent volumes in the series:

Elaine A. Heath
Naked Faith: The Mystical Theology of Phoebe Palmer

Ryan A. Neal
*Theology as Hope: On the Ground and Implications
of Jürgen Moltmann's Doctrine of Hope*

Jeff B. Pool
*God's Wounds: Hermeneutic of the Christian Symbol of Divine Suffering,
Volume One: Divine Vulnerability and Creation
Volume Two: Evil and Divine Suffering,*

Todd Pokrifka
*Redescribing God: The Roles of Scripture, Tradition, and Reason
in Karl Barth's Doctrines of Divine Unity, Constancy, and Eternity*

David H. Nikkel
Radical Embodiment

William A. Tooman
*Transforming Visions: Transformations of Text, Tradition,
and Theology in Ezekiel*

Christopher L. Fisher
Human Significance in Theology and the Natural Sciences: An Ecumenical Perspective with Reference to Pannenberg, Rahner, and Zizioulas

Myk Habets
The Anointed Son: A Trinitarian Spirit Christology

Trinitarian Theology after Barth

Edited by
MYK HABETS *and* PHILLIP TOLLIDAY

Foreword by John Webster

PICKWICK *Publications* • Eugene, Oregon

TRINITARIAN THEOLOGY AFTER BARTH

Princeton Theological Monograph Series 148

Copyright © 2011 Wipf and Stock. All rights reserved. Except for brief quotations in critical publications or reviews, no part of this book may be reproduced in any manner without prior written permission from the publisher. Write: Permissions, Wipf and Stock Publishers, 199 W. 8th Ave., Suite 3, Eugene, OR 97401.

Pickwick Publications
An Imprint of Wipf and Stock Publishers
199 W. 8th Ave., Suite 3
Eugene, OR 97401

www.wipfandstock.com

ISBN 13: 978-1-60899-490-8

Cataloging-in-Publication data:

Trinitarian theology after Barth / edited by Myk Habets and Phillip Tolliday; foreword by John B. Webster.

Princeton Theological Monograph Series 148

xviii + 400 p. ; 23 cm. Includes bibliographical references and indexes.

ISBN 13: 978-1-60899-490-8

1. Trinity. 2. Barth, Karl, 1886–1968. 3. Holy Spirit. I. Habets, Myk. II. Tolliday, Phillip. III. Webster, J. B. (John Bainbridge), 1955– . IV. Title. V. Series.

BT111.3 T71 2011

Manufactured in the U.S.A.

Contents

List of Contributors / vii

Foreword—John B. Webster / *xi*

Preface—Myk Habets and Phillip Tolliday / *xiii*

Acknowledgments / xvi

Abbreviations / xvii

PART ONE: Theology with Barth

1. The Role of the Holy Spirit in Knowing the Triune God—*Paul D. Molnar* / 3

2. Divine Light: Some Reflections after Barth—*Ivor J. Davidson* / 48

3. The Spatiality of God—*Murray Rae* / 70

4. The Doctrine of the Trinity after Barth: An Attempt to Reconstruct Barth's Doctrine in the Light of His Later Christology—*Bruce L. McCormack* / 87

PART TWO: Theology after Barth

5. Election, Trinity, and the History of Jesus: Reading Barth with Rowan Williams—*Benjamin Myers* / 121

6. Obedience and Subordination in Barth's Trinity—*Phillip Tolliday* / 138

7. *Filioque? Nein*: A Proposal for Coherent Coinherence—*Myk Habets* / 161

8. The Triune Savior of the World—*Andrew Burgess* / 203

9. The Contribution of Karl Barth's Doctrine of Appropriation to a Trinitarian Ecclesiology—*Adam McIntosh* / 221

10 Why Do Humans Die? An Exploration of the Necessity of Death in the Theology of Robert Jenson with Reference to Karl Barth's Discussion of "Ending Time"
—*Andrew Nicol* / 241

11 Prayer, Particularity, and the Subject of Divine Personhood: Who Are Brümmer and Barth Invoking When They Pray?—*John C. McDowell* / 255

PART THREE: Theology beyond Barth

12 The Doctrine of the Trinity—The Major Stumbling Block in Inter-Religious Dialogue? Reflections on the Methodological Function of Theological Concepts
—*Ulrike Link-Wieczorek* / 287

13 Temporality, Triunity, and the Third Article: The Mediatorial Work of the Holy Spirit in Karl Barth's *Church Dogmatics*—*Antony Glading* / 311

14 The Dynamic Stillness of God: Trinitarian Conceptions of Divine Immutability and Impassibility
—*Haydn D. Nelson* / 332

15 Reconciling Normative Tensions in Biomedical Ethics: Constructing an Ethics of Coinherence Informed by the Trinitarian Theology of Karl Barth—*Ashley Moyse* / 355

16 Vestiges of Trinity—*Nicola Hoggard-Creegan* / 377

Subject Index / 393

Author Index / 397

Contributors

ANDREW BURGESS, Vicar of All Saints Anglican Parish, Nelson, New Zealand, and Lecturer in Systematic Theology at Bishopdale Theological College. His publications include *The Ascension in Karl Barth* (Ashgate, 2004).

IVOR J. DAVIDSON, Professor of Systematic and Historical Theology and Head of the School of Divinity at the University of St. Andrews, Scotland. His publications include *Ambrose: De Officiis*, edited with an introduction, translation, and commentary (Oxford University Press, 2002); and numerous other studies in patristics and modern theology. He is a series editor for T. & T. Clark's Studies in Systematic Theology Monograph Series.

ANTONY GLADING, Pastor of Otahuhu Baptist Church, Auckland, New Zealand. He is completing an MTh from Laidlaw-Carey Graduate School with a thesis entitled "The Meaning and Significance of Jesus Christ as the Subject of Election in Karl Barth's Church Dogmatics."

MYK HABETS, Lecturer in Systematic Theology, and Director of the R. J. Thompson Centre for Theological Studies, Carey Baptist College and Graduate School, Auckland, New Zealand. His publications include: *Theosis in the Theology of Thomas Torrance* (Ashgate, 2009), *The Anointed Son* (Pickwick, 2010), and *The Spirit of Truth*, editor (Pickwick, 2010). He is currently working on a series of edited books to do with Calvinism, gender, culture, and the *filioque*.

NICOLA HOGGARD-CREEGAN, Senior Lecturer in Systematic Theology at Laidlaw College and Graduate School, Auckland, New Zealand. She chairs a Local Society Initiative in theology and the natural sciences (TANSA), and writes a column on science and faith issues for the NZ journal *Stimulus*. Her publications include *Evangelicalism and Feminism: Living on the Boundary* (IVP, 2005), with Christine Pohl, and a forthcoming work entitled *Animal Suffering and the Problem of Evil* (Macmillan).

ULRIKE LINK-WIECZOREK, Professor of Systematic Theology, Institute of Evangelical Theology and Religious Education, Carl von Ossietzky University, Oldenburg, Germany. Her publications include *Reden von Gott in Afrika und Asien* (1991), *Inkarnation oder Inspiration? Christologische Grundfragen in der Diskussion mit britischer anglikanischer Theologie* (1998), and *Profilierte Ökumene. Bleibend Wichtiges und jetzt Dringliches, FS für Dietrich Ritschl zum 80*, edited with Fernando Enns and Martin Hailer (2009).

BRUCE L. MCCORMACK, Charles Hodge Professor of Systematic Theology, Princeton Theological Seminary, Princeton, NJ. His publications include *Karl Barth's Critically Realistic Dialectical Theology: Its Genesis and Development, 1909–1936* (Clarendon, 1995) and *Orthodox and Modern: Studies in the Theology of Karl Barth* (Baker Academic, 2008).

JOHN C. MCDOWELL, Morpeth Professor of Theology at the University of Newcastle. He is the author of *Hope in Barth's Eschatology* (Ashgate, 2000) and *The Gospel according to Star Wars* (Westminster John Knox, 2007), and the co-editor of *Conversing with Barth* (Ashgate, 2004). He has authored numerous articles on Barth—on the doctrine of election, hope, the theological relation to Brünner, *das nichtige*, and wickedness, natural theology, political agency, and prayer—in academic journals such as *Modern Theology, Scottish Journal of Systematic Theology*, and *International Journal of Theology*. Among other things, he is presently writing two books on Barth—Barth as a conversational theologian, and Barth's account of prayer as shaping political agency.

ADAM MCINTOSH, Minister of the South Ballarat Uniting Church, Victoria, Australia. He has published articles on theology in journals such as *Pacifica* on topics including trinitarian theology, ecclesiology, and theology of human and animal relations.

PAUL D. MOLNAR, Professor of Systematic Theology, Department of Theology and Religious Studies, St. John's University, New York. His publications include numerous articles in professional journals and *Divine Freedom and the Doctrine of the Immanent Trinity: In Dialogue* with *Karl Barth and Contemporary Theology* (T. & T. Clark, 2002); and *Thomas F. Torrance: Theologian of the Trinity* (Ashgate, 2009).

ASHLEY J. MOYSE, PhD student at the University of Newcastle, Australia. His research, under the supervision of John C. McDowell, focuses on the intersection of theology and medicine with particular interest in Karl Barth's theological anthropology. He is also a Sessional Instructor in the Faculty of Science, the University of the Fraser Valley, BC, Canada, where he teaches courses in human anatomy and physiology, applied physiology, and health ethics.

BENJAMIN MYERS, Lecturer in Systematic Theology, Charles Sturt University School of Theology, Sydney, Australia. He is author of *Milton's Theology of Freedom* (de Gruyter, 2006), a forthcoming book on the theology of Rowan Williams (T. & T. Clark), and many journal articles on modern theology.

HAYDN D. NELSON, Lecturer in Theological Ethics and Apologetics, Vose Seminary, and Executive Minister, Riverview Church, in Perth, Western Australia. His publications include "A Trinitarian Perspective on the Destiny of the Unevangelised," in *Text and Task: Scripture and Mission*, edited by Michael Parsons (Paternoster, 2006), and *The Problem of the Providence of God: How Can a God outside This World Also Be Present in It?* (Edwin Mellen, 2010).

ANDREW NICOL, PhD student at the University of Otago, Dunedin, New Zealand. His research evaluates the identification and significance of the "God of Israel" in Robert W. Jenson's theology. He was previously Head of Religious Studies at St. Bede's Prep School, East Sussex, England.

MURRAY A. RAE, Associate Professor of Theology at the University of Otago, Dunedin, New Zealand. His publications include *History and Hermeneutics* (T. & T. Clark, 2005), *The Person of Christ*, edited with Stephen R. Holmes (T & T. Clark, 2005), *Kierkegaard's Vision of the Incarnation: By Faith Transformed* (Clarendon Press, 1997), and *The Practice of Theology: A Reader*, edited with Colin E. Gunton and Stephen R. Holmes (SCM, 2001).

PHILLIP TOLLIDAY teaches Anglican Studies and Systematic Theology, St. Barnabas' College, School of Theology, Flinders University. His publications include work on Paul Tillich, Augustine, Jean-Luc Marion, the trinitarian doctrine of God, and philosophical-theological aspects of forgiveness. He has been co-editor of *Dialogue Australasia*, and is currently the series co-editor for volumes on the interface between philosophy and theology, which is a joint project between ATF Press and the Department of Modern Languages and Cultures at Hong Kong University.

JOHN B. WEBSTER, Professor of Systematic Theology, the University of Aberdeen, Scotland. He has written a number of books on Barth, including *Barth's Ethics of Reconciliation* (Cambridge University Press, 1995) and *Barth's Earlier Theology* (T. & T. Clark, 2004).

Foreword

John B. Webster

LIKE THE DOGMATICS IN WHICH IT IS ARGUABLY THE DRIVING FORCE, Barth's doctrine of the Trinity is a magisterial but incomplete achievement. Why magisterial? Partly because of its sheer scale and artistry. Partly because Barth understood very clearly at a critical point in the history of Protestant theology that it is from trinitarian teaching that Christian dogmatics derives not only the entirety of what it has to say about God, but also what it has to say about the relation of God and creatures; others before him in the modern Protestant tradition had let the doctrine of the Trinity loose in this way (Dorner's seriously neglected *System of Christian Doctrine* is a case in point), but Barth did so with consummate skill and sense of occasion. Partly, again, because of the descriptive depth of what Barth has to say. Throughout the *Dogmatics* Barth exercised a capacity for astonished portrayal of the substance of trinitarian teaching—not only in the doctrine of reconciliation, considered by many to be his most satisfying account of God's triune being, but also in the early treatment in I/1 which, despite its stiffness at certain points, contains some of the finest passages of dogmatic writing Barth ever produced. Barth is very far indeed from the flat-footed Latin trinitarian he is sometimes judged to be by those hoping to find in his teaching something more agreeable to social trinitarian sensibilities.

If Barth's trinitarian achievement remains incomplete, it does so, I think, for at least a couple of reasons. One is that, despite powerful countervailing currents in his conception of Christian doctrine, Barth was at some points so committed to the identity of God's being and God's outer works that he risked saying too little about the *opera Dei ad intra*. Precisely where, and to what extent, and for what reasons, and with what benign or malign results, his doctrine of the Trinity is affected by this are matters of contemporary dispute; but that it is so affected is incontrovertible. Second, it should be asked whether Barth's sense of dogmatic proportion and placement may sometimes have been less than secure, with the result that the second article is too expansive and is allotted too many dogmatic tasks. Earlier readers of Barth sometimes worried that Christology swamped anthropology—a concern which may be largely laid to rest when we keep in mind Barth's interest in moral theology. But there are perhaps occasions when, *malgré tout*, Barth concentrated with such loving attention on the temporal mission of the Son that he passed too swiftly over the "whence" of that transitive divine act in the eternal plenitude of God's triune processions. *Perhaps*: only the most delicate reading of Barth, alert both to the scope and the details of his writings and to his peculiar rhetoric and modes of argument, would be adequate to reach a judgment.

Whatever the judgment may be, Barth's trinitarian theology continues to be a commanding presence. The essays which follow, with, after and beyond Barth, testify both to the fact that interpretation of one of Barth's doctrinal convictions is an open matter, and to the seemingly inexhaustible resourcefulness of what he has to say.

Preface

Myk Habets and Phillip Tolliday

COLIN GUNTON ONCE, NOW FAMOUSLY, REMARKED THAT EVERYTHING "looks different when theologized with and through the doctrine of the Trinity."[1] It could also be said that "everything looks different when theologized with and through the theology of Karl Barth." This is, at least in some quarters, a fair assessment of his influence. The most outstanding church thinker of the twentieth century is proving to be the most pivotal theological figure of the twenty-first century as well. It is no wonder some have referred to Karl Barth as a "Father" of the church. Such is the influence of Barth on the theological world. It is this conviction that stands behind the rationale for the present volume.

Karl Barth is acknowledged as the most influential theologian of the modern era. His work has occasioned appreciation, critique, and rejection; and works on aspects of his theology threaten to fill entire libraries. Indeed, the appreciation for Barth and the resurgence of his theology in recent years is remarkable. As just one example note the following comments from Barth's English interpreter (and fan!), Thomas Torrance:

> Karl Barth is the greatest theological genius that has appeared on the scene for centuries. He cannot be appreciated except in the context of the greatest theologians such as Athanasius, Augustine, Anselm, Aquinas, Luther, Calvin, Schleiermacher, Kierkegaard, nor can his thinking be adequately measured except in the context of the whole history of theology and philosophy. Not only does he recapitulate in himself in the most extraordinary way the development of all modern theology since the Reformation, but he towers above it in such a way that he has created a situation in the Church, comparable only to the

1. Gunton, *Father, Son, and Holy Spirit*, 22.

Reformation, in which massive clarification through debate with the theology of the Roman Church can go on. Karl Barth has, in fact, so changed the whole landscape of theology, Evangelical and Roman alike, that the other great theologians of modern times appear in comparison rather like jobbing gardeners.[2]

It is now possible for scholars to deliberately work in the wake of Barth in areas of constructive trinitarian theology. This volume draws together scholars whose essays exhibit work "after Barth" in the doctrine of the Trinity and its related themes. That is not to say each contributor is a "Barthian," whatever such an epithet means. But it is to say that Barth has been encountered along the theological journey and has affected such a journey one way or the other. For some contributors Barth's theology is the mainspring of their academic career and they are amongst the rare few today who may genuinely be considered experts on his theology. To conclude, however, that there is a univocal interpretation of Barth's theology would be a grave mistake. Barth's thought, as evidenced amongst his most expert commentators, allows for a variety of interpretations, the details of which are being hammered out on the pages of academic journals and volumes such as the one you presently hold in your hands. Other contributors may be described as observers of Barth, while others still would accept a stance in critical but appreciative opposition to Barth. It is this variety of responses to and interpretations of Barth's theology that gives such vibrancy to the essays in this volume. This echoes something of the sentiment of William Stacy Johnson, who wrote:

> It should be clear by now that Barth's theology is being read today in provocative new ways by a generation of interpreters who see well the contradiction in trying to recapture the doctrinal propositions of Barthianism without the dynamic movement of revelation in which Barth himself was caught up and in which he placed his hope. If there is to be any future for Barth's theology, therefore, it lies in looking far beyond the theology itself and toward the grace to which Barth was seeking to bear witness.[3]

Barth's influence has been particularly influential in regard to the doctrine of the Trinity. James Packer, for instance, once remarked that

---

2. Torrance, "Introduction," 7.
3. Johnson, "Barth and Beyond," 17.

Barth provided contemporary theology with a "powerful Bible-based restatement of trinitarian theism," before going on to note that "Barth's purpose of being rigorously, radically, and ruthlessly biblical and his demand for interpretation that is theologically coherent, is surely exemplary for us."[4] And he was right of course, but not if by "exemplary" is meant all must follow in his precise footsteps. Such a following would amount to the form of "Barthianism" Barth so famously despised.

Bibliography

Gunton, Colin E. *Father, Son, and Holy Spirit: Toward a Fully Trinitarian Theology.* London: T. & T. Clark, 2003.

Johnson, William Stacy. "Barth and Beyond." *The Christian Century* (May 2, 2001) 16–17.

Packer, James I. "Theism for Our Time." In *God Who Is Rich in Mercy*, edited by Peter T. O'Brien, 1–23. Homebush, Australia: Lancer, 1986.

Torrance, Thomas F. "Introduction." In *Karl Barth, Theology, and Church: Shorter Writings, 1920–1928.* Translated by Louise Pettibone Smith. New York: Harper & Row, 1962.

---

4. Packer, "Theism for Our Time," 10.

Acknowledgements

THANKS TO MYK HABETS FOR CONVENING THE SYMPOSIUM AT WHICH the essays in this collection were first presented, to Laidlaw-Carey Graduate School and the R. J. Thompson Centre for Theological Studies, Carey Baptist College, New Zealand, for hosting the Symposium, and a special thanks to those contributors who travelled so far to meet with us for these few stimulating days. Thank you to Professor John Webster for writing the Foreword to this collection. Special thanks go to Mrs. Odele Habets, who worked tirelessly behind the scenes for the duration of the Symposium, offering hospitality and providing support. Finally, to the staff at Wipf and Stock—especially Christian Amondson, Charlie Collier, Patrick Harrison, Nathan Rhoads, Robin Parry, Kristen Baremen, and Diane Farley—thank you for making the task of academic publishing so efficient and joyful.

Abbreviations

Karl Barth, *Church Dogmatics*, 4 vols. (Edinburgh: T. & T. Clark, 1956–75), and *CD* refers to:

Church Dogmatics vol. I. Part 1. *The Doctrine of the Word of God*, 2nd ed. Translated by G. W. Bromiley. Edited by G. W. Bromiley and T. F. Torrance. Edinburgh: T & T. Clark, 1975.

Church Dogmatics vol. I. Part 2. *The Doctrine of the Word of God*. Translated by G. T. Thompson and H. Knight. Edited by G. W. Bromiley and T. F. Torrance. Edinburgh: T. & T. Clark, 1956.

Church Dogmatics vol. II. Part 1. *The Doctrine of God*. Translated by T. H. L. Parker, et al. Edited by G. W. Bromiley and T. F. Torrance. Edinburgh: T. & T. Clark, 1957.

Church Dogmatics vol. II. Part 2. *The Doctrine of God*. Translated by G. W. Bromiley, et al. Edited by G. W. Broliley and T. F Torrance. Edinburgh: T. & T. Clark, 1957.

Church Dogmatics vol. III. Part 1. *The Doctrine of Creation*. Translated by J. W. Edwards, et al. Edited by G. W. Bromiley and T. F. Torrance. Edinburgh: T. & T. Clark, 1958.

Church Dogmatics vol. III. Part 2. *The Doctrine of Creation*. Translated by H. Knight et al. Edited by G. W. Bromiley and T. F. Torrance. Edinburgh: T. & T. Clark, 1960.

Church Dogmatics vol. III. Part 3. *The Doctrine of Creation*. Translated by G. W. Bromiley and R. J. Ehrlich. Edited by G. W. Bromiley and T. F. Torrance. Edinburgh: T & T. Clark, 1960.

Church Dogmatics vol. III. Part 4. *The Doctrine of Creation.* Translated by A. T. Mackay et al. Edited by G. W. Bromiley and T. F. Torrance. Edinburgh: T. & T. Clark, 1961.

Church Dogmatics vol. IV. Part 1. *The Doctrine of Reconciliation.* Translated by G. W. Bromiley. Edited by G. W. Bromiley and T. F. Torrance. Edinburgh: T. & T. Clark, 1956.

Church Dogmatics vol. IV. Part 2. *The Doctrine of Reconciliation.* Translated by G. W. Bromiley. Edited by G. W. Bromiley and T. F. Torrance. Edinburgh: T. & T. Clark, 1958.

Church Dogmatics vol. IV. Part 3.1. *The Doctrine of Reconciliation.* Translated by G. W. Bromiley. Edited by G. W. Bromiley and T. F. Torrance. Edinburgh: T. & T. Clark, 1961.

Church Dogmatics vol. IV. Part 3.2. *The Doctrine of Reconciliation.* Translated by G. W. Bromiley. Edited by G. W. Bromiley and T. F. Torrance. Edinburgh: T. & T. Clark, 1961.

Church Dogmatics vol. IV. Part 4. *The Doctrine of Reconciliation.* Translated by G. W. Bromiley. Edited by G. W. Bromiley and T. F. Torrance. Edinburgh: T. & T. Clark, 1969.

PART ONE

Theology with Barth

1

The Role of the Holy Spirit in Knowing the Triune God

Paul D. Molnar

IF CONTEMPORARY THEOLOGIANS WERE TO MAKE EXPLICIT THE ROLE of the Holy Spirit in enabling our knowledge of the triune God, then there could be wide agreement that natural theology of whatever stripe is not only unhelpful, but is directly excluded from any serious understanding of theological epistemology. To develop this thesis I will mine the theologies of Karl Barth and Thomas F. Torrance. My aim is to stress why it is crucial to recognize the epistemological relevance of the Holy Spirit in our knowledge of God. In this remark I deliberately follow Torrance who, in agreement with Barth,[1] believes that there can be no epistemology *of* the Spirit because, while the Spirit is active enabling our knowledge of God, that divine action cannot be explained from the human side.[2] My point here is that Torrance maintains that we may only speak of an "epistemological relevance of the Spirit" and not an "epistemology of the Spirit as such" since we cannot attribute actual knowledge of God to ourselves but only to the fact that such knowledge is actually a "freely given participation in [God's own] self-knowledge."[3]

Before developing these ideas let me first explain why I have chosen Barth and Torrance to explicate this theme. My reason is simple. They are excellent examples of contemporary theologians who not only explicitly direct our attention to the role of the Holy Spirit in knowing God, but they allow their own dogmatic thinking to be governed by what

---

1. See esp. *CD* I/2, 244–79, and 201.
2. Torrance, *God and Rationality*, 166.
3. Ibid., 166.

they assert to be true of the Holy Spirit as the enabling condition of such knowledge. While there are some differences between them regarding our natural knowledge of God, those differences, as far as I can tell, never surface in their strict dogmatic considerations. For instance, in his quest for a "new natural theology" Torrance refuses to embrace a traditional natural theology which claims that God can be known outside of faith and apart from revelation. But at the same time he accepts remnants of that old natural theology with the claims that natural knowledge of God can be bracketed from revelation for purposes of clarification and that we find ourselves under an imperious constraint from beyond when we consider the intelligibility of the universe and this suggests some reliable knowledge of God in that experience.[4] Barth certainly would not accept either of these claims since for him there is no true knowledge of God apart from revelation and any claim to knowledge of God based on the intelligibility of the universe could just as easily be knowledge of the devil as knowledge of the triune God. Nonetheless, these claims are seen in Torrance's thought only when he is trying to show the commonality of approaches to reality between theological and natural science. They never appear in his dogmatic work. Since Torrance's dogmatic theology is shaped by his understanding of the Trinity, there is substantial agreement between him and Barth on the role of the Holy Spirit in our knowledge of God, which will help us see why a proper understanding of this matter marginalizes natural theology in the traditional sense and also shows why we can have true knowledge of God only as the Holy Spirit unites us to Christ and through him to the Father.

An Example of a Traditional Natural Theology

Let us begin with a very brief example of the kind of thinking I believe is excluded and avoided when one's theological epistemology takes the Holy Spirit's activity seriously. I cite a book that was very popular in Roman Catholic circles some forty years ago, namely, John Courtney Murray's *The Problem of God*. I am aware that contemporary Thomists likely would not accept his basic premises because they tend to believe that even Thomas's so-called natural theology presented in his five ways was shaped by his faith commitments. That is pretty common fare

---

4. See Molnar, "Natural Theology Revisited."

today.⁵ Whether that interpretation of Thomas is ultimately correct, I will leave to Thomists. I am interested in thinking that still pervades Catholic theology and perhaps not a few Protestant theologians today, with or without explicit reference to Thomas Aquinas. Let me explain that now. More than midway through his book, Murray explains that "we can know that God is but we cannot know what he is."⁶ He explicitly follows Thomas's belief that "our presence to him [God], which is real, is a presence to the unknown: 'to him we are united as to one unknown.'"⁷ Therefore we must negate everything in this world as we know it and then what remains in our minds is only the affirmation "that he is, and nothing more. Hence the mind is in a certain confusion."⁸ The confusion is this: how can we affirm "that God is" while simultaneously claiming that God is not like anything else we know? His answer, according to Murray, is that it is by this very "ignorance" that we are united to God. Murray continues: 'Ignorance of God becomes a true knowledge of him only if it is reached, as Aquinas reached it, at the end of a laborious inquiry that is firmly and flexibly disciplined at every step by the dialectical method of the three ways. This method not only governs the search for the supreme truth but also *guarantees* that the search will end in a discovery."⁹

---

5. See, e.g., Healy, *Thomas Aquinas*, 5ff. While Healy contends that the *Summa Contra Gentiles* "amounts in effect to a demonstration of our need for revelation" (5), this does not explain Thomas's division of knowledge assigning knowledge "that God exists" to natural reason and knowledge that God is triune to our knowledge of God through revelation. Thus "Some truths about God exceed all the ability of the human reason. Such is the truth that God is triune. But there are some truths which the natural reason also is able to reach. Such are that God exists, that He is one, and the like. In fact, such truths about God have been proved demonstratively by the philosophers, guided by the light of the natural reason," *Sc. G.* Book I, ch. 3, 2. Here the question concerns whether or not we know God's *actual* oneness apart from the Holy Spirit empowering us to know the Father through union with his Son. Eugene Rogers in *Thomas Aquinas and Karl Barth* attempts to show that Thomas's theology was grounded in Scripture rather than in an independent natural theology and then attempts to show that Thomas was really closer to Barth than is usually thought when considering the issue of natural theology. See my review of this book (Molnar, "Review").

6. Murray, *Problem of God*, 71.

7. Ibid.

8. Ibid., 72.

9. Ibid., 73, emphasis mine. Murray describes this "first aspect of Thomist thought" as "definitional agnosticism" (73).

Our question is: what exactly is it that can be discovered by a method of negative theology that very clearly has not begun by acknowledging that the only guarantee of true knowledge of God is in reality the Holy Spirit? If this had been Thomas's working assumption, then both he and Murray would have had to admit that no method, not even a dialectical method, could be that guarantee. It is here that the problem of natural theology still rears its ugly head. Let us listen for a few more moments to Murray's reflections. He states that, unlike the "biblical problematic, which came down from heaven in a theophany, the Thomist statement rises up out of the earthly soil of experience."[10] And behind this, Murray says, is Thomas's assurance "that it is within the native powers of the human intelligence, if it be trained in the discipline of philosophy, to make and to demonstrate the highest of metaphysical affirmations—to posit and to prove the judgment that God is; that it is further possible for reason to go on to articulate a complex of what God is not—a conception that, despite its negative form, is of positive cognitive value."[11]

Murray goes on to say that among Protestants this type of natural theology is impossible because a philosophy of religion may be a possibility but "not a philosophy of God."[12] There is, he says, a gulf between what the philosopher recognizes by reason and the notion of God recognized in faith. But if this gulf exists, he says, then philosophers, who "must stand by reason, should also stand for atheism."[13] From this he concludes that "If the universe of reason and the universe of faith do not at any point intersect, it is unreasonable to accept any of the affirmations of faith, even the first, that God is."[14] It is in this context, Murray believes, that Thomas Aquinas set out to demonstrate that "atheism is not the reasonable conclusion from the data of common human experience." And this is the case because while faith and philosophy are distinct, they nonetheless intersect "in the crucial instant when reason affirms, what faith likewise affirms, that God is."[15]

---

10. Ibid., 73–74.
11. Ibid., 74.
12. Ibid.
13. Ibid., 74–75.
14. Ibid., 75.
15. Ibid.

Connecting Reason and Faith without According Primacy to Reason

With the help of Barth and Torrance we can see our way through this maze quite easily and quickly. *First*, for them it is impossible to assert "that God is" without first knowing "who God is" in faith. That means that while there is indeed an intersection of faith and reason in the affirmation "that God is," that point of intersection is not to be found either in human reason or in human experience but rather objectively in Christ and subjectively through his Holy Spirit. *Second*, to separate the questions "that God is" from "what God is" or "who God is" is the first mistake that follows from failing to realize that our knowledge of who or what God is comes positively to meet us in Christ and thus through his Spirit as an act of God. *Third*, for that very reason, one can never discern either "that God is" or "who God is" by negating our experience of ourselves. Both Torrance and Barth are consistently clear about this in their writings. And it is my contention that they are very clear about this because they both explicitly acknowledge, along with Irenaeus, Hilary, and Athanasius, that it is *by God* that God is known.[16] They both explicitly claim our knowledge of God comes to us through a miraculous action of the Holy Spirit uniting us to Christ and through him to the Father. They also realize that as sinners we need to be reconciled to God by God actually to know God accurately.

What if John Courtney Murray had begun his reflections by acknowledging the role that the Holy Spirit plays in our knowledge of God? Then perhaps he could have seen that a proper doctrine of the Trinity would lead us to insist upon the integrity of human reason, but not at the expense of faith's affirmation that God is both immanent and transcendent in his Word and Spirit in such a way that none of this can be explicated apart from faith. In other words human reason cannot simply reach the true God by analyzing or by negating human experience. Thomas F. Torrance captures this situation perfectly when he says that we cannot have precise theological knowledge of God as the almighty creator "in terms of abstract possibilities and vague generalities—from what we imagine God is not, or from examining what God has brought

---

16. Hilary, *De. Trin.* 5.20f., cited in Torrance, *Trinitarian Faith*, 21. This is also a theme that appears in Irenaeus. See Irenaeus, *Adversus haereses*, 4.11 as cited in Torrance, *Christian Doctrine of God*, 13. Athanasius will be cited below.

into being in complete difference from himself."[17] It was the Gnostic Basileides from Alexandria who, relying on Plato's notion that "God is beyond all being," taught that "we cannot say anything about what God is, but can only say something about what he is not."[18] But Torrance insists that Gregory of Nazianzen (*Or.* 28.9) held in opposition to this thinking that "if we cannot say anything positive about what God is, we really cannot say anything accurate about what he is not."[19] As Torrance rightly explains, Nicene theologians refused to speak of God in empty negative conceptions because if we do not think of the Father in his relation to the Son but only as creator in relation to creatures, then we will think of the Son himself as one of the works of the Father. And this will mean that we are then speaking of God "in a way that is not personally grounded in God himself, but in an impersonal way far removed from what he is in himself."[20] Further, if we try to reach knowledge of God from some point outside of God, then there is no point within God "by reference to which we can test or control our conceptions of him" and so we "are inevitably flung back upon ourselves."[21] In this case our God-talk will be arbitrary and grounded in human experience rather than God himself. And this is just what Athanasius accused the Arians of doing. Hilary was also unhappy with such a procedure, arguing that "the action of God must not be canvassed by human faculties; the Creator must not be judged by those who are the work of his hands."[22]

The important point to be made here is that for Torrance we cannot attribute knowledge of God to ourselves since such knowledge is a "freely given participation in [God's] self-knowledge."[23] Consequently, knowledge of God takes place only in obedience to Christ as our minds conform to him. And this can happen, Torrance says, "only as in the Spirit the being and nature of God is brought to bear upon us so that we think under the compulsion of His Reality. That is the activity of

---

17. Torrance, *Trinitarian Faith*, 78.
18. Ibid., 50.
19. Ibid.
20. Ibid.
21. Ibid., 51.
22. Hilary, *Trinity*, Book III, 26, at 70.
23. Torrance, *God and Rationality*, 166.

the Holy Spirit whom Jesus spoke of in this connection as the Spirit of Truth."[24] We will explore Torrance's thinking further later.

For now it is important to note that left to itself, reason will always affirm "that God is" based on a set of experiences that also could be interpreted as pointing to any one of a number of gods or idols or perhaps even the devil as Barth once said.[25] Therefore it will never be compelling as true knowledge of the Christian God. At the end of such a reasoning process, one may not be an atheist formally speaking. But materially, one might just as well be an atheist with regard to that very knowledge as far as Barth was concerned. Barth saw the matter very clearly when he insisted that his starting point for learning "the lofty but simple lesson that it is by God that God is known . . . was neither an axiom of reason nor a datum of experience. In the measure that a doctrine of God draws on these sources, it betrays the fact that its subject is not really God . . ."[26] For Barth, as we shall see, it is the deity of the Holy Spirit which creates faith. That, unfortunately, is precisely what was systematically excluded from John Courtney Murray's reflections.

And to those who might say that contemporary Roman Catholic theology has changed radically in the last forty years such that this example does not speak to us today, I would simply respond that you should read Elizabeth Johnson's recent *Quest for the Living God*.[27] The only difference between her and Murray is that she negates personal experiences of depth in order to attain knowledge of God. Thus she follows Rahner's basic turn to the subject to explain the meaning of Christianity. While claiming that the God she knows is the God of salvation history,[28] her theological method explicitly negates human experience on the assumption that we are basically good and that we therefore participate in the goodness of God so that we actually can know God's goodness by negating the goodness we experience humanly. In her words: "Based on a belief that the created world is fundamentally

---

24. Ibid., 167.

25. Speaking of the relation of science and philosophy to theology in answer to a question about the thinking of Karl Heim, Barth responded "is the presupposition true, that at the end of our thoughts we will always meet God? After all, it may be the devil!" *Karl Barth's Table Talk*, 20.

26. CD II/2, 3. See also Molnar, *Divine Freedom*, 129.

27. See Johnson, *Quest*.

28. Ibid., 210.

good, analogy holds that all creatures participate in some way in the overflowing goodness, truth, and beauty of the One who made them. Therefore, something of the creature's excellence can direct us back to God."[29] Moreover, she explicitly argues both that "no expression for God can be taken literally"[30] and that:

> From our experience of our own self and our interactions with other human beings, we develop an idea of what it means to be a person. Then we attribute this excellence to God. . . . We affirm: yes, God is a person. We negate: no, God is not a person in the finite way we know ourselves to be persons. We counternegate in order to affirm: still, God is a person in a supereminent way as Source of all who are persons. At this point we've lost the literal concept. We don't really understand what it means to attribute personhood to God. But in the very saying, our spirits are guided into a relationship of personal communion with the Holy.[31]

But that is precisely the problem—we may envision ourselves in personal communion with the holy, but that hardly means we have thereby described our relationship with the triune God who alone can unite us to himself precisely through the action of the Holy Spirit uniting us to his Son and thus to the Father. While Johnson claims she is thinking from the economy, she actually assumes that we can know God from our experience of ourselves and that indeed, "If the Trinity is not grounded in the experience of salvation, the triune symbol will remain in the dust, defeated."[32] How can anyone claim that the Trinity is grounded in our experience of salvation without reducing the content of the doctrine to a description of experience? No wonder she thinks that God is *like* a Trinity,[33] and no wonder she espouses an agnosticism that leaves it to us to construct the symbol God according to our social and religious

29. Ibid., 18.
30. Ibid.
31. Ibid., 19.
32. Ibid., 211.

33. See Johnson, *She Who Is*. She writes: "the symbol of the Trinity is not a blueprint of the inner workings of the godhead, not an offering of esoteric information about God. In no sense is it a literal description of God's being *in se*. As the outcome of theological reflection on the Christian experience of relationship to God, it is a symbol that indirectly points to God's relationality. . . . God is *like* a Trinity . . ." (204–5). But isn't the whole point of the doctrine to say that God *is* the Trinity? Grenz recognizes this problem in her thought, *Rediscovering the Triune God*, 181.

agenda. No wonder also that she thinks we can never literally know who God is. There must be many names for God, she claims, because "there is no one such name" since "If human beings were capable of expressing the fullness of God in one straight-as-an-arrow name, the proliferation of names, images, and concepts observable throughout the history of religions would make no sense at all."[34] That is why human beings name God with many names she says. By contrast, Barth and Torrance insist that because God *is* the Trinity, God can and does freely relate with us in the economy in his Word and Spirit and thus can be known only in faith through the Holy Spirit and not by negating any human experience, but by knowing God as *he has named himself* to us in Jesus Christ and through his Holy Spirit. To speak of God as Father, Son, and Spirit refers neither abstractly to relationality nor to some freely chosen object of our experience, but to the one true God alone.

Let me summarize the issue. If reason affirms "that God is" without faith in "who God is" as the eternal Father, Son, and Holy Spirit, then the Holy Spirit, who unites reason and revelation as well as faith and knowledge, has been left out of the epistemology that is then presented. And the crucial question then becomes whether or not the God affirmed by reason is the true God. In this approach to understanding God we will have no genuinely certain knowledge of God because it will always be thought in some way that reason can establish "that God is" without actually knowing "who God is" in faith as this is positively given to us in Christ objectively and through the Spirit subjectively.

Mapping the Terrain

Thomas F. Torrance frequently cited Athanasius' statement that "'It would be more godly and true to signify God from the Son and call him Father, than to name God from his works alone and call him Unoriginate.'"[35] There is a great deal in this statement to be sure. And it is full of ecumenical significance because the truth of that statement rests on the church's confession of the triune God as the source, meaning, and goal of all its knowledge and action. When taken seriously, as both Barth and Torrance did in their theologies, this statement is full of meaning. *First*, this statement rules out any natural theology as a

34. Johnson, *Quest*, 21.
35. See, e.g., Torrance, *Trinitarian Faith*, 49.

way to know God with accuracy. And natural theology is ruled out not on negative grounds but on very positive grounds: it is because God has made himself decisively known and knowable in his Son and by his Spirit and thus by grace and revelation that any other avenue into knowledge of God is recognized in faith to be at variance with the truth. That is, it is at variance with the truth of God's own self-knowledge into which we are drawn by grace through the Holy Spirit. *Second*, it implies, though it is not always stated in so many words, that one can really have true knowledge of God only through a special and miraculous action of the Holy Spirit.

Third, it further implies that all knowledge of God is a kind of obedience; it is thus not simply theoretical and so Barth could never be charged, as he sometimes is, with equating justification and sanctification merely with our knowledge and nothing more.[36] This has far ranging implications for our understanding of how experience relates with doctrine in contemporary theology. The fact that knowledge of God can take place only in obedience illustrates that we are dependent upon the Holy Spirit at every moment really to relate with God and to know God. We cannot and indeed we must not attempt to do away with this neediness for the coming of the Spirit in any area of theology, but this is especially important in a Christian theological epistemology.

Fourth, any claim to have the Holy Spirit and thus to know the triune God would be exposed as problematic if and to the extent that one is not immediately and self-evidently speaking of one's fellowship or communion with Christ himself. This implies that while we, with the full range of our experience, are fully involved in the present prophetic activity of Christ, the light of the world, the validity of our activity can never be traced to anything within that activity as such. Hence, there is no knowledge without experience of God. But, when God is known through God, we immediately know that the *guarantee* of that knowledge is and remains God and not our experience of God. This is why Barth insists that "To have the Holy Spirit is to let God rather than our having God be our confidence."[37] Any attempt to appeal to experience as the guarantee in this matter will always result in some false form of knowledge whether it be pantheistic, panentheistic, dualistic, or idealis-

---

36. See McGrath, "Karl Barth's Doctrine of Justification," 182, 187f.
37. *CD* I/1, 462–65, and I/2, 249.

tic, because it will formulate its understanding without actually relying on the Holy Spirit who alone unites us to Christ and thus to the Father.

Finally, if the Holy Spirit is seen as the enabling factor in our knowledge of God, it will be extremely important to see that what Barth considered one of the hardest problems of Christology, namely, the issue of whether or not Jesus is the revealer in his humanity as such, must be addressed in such a way that revelation has to be seen always as an act of God in the humanity of Jesus which empowers our human being and actions without becoming confused with our self-experience.[38] Barth's insistence that there are no concepts or analogies that are true in themselves follows directly from this christological insight.

Here, I would like to demonstrate that each of these points can be seen working together in the reflections of both Barth and Torrance; in fact each of these points necessarily operates in unison because and to the extent that a theological epistemology recognizes and maintains its theological possibilities and limits on the basis of faith, grace, and revelation. If one were to isolate any one of these insights, one might then castigate Barth and Torrance perhaps for undercutting reason in their opposition to natural theology. Or one might chastise them for placing too much stress on faith, to the exclusion of reason. But if one takes the factors just noted together and sees that opposing natural theology does not mean opposing human nature or human reason, and that stressing faith does not undermine human nature or human reason, then perhaps Christian theologians can find that they will agree about the truth of our knowledge of God when and to the degree that they specifically understand that such knowledge is a miracle in the sense that it cannot be explained from the human side, but can only be acknowledged and then genuinely understood. In this context, I hope to show that the attention Barth and Torrance pay to the Holy Spirit as the decisive factor in our knowledge of the Trinity will be extremely useful for a contemporary theological epistemology.

Knowledge of God and the Holy Spirit for Barth

For Barth "The knowledge of God occurs in the fulfillment of the revelation of His Word by the Holy Spirit, and therefore in the reality and

---

38. Ibid., II/1, 56.

with the necessity of faith and its obedience."[39] Barth argues that since the triune God alone is the source and goal of true and certain knowledge of God, therefore "Knowledge of God is ... an event enclosed in the mystery of the divine Trinity."[40] In speaking of God's hiddenness Barth concludes that "The beginning of all knowledge of God has now to be understood as its end and goal—God the Father and God the Son by the Holy Spirit as the object of the knowledge of God." He continues by explaining that we humans are included secondarily, subsequently, and improperly in this event "in the height, in the being and essence of God, so that God is now the object not only of His own cognition, but also of that of man.... For if this is not the case he does not know God. Knowledge of God is then an event enclosed in the bosom of the divine Trinity."[41]

This thinking reiterates an earlier position presented when Barth stated that "According to Scripture, everything which can be, everything which is either objectively or subjectively possible in relation to revelation, is enclosed in the being and will of the triune God."[42] If knowledge of God is an event enclosed within the bosom of the divine Trinity, then Barth must mean that we can have what he calls apodictically certain knowledge of God only in faith, by grace, and therefore through the action of the Holy Spirit uniting us to the incarnate Son and thus to the Father (*CD* II/1, 162). Genuine knowledge of God then is a happening that is begun, upheld, and completed by God himself.

That does not mean that it is an event that does not include us humanly with all we have and are so that one might mistakenly criticize Barth for displaying an Apollinarian tendency in his theology of revela-

---

39. Ibid., 3.

40. Ibid., 181.

41. Ibid., 205. In this context Barth is stressing that we are in the height with God because Jesus Christ is our reconciler and mediator. In other words because of Christ our thinking is empowered to reach God in spite of our sinful tendency to create God in our own image.

42. Ibid., I/2, 247. This is why Barth speaks of the fact that the Spirit is not only the Spirit of the Father and Son here and now for us "but also for all eternity, in the hidden triune being of God which is revealed to us in revelation. It is because the Holy Spirit is from all eternity the communion between the Father and the Son and therefore not only the Spirit of the Father but also the Spirit of the Son, that in God's revelation He can be the communion between the Father and those whom His Son has called to be His brethren." *CD* I/2, 250.

tion.⁴³ One has only to pay attention to the fact that Barth insists that revelation claims us in our entirety without in any way changing our human being into something more or less than human (CD I/2, 266).⁴⁴ What it does mean is that since our inclusion in this event takes place by an act of God, that is, by God's grace, it is not something that can be traced directly to us in our experiences of God in Christ. It requires faith and the present activity of the Holy Spirit in order to be properly appreciated. Consequently, it rests upon a miracle and thus is not in any sense under our control. Why does Barth insist that our knowledge of God rests on a miracle? We might say that it is because our knowledge of God or readiness for God is enclosed in God's readiness for us. Barth says that God is "ready within Himself to be known by man" and that with and in that fact, we are actually ready to know him. The error of natural theology Barth stresses is not that it treats the problem of our human readiness to know God, but that it treats it by elevating human readiness for God "into an independent factor" so that God's actual

---

43. See Alan Torrance, *Persons in Communion*, 193; and Molnar, *Divine Freedom*, 254f.

44. See esp. *CD* I/1, "The Word of God and Experience," 198–226. Barth insists that experience of God's Word takes place in a human act of self-determination but that in no way is it an experience of God's Word "as this act" (*CD* I/1, 199) because we do not give ourselves this determination—we cannot accomplish this in whole or in part; but neither does this mean that human self-determination is eliminated (*CD* I/1, 200). And for Barth no anthropological sphere is excluded from being determined by the power of the Word: will, conscience, subconscious, intuition and feeling included. Yet there is no hidden anthropological center where the Word may be found either, because it is the act of God whereby we are upheld by God in our self-determination. In this regard Barth emphatically maintained that our new life as those who experience the Word and know God is not to be found in our "immanent constitution" (*CD* I/1, 212) but only in Christ. In Barth's view "The possibility of knowledge of God's Word lies in the God's Word and nowhere else" (*CD* I/1, 222). Therefore it can take place "only as a miracle before the eyes of every man" (*CD* I/1, 223), and thus it takes place in faith. Hence one is "not sure of himself but of the Word of God, and he is not sure of the Word of God in and of himself but in and of the Word. His assurance is his own assurance, but it has its seat outside him in the Word" (*CD* I/1, 224–25). Faith, Barth says is "not one of the various capacities of man" but in faith we actually receive the Word which is grounded only in itself (*CD* I/1, 238). In this section Barth speaks of faith as completely grounded in the objectivity of the Word. It is not until later in the volume that he specifically notes that "We may, of course, be strong and sure in faith—that we are so is the act of God we are confessing, the work of the Holy Spirit—but we cannot try specifically to make ourselves strong and sure again by contemplating ourselves as the strong and the sure. To have the Holy Spirit is to let God rather than our having God be our confidence" (*CD* I/1, 462).

readiness for us in his Word and Spirit is not the only possible basis for our knowledge; consequently it does not see human readiness as exclusively enclosed within this divine readiness (*CD* II/1, 129).

Knowledge of God, Miracle, and Grace

Barth says that God's readiness for us is "God's grace." Therefore our readiness must be readiness for grace. It must refer to our "openness for grace . . . openness for the majestic, the free, the undeserved, the unexpected, the new openness of God for man established entirely in God's own authority."[45] It is here that Barth uses the word "miracle" to describe the fact that God is "not only open to Himself as the Father, the Son and the Holy Spirit, but that He is all this for men also" as "the Lord, the Creator, the Reconciler and Redeemer" (*CD* II/1, 129). This is a miracle because it is a free act of God for us that is neither demanded by God's essence nor conditioned by anything outside of God and apart from God. It is something that is undeserved and is to be seen as God's movement toward us in the incarnation, death, and resurrection of Jesus himself (*CD* I/2, 240–80). It is striking how many times Barth refers to our human inclusion in the event of revelation as a miracle in *CD* I/2. I think what he says there can be directly related to his understanding of our readiness for God in *CD* II/1 and illustrates why his theological epistemology is very precisely centered around his view that it is the Holy Spirit in union with the Father and Son who creates in us the possibility and actuality of our knowledge of God. For Barth this movement of God toward us in Christ is and remains offensive to us because it meets us in Jesus Christ and only in him. And it meets us as those who are sinners, those who actually resist God and are at enmity with God. This fact is not something that can be known in advance, Barth insists, because it is something that is revealed to us by Christ himself. It is and remains an act of God who veils himself and who alone unveils himself to us. "The Holy Spirit," Barth writes, "is holy because He is God's Spirit, and therefore the Spirit, the moving and unity of the Father and of the Son from eternity and in eternity. The fact that by the Holy Spirit we are ready for God in Jesus Christ is in the first instance and in itself only a confirmation of what we have just said. . . . In the Holy Spirit as the Spirit

---

45. *CD* II/1, 129.

of the Father and of the Son there is, in the height of God, no 'Against us' but only the 'For us.'"[46]

Here is where revelation and reconciliation must be seen together since we are sinners who need to be reconciled with God in order to know God. That, for Barth, one might say is the epistemological relevance of our justification by faith.[47] It is just this important fact disclosed to us in revelation that is always missing from theologies that claim reason knows "that God is" but not "what God is."

Barth is not only clear that knowledge of God takes place through a miraculous action of the Holy Spirit; his work is shaped by the fact that at every point in his consideration of our knowledge of God, his thinking actually bears the mark of this particular truth because it operates under what he calls the constraint of the Word of God (*CD* II/1, 7ff.). Barth is simply being faithful to his insight that "the work of the Spirit is nothing other than the work of Jesus Christ. . . . By the Holy Spirit whom He has given us, we know that the Word, that is Christ, abides with us, and so becomes ours and we His. . . . He Himself must give us light to believe the Gospel, which is to make us new creatures, the temples of God."[48]

Because he is the objective revelation of God for us, Barth maintains that we are subjectively included in the fact that God was in Christ reconciling the world to himself and that therefore our lives really are hidden with Christ in God. For this reason, in him we are already "hearers and doers of the Word of God" (*CD* I/2, 240). "When the Holy Spirit draws and takes us right into the reality of revelation by doing what we cannot do, by opening our eyes and ears and hearts, He does not tell us anything except that we are in Christ by Christ."[49] Barth is adamant that the subjective reality of revelation, i.e., our human inclusion in the truth

---

46. Ibid., 157.

47. Later, in his *Doctrine of Reconciliation*, Barth identifies the sin known in light of the incarnation as pride and sloth—pride in the form of active displacement of God in his revelation and sloth in the form of evil inaction. God's response was to justify and sanctify us in the humiliation and exaltation of his Son. That is God's reconciling grace. See *CD* IV/2, 403. Importantly, Barth says that "The error of man concerning God is that the God he wants to be like is obviously only a self-sufficient, self-affirming, self-desiring supreme being, self-centered and rotating about himself. Such a being is not God. *God is for Himself, but He is not only for Himself.*" *CD* IV/1, 422, emphasis mine.

48. *CD* I/2, 241–42.

49. Ibid., 240.

of our existence in Christ, is not something that has to be added to who Christ is as our savior and what he does for us; it is distinct from but not separable from "objective revelation." Indeed, "Revelation is objective only in its irruption into the subjective, in its redemptive objective assault upon man. We have to follow objective revelation through its whole unified movement from God to man,"[50] Barth says. In this sense objective revelation comes to us and is in fact "recognised and acknowledged by [us]. And that is the work of the Holy Spirit."[51] The work of the Holy Spirit opens our blind eyes and empowers us thankfully to surrender and "acknowledge that it is so."[52] The truth of revelation as it is in God's actions in Christ can never be added to, since "It is the truth, even if man is not in the truth" and "It is true from all eternity, for Jesus Christ who assumed our nature is the eternal Son of God . . . it is always true in time, even before we perceive it to be true."[53] Moreover, our perception that it is true is inexplicable from our side since this is the work of the Holy Spirit (*CD* I/2, 239). When we thankfully acknowledge the truth of our freedom for God as it is in Christ, then we are living by faith, which itself is the work of the Holy Spirit within us (*CD* I/2, 242–43).

In speaking of the way objective revelation reaches us in the Holy Spirit, Barth insists that the subjective reality of revelation "is simply the process by which that objective reality becomes subjective. The Holy Spirit is the Spirit of the Father and of the Son, of the Father who reveals Himself in His Son and only in His Son. But that means that He is the Spirit of Jesus Christ."[54] This is why Barth points firmly to the church as the place "which corresponds to the particularity of the incarnation."[55] "The Church is the historical form of the work of the Holy Spirit and therefore the historical form of faith" because the Holy Spirit gathers people on the ground of what "in Jesus Christ is their common eternal truth."[56] The church is the body of Christ as it is united to its heavenly head. But Barth does not fall into the trap of saying that Christ needs no other body than the church to be visible to us, since for Barth, the

---

50. Ibid., 239.

51. Ibid.

52. Ibid.

53. Ibid., 238.

54. Ibid., 246–47.

55. Ibid., 247. Barth works out the details of how he understands the church as the earthly-historical form of Christ's heavenly existence in *CD* IV/1, 150ff., and 650ff.

56. *CD* II/1, 160.

church is Christ's earthly, sacramental body precisely by being united to him as the risen and ascended Lord in his heavenly body.[57] Hence, "everything which can be, everything which is either objectively or subjectively possible in relation to revelation, is enclosed in the being and will and action of the triune God."[58] Moreover, "The work of the Holy Spirit means that there is an adequate basis for our hearing of the Word, since it brings us nothing but the Word for our hearing."[59] Furthermore, it means that "there is an adequate basis for our faith in Christ and our communion with Him, because He is no other Spirit than the Spirit of Jesus Christ."[60] That precisely is the "life of the body of Christ, the operation of the prophetic and apostolic testimony, the hearing of preaching, the seeing of that to which the sacraments point."[61] For Barth, "The Holy Spirit is the Spirit of God, because He is the Spirit of the Word. And that is the very reason and the only reason why we acquire eyes and ears for God in the Holy Spirit."[62]

Importantly, however, it is here that Barth insists that we will never truly understand the Holy Spirit and his work upon us if we "try to understand them abstractly and in themselves." What we will discover is "something extremely human, in which Christ is unrecognizable" and thus we will misunderstand the work of the Spirit or we will "confuse and equate the occurrence which we know, and therefore our human something, with Christ Himself, which means that we will seek Christ anywhere and everywhere and expose ourselves to every possible heresy."[63] This will lead only toward skepticism or "mild or even a violent fanaticism."[64] Here Barth resolutely insists that to avoid this problem "we must look at Christ Himself" and not our experiences of him because the love of God is shed abroad in our hearts by the Holy Spirit (CD I/2, 248–49, and Rom 5:5). We must, Barth says, point away from

57. See CD II/1, 161, "As the earthly body of Jesus Christ it [the church] may—as is believed and proclaimed in the Lord's Supper—be nourished by its own eternal truth in its form as the heavenly body of Jesus Christ. It cannot be nourished in any other way. If it nourishes itself in any other way it can only die as the Church."

58. CD I/2, 247.
59. Ibid., 248.
60. Ibid.
61. Ibid.
62. Ibid.
63. Ibid.
64. Ibid., 249

our or other people's "seizure" toward the "divine seizing, and therefore once again to Christ Himself" (*CD* I/2, 249). Barth never wavered on this point.

The Necessity of Faith

That is why, in his doctrine of God, Barth insisted that "Faith does not consist in an inward and immanent transformation of man, although there can be no faith without such a transformation."[65] For Barth, however, "faith is more than all the transformation which follows it" precisely because it is "the work of the Holy Spirit" as our new birth from God "on the basis of which [we] can already live here by what [we] are there in Jesus Christ and therefore in truth."[66] Faith is indeed the temporal form of our "eternal being in Jesus Christ"—a being "which is grounded on the fact that Jesus Christ intercedes for us before the Father. . . . Faith extinguishes our enmity against God by seeing that this enmity is made a lie, a lie confessed by ourselves as such, expiated and overcome by Jesus Christ."[67] That is why Barth insists that the truth cannot be found within us. What we find in ourselves, he insists, "will only be our enmity against God." That very being, he says, "is a lie. It is the lie which is seen in faith. Our truth is our being in the Son of God, in whom we are not enemies but friends of God, in whom we do not hate grace but cling to grace alone, in whom therefore God is knowable to us."[68] This, Barth writes, "is man's truth believed by faith. And it is the work of the Holy Spirit that the eternal presence of the reconciliation in Jesus Christ has in us this temporal form, the form of faith. The man in whom Jesus Christ has this temporal form does not then in any sense believe in himself."[69] Faith means not standing at all upon ourselves but only on Christ. And the power to do this comes only from the Holy Spirit and not at all from ourselves. Thus, "We have to believe; not to believe in ourselves, but in Jesus Christ."[70]

65. *CD* II/1, 158.
66. Ibid.
67. Ibid.
68. Ibid., 159.
69. Ibid.
70. Ibid.

In his doctrine of reconciliation Barth takes a similar line, insisting that the necessity of faith does not lie within us at all: "It is to be found rather in the object of faith. It is this object which forces itself necessarily on man and is in that way the basis of his faith. This object is the living Lord Jesus Christ, in whom it took place, in whom it has taken place for every man, in whom it confronts man as an absolutely superior actuality, that his sin, and he himself as the actual sinner he is, and with his sin the possibility of unbelief, is rejected, destroyed and set aside."[71] Because Christ has died and risen for all, he is not just one alternative put before us to choose, Barth says—rather, the choice of unbelief, which is the choice not to acknowledge him, is rendered ontologically impossible. The only real possibility is faith and thus obedience. That is our only justification. Yet the power to do this "is the awakening power of the Holy Spirit. . . . The Holy Spirit is the power in which Jesus Christ the Son of God makes a man free, makes him genuinely free for this choice and therefore for faith."[72] Barth concludes his discussion of faith at the end of *CD* IV/1 with his understanding of confession, saying that "confessing is the moment in the act of faith in which the believer stands to his faith, or, rather, to the One in whom he believes, the One whom he acknowledges and recognises, the living Jesus Christ; and does so outwardly, again in general terms, in face of men."[73] To Barth this means that someone who only acknowledges and recognizes but does not confess Jesus Christ by living as his witness in the genuine freedom that comes from Christ through his Spirit is not really a Christian at all. And it does not matter how a person feels about this since we are not asked about our own wishes or aversions. Faith itself is the free act of confession. Barth concludes that "It is not on the basis of his own discovery and private revelation, but by the mediatorial ministry of the community which is itself in the school of the prophets and apostles, that a man comes under the awakening power of the Holy Spirit and therefore to faith."[74]

71. *CD* IV/1, 747.
72. Ibid., 748.
73. Ibid., 777.
74. Ibid., 778.

Knowledge of God and Apologetics

Thus, for Barth, there is a good apologetics and a bad one. The former has "the character of a supplementary, incidental and implicit apologetics, comparable to the subsequent substantiation of a judgment of the supreme court which has already been given and come into force and hence whose validity cannot be questioned."[75] The latter will not be bound by what has happened, namely, God's actually speaking his Word by his Holy Spirit, and so will think that knowledge of God is based on a person's free choice. Barth says that this approach to the knowledge of God not only will ask the false question of whether God is known (when it should be asking how it is that God has made himself known), just as a false understanding of revelation will lead one to ask whether or not he or she has understood, instead of beginning in and by the Holy Spirit and asking about the fact that the Holy Spirit who does this has the power to do it (*CD* I/2, 243). But this approach will create anxiety and doubt since it will be unsure of its object and it will thus be open to questioning from without. That, Barth claims, is the sure sign of all false knowledge of God as idolatry. Wisely, Barth depicts false apologetics by noting that its approach to understanding God will operate with "sublime, sovereign freedom, open on every side, interested in anything and everything, taking every possible and impossible knowledge of 'God' with a tragic seriousness,"[76] until it finally reaches the point of a "*sacrificium intellectus*" as its own final possibility. This final possibility may even take the form of a "leap into faith" (*CD* II/1, 9). At that point, "probably assuming a parsonic voice, it will praise this very *sacrificum* as the last and best choice" and will then speak of a "necessary constraint of the Word of God" and start talking about Jesus and the Bible or even church dogma. But, Barth says, then it is too late, since such thinking was not *originally* constrained by the Word, "even though it now declares and designates itself to be such."[77] His point is simple, but with profound consequences: "We can only come from the real and original constraint by the Word; *we cannot come to it.*"[78]

---

75. *CD* II/1, 8.
76. Ibid.
77. Ibid.
78. Ibid., 9, emphasis mine.

For the very same reason, Barth not only insists that our knowledge of God is based on his knowing us and enabling such knowledge, but that the same is true regarding our knowledge of Christ's deity. We do not know this "on the basis of [our] knowledge and choice, but on the basis of [our] being known and chosen (not as the result but as the beginning of [our] thinking about Him)."[79] This, of course, sets Barth apart from those who certainly would admit that our knowledge of the Trinity comes from and through the Holy Spirit but then proceed to develop their knowledge of God from elsewhere than from the revelation of God in Jesus Christ. For Barth this is impossible because the Holy Spirit, who includes us in revelation as its "subjective reality," is the Spirit of the Father *and* the Son and simply cannot be separated under any circumstances from the Word who is the Son.[80] This happens quite frequently however. I will just highlight one example.

Pannenberg, Apologetics, and the Knowledge of Faith

Consider Wolfhart Pannenberg's approach elaborated in his *Systematic Theology*, volume 1. Pannenberg claims that "Dogmatics, although it treats all other themes from the standpoint of God and thus discusses them in exposition of the concept of God, cannot begin directly with the reality of God."[81] It must instead recognize that God is present initially only as "a human notion, word, or concept" and that to escape from confusing God with our ideas we must "engage in controversy" by clarifying "how we come to count on God as a reality" by publicly discussing the reality of God witnessed in Scripture. This sounds acceptable, I realize, to many modern ears. But it is exactly the point that Barth emphatically contests because it represents a kind of apologetics that refuses to begin in faith with the reality of God made known in his Word and by his Spirit.[82] Thus, Pannenberg can sound as though

79. *CD* I/1, 461.

80. Cf. e.g., *CD* I/2, 244.

81. Pannenberg, *Systematic Theology*, 1:61.

82. Pannenberg mistakenly accused Barth of "faith subjectivism" for beginning his theology in faith with the reality of God (ibid., 44–45). What Pannenberg did not realize is that unless one begins theology in faith with the reality of God revealed in his Word and by his Spirit and therefore as a witness (*CD* I/2, 817ff.), one will always be supposing that one can freely choose which concept of God one wishes based on a series of rational arguments (Cf. also *CD* IV/3, 1). But in Barth's thinking that very

he is saying the same thing as Barth when he writes: "Materially only God, or his self-revelation in Jesus Christ, is fundamental" for a "fundamental theology" that seeks to lay the groundwork for dogmatics.[83] But Pannenberg is not even remotely close to Barth's position because he believes that "The designation of Yahweh as God and the Christian attributing of deity to Jesus Christ make sense only on the condition of an established pre-Christian and extra-Christian use of the word 'God.'"[84] No wonder Pannenberg reaches this conclusion: "The natural theology of the philosophers had formulated a criterion for judging whether any God could be seriously considered the author of the whole cosmos, and Christian theology had to meet this criterion if its claim could be taken seriously that the God who redeems us in Jesus Christ is the Creator of heaven and earth and thus the one true God of all peoples."[85]

This is exactly the thinking that Barth rejected as false apologetics precisely because of its refusal to begin thinking about God under the constraint of the Word of God. It refuses to acknowledge that it is the Holy Spirit *alone* who actually enables us to know this God. And it is no accident that Barth's entire theology is marked by the fact that he steadfastly refuses to begin thinking about God apart from Jesus himself as the incarnate Word, insisting that all thinking about God must begin with him because he is God's Son (*CD* I/1, 415). Indeed this is not something we can establish, as Pannenberg seems to believe, because Jesus simply is who he is, and that fact is grounded within the eternal relation of the Father to the Son and in the Spirit and can only be acknowledged in faith.[86] This is why there is an air of adoptionism that pervades Pannenberg's Christology, as when he expresses his belief that the resurrection constitutes Jesus' Sonship.[87] There is no such ambiguity

---

approach displaces the Holy Spirit from the scene as the sole miraculous (because it cannot be explained or proven but only accepted as an act of God in faith) action which enables true and certain knowledge of God. See Molnar, "Some Problems."

83. Pannenberg, *Systematic Theology*, 1:61.

84. Ibid., 68.

85. Ibid., 79. Barth was always very clear about the fact that "God can never be for dogmatic thinking and speaking an object which can be affirmed apart from God" (*CD* I/2, 819).

86. This is a point also stressed by Thomas F. Torrance. See, e.g., Torrance, *Christian Doctrine of God*, 194ff.

87. See Molnar, *Incarnation and Resurrection*, 283f. See also Taylor, *Pannenberg on the Triune God*, 111ff.

in Barth's thought because Barth insists that the deity of the Holy Spirit can be contested (and is contested whenever one does not begin thinking about God from and through Jesus himself) "only if one has first explained away the fact that with its Ἰησους Κύριος the New Testament community confessed its faith in Jesus Christ as faith in God Himself. If the Christ of the New Testament is a demi-god from above or below, then naturally faith in Him becomes a human possibility."[88] In Barth's words:

> The Spirit guarantees man what he cannot guarantee himself, his personal participation in revelation. The act of the Holy Spirit in revelation is the Yes to God's Word which is spoken by God Himself for us, yet not just to us, but also in us. This Yes spoken by God is the basis of the confidence with which man may regard the revelation as applying to him. This Yes is the mystery of faith, the mystery of the knowledge of the Word of God, but also the mystery of the willing obedience that is well-pleasing to God. All these things, faith, knowledge and obedience, exist for man "in the Holy Spirit."[89]

That is why, in his concept of analogy, Barth took a position diametrically opposed to Pannenberg's. "Can the ideas of lords and lordships even help us to know God?" Barth asks, before answering: "Of themselves they can only hinder. For in the last resort they do not point us to God, but to ourselves."[90] Here Barth applies his doctrine of justification by faith to our knowledge of God and he thus refuses to allow any self-grounding or any apologetic concern that would attempt to secure us from our neediness. In other words we need God's grace and revelation. We need the Holy Spirit to have apodictic certainty here. We need to know the true God and our actual freedom as it exists in Christ for us. But for all this we must pray. And when we pray we actually rely on God's promise to be our God and so we believe and obey God's command and we are thus in the truth—not, however, a truth that needs

---

88. CD I/1, 460.

89. Ibid., 453. See Barth, *Credo*, where he says that when we confess the Holy Spirit we recognize that human beings now come on the scene, but that this is no warrant for pursuing an anthropology or theological anthropology in order to understand God and our relations with God (127–29). Is it any surprise that Barth reacted negatively to Pannenberg's Christology by stating that it appeared to him to be an outstanding example of a presupposed anthropology and cosmology? See *Karl Barth Letters*, 178.

90. CD II/1, 76.

to be debated before freely deciding to commit ourselves—but a truth which constrains us to belief and thus to obedience to God's Word and Spirit and therefore to the Father as the sole Lord of the covenant. Barth works these insights out with amazing consistency in his doctrine of reconciliation.[91]

Barth and the Knowledge of God

In Barth's understanding, God knows himself immediately and we never know God as God knows himself. Nonetheless, on the basis of revelation we do know God "mediately" as an "object" because God presents himself to us "in a medium" so that God is present to us in a "double sense. In His Word He comes as an object before man the subject. And by the Holy Spirit He makes the human subject accessible to Himself, capable of considering and conceiving Himself as object" (*CD* II/1, 10). "As He is in the essence of God Himself the Spirit of the Father and of the Son, the Holy Spirit does not come independently, or for Himself, as immediate truth to man, but through the Son, and as the Spirit of the Son, as the power in which the truth of God lays hold of man in this very mediacy, in the incarnate Son of God."[92]

Barth insists upon two crucial points here. First, real knowledge of God thus described involves both God's relationship to us and his distinction from us. This rules out all claims to knowledge of God that understand this as "the union of man with God" but "which do not regard it as an objective knowledge" since they "leave out the distinction between the knower and the known."[93] Importantly, Barth is claiming that all attempts to know God which bypass Jesus Christ, the incarnate Word, will necessarily lead in this direction, namely, toward a non-objective knowledge and toward some form of confusion of divine and human being. This is why Barth insists that knowledge of God is knowledge of faith. "Faith is the total positive relationship of man to the God who gives Himself to be known in His Word. It is man's act of

---

91. See, e.g., *CD* IV/1 §61, "The Justification of Man," esp. 608ff., and §62 "The Holy Spirit and Christian Faith," 725–79; *CD* IV/2 §68 "The Holy Spirit and Christian Love," 727–840; *CD* IV/3, §71 "The Vocation of Man," §72 "The Holy Spirit and the Sending of the Christian Community"; and §73 "The Holy Spirit and Christian Hope."

92. *CD* II/1, 101.

93. Ibid., 10.

turning to God, of opening up his life to Him and of surrendering to Him."[94] Indeed, "Knowledge of faith means fundamentally the union of man with the God who is distinct from him as well as from all his other objects."[95] But this faith itself comes from God. In reality "it is utterly and entirely grounded in the fact that God encounters man in the Word which demands of him this turning, this Yes, this obligation; becoming an object to him in such a way that in His objectivity He bestows upon him by the Holy Spirit the light of the clarity that He is God and that He is his God."[96]

Barth proceeds to speak of God as an utterly unique object by positing what he calls God's "primary objectivity" in distinction from his "secondary objectivity." "In his triune life as such, objectivity, and with it knowledge, is divine reality before creaturely objectivity and knowledge exist"[97] Barth writes. That is God's primary objectivity. Yet God "gives Himself to be known by us as He knows Himself." That is God's secondary objectivity. Barth maintains that God is "first to Himself, and then in His revelation to us . . . nothing but what He is in Himself. It is here that the door is shut against any 'non-objective' knowledge of God."[98] With this distinction between primary and secondary objectivity in place Barth asserts that all our knowledge of God is knowledge of faith that rests upon God's objectivity. But since it is mediated through the veil of secondary objectivity, it is indirect and not direct knowledge of God's "naked objectivity." That is why he says that "the Word does not appear in His eternal objectivity as the Son who alone dwells in the bosom of the Father. No: the Word became flesh. God gives Himself to be known, and is known, in the substance of secondary objectivity . . . in the manhood which He takes to Himself, to which He humbles Himself and which He raises through Himself."[99]

Knowledge of God, however, takes place, Barth notes, as primary and secondary objectivity are distinguished without being separated and as long as God is understood as the living God, i.e., as the Creator from whom we come even before we know him; he is our "Reconciler, who

94. Ibid., 12
95. Ibid., 15.
96. Ibid., 12.
97. Ibid., 16.
98. Ibid.
99. Ibid., 19–20.

through Jesus Christ in the Holy Spirit makes knowledge of Himself real and possible," and he is our "Redeemer, who is Himself the future truth of all present knowledge of Himself. He and none other is the object of the knowledge of faith."[100]

This knowledge of God is true and certain only as and because God in free grace "posits Himself as the object" of our knowledge (*CD* II/1, 22). Without any constraint and in the freedom of his love, God gives himself to be known and can be known as God only in this giving "which is always a bestowal, always a free action." This action of his can never be separated from his being and we are completely unable to contemplate God *in abstracto* as if we might know God's being according to some pre-arranged "being of the contemplating man himself" (*CD* II/1, 22). Because our knowledge of God always depends upon this preceding act of God to be true, we "must of necessity pray for its fulfillment as real knowledge of God . . . the position of grace cannot be taken up and held in any other way than by asking and praying for it."[101] This is one of the reasons that Barth is so insistent upon the fact that such knowledge must always be seen as a miracle (*CD* I/2, 258, 65–66, 68–69). "Necessarily, it is all up with the truth of God's work and sign if we cease to adore its grace. For just as certainly as grace is truth, so certainly can truth only be had as grace."[102] In the Bible, Barth insists, knowledge of God differs from all other human knowledge by the fact that "it coincides with some action of God. God is known, not simply because He is God in Himself, but because He reveals Himself as such; not simply because his work is there, but because He is active in His work."[103] This is why Barth asserts further that knowledge of God is "obedience to God." And for Barth this is no coerced obedience but the free obedience that springs from one who has been set free for the service of God by the grace of God. Hence, for Barth, justification does not simply apply to human knowledge but to human being as it is in Christ. Human knowledge without corresponding acts of faith and obedience would not be true knowledge of the living God. Consequently, Barth insists that "Knowledge of God according to the teaching of the Reformation does not therefore permit the man who knows to with-

100. Ibid., 21
101. Ibid., 22; I/1, 108; and III/3, 266.
102. *CD* II/1, 23.
103. Ibid.

draw himself from God, so to speak, and to maintain an independent and secure position over against God so that from this he may form thoughts about God, which are in varying degrees true, beautiful and good. This later procedure is that of all natural theology.... Knowledge of God according to the teaching of the Reformation is *obedience* to God and therefore itself already service of God."[104] When God as object reaches out and grasps us, then knowledge of God takes place. But in that very occurrence we become new human beings, according to Barth. All of this is tied to faith of course. And that means that we are set face to face with Jesus Christ as prophet, priest and king who not only tells us what we need to know, but makes amends for us and will do so for everything and has the power of God actually to accomplish all this. "That is why knowledge of God is nothing else than service of God."[105] Unless knowledge of God means service of God in Christ, our freedom in the Holy Spirit would only become a pretext for "new unfreedom" (*CD* I/1, 457). Moreover, unless we see knowledge of God as service of God, we would miss the fact that when the Holy Spirit actually is at work in our lives and thus when we "have our master unavoidably in Jesus Christ," we exist "in an ultimate and most profound irresponsibility" (*CD* I/2, 274). What could Barth mean by this?

He means that all other teachers or masters actually burden us with obligations and responsibilities that we must fulfill by means of our own activities and achievements. But Jesus Christ, when he comes to us in his Holy Spirit, actually "claims our response; . . . claims the achievement which is, of course, required of us."[106] Notice that Barth is no Apollinarian or Docetist in his thinking. He really thinks that works follow from faith. But they follow from faith not as autonomous activities that we must guarantee, but rather as acts of service "in the fulfillment of which we are borne and covered by the work it does itself."[107] In this sense he states that the outpouring of the Holy Spirit relativizes "the question who and what we are in ourselves" because by this action we are placed under the "command of the Word."[108] We really "participate in the work of the Word." But we do so, "Not as those who have to finish

104. Barth, *Knowledge of God*, 104. See also *CD* I/2, 846.
105. Barth, *Knowledge of God*, 104.
106. *CD* I/2, 274.
107. Ibid., 274–75.
108. Ibid., 275.

the work, to reach the goal, to bring in the results." Our participation does not rest on our fitness for revelation, since we know we are unfit for it. Our participation rests on our forgiveness. It is, Barth says, "grace." What preserves us from the anxiety and worry about whether or not we are truly able to do what God requires here is that we are permitted and enabled to do exactly what we are unable to do of ourselves. "As those who cannot do it of ourselves, and never could, we have to participate when the Word does it."[109] When we are placed under the command of the Word we are genuinely free, that is, we do not have to worry about ourselves or others or the development of the church or world because we can pray "Thy will be done." In that prayer we admit that we need not worry about these things "because that is not [our] business. I am not responsible. This burden, the burden of my own and others' sins, does not lie upon me. It lies solely and entirely upon Jesus Christ, upon the Word of God. . . . Jesus Christ alone bears it and can bear it."[110] This freedom is our "ultimate absence of responsibility," says Barth, because we know in faith that Christ cares for us. And this is what the Holy Spirit of Christ discloses to us. Of course, Barth is not saying that we are not to be responsible to the Word of God. But that responsibility is our obedience of faith and thus it cannot be traced back to us in some self-justifying fashion.

The key question in this context is, from where does faith come? Barth's answer is direct and simple. It comes from the Holy Spirit, so that the person who lives by faith sees himself "convicted of his own unfaithfulness" and also sees that "he is in no position to have faith in himself, or to ascribe to himself a capacity or power by means of which he himself could somehow bring about his salvation, or co-operate in bringing it about."[111] Very bluntly, Barth states that "Faith, New Testament πίστις, is . . . to be understood as a possibility which derives from a mode of being of God, from a mode of being which is in essential unity with Him who in the New Testament is described as Father and as Son" (*CD* I/1, 461).

We have already seen that unlike those who think that some theological or philosophical method might guarantee our knowledge of God, Barth insists that only the Spirit is that guarantee and that our

---

109. Ibid.
110. Ibid.
111. Barth, *Knowledge of God*, 105.

yes to God is the mystery of faith in which we are miraculously enabled by God to know him in spite of our sin and our tendencies to be self-reliant. "It is God Himself who opens our eyes and ears for Himself. And in so doing He tells us that we could not do it of ourselves, that of our selves we are blind and deaf. To receive the Holy Spirit means an exposure of our spiritual helplessness, a recognition that we do not possess the Holy Spirit."[112] This is why Barth says it is a miracle. "It is a reality to be grounded only in itself" (*CD* I/2, 244). Thus, apart from this action of the Spirit including us in the life of Christ, "there is no other possibility of being free for God" (*CD* I/2, 244). Importantly, Barth insists here that he is not making a generally self-evident statement "after the manner of philosophical agnosticism" (*CD* I/2, 244). What the philosophical agnostic recognizes, Barth asserts, is not God because we can have no actual view of God by speaking of our incapacity for God. The certainty of this agnosticism which speaks of "the above which is barred to us" is of our own disposing exactly because it is made so absolutely. Barth says that if the philosopher "did mean God, he would have to allow the renunciation he makes so absolutely to be bracketed and relativised by the reality of the Holy Spirit" (*CD* I/2, 244). An actual encounter with the Holy Spirit, Barth insists, would cause the agnostic to speak quite differently. Instead of making "an absolute claim to renunciation, he would have to forego all claims and speak about the humility enjoined upon us. Instead of eyes which blink (and blink continually), he would have to speak about our blindness and the healing of the blind. In fact, he would have to surrender his agnosticism all along the line."[113]

Barth adds that he is not engaging in apologetics here, because he simply wants to make it clear that his statement that we cannot be free for God without the Holy Spirit has nothing to do with philosophical agnosticism. Hence while it may seem that the philosophical agnostic and the theologian agree that we are not free for God, Barth maintains that the agnostic knows nothing about this because this can only be known by revelation and thus "by the Holy Spirit" (*CD* I/2, 245). Moreover and importantly, the fact that anyone really knows this is due to a miracle. The Holy Spirit is the "Teacher of the Word who reconciles us to God" and "He informs us both about God and also about ourselves" (*CD* I/2, 245). But he does not reveal to us that we are "petty finite creatures of

112. *CD* I/2, 244.
113. Ibid.

little account in His presence (for this contrast would still not signify that we are not free for Him; the infinite needs the finite just as the finite needs the infinite)."[114] What is revealed is that we are "rebels against this Lord" as those who are "unthankful for his kindness" and "as resisters of His call" (*CD* I/2, 245). "In the Holy Spirit we are confronted by what we cannot deny even if we willed to do so. We know, therefore, that we cannot ascribe to man any freedom of his own for God, any possibility of his own to become the recipient of revelation. And we know it in a way which does not admit of any question. For the Holy Spirit is not a dialectician. And the negation is not our own discovery. Unlike our own positive or negative discoveries, it is not open to revision."[115]

But there is more to be said about the action of the Holy Spirit here. Barth also insists that "The Spirit gives man instruction and guidance he cannot give himself" (*CD* I/1, 454). However, this presupposes that "the Spirit is not identical, and does not become identical with ourselves.... As our Teacher and Leader He is in us, but not as a power of which we might become lords. He remains Himself the Lord."[116] In this sense the Spirit is the power in which God "establishes and executes His claim to lordship over us by His immediate presence" (*CD* I/1, 454). In addition, "the Spirit is the great and only possibility in virtue of which men can speak of Christ in such a way that what they say is witness and that God's revelation in Christ thus achieves new actuality through it" (*CD* I/1, 454). The Holy Spirit authorizes us to speak about Christ and summons us to be ministers of the Word. Therefore the very existence of the church consists in the fact that as individuals part of this community of faith, we are constrained by the Holy Spirit to speak about the "wonderful works of God" (*CD* I/1, 456). By the Holy Spirit we really become recipients of revelation, Barth says. How can a sinner become capable of receiving the Word of God? Barth answers by saying that we do not first become this in order to be it but that we are already capable of this because, in Christ, God has made us his children. As such Barth says we are free and therefore we can believe. We are God's children as we receive the Holy Spirit. But in receiving the Holy Spirit "he is what in himself and of himself he cannot be, one who belongs to God as a child to its father, one who knows God as a child knows its father" (*CD* I/1,

---

114. Ibid., 245.
115. Ibid., 246.
116. *CD* I/1, 454.

457). Interestingly, Barth identifies this freedom of ours as "the power of the resurrection" because it consists in a "transition from death to life," because the Holy Spirit sets us in Christ who died for us and also rose for us. This freedom cannot be seen as an "immanent freedom of his own, but as that which is conferred upon him by God" (*CD* I/1, 458). Hence, for Barth, "to stand under this Master is not only the normal thing, it is the only possible thing. The outpouring of the Holy Spirit exalts the Word of God to be the master over men, puts man unavoidably under His mastery. The miracle of the divine revealdness, the power of Christ's resurrection in a man, consists in this event. In it the 'God became man' is actualised in us as 'man has a God.'"[117] In this event we participate "in this divine possibility" in spite of the fact that we exist as those who, as unredeemed, are unworthy of this.

Thomas F. Torrance's Views

Now let us explore some of what Thomas F. Torrance has to say about the role of the Spirit in our knowledge of God. Torrance begins his chapter on the Holy Spirit and knowledge of God in his important book *God and Rationality* insisting, as he frequently does, that only God reveals God, and he proceeds to explain why he thinks we must speak of an "epistemological relevance of the Spirit."[118] We cannot attribute knowledge of God to ourselves since such knowledge is a "freely given participation in [God's] self-knowledge."[119] Consequently, knowledge of God takes place only in obedience to Christ as our minds conform to him. And this can happen, Torrance says, "only as in the Spirit the being and nature of God is brought to bear upon us so that we think under the compulsion of His Reality. That is the activity of the Holy Spirit whom Jesus spoke of in this connection as the Spirit of Truth."[120] In this context, Torrance mentions what we may say about the Spirit. *First*, "The Holy Spirit is not cognisable in Himself."[121] As the Spirit of Jesus Christ, the Holy Spirit bears witness to Christ and not to himself. We do not know the Spirit directly because, according to Torrance, he

117. *CD* I/2, 270.
118. Torrance, *God and Rationality*, 166.
119. Ibid.
120. Ibid., 167.
121. Ibid.

hides himself. It is through the Holy Spirit that the Word became flesh and that the Word continues to be heard. It is by the operation of the Spirit that we know the unknowable God. We are confronted by the Holy Spirit in his own person since the Spirit is of one substance with God. Yet unlike the Son, the Spirit did not become incarnate and therefore he is not of one substance with us. This is an extremely important point when you consider how many contemporary theologians opt for indwelling Christologies claiming that Jesus differs from the rest of us only by the extent to which he was indwelt by the Spirit. Such thinking clearly rests on a confusion of the work of the Holy Spirit with the work of the incarnate Word. For Torrance, the Spirit "incarnated the Son" and "utters the Word" and directs us to Christ.[122] Both he and Barth are consistent in stating this since both theologians hold that there is an essential *perichoretic* relation both in eternity and in time of the Father, Son, and Holy Spirit.

Second, with regard to our knowledge of God, Torrance insists that such knowledge is a miracle.[123] The Holy Spirit functions here as the one who points us outside our human knowledge to reality beyond. It is the Spirit who enables us to distinguish what we know, namely, God himself, from our knowledge of him and from what we say about God. Through cognition and speech we are directed to objective realities and thus we "speak of them under the compulsion of their being upon us."[124] In Torrance's view two things must be avoided: 1) any attempt to "close the gap" between thought and being, and 2) any attempt to "make the gap complete." In both cases, Torrance contends, knowledge is not just disrupted, but it is destroyed. In both cases we become "imprisoned in ourselves," either by reducing everything to the forms of our own thought and speech or, if we try to escape those forms to some world of "non-formal" reality beyond, "we grasp nothing and only engage in empty movements of thought."[125] In all genuine knowledge, Torrance insists, we need our "frames of thought" but we recognize that we must always be critical so as to not confuse those frames with reality, which must be allowed to break through our interpretations. In this context, Torrance maintains that reality must show through our knowledge

122. Ibid.
123. Ibid., 168.
124. Ibid., 169.
125. Ibid.

without being identified with it or separated from it.[126] But he insists no one can say *how* knowledge is related to reality. This is where the Holy Spirit functions.

Torrance maintains that it is the Holy Spirit who makes God's being knowable to us, so that "Apart from the Spirit we would not break through to the divine Being, or rather the divine Being would not break through to us."[127] While it is true that not everything we know can be objectified, Torrance insists that we cannot equate that limitation with the work of the Holy Spirit because in the Holy Spirit we are up against God's very own transcendent truth and majesty so that it is *only* from the Spirit "that we learn what objectivity in knowledge really is."[128] The Holy Spirit therefore both creates the relation between us and God that is necessary if there is to be knowledge of God and simultaneously reinforces the fact that we cannot explain "how our thought and speech are related to God."[129] In this sense all our thoughts and speech must point beyond themselves to God. We have what Torrance calls intuitive knowledge of God—but that does not mean we can control God by equating the Spirit with our intuitions. Rather it means that we come under God's control in our experience and knowledge. Had Torrance confused knowledge of God with our intuitions, he would not have claimed that our thoughts and speech must always point beyond themselves to God and he would not have insisted that the Holy Spirit and not our experience dictates the truth of what is known.

Torrance rejects what he calls "non-conceptual experience of God" as a leap into irrationality.[130] We cannot experience God or know God, Torrance claims following Anselm, without concepts. And that is where the Spirit functions. For it is by the power and enlightenment of the Spirit that we think and speak "directly of God in and through the forms of our rational experience and articulation and we do that under the direction and control of the inner rationality of the divine Being, the eternal *Logos* and *Eidos* of Godhead."[131] Only through the

---

126. Ibid., 175.

127. Ibid.

128. Ibid., 176.

129. Ibid.

130. Ibid., 170. This is fully in accord with Barth's rejection of non-objective knowledge of God discussed above.

131. Ibid.

Spirit then can we know the rational truth of God and distinguish this from our knowledge of it. In this way our knowledge is transformed by being rooted in the eternal Word and thus in the being of God.[132] Here Torrance makes four crucial points regarding the Holy Spirit that will enable him to explain the epistemological relevance of the Holy Spirit.

First, the Holy Spirit is not only the free and sovereign Creator acting toward us, but is God enabling us to relate with God. Following Athanasius, Torrance notes that, "For the grace and gift that is given is given in the Trinity, from the Father, through the Son, in the Holy Spirit. As the grace given is from the Father through the Son, so we can have no communion in the gift except in the Holy Spirit. For it is when we partake of him that we have the love of the Father and the grace of the Son and the communion of the Spirit himself."[133] We have no *continuity* with God "that belongs to the creature in itself"; this must be "continuously given and sustained by the presence of the Spirit within creation bringing creaturely relations to their *telos* in God."[134] For this reason, Torrance insists that there can be no concept of "a mutual correlation between the creature and the Creator." This is why Torrance insists that there is "no necessary relation between God and the world he has created, for he had no need of the creation to be who he is, while the world he creatively brought into existence out of nothing contains no reason in itself why it should be what it is and should continue to exist as it does."[135] Here Torrance's thinking is fully in accord with Barth's. He even appeals to Barth's own understanding of the matter to say: "Coming from the inner Life and Communion of the Trinity, the Holy Spirit is the Creator God who in virtue of his presence to the creature, not just externally nor just from above, but from within and from below, effectuates the relation of the creature to himself by way of a relation of himself to himself."[136]

Second, the Holy Spirit is God himself freely opening creatures to know and love God, creating in them a "capacity for God" and thus enabling knowledge of God. The basis of this, says Torrance, is "the inner personal relations of the Holy Trinity" in creation and revelation. And

132. Ibid., 170–71.
133. Torrance, *Christian Doctrine of God*, 197.
134. Torrance, *God and Rationality*, 171.
135. Torrance, *Christian Doctrine of God*, 216.
136. Ibid., 218.

because the Father has created and revealed himself in creation in his Word, all of this occurs only "in the inseparable relation of the Spirit to the Word." Therefore the Spirit does not come in his own name but "in the name of the Son."[137] This is an extremely important point. As the Spirit is the Spirit of the Father and Son in eternity, so the Spirit in creation and revelation cannot be conceptualized independently from the work of the Son "or apart from the incarnation of the Word."[138] As seen above, this thinking is wholly in line with Barth's insistence that the Spirit in no way and at no time can be separated theoretically or practically from the Son or from the Father.

What does this imply? For Torrance it means that we cannot think of the Spirit as a rational principle that informs all things with rationality and imparts form to humanity "which can be brought to expression within the cosmos as its inherent entelechy."[139] This statement of course eliminates at root the attempt of natural theology to approach knowledge of God with the claim that reason may know "that God is" but not "what God is." Because the Spirit actualizes within creation "its bond of union with the *Logos*," our minds learn of the truth of God only through God's Word and thus through union with Christ by the Spirit who recreates us in his image. Even though we are unable to relate our thoughts and speech to God, God himself acts upon us and within us to enable us to know him.[140] That indeed is the epistemological function of the Spirit. Here in the activity of the Holy Spirit, God himself is the object of our knowing in his activity of "creating from our side a corresponding action in which our own being is committed."[141] Torrance calls this "kinetic" thinking because it involves a movement of thought and experience that "corresponds to the movement of the Spirit and indeed participates in it."[142] In this sense, theology is a spiritual activity. We know God by participating in what we seek to know. In this view Torrance says we may only know Jesus Christ as the eternal Word who became flesh according to the Spirit and in faith. Torrance says that what we have here is a leap of faith that is neither blind nor irrational.

137. Torrance, *God and Rationality*, 171.
138. Ibid., 172. See also Torrance, *Trinitarian Faith*, 200–203.
139. Ibid.
140. Ibid., 176. This is a persistent theme in all of Torrance's writings.
141. Ibid., 177.
142. Ibid.

Importantly, Torrance understands that none of this depends on us but only upon God who acts upon us. Were true knowledge of God here to depend on us, we would, as Heidegger claims, "leap into nothing or into death."[143] Here again Barth and Torrance are one in rejecting any notion that we can rely on ourselves to understand God in truth.

Torrance maintains that when we think of God on the basis of revelation, we are confronted with something so totally *new* that we must engage in a "repentant rethinking" of all our presuppositions. We must, Torrance says, be carried beyond ourselves "to what is utterly beyond us."[144] Admittedly, Torrance is not always this careful, as when he says "we bring our thinking under the compulsion of the inherent rationality of the divine Being."[145] But there can be no doubt that he intends to allow the doctrine of justification to shape his epistemology here just as Barth had done. Hence he insists that the Spirit comes to us from beyond our being to give us God's own Being as an object of knowledge and to realize our knowledge of God from our side. Here, Torrance notes that we are at enmity with God without this knowledge which is based on our reconciliation with God in Christ.[146] As seen above, this thinking reiterates Barth's important point that we may only know our enmity with God from the reconciliation of God that has taken place in Christ himself. And this is the place from which we may know God with certitude. It is here that all approaches to God that claim to know "that God is" without knowing "who God is" in faith falter because their claim ultimately disregards God's movement toward us in his Word and Spirit.

Third, because the Spirit "hides Himself from us" we are not informed with "his own Form" but with the "Form of the Word." In this way we "participate in the communion of the Father and the Son." The Spirit never ceases being God himself even when he enables us who are incapable of relation with God to become free "from imprisonment in themselves" and "partake of His creative and eternal Life."[147] In the Holy Spirit we "come up against God in the most absolute and ultimate

---

143. Ibid., 178.
144. Ibid.
145. Ibid., 170.
146. Ibid., 179.
147. Ibid., 172.

sense."[148] Thus, God "resists all our attempts to be independent of him or to get alongside of Him or to manipulate Him."[149] The Holy Spirit distinguishes his own activity from all our "creative spirituality." God is thus revealed within the structures of our own experience, but in such a way that he always encounters us as the Lord in his own way through his own Word of self-revelation. This thinking is fully in accord with Barth's view that although we experience and know God in faith, we can never control God or our knowledge of God and so must pray for the Spirit to come upon us again and again.

Fourth, The Holy Spirit actually operates within us to realize our human response to God. He turns us away from our "in-turned" and "in-grown existence" toward God. Because the Holy Spirit "is the eternal communion of the Father and the Son,"[150] when he is sent into our hearts "by the Father in the name of the Son we are made partakers with the Son in His Communion with the Father and thus of God's own self-knowledge."[151] In this way we are "converted from ourselves to thinking from a centre in God and not in ourselves, and to knowledge of God out of God and not out of ourselves."[152] In the Spirit we actually know God in truth "together with Christ" and thus "always out of a centre in Him."[153] This thinking surely corresponds with Barth's view that the truth cannot be found directly within our self-experience and knowledge, but must always be sought and found in Christ himself and thus through the Spirit and in faith.

I have noted the importance of holding together God's Word and Spirit for Torrance. This means that God's being is not dark or mute but eloquent because God speaks himself and utters himself both within the eternal Trinity in one way and in our hearts in another.[154] While "the Word of God remains eternally Word and does not disappear into Spirit," God nevertheless speaks in a way appropriate to his nature as Spirit. In us, however, the Spirit remains distinct from our spirits. Several crucial implications follow. *First*, because the Word is within God's eter-

---

148. Ibid., 173.
149. Ibid.
150. Ibid.
151. Ibid., 174.
152. Ibid.
153. Ibid.
154. Ibid., 180.

nal being, God himself is the Word he utters. Hence "The Word is not just the form that the shining of God's light or the going forth of His Spirit takes in the *opera Trinitas ad extra* but is eternally in the depth of the divine Being what it is as Word towards us."[155] Through his Spirit and Word, Torrance insists, following Anselm and Calvin, God speaks to us—God "articulates Himself within our minds and makes Himself understood by us in accordance with His self-revelation."[156] This factor prevents genuine knowledge of God from becoming a human construct projected into God. *Second*, "the co-ordinating principle of theological knowledge does not lie in theological activity itself but in the speaking of the Word by the Spirit and our participation in the Word through the Spirit."[157] In other words we cannot think our way into God. That would be a form of self-justification, which Torrance abhors. Torrance asserts, "Theological knowledge must take the road from God to man before it takes the road from man to God."[158] For Torrance, theology takes place in *acknowledgment* that we do not know God by the power of our own thought or spirituality but only by allowing the Spirit to lead us to recognize and respond to the truth of God's Word. The basis of theology therefore is "not in itself but in God."[159] All genuine theology must be open to "the questioning and speaking of the Spirit" and thus it can only be "*obedient* service to God's own testimony to himself."[160]

Third, theological knowledge can only take place in the form of "*recognition-statements.*"[161] This is an enormously important point because what Torrance means here is that genuine theological knowledge is neither creative nor inventive. If that were to happen, then theology would be self-grounded and would attempt to establish itself "as the basis of reality by building a world of reality on its own inventions and achievements."[162] For Torrance, theology must allow its knowledge to

---

155. Ibid. This is a frequently repeated insight found in all of Torrance's major works. See, e.g., Torrance, *Christian Doctrine of God*, 130; *Trinitarian Perspectives*, 38; and *Trinitarian Faith*, 233.

156. Torrance, *God and Rationality*, 181.

157. Ibid.

158. Ibid.

159. Ibid., 182.

160. Ibid., emphasis mine.

161. Ibid.

162. Ibid.

be shaped by the given reality, namely, by God's own Word and Spirit. Theological knowledge in the form of recognition statements takes place only in acknowledgment[163] as our thinking points beyond itself to the Word "as their sole justification and truth."[164]

Fourth, the Holy Spirit works in our knowledge of God by personally being present to us and acting to open our minds to understand his revelation and to respond to God in faith and love. God uses the media of creation to do this in such a way that our minds do not "terminate on the media but on the Being of God Himself."[165] According to Torrance, God is personally present to us in space and time and uses "the sign-world of inter-human communication" to speak to us. God directs us, Torrance believes, "to immediate intuitive knowledge of Himself in His own ultimate Objectivity and Reality."[166] The sign-world God uses is the history of the covenant fulfilled in the incarnation and as witnessed in the Bible as inspired by the Spirit. Even now, Torrance says, God comes to us "clothed in the historical and biblical forms of His revelation which (whether BC or AD) direct us to Jesus Christ in the centre."[167] And it is the Holy Spirit who enables us to know God "directly and immediately in Jesus Christ." This is how God meets us in history objectively and so this knowledge excludes "any possibility of non-objective knowledge." But God also meets us in his Spirit "as Supreme Subject, and thus in all His ultimate objectivity as Lord God."[168] Again, from what was said above, this thinking is fully in accord with Barth's understanding of our knowledge of God as mediated through history and thus through the prophetic and apostolic testimony and ultimately through the incarnate Word.

All historical signs, however, in themselves cannot refer us to God because they refer only to intra-worldly reality. To function properly they must (and this includes biblical statements) be made to point beyond themselves to God. That, according to Torrance, is where the Holy Spirit enters along with his "propriety to the Word of God."[169] He

163. Ibid.
164. Ibid., 183.
165. Ibid., 184.
166. Ibid.
167. Ibid.
168. Ibid.
169. Ibid., 185.

speaks the Word "in all His divine ineffability and transparence" so that through the created media, he discloses himself to us by making us capable of "knowing Him beyond ourselves. Apart from the work of the Holy Spirit all the forms of revelation remain dark and opaque but in and through His presence they become translucent and transparent."[170]

How then can we think about that which utterly transcends our own thoughts by means of those same thoughts? How can we use human language with merely intra-worldly reference to speak of God who transcends it altogether? These are our most difficult questions, Torrance says, and the answers can be found only in the "operation of the Holy Spirit."[171] What we cannot do "by our thinking and stating is done by his *action* as Spirit of God."[172] This means that a proper interpretation of Scripture cannot simply look at linguistic and logical facts and the intentions of the authors, but to God himself and his truth. We must learn, Torrance says, that "the truth of realities is independent of the statements we make in signifying them." True statements about God thus have a "dimension of depth"[173] since they point beyond themselves to the truth of God.

Our concepts, Torrance believes, must be kept open. On our side they are closed since we need to formulate them exactly and carefully. But they are open on God's side. What does this mean? For Torrance it means that "our acts of cognition are formed from beyond them by the reality disclosed so that the content of what is revealed constantly bursts through the forms we bring to it in order to grasp it."[174] And the only way this can happen is "under the power of the Spirit."[175] It is the Spirit who actually keeps our concepts open, thus enabling us to know what is beyond them. Without this action of the Spirit, our concepts either obscure or obstruct revelation. Open concepts importantly are not irrational because they are open; rather openness to God "is the true mode of their rationality." This indicates that our concepts cannot control God's rationality and thus are limited. Open concepts "do not

170. Ibid.
171. Ibid., 186.
172. Ibid.
173. Ibid.
174. Ibid., 187.
175. Ibid.

describe, delimit, or define the Reality we seek to understand."[176] Rather, through them "we allow our minds to come under the compulsion of the Reality so that we may think of it only as we are forced to."[177] And when this happens, these concepts will necessarily point beyond themselves. This can happen only through the Spirit. Knowledge of God is rational and conceptual but it is also "apposite to the nature of God as *Spirit*" and so "we are carried right over to what transcends us."[178]

Fifth, knowledge of God takes place within the rational, personal, and social structures of human life. This happens through the "personalizing Spirit."[179] This means that as "the living presence of God confronts us with His personal Being, addresses us in His Word, opens us out toward Himself, and calls forth from us the response of faith and love, He rehabilitates the *human subject*, sustaining him in his personal relations with God and with his fellow creatures."[180] As human subjects, Torrance thinks, we can easily become concerned only with things and think mechanically and impersonally. Or we might react against such false objectivism and try to "subdue everything to [our] own subjectivity and so get locked up in [ourselves]."[181] Then we might actually objectify our own subjective states, cutting ourselves off from objective reality. It is the Spirit who both frees us from our "in-turned subjectivity"[182] for "genuinely objective experience" and from the "threat of impersonalizing objectivism and determinism"[183] so that we become free to stand before God and capable of spontaneous personal relations with others.

The personalizing work of the Spirit comes from "the inter-personal Communion of the Holy Trinity" and "establishes divine communion among us by reconciling us with God"[184] and creating social structures that are sustained through God's presence. While "theological statements take their rise from a centre in God and not in ourselves, the very nature of the divine Object makes it impossible for us

176. Ibid.
177. Ibid.
178. Ibid., 188.
179. Ibid.
180. Ibid.
181. Ibid., 189.
182. Ibid., 188.
183. Ibid., 189.
184. Ibid.

to abstract them from the personal and community setting in which they take place."[185] A distinction between judgment and proposition is necessary. Judgments involve decisions within each individual's mind. But propositions occur within objective relations "between two or more subjects" so that together they "come under the compulsive reality of what is given in common to them."[186] Theology necessarily involves propositions that develop out of the church's obedient acknowledgment of God's self-revelation and are clarified and deepened through worship, dialogue, and "repentant rethinking within the whole communion of saints."[187] This requires them to be ecumenical or open to the entire community to avoid distortion through a "false in-turned subjectivity." But ultimately "it is not the Church but God Himself who is the Object of their reference."[188] There is a danger here. The church could end up reinterpreting God's Word "to suit contemporary thought and culture."[189] The temptation is for the church to "transfer the locus of authority from the Word and Truth of God to its own collective subjectivity, and to identify the Spirit of God with its own spirit."[190] Torrance maintains that the church must also be on guard against this danger by being critical of its own thinking in a disciplined manner by testing its thought and speech to make sure that it is really speaking about God and not itself. This, however, cannot simply be achieved "by method, no matter how rigorous and scientific, for it is only by divine *action* that man's thought may be related to God's Truth and his speech may actually refer to God's Being."[191] That is precisely why the church must continually pray for the Holy Spirit. It is the Holy Spirit alone who can free the church "from imprisonment in itself or deliver its mind from being engrossed in its own subjectivity by confronting it with the implacable Objectivity of the divine Subject, and call forth from it a faithful response to the divine self-revelation."[192] It is in this regard that the role of the Holy Spirit in our knowledge of God is eschatological. It is eschatological in the sense

185. Ibid.
186. Ibid., 188–89.
187. Ibid., 190.
188. Ibid.
189. Ibid.
190. Ibid., 191.
191. Ibid.
192. Ibid.

that only God himself can judge our theological statements in such a way that they may actually signify God who transcends this world of time and space. The result of true knowledge of God will be the recognition that when we really know God's being and act, we know that this being and action cannot pass over into the church. If that were to happen we would be thrown back upon ourselves. But the Spirit constantly judges us and points us to Christ as the objective source of our knowledge of God and thus the Spirit enables us to distinguish God's truth from our knowledge of it, "and so to live ever out of Christ and not out of ourselves."[193]

Conclusion

What I hope can be seen from this presentation of the function of the Spirit in knowledge of the triune God is that all genuine knowledge of the Christian God always begins in acknowledgment, in the sense that it can only begin in faith in Christ and not at all in itself. And this beginning itself is not under anyone's power because it is itself a miracle enabled by the present action of the Holy Spirit uniting us to Christ and thus to the Father. When knowledge of God is understood in this way, natural theology is simply marginalized as a way to understand God in truth. And as long as theologians recognize and maintain the importance of the Holy Spirit in knowing God, they will to that extent never attempt to know God outside of faith in his Word and Spirit, and so their knowledge will never be grounded in reason or experience but only in grace as it meets us and heals our reason and enables our experience. Practically speaking this means that any attempt to know "that God is" that abstracts from "who God is" as the eternal Trinity will always end in some form of self-justification, attempting to know God by relying on reason rather than the Spirit, thus engaging in false forms of apologetics that aim to find ways to God that evade the need for faith and for exclusive reliance on the Holy Spirit from beginning to end.

---

193. Ibid., 192. For more on Torrance's notion of the Spirit as it relates to our knowledge of and relationship with the triune God see Torrance, *Christian Doctrine of God*, 147–55; and Torrance, *Theology in Reconstruction*, 39ff.

Bibliography

Barth, Karl. *Church Dogmatics*. 4 vols. Edinburgh: T. & T. Clark, 1956–75.

———. *Credo*. Translated by J. Strathearn McNab. 1962. Reprinted, Eugene, OR: Wipf & Stock, 2005.

———. *Karl Barth Letters 1961–1968*. Edited by Jürgen Fangmeier and Hinrich Stoevesandt. Translated and edited by Geoffrey W. Bromiley. Grand Rapids: Eerdmans, 1981.

———. *Karl Barth's Table Talk*. Edited by John D. Godsey. Richmond: John Knox, 1962.

———. *The Knowledge of God and the Service of God according to the Teaching of the Reformation*. Translated by J. L. M. Haire and Ian Henderson. London: Hodder & Stoughton, 1949.

Grenz, Stanley J. *Rediscovering the Triune God: The Trinity in Contemporary Theology*. Minneapolis: Fortress, 2004.

Healy, Nicholas. *Thomas Aquinas: Theologian of the Christian Life*. Aldershot, UK: Ashgate, 2003.

Johnson, Elizabeth A. *Quest for the Living God: Mapping Frontiers in the Theology of God*. New York: Continuum: 2008.

———. *She Who Is: The Mystery of God in Feminist Theological Discourse*. New York: Crossroad, 1992.

McGrath, Alister E. "Karl Barth's Doctrine of Justification from an Evangelical Perspective." In *Karl Barth and Evangelical Theology: Convergences and Divergences*, edited by Sung Wook Chung, 172–90. Milton Keynes, UK: Paternoster, 2006.

Molnar, Paul D. *Divine Freedom and the Doctrine of the Immanent Trinity: In Dialogue with Karl Barth and Contemporary Theology*. London: T. & T. Clark, 2005.

———. *Incarnation and Resurrection: Toward a Contemporary Understanding*. Grand Rapids: Eerdmans, 2007.

———. "Natural Theology Revisited: A Comparison of T. F. Torrance and Karl Barth." *Zeitschrift für Dialektische Theologie* 20 (2005) 53–83.

———. Review of *Thomas Aquinas and Karl Barth: Sacred Doctrine and the Natural Knowledge of God*, by Eugene F. Rogers. *Scottish Journal of Theology* 55 (2002) 496–98.

———. "Some Problems with Pannenberg's Solution to Barth's 'Faith Subjectivism.'" *Scottish Journal of Theology* 48 (1995) 315–39.

Murray, John Courtney. *The Problem of God Yesterday and Today*. New Haven: Yale University Press, 1965.

Pannenberg, Wolfhart. *Systematic Theology*. Vol. 1. Translated by Geoffrey W. Bromiley. Grand Rapids: Eerdmans, 1991.

Rogers, Eugene F. *Thomas Aquinas and Karl Barth: Sacred Doctrine and the Natural Knowledge of God*. Notre Dame: University of Notre Dame Press, 1995.

Taylor, Iain. *Pannenberg on the Triune God*. London: T. & T. Clark, 2007.

Torrance, Alan. *Persons in Communion: Trinitarian Description and Human Participation*. Edinburgh: T. & T. Clark, 1996.

Torrance, Thomas F. *The Christian Doctrine of God: One Being, Three Persons*. Edinburgh: T. & T. Clark, 1996.

———. *God and Rationality*. London: Oxford University Press, 1971.

———. *Theology in Reconstruction*. Eugene, OR: Wipf & Stock, 1996.
———. *The Trinitarian Faith: The Evangelical Theology of the Ancient Catholic Church*. Edinburgh: T. & T. Clark, 1988.
———. *Trinitarian Perspectives: Toward Doctrinal Agreement*. Edinburgh: T. & T. Clark, 1994.

2

Divine Light
Some Reflections after Barth

Ivor J. Davidson

BARTH MADE IT EASIER AND HARDER TO TALK ABOUT THE DOCTRINE of God. Easier, in so far as his theology identifies with such sharpness so many of the dogmatic imperatives of the gospel; harder, in that the range and eloquence of his presentation have sometimes left the sympathetic wondering quite what is left to say. Doing theology "after Barth" means many things, of course, the very last of which ought to be slavish adherence to Barth's wisdom, or the naïve supposition that Barth spoke the final word on anything. Barth is taken seriously when we pursue with proper attentiveness the always unfinished, always costly business to which his theology issued its relentless summons: reckoning with the uniqueness of the God who presents himself to us in the gospel.

That task is, by definition, never reducible to the computation of domestic capital, or the mere repetition of inherited insight. It involves engagement with a living presence, with the ever-fresh and inexhaustible reality of the One who, in free majesty, gives himself on no terms other than his own: not as an object for possession, but as the God whose revealed fullness always exceeds our measure. Appropriate response to the staggering reality of God's mercy means the demanding yet delightful work of submitting our minds to the living Word of God, whose glory is transcendent of any contingent representation, no matter how faithful. It is ironic that Barth himself should ever be treated as a kind of final authority, or—for all his magisterial gifts—as some sort of ultimate artisan of theological profundity in a modern key. To learn from Barth at all is to go on wondering at the fathomless marvel the evangel announces: the triune God, who is who he is, determines to be

God for and with us. Barth's significance as a Christian theologian bears the weight it does not because of the expansiveness or color or influence of his work, but in so far as his dogmatics represents an exceptionally dogged pursuit of the unending question posed by this God's arrival in our midst: "What does this mean?" (Acts 2:12).

In what follows, I want to consider some of the ways in which Barth's mature theology might help us gloss a primordial response of faith to divine encounter: "God is light" (1 John 1:5). The implications of that confession, along with its obvious hinterlands in Johannine theology and in Israel's Scripture, have of course had a very high profile in classical doctrinal argumentation, and huge significance in historic Christian spirituality. In modern dogmatics the theme has received somewhat less attention than we might expect. Barth himself presents relatively little by way of direct commentary upon it in *Church Dogmatics*, but the idea of divine light occupies an important place in two sections of the work: in II/1, in Barth's treatment of the divine perfections, particularly §31.3, on the Glory of God; then—much more extensively—in the Christology of IV/3: §69.2, on "The Glory of the Mediator," "the Light of Life," and in its corresponding paragraph, §71.1: "Man in the Light of Life." Barth's theology is, however, instructive on the subject in ways that far transcend these tracts. In pressing us to ponder what is and is not occurring in the dazzling reality of God's self-giving, Barth's dogmatics as a whole invites us to trace the antecedent conditions of that bestowal in the identity of the One who, just as he is, shines forth towards creatures. What might an account of divine luminosity look like after an appreciative albeit leisurely reading of Barth? I shall begin by rehearsing some basic moves in Barth, then offer a very rudimentary sketch in response to the question.

Encountering God: Revelation and the Divine Perfections

At the heart of Barth's exposition of the doctrine of God in *Church Dogmatics* II lies the claim that divine objectivity, properly understood, is the sole basis for the knowledge of God by human beings. God is, and is of himself objective to himself. The God who is, and who in his eternal being knows himself immediately, moves in mercy to posit himself as an object for human minds: creatures are constituted knowers, and that of God. God's immediate self-knowledge, his "primary objectivity" for himself, is unattainable by us, but it is the essential ground of God's preparedness to be secondarily objective for us; the latter is mediated, clothed, yet stands in vital correspondence with the former. Thus is shattered the supposition that creaturely knowledge of God can only be appraised as an activity of free projection, an attempt to put flesh upon such intuitions as may putatively be had of an entirely transcendent reality, or (to cite a somewhat different preference) to render worldly experience in the necessary yet porous symbolism of moral or existential categories. Thus is shattered also the drastic inference that if the implications of such supposedly obligatory constructivism are taken with full seriousness, extreme epistemic ascesis—negativity—emerges as the only intelligent option. *Au contraire*: when the God who knows himself elects to be known by others, cognitive possibilities lie in his hands.

Knowledge so afforded is of course, as Barth emphasizes, a matter of sheer grace. It is visible to faith, not to sight; it is afforded to those who have no readiness of their own, but are made ready by the particular acts in which God engages when he manifests for creatures his eternally antecedent readiness to be known. God's acts of self-disclosure in no wise place him at our disposal, or dissolve the concealment that is also present in his movement towards us: "In all our thinking and speaking about Him" consequential upon his revelation, "we never become His masters."[1] Nevertheless, to encounter God is to be granted, by the miracle of divine agency, a creaturely version of God's unique knowledge of himself.

God's works of self-presentation are thus not merely ostensive, a (necessarily ineffectual) display of the divine character before a world of obtuse—spiritually unsighted—spectators. They are generated by a divine determination to bestow upon contingent beings such share as God chooses in his essential self-understanding—in more familiar register, they enact God's wholly merciful will to seek and save the lost—and just so they effect a radical transformation of creaturely circumstances. God's self-presentation includes its own efficaciousness. Revelation and reconciliation, as Barth discerns, are of a piece; more precisely, revelation *is* reconciliation in its cognitive effect. Against those enduring critics of Barth who suppose such idiom to reduce soteriology to an overtly modern obsession with *Erkenntnis* stands Barth's delimitation of what

1. *CD* II/1, 342.

it in fact means to know the triune God: revelation is not the mere provision of information to agents somehow capable in themselves of appropriate response; it occurs in the drawing of the alienated, the confused and the helpless into saving fellowship with the Father through the Son by the Spirit. In that process occurs a definitive reordering of the standing of such creatures in regard to God, and thus, simultaneously, of their apprehension of who God is. In turn—crucially—new kinds of creaturely action are evoked, reflective of the genuine freedom and responsibility into which creatures are brought, covenant-partners of God. In sum, questions of knowledge can only be settled where they *are* settled: in a divine self-giving that decisively alters the conditions of those who, in their native sphere, do not know God.[2]

Describing the character of the God who is who he is in the act of his revelation—"the One who loves in freedom"—means describing God's perfections. Barth delineates twelve of these in particular, organized under the respective, inseparable themes of divine loving and divine freedom: under the first head come grace and holiness, mercy and righteousness, patience and wisdom; under the second, unity and omnipresence, constancy and omnipotence, eternity and glory (CD §29–31). Whatever may be said about the success of Barth's arrangement—the elevation of a complex of "major" perfections; the isolation of these particular ones as central; the dialectical pairing of concepts; the putative associations with loving or freedom primarily; the efforts to mark off properly theological (as distinct from general) uses of terms; the intricate movements backwards and forwards with which Barth develops and qualifies his case; the details of the scriptural exegesis that occupies swathes of the discussion—the most compelling feature of Barth's treatment is his insistence that the divine perfections as we encounter them are indeed defining features of God's Godness. Divine revelation is no phenomenal display, the assumption of qualities "merely in connexion with [God's] self-revelation to the world,"[3] or simply (*pace* some major

---

2. If such a vision implies that Barth remains captive to modern preoccupation with knowledge, it is thus a decidedly odd captivity. His acute consciousness of the Kantian challenge and the lingering influence of later Marburg Neo-Kantianism certainly reflect his intellectual roots in the nineteenth century; but there is also an explicit subversion of the basic assumption on which the epistemological strategies of his theological mentors had, to his mind, ultimately foundered: the notion that God could ever be, in any sense, at the *disposal* of human subjects.

3. CD II/1, 327.

figures in the Christian tradition) a matter of divine accommodation to creaturely capacities.[4] Precisely inasmuch as creaturely knowledge of God is a consequence of God's loving and free resolve to afford us a genuine taste of his boundless self-understanding, "God is actually and unreservedly as we encounter Him in His revelation."[5]

Barth is conscious of the contingency of his way of organizing things: his approach does not bear express scriptural or traditional warrant, and "can possess and claim only the character of an attempt or suggestion."[6] He goes to considerable lengths to emphasize the vital coinherence of loving and freedom, and to sketch the interrelationship that must be deemed to exist between themes; the proposed orientations towards loving or freedom respectively are said to be primary, not exclusive; the overlapping of territory is reflective of the essential simplicity as well as relational complexity and differentiable abundance that characterizes God's being (just as God's oneness includes his threeness, so the one God subsists in a multitude of inseparable perfections). More significant than the form of the treatment is the fundamental motivation of its content: to map "the contours of [God's] being"[7] responsibly is to reject any nominalistic construal of the derivation and distribution of divine perfections, any idea of divine "attributes" as mere features of creaturely ascription to one conceived as a maximally perfect or supreme being. Appropriate language about God's characteristics is not extrapolated from psychological, religio-genetic, or historico-intuitive appraisal of a divine being capable of being known in general;[8] it derives from the specific sequence of divine self-identification that occurs in the history of God's creating, reconciling, and redeeming acts attested in Holy Scripture.[9]

The content of love and freedom is not to be filled out with reference to generic concepts; it is defined in the dramatic sequence of God's

4. Ibid., 327–30.
5. Ibid., 325.
6. Ibid., 441; cf. also 657–58.
7. Ibid., 336.
8. Ibid., 335–41.

9. It is this concern to underscore the uniqueness of God's enacted identity that lies behind Barth's preference for the language of "perfections" (*Vollkommenheiten*) over the more familiar terminology of "attributes" (*Eigenschaften*): other beings may formally have attributes; the being of God alone is revealed to be "identical with" a multitude of perfections (ibid., 322).

presentation of himself to us. The divine glory that meets us there is the Lord of glory himself:[10] there is no other God behind the perfections as encountered in the economy of God's action; the perfections of the economy are not, as it were, ends in themselves, but God in person. The God who lives his perfect life in the plenitude of his manifold perfections does not merely *have* his perfections—as Anselm rightly discerned,[11] he *is* his perfections. The manifestation of those perfections occurs as God's choice to live his life—without detriment to his intrinsic completeness—in fellowship with us.

Talk of the divine perfections must accordingly be trinitarian at its core. It is as Trinity that God makes himself known; in so far as God actually does make *himself* known, his self-disclosure as triune is grounded in his triune character *in se*. God is "the One who, both in His revelation and in eternity, is the same."[12] God's loving is specified in God's works of seeking and establishing fellowship between himself and creatures. Yet the source of those acts is the God who already exists not in solitude but in fellowship, as Father, Son and Holy Spirit, "alive in His unique being with and for and in another."[13] God's freedom finds its positive expression in God's enacted determination to be what God is found to be in Jesus Christ: free for and with humanity. Yet the bedrock of that freedom is an aseity that is not reducible to mere absence of external causation or constraint, but is God's singular capacity to live the triune life God does. God's self-existence is no abstract (monistic) independence or absoluteness, but the living energy of eternal self-communication that characterizes God's ever-sufficient, ever-realized yet ever-mobile being-in-relation.

Barth's foundational exposition of that divine relationality in the idiom of divine self-reiteration and "ways of being" (*Seinsweisen*) presents to many critics a less robust account of divine personal fellowship than such investments require. Whether Barth's ensuing treatment of individual perfections turns out to be as explicitly and consistently trinitarian in its details as one might expect,[14] and whether his overall

10. Ibid., 322.
11. *Proslogion* 12, at ibid., 323.
12. *CD* II/1, 324.
13. Ibid., 275.
14. The trinitarian doctrine set out at such length in *CD* I is plainly assumed by Barth to be fundamental for all his talk of God "in the correct sense" in *CD* II/3; at least

account devotes nearly enough space to the Holy Spirit in particular,[15] are matters of interpretative debate. What is undeniable is that Barth's depiction of the reality of God is founded on an immensely strong claim that God is indeed the triune God he shows himself to be, *and* that the triune economy is just what it is because of its basis in the relations that constitute God's inner life. God does not constitute his own being in history: he subsists complete in his triune perfections regardless of any world, opening up those perfections to creaturely apprehension as a matter of loving freedom. But that loving freedom is itself God's true nature, the identity he essentially bears as Father, Son, and Holy Spirit. Without *collapsing* talk of divine identity into talk of the functions of God in creating, sustaining, and redeeming contingent reality (and thus compromising fatally, as a good deal of modern theology does, the completeness of God's immanent being), Barth seeks to affirm that there is no *gap* between who God is and what God does, between God's eternal character and what God makes himself known to be. God does what he does solely because he is—in anterior fullness—the God he shows himself to be.

If this is the relationship between God *ad intra* and God *ad extra*, *glory* assumes a particular significance in discourse on the divine perfections. Glory is not merely a perfection in itself, one more feature in a series of inseparable divine characteristics; it is a synonym for the perfections as a whole,[16] "the self-revealing sum of all divine perfections."[17] Barth's entire discussion of the perfections is framed by its importance,[18] for the divine glory *is* God's being in so far as that being is, in its essence, a being that declares itself.[19] God's glory "is His dignity and right not only to maintain, but to prove and declare, to denote and almost as it were to make Himself conspicuous and everywhere apparent as the One He is."[20] Barth grounds his exposition in the biblical associations (*kabod, doxa*) with light; "glory" and "light" serve more or less as

---

part of the question then is whether he is to be criticized for failing to repeat himself—a fairly unusual charge if so.

15. See, e.g., Gunton, *Act and Being*, 97–104.
16. *CD* II/1, 327.
17. Ibid., 643; cf. 652.
18. Ibid., 324, and 640–77.
19. Ibid., 643.
20. Ibid., 641.

interchangeable terms in his discussion.[21] Critical elsewhere of the vestigial nominalism that he detects in Protestant Orthodoxy's reluctance to take seriously the unity of essence and attributes,[22] Barth here finds inspiration from Petrus van Mastricht for four contentions:[23] (1) God's glory consists in the fact that God's being is his utter fullness and self-sufficiency as God, the unique source of light, the only being who is light in himself; (2) God's glory is the radiance of God, his splendor as the one who shines forth, omnipotently reaching into the darkness, overcoming the distance between himself and others, seeking and at once finding those to whom he declares himself; (3) God's glory is God's coming to creatures in person, to show them not something other than himself but the very glory of his own "face"; (4) God's glory is the consequence of God's outshining in the actual illumination of creatures, the eliciting of glory from them, the bringing of them to their intended destiny as sharers in God's eternal joy in himself. God's glory is, in the end, his overflowing, self-communicating delight; what is made known in his essential radiance is his *beauty*, a reality which "speaks for itself": the One who gives pleasure, creates desire and rewards with enjoyment does so "because first and last He alone is that which is pleasant, desirable and full of enjoyment."[24]

Barth's account of God's revealed splendor seeks to be governed at every point by the person in whom this divine *kabod* has its "middle point, . . . concrete form and name":[25] Jesus Christ. A doctrine of God, if it is to be properly Christian, must not, as Barth puts it, be "only a doctrine of God":[26] it must be a doctrine of the God made known in the incarnation, "the center and goal of all God's works, and therefore the hidden beginning of them all."[27] This concern is basic to the reasoning of *CD* II/1; in *CD* II/2 the point is pressed considerably further. The particularity of the gospel, Barth insists, must govern everything; the gospel speaks of God's loving and free resolve to be God not merely

---

21. On the semantic context, see ibid., 641–43.
22. See further Holmes, "Theological Function of the Doctrine of the Divine Attributes," 206–23.
23. *CD* II/1, 646–49.
24. Ibid., 650–51.
25. Ibid., 643.
26. *CD* II/2, 5.
27. *CD* II/1, 661.

for himself but also for creatures. The theology of election accordingly lies at the heart of the doctrine of God, as "the sum" of that good news. Election is properly focused in the twofold reality made known in Jesus Christ, at once the subject and the object of election, the electing God and the elect human. First, God has primally determined himself, in utterly loving freedom, for relation to humankind: to enact his being in the entirely gracious movement that climaxes in the death, resurrection, and ascension of Jesus Christ. Second, since the agent of election is not some absolute God but the God who takes human flesh in Jesus Christ, election is the election of humanity to the particular form of human life which Jesus Christ establishes: covenant fellowship with God. In Jesus, the election of human beings is seen not as the settling of eschatological fates by inscrutable divine decree, but as the choice of humanity for life with God.

The interpretation of the significance of Barth's theology of election for his (and potentially for all) trinitarian theology has occasioned very vigorous debate in recent years.[28] The origins of aspects of Barth's thinking in his hearing of Pierre Maury in Geneva in 1936; his turn towards a much more explicitly christological construal of the doctrine of God as anticipated in *CD* II/1 but only made explicit in *CD* II/2; the long-term consequences as witnessed in the mature narrative theology of *CD* IV/1–3; the implications of the whole for the periodization of Barth's work and the internal consistency or otherwise of his thinking in *Church Dogmatics*—all are properly matters of serious genetic-historical investigation. What is of much larger pertinence is the theological weight attached to the conclusions. What degree of inspirational creativity ought to be attributed to Barth's so-called actualistic divine ontology as it takes shape from *CD* II/2 onwards? To what extent does his supposed handling thereafter of the logical relationship between election and Trinity represent a brilliant (if not always consistent) move beyond essentialist metaphysics, one which takes with fully "modern" seriousness God's commitment of himself to history yet manages to avoid a collapse into Hegelianism? Or, to the contrary: to what extent does the attempt to see it as such reflect a misreading of Barth's work, which carries with it severe consequences for a responsible articulation

---

28. A debate launched in large measure by McCormack, "Grace and Being," 92–110, an essay which has given rise to an ongoing stream of discussion from both critics and defenders, and significant further elaboration of the issues from McCormack himself.

of the very freedom of God's immanent being which Barth never ceased to prize?[29]

How these questions are answered will clearly depend on assessments of the degree of development discerned within Barth's thought in the *Church Dogmatics*, and of the extent to which material may legitimately be synthesized across the work as a whole. More specifically, it will depend on how one reads the relationship between the foundational account of divine aseity proposed in *CD* I–II/1 and the implications of Barth's subsequently intensifying case about God's self-determination to be only what God is found to be in Jesus Christ. Fundamentally, it will turn on whether—regardless of what Barth may be deemed to be implying at certain (rather cryptic) moments—it is *ever* sustainable from Barth's perspective to speak of God's being as "event" in the sense of an eternal decision on God's part "to give himself his being," and thus "to be triune for us," without somehow conflating being and time and dissolving God's essential (though *not* thereby "timeless") freedom and plenitude as the one who is inherently triune regardless of any world. To my mind it is not, and the endeavor to read the later Barth's theological ontology[30] that way is a mistake. Taking divine self-determination seriously entails, as Barth was acutely aware, a radical shake-up in traditional handling of the doctrine of election.[31] It means a repudiation of fallacious ideas (strangely persistent in many quarters) that Barth's convictions about divine aseity somehow represent a devaluing of worldly history or human creaturehood.[32] Above all, it means locating an entire theology of creation and reconciliation in its proper place: in God's unfathomably loving and free commitment of himself to live his

---

29. See, e.g., Molnar, *Divine Freedom and the Doctrine of the Immanent Trinity*, 61–64; Hunsinger, "Election and the Trinity." The full literature arguing for and against McCormack's position is too substantial to document here.

30. Which indubitably does develop within *CD*, its mature expression taking explicit impetus from the formulation of election presented in II/2. Whether such development represents, at its christological climax in IV/1–3, a fundamental revision of Barth's earlier ontological commitments is another matter.

31. "Because there is no darkness in God, there can be no darkness in what He chooses and wills. Nor is there anything midway, anything neutral, between light and darkness. In aim and purpose God is only light, unbroken light" (*CD* II/2, 169).

32. The "outward cause and object" of the overflowing of the divine glory, the human creature is appointed, *in* its otherness from God, to "participation in [God's] own glory," to existence "in the brightness of this glory and as the bearer of its image" (ibid.).

triune life with others, to utter the concrete decree that *is* Jesus Christ.[33] It does not mean, I believe, that God's being-in-act is ever, for Barth, a divine decision *to be triune* in anticipation of such fellowship.

The temporal history of God's outshining is nonetheless of the utmost importance, for it is in the concretions of that history that God is indeed found to be the God who, in utterly momentous grace, has determined himself for us. The narrative of reconciliation has as its center the story of Jesus Christ, the divine-human mediator in whom the covenant is fulfilled, the one who as Son of God ventures into the far country and as Son of Man returns home. His story includes the history of his free and sovereign self-communication in world-occurrence, his declaration of himself to creatures as the living one, whose glory "embraces both the *gloria* of God and the *glorificatio* which it deserves and exacts."[34] As God and man, humiliated and exalted, the Lord as Servant and the Servant as Lord, Jesus is the light of life, the one who shines out, "not with an alien light which falls upon Him from without and illuminates Him, but with His own light proceeding from Himself."[35] Agent of his own disclosure, the risen and ascended one announces himself victor over the world's darkness; the reconciliation that has occurred and does occur in him is radiant and perspicuous, "a fact which speaks for itself."[36] His prophetic work of attesting his own reality faces opposition and conflict, but must in the end prevail, for it is the revelation of an invincible reality: God's infinite commitment of himself to the world's blessing.[37]

Criticisms of this narrative Christology, and of Barth's treatment of the *munus propheticum* in *CD* IV/3 in particular, are common enough. The most familiar concern relates to the adequacy of Barth's pneumatology. Determined to avoid the collapse of talk of the Holy Spirit into a vague appeal to divine immanence—a fate he discerned widely in nineteenth-century divinity—and to offer a responsible alternative to the sorts of obsession with creaturely interpretation and existential experience evident in Bultmann and others in his own time, Barth focuses on the self-authenticating work of the exalted Christ. But does his

33. Cf. ibid., 158.
34. *CD* IV/3, 48.
35. Ibid., 46.
36. Ibid., 221.
37. On the irresistibility of divine glory, cf. earlier *CD* II/1, 645–46.

(notably Western and Reformed) idiom not seriously erode the place of the Spirit, perhaps even blur the Spirit's hypostatic identity? Does not Barth also, by extension, offer a markedly slim depiction of ecclesial agency, of the work of the Spirit-constituted body of the risen one, in the proclamation of the gospel, even as he labors to give due shape to human vocation in union with Christ? And does not his exposition of the mediator's glory, concerned as it is to explore the significance of divine *enanthropesis* for ethics, so emphasize the transcendent splendor of the exalted Christ that it runs into problems of its own: a risk of triumphalism, a sense of reconciliation's message as declaration of past achievement more than of present-tense socio-ethical reality? Does Barth's stress on the divine victory, his preoccupation with the heavenly power of the divine light, perhaps neglect the vital import of the humanity of the Savior—not least, in the context of Christ's priesthood, his ascended humanity and ongoing work as forerunner of his people, their brother-man at God's right hand?[38]

There is no doubt that Barth's approach is profoundly different from that of many theologies after him, particularly those concerned to offer unabashedly strong accounts of churchly mediation or overtly "social" treatments of creaturely participation in God. Some of these subsequent strategies have of course been developed in conscious correction of Barth, sometimes by those who in other respects seem honored to stand in his debt. The issues are too large to be addressed *en passant*. Whatever is to be said about the possible weaknesses of Barth's presentation,[39] his doctrine of reconciliation is remarkable not least for

---

38. See, e.g., Torrance, *Karl Barth, Biblical and Evangelical Theologian*, 133–35.

39. As various treatments of Barth's ethics have amply shown, the critiques of his accounts of human responsibility in particular are generally well wide of the mark, missing the point of his core claims about the nature of moral space: see, e.g., Webster, *Barth's Ethics of Reconciliation*. Nor is it remotely sustainable to accuse Barth of historical narrowness, for his account of the particularity of the mediator expressly includes Christ's universal pertinence, his constitutive significance for all the world's darkness. Christology certainly takes firm control over any metaphysics of history, and there is no shortage of a *grand récit*; but objections to such investments may reflect philosophical more than doctrinal commitments. As Barth's much-discussed remarks on "secular parables" and "lesser lights" suggest (and his political thought and activity abundantly bear out), attention to the specificity of the one who is "the one and only light of life" (*CD* IV/3, 86) does not at all mean cultural insularity, the consignment of the world as such to a realm of utter darkness from which nothing can be learned of God's glory or in which nothing Christianly ought to be done.

its massive expansion of themes with long-standing roots in his dogmatics; among these is the insistence that the objectivity of God's salvific outreach necessarily includes its completion in the realm of human subjectivity. Once again, when God elects to communicate himself, he brings to fruition what he wills and effects, seeking and at once finding those to whom he declares himself.[40] What occurs in this omnipotent divine act is not merely the establishment of cognitive union, but the bestowal of the gift of faith, which in turn gives rise to new forms of life, with new responsibilities, new joys and new patterns of social existence, all of them thoroughly human. If the description of the ministry of the Spirit as the distinctive personal instrument of such fruits turns out in the narrative ontology of *CD* IV to be slighter than some might wish, and if the consequent mapping of ecclesial agency is (quite deliberately) much more restrained than it might be, the underlying contention is consistent: divine luminosity is primary; divine luminosity does its own—unsubstitutable—work.

Analysis of the success of Barth's insistence upon the inseparability of the knowledge of God from the doctrine of God involves, in the end, an assessment of much of what Barth is about in the *Church Dogmatics* as a whole. The boundaries he erects around creaturely knowledge—his concerns to avoid the wrong kinds of theological realism, his determination not to collapse the immanent Trinity into the economic—have certainly been much misconstrued. Where they have not been missed altogether (by those who suppose him to know too much about the being of God), they have been seen, quite to the contrary, as vestiges of an ironic reticence (classical as well as modern) to take the history of revelation seriously enough—hence Barth's theology is alleged to leave us with the specter of a God who is unitary more than he is triune, a mysterious transcendent subject more than a genuinely knowable fellowship of persons in communion. Alternatively (and generally with much more enthusiasm), Barth's qualifications have been read as evidence of his anticipation of postmodern concerns about negative theology and the limitations of human language.

Responses to such misreadings are ready at hand—and in a contemporary context are likely to need to go on being offered—but can only amount to careful restatements of the basic logic of Barth's arguments about revelation and hiddenness, and about what it is that God is

---

40. *CD* II/1, 646.

doing and not doing in freely and lovingly reconciling estranged creatures to himself. There is for Barth (even in the allegedly underdeveloped relational differentiation of *CD* I) no God *beyond* the distinctions of Father, Son, and Holy Spirit (each of whom only *is* in perichoretic relation to the other two),[41] no monistic "hidden Fourth," no "economy which is foreign to [God's] essence,"[42] no knowledge of God that is not *ipso facto*, for creatures, a matter of properly responsive fellowship with God's triune life (censures of Barth for missing the point of *koinonia* are decidedly off-target). In *CD* II/1, the revelation of God's intrinsic triunity is said to occur in hiddenness in the sense that its source lies in this God alone, not in any creaturely capacities, and insofar as God is not an object capable of being reduced to or controlled by the words and images that are the necessary stuff of human cognition. But the external limitations of revelation are a function neither of creaturely finitude in general (a limitation perceived naturally) nor of a divine unwillingness to be apprehensible: they are a feature of the specific self-disclosure God enacts, a movement in which God freely and lovingly shows himself to be ontologically self-sufficient and beyond creaturely captivity, yet one who is indeed knowable by faith, personally and genuinely.

Veiling and unveiling are not "equally balanced" moments in that process: "Not the veiling . . . but the unveiling is the purpose of [God's] revelation, the direction of His will."[43] Talk of revealed hiddenness is no image of a *Deus absconditus* lurking behind the God who encounters us, or a pretext for the celebration of divine absence; it is talk of the judgment and the grace of the one who, in revealing himself in and through the veil of creaturely form as the incomprehensible and sovereign God that he is, makes possible and actual a true knowledge of his character by creatures.[44]

In turn, contentions that human thought and speech possess no adequacy of their own are, for Barth, license for neither resigned silence nor arbitrary play. Frail creaturely media are annexed by God, rendered instruments of a divine self-communication that, indirect and partial, is yet real and reliable. In the case of Holy Scripture, the human text through which God is pleased to speak his Word as nowhere

---

41. Cf., e.g., *CD* I/1, 370–71.

42. Ibid., 382.

43. *CD* II/1, 215.

44. For a valuable overview of core elements of Barth's reasoning in the crucial *CD* §27, see, e.g., McCormack, "Limits of the Knowledge of God," 167–80.

else, images and metaphors of God—such as the statement that God is light—are not true in univocal or equivocal fashion, as though there were some simple identity between the content of human words and their transcendent referent; but they are genuinely true nevertheless, as by divine grace they are taken up by God and given partial yet vital correspondence to the one of whom they speak. Their analogical force does not derive from the native possibilities of language in general, or from human resourcefulness, but from the sovereignty of God's gracious determination to commandeer these particular forms and restore them to their proper primary use in reference to himself.[45]

The alternative to naïve literalism or the putative domestication of divinity in linguistic categories is not the indulgence of endless deferral or whimsical inventiveness (the latter as much as the former might be seen as a celebration of human incapacity over divine capacity, and thus also, for Barth, an expression of human wickedness).[46] It is, rather, the *right kind* of positivity: a God who is never in our grasp, but the one who, in the specificity of his triune act of self-bestowal in the event that is his Word, gives us "permission and command . . . and therefore . . . capacity to see and speak" of who he really is.[47]

All this in mind, we come at last to the scriptural text: "God is light."

Divine Luminosity: A Brief Sketch

Like the other (few) divine identity statements of the New Testament—God is spirit, God is love, God is a consuming fire—the predication is anarthrous and wholly irreversible. Created light is not divine; what it is may be hard enough to fathom, but whatever it is, God is not an exponential expansion of it—"that than which a brighter cannot be conceived." God's being is strictly non-commensurable, his features non-specifiable by empirical synthesis. Divinity and light may be widely associated in the world's religions, but Scripture's God is irreducibly different from any light that he fashions; cultic veneration of light, his

---

45. The matter is helpfully surveyed by Hunsinger, "Beyond Literalism and Expressivism," 210–25; more briefly, Hunsinger, *How to Read Karl Barth*, 43–49.

46. Cf. *CD* II/1, 201.

47. Ibid., 190. For some salutary orientation, see Webster, "Barth, Modernity and Postmodernity," 1–28.

Word declares, is an act of false worship, the service of created thing rather than creator.

This God's way of being light is his own. His appointment of this specific image in description of himself implies no simple semantic equation; it is resistant to domestication as conventional trope, or complacent classification within the categories of the general—purity, truth, knowledge, goodness, vitality. The acknowledgement of its essential veracity, its status as more than mere accommodation to human sensibilities, is a matter of confession, not ascription; its content is a content that is given in the work that the God who is light effects and confirms in the singularity of his impact upon us. If the statement is an axiom, it is an axiom of faith, not the enunciation of a natural principle. It is the thrilled cry of those whose native sphere is dark, whose minds are dim, who yet learn that this, their perversely chosen state, is not the final measure of the real. To probe the entailments of such wonder is a task of reason sanctified, of minds in process of renovation.

What might we try to say? First, that God is indeed light in himself, and his character as light is, like all his perfections, trinitarian through and through. One God in threefold repetition, eternally complete in the enactment of his being, Father, Son, and Holy Spirit, God is perfectly immediate to himself. Quintessential transparency characterizes his inner life. The Father *knows* the Son; the Son, Light from Light, *knows* the Father; unifier of their relation, the Spirit *knows* and *is known* by the Father and the Son. There is nothing the Father knows which the Son, by the Spirit, does not. There is also nothing the Father *wills* which the Son, by the Spirit, does not. Nothing occludes or blocks the inner-divine pathways of fellowship, peace, and unity; no conceivable moral tension or gradation of goodness affects their ways of subsisting: "in him there is no darkness at all" (1 John 1:5). For Father, Son, and Spirit to dialogue is not for them to deliberate as dissenting interlocutors; for them to agree is not for them to strike a bargain.[48]

The Father begets, the Son is begotten, the Spirit is breathed; the Father sends, the Son and the Spirit are sent—but such relations bespeak no society of individuals, no ontological hierarchy, only the unparalleled structure in which the one God is pleased to have his three

---

48. Cf. Barth's opposition to the idea of an inner-divine *pactum salutis* as "mythology" (*CD* IV/1, 65). Whether the crass pluralism and voluntarism to which Barth objects are inevitable features of such a *theologoumenon* remains an open question.

ways of being, a structure of life in which generation and derivation, commission and obedience, co-exist in perfect simultaneity and equality. In the unfathomable love and freedom of God's self-repetition, God communicates himself to himself, giving and receiving, sharing with himself the fullness of who he is, having his being in the ever-mobile repose of his relational self-sufficiency, the ordered abundance of his unqualified completeness. God is light primordially in the infinite liberty and uninhibited intimacy of his triune fellowship with himself.

Light of this order is impenetrable ("unapproachable": 1 Tim 6:16). As creatures—*fallen* creatures—we are puzzles to ourselves; the inner depths of our psyches are opaque to our introspection. We have no comprehension of what it is to be perfectly self-aware, reel at the notion of a being in whose single yet differentiable identity there is absolute understanding, unimpeded harmony of purpose, unfettered moral integrity. That mystery, the irreducible otherness it represents, is not (never shall be) resolved by God's choice to make himself known, a reality around which God is pleased to place such cognitive boundaries as he chooses, according to the manner of his coming—in material history, in frail flesh, in human words. But the primacy of God's intra-divine luminosity for his gracious self-disclosure is of critical significance. God does not come to know himself in shining forth to that which lies outside himself, nor does he realize a mere potential for self-understanding, peace, or fulfillment in his outreach to the world. Perfectly clear to himself, God's external radiance does not perfect the light that he antecedently is, or illumine for divine *hypostaseis* what it means to be who they are.

There is no augmentation of the light, for there can be none for God. Nor is there detriment to the light: effulgence represents no jeopardy to God's intrinsic perfection, no voltage drop in his inner glory. Rather, it is *because* God is perfect light in himself that he is able to turn as he does towards that which is other. God's creating, reconciling, and redeeming works are a reiteration in contingent time and space of what God is in his own eternal time and space; their grounding lies in the relations of ineffable love, unity, and reciprocity that constitute God's life in himself.

The Father wills that there should be fellowship for creatures with his eternal light; the Son, who actively shares that will, comes to carry it through; the Spirit, the one in and through whom the Father and the

Son are turned towards, open to, freed for each other eternally, brings to perfection the purpose here enacted. All the markers on the plotline—election, creation, reconciliation, redemption—are expressions of the unqualified majesty of God's being in himself. God's radiance *ad extra* is utterly gracious, but it is the work of One who is naturally resplendent, whose will to reach out towards creatures lies in his relational character as God, and whose revealed perfections—all the inseparable excellencies of his disclosed immensity, eternity, holiness, and love—are but a demonstration of the essential clarities of his triune being.[49]

Second, the triune God really does shine forth, dispelling creaturely darkness by the sheer potency of his inner splendor, reaching us as he really is. The distinction between that outshining towards creatures and God's inner glory is best elaborated not by a distinction between essence and energies, far less between uncreated and created light, but by speaking of the freedom of God's will to make visible for creatures something of what is eternally visible to God himself. This movement is neither necessary nor automatic, nor is it summoned by the conditions of darkness that it reaches, as some divine reflex to the self-chosen murk of contingency. God is resplendent in himself, his commitment to scatter the absurdity of the darkness is grounded in his primary purpose in creating at all; but his refulgence towards the creature's world is a matter of his inner integrity, of the surety of his determination to bind himself to that world in spite of everything, and that resolve is a matter of fathomless love, not an obligation governed by the world's intrinsic merit or elicited proleptically by its foreseen response. What we see is what we get, God as he truly is; what we get is mercy all the way down. Mercy shines supremely in the face of Jesus Christ, in whom God's aseity is seen not as naked absoluteness but as freedom for creatures; yet God's election to be the God made known in Jesus Christ is not thereby a constitution of God's being: it is his commitment to share the eternal repleteness of his being with others. It is *free* mercy that we get.

As creaturely history attests, God's luminosity *pro nobis* is sovereign and invincible, but it is in no sense effortless or without cost.

---

49. I take the language of "clarities" from the impressive work of Krötke, *Gottes Klarheiten*—though Krötke's concentration on the historical disclosure of God's triune truth, love, power, and eternity may need to be enriched by a somewhat stronger account of the completeness of such clarities for God *in se*. For critical assessment, see Holmes, *Revisiting the Doctrine of the Divine Attributes*; Holmes, "God's Attributes as God's Clarities," 54–72.

Divine energy of an exquisite order is deployed. God's radiance encounters contradiction and defiance, the willful resistance of creatures who, ruinously, prefer darkness rather than light. God's glory has a worldly story; at its mid-point lie the events of Jesus Christ, the one who enacts a proper creaturely response to God in a realm that exists under the shadow of death. Within the conditions of this environment, partaker of the same humanity as those he comes to save, shines the true light, the light of the world. He is detested for it. His character appears as no long-awaited ideal, the welcome embodiment *par excellence* of native intuitions of the good. Uncomprehending and hostile, the world, which does not know where it is going (cf. John 12:35), finds him the antithesis to all that it considers admirable or illuminating. Confronted by the covenant-keeper, covenant-breakers display the ultimate madness of their estate; they seek to extinguish the light that takes away—though it also exposes—their darkness: "Away with him!" (Luke 23:18; John 19:15). Calvary's cross and Joseph's tomb are testimony to their seeming success; in the fate of the one cut off, the power of darkness seems to reign supreme. Impenetrably black that site is, its measure a "Why?" that finds no immediate answer save the silence of the grave.

But this is not all: God raises the dead Jesus; dazzling angelic testimony declares that the crucified one lives. He is encountered as such, "seen" in majesty by those who did not know him as well as those who did (cf. Acts 9:1–19; 22:6–11; 26:12–19; 1 Cor 9:1; 15:5–8), demonstrably alive with all the "aliveness" of God. The consequences are transformative for creatures everywhere; a different end is available from that which the world's crazed dwellers have chosen for themselves. By the work of this subject, God's light in himself, invisible to the spiritually unsighted, is now rendered visible to faith; faith is given as eyes are opened by the sovereign manifestation of the risen Jesus by his Spirit. In giving himself, God does not give himself away; the resplendence of God's light also does in one sense hide him; there remains indeed immensity in God that is known to God alone. But there is no other God than the one who shines out, and his outshining spells liberation for captives. Those who sit in darkness are effectually called into God's marvelous light; the divine radiance generates in turn a genuine response of glory in those it reaches. All along the line, the realization of divine disclosure, like its origins and execution, lies with God.

Fierce opposition remains, certainly, but that cause is hopeless. The risen and ascended one makes himself known in the power of his Spirit. He is also the coming one, destined to present himself in final, public splendor, to demonstrate his majesty and confound his enemies. The mission of his Spirit, the revealer of his victory over death and all evil, the agent and enabler of living relation with him and bestower of all its fruits, is in the end unassailable; the same energy at work in creation's *fiat lux* is operative in the sovereign redemptive summons to all creation to arise and shine for its light has come. The Spirit calls forth emissaries of that light, charging them to live as children of light, to join in personal and corporate attestation of the present and coming reality of evil's conquest, the triumph of God's majesty.

In that vocation they are, in great measure, a dismal failure, the assurance of divine accompaniment and the promise of heavenly intercession notwithstanding. But the meaning of their communal existence and the worldly success of their message do not hang upon creaturely resources, nor is the subject who constitutes, commissions, and empowers dependent on the capabilities of those he calls. Popular as it presently remains, darkness will not ultimately overcome the steadfast determination of the One who is light to shed his beams abroad; it will not withstand his capacity to outbid every competitor at last by the magnificence of his glory.

By Way of a Conclusion

A fair bit of theology, modern and postmodern, might be said to have proceeded pretty much as if God were not light at all. If all we are about is a human endeavor to name the unknowable, a project irreducibly restricted to—or freed by—the possibilities of human imagining, it is hard to see what role, if any, is played by divine luminosity. If all we ever have are our efforts to fashion experiential symbols and metaphors for God, to throw words up to the clouds to see if any stick in ways we find appealing, in what sense is God light? God might conceivably be thought of as somehow grounding the religious or moral experiences with which we work, even in some sense as offering episodic pedagogy in the ways in which we are enabled to process that which presents itself to our minds; but there is, on such reckoning, little or no clarity as to the criteria for truth and error, little if any check upon the nagging suspicion that we may be making things up as we go along.

The motivations of some forms of theological reserve (if not of theological license) can, it is true, be commendable: a concern to avoid idolatry, and the ideological abuses to which it invariably gives rise; an effort to resist domestication, or the reduction of divinity to a dubious metaphysics of substance or presence. But extreme forms of negative theology or celebrations of private or contextual *poiesis* as the preferred options in an epistemically complex world are, in the end, refusals of the gospel's primary announcement: the light is here, non-domesticable, transcendent, yet gloriously real, and destined ultimately to prevail over its every foe.

More than the work of most theologians in the twentieth century, Barth's dogmatics offers a sustained endeavor to grapple with what it is to confess that the God who is all-glorious in himself invades and dispels our darkness. We do not need to call ourselves by the dubious name of "Barthians," or to be uncritical of the details of Barth's thought, to find rich stimulus in his remarkable endeavor to probe that wonder, and to set it out in robustly trinitarian doctrinal form. To think after Barth is not to be his follower; it is to pursue the utterly demanding yet utterly joyful and compellingly beautiful reality to which his theology points. The divine self-declaration is the declaration of the One who is, in his splendor, infinitely sufficient; and so: "[the person] who has God has really everything."[50]

---

50. *CD* II/1, 644.

Bibliography

Barth, Karl. *Church Dogmatics*. 4 vols. Edinburgh: T. & T. Clark, 1956–75.
Gunton, Colin E. *Act and Being: Towards a Theology of the Divine Attributes*. Grand Rapids: Eerdmans, 2002
Holmes, Christopher R. J. "God's Attributes as God's Clarities: Wolf Krötke's Doctrine of the Divine Attributes." *International Journal of Systematic Theology* 10 (2008) 54–72.
———. *Revisiting the Doctrine of the Divine Attributes: In Dialogue with Karl Barth, Eberhard Jüngel, and Wolf Krötke*. New York: Lang, 2007.
———. "The Theological Function of the Doctrine of the Divine Attributes and the Divine Glory, with special reference to Karl Barth and His Reading of the Protestant Orthodox." *Scottish Journal of Theology* 61 (2008) 206–23.
Hunsinger, George. "Beyond Literalism and Expressivism: Karl Barth's Hermeneutical Realism." In *Disruptive Grace: Studies in the Theology of Karl Barth*, edited by George Hunsinger, 210–25. Grand Rapids: Eerdmans, 2000.
———. "Election and the Trinity: Twenty-Five Theses on the Theology of Karl Barth." *Modern Theology* 24 (2008) 179–98.
———. *How to Read Karl Barth: The Shape of His Theology*. Oxford: Oxford University Press, 1991.
Krötke, Wolf. *Gottes Klarheiten: Eine Neuinterpretation der Lehre von Gottes "Eigenschaften."* Tübingen: Mohr/Siebeck, 2001.
McCormack, Bruce L. "Grace and Being: The Role of God's Gracious Election in Karl Barth's Theological Ontology." In *The Cambridge Companion to Karl Barth*, edited by John Webster, 92–110. Cambridge: Cambridge University Press, 2000.
———. "'The Limits of the Knowledge of God': Theses on the Theological Epistemology of Karl Barth." In *Orthodox and Modern: Studies in the Theology of Karl Barth*, edited by Bruce L. McCormack, 167–80. Grand Rapids: Baker Academic, 2008.
Molnar, Paul. *Divine Freedom and the Doctrine of the Immanent Trinity: In Dialogue with Karl Barth and Contemporary Theology*. London: T. & T. Clark, 2002.
Torrance, Thomas F. *Karl Barth, Biblical and Evangelical Theologian*. Edinburgh: T. & T. Clark, 1990.
Webster, John. *Barth's Ethics of Reconciliation*. Cambridge: Cambridge University Press, 1995.
———. "Barth, Modernity and Postmodernity." In *Karl Barth: A Future for Postmodern Theology?*, edited by Geoff Thompson and Christiaan Mostert, 1–28. Hindmarsh, SA: Australian Theological Forum, 2000.

3

The Spatiality of God

Murray Rae

A STRIKING FEATURE OF THE BIBLICAL STORY OF GOD AND OF GOD'S relation to the world is the prevalence in that story of spatial language. Even at the dawn of creation when the earth was without form, there is, according to Genesis 1:2, a spatial relation between it and the *ruach* of God that hovers or sweeps over the face of the deep. Again and again, thereafter, the relation between God and creation is portrayed in spatial terms. "Why O Lord do you stand far off?" the Psalmist cries, "Why do you hide yourself in times of trouble?" (Ps 10:1), while elsewhere the Psalmist confesses. "The Lord is in his holy temple; the Lord's throne is in heaven" (Ps 11:4). Later still the Psalmist testifies that there is no place where God is not:

> Where can I go from your spirit?
> Or where can I flee from your presence?
> If I ascend to heaven, you are there;
> if I make my bed in Sheol, you are there.
> If I take the wings of the morning
> and settle at the farthest limits of the sea,
> even there your hand shall lead me,
> and your right hand shall hold me fast. (Ps 139:7–10)

Then in the New Testament "the Word who was in the beginning *with* God . . . became flesh and lived among us" (John 1:2, 14). This Word, the Son is also "*close* to the Father's heart" (John 1:18), and on account of his mediation, "you who were once far off have been brought near by the blood of Christ" (Eph 2:13). Jesus, in his discourse with the disciples, tells them that he is "going to him who sent me" (John 16:5), but he has assured them earlier that in his Father's house "there are many dwelling places" and that he will "go to prepare a place for them." He promises further that "if I go to prepare a place for you, I will come again and take you to myself, so that where I am, you may be also" (John 14:2–3). Following his death and resurrection Christ *ascends* into heaven (Acts 1:6–11) where he sits "at the right hand of the throne of God" (Heb 12:2; cf. Eph 1:20), and from where, at the sound of God's trumpet, he "will descend," once more to be with his people for ever (1 Thess 4:16). Both in the Bible and in the subsequent theological tradition, many more examples may be found of spatial language employed to speak of God and of God's relation to the world.

It is to be noted that the spatial language refers not only to the economic being of God—God's relation to the world—but also to the immanent being of God, to God's being in himself. "In the beginning, the Word was with God," and, "the Son sits at the right hand of the throne of God," for instance. These affirmations have enormous importance for God's relation to the world of course, but they propose also a spatial relation between the persons of the Trinity themselves. Spatial language of this kind occurs frequently in biblical and in subsequent theological speech. What is more, it would seem very difficult to do without it. Central concepts in the theological vocabulary have spatial roots and retain spatial overtones still. The most important cluster of Hebrew words for salvation have the root ישע (*yasa*) which has the fundamental meaning to become spacious, to enlarge. Cognates of this root, translated into English as "salvation," refer to God's deliverance of his people from confinement. Salvation is said to be necessary on account of humanity being *separated* from God, or on account of its *fallenness*, a state of affairs recorded in the primal history cf Genesis 3 as leading to their *exile* from the garden of Eden, spatial language again being used to testify to the distancing of the creature from its place with God. And so on.

The question I wish to explore in this essay is this: in what way does the spatial expression of the conceptual reality with which theology is concerned correspond to the being of God? Does the spatial language commonly used in theology have some purchase on the reality of God beyond what we might call the *merely* metaphorical? I do not intend to cast aspersions on the value of metaphorical speech at this point. Such language is indispensable in theology as the means by which we may tell the truth. The question before us, however, is whether spatial language used of God can have a legitimate non-metaphorical sense.

The Dangerous Idea that God is Non-Spatial.

The tradition has largely followed Augustine in this matter, or at least, it has extrapolated from Augustine's thesis that the world was created with time rather than in time (*non est mundus factus in tempore, sed cum tempore*) to the parallel thesis that the world was created with space rather than in space.[1] Just as God is eternal, that is to say, non-temporal, so also God is immense, that is, non-spatial.[2] Space and time are thereby identified as predicates of the created order and may be applied to God, who is *increatus*, only figuratively or metaphorically. God's immensity is to be understood, accordingly, as his qualitative distinction from created, spatial reality.[3] The absolute, qualitative distinction between divine and creaturely reality was a principle affirmed of course by Karl Barth who had learned the principle from Søren Kierkegaard. It then became, by Barth's own admission, the nearest thing, in his early years at least, to the systematic core of his theological thought:

> If I have a system, it is limited to a recognition of what Kierkegaard called the "infinite qualitative distinction" between time and eternity, and to my regarding this as possessing negative as well as positive significance: "God is in heaven, and thou art on earth." The relation between such a God and such a man, and the relation between such a man and such a God, is for me the theme of the Bible and the essence of philosophy.[4]

Barth thus upholds the infinite, qualitative distinction between God and the creaturely realm. But that does not preclude him from applying spatial predicates not only to the creaturely reality, but also to the divine: "God is in heaven, and thou art on earth." He says this precisely

---

1. See for contemporary instance, Küng, *Beginning of All Things*, 120–21. In *Civitas Dei*, 11.5, Augustine himself dismissed the idea of there being space antecedent to the creation.

2. As an aside here, Augustine's deliberations reveal, contra Rudolf Bultmann, that theologians did not need to learn from Copernicus that we do not live in a three-decker universe.

3. See Webster, "Immensity and Ubiquity of God," 94.

4. Barth, *Epistle to the Romans*, 10.

to uphold the qualitative distinction, so whatever the distinction means for Barth, it does not preclude him from applying to God predicates that have been regarded traditionally as properly belonging only to the creature. Indeed, in his discussion of 'the unity and omnipresence of God' in *Church Dogmatics* II/1 Barth argues that "God has his own space." Barth writes,

> God is spatial as the One who loves in freedom, and therefore as Himself. . . . He is spatial always and everywhere in such a way that His spatiality means the manifestation and confirmation of His deity. God possesses His space. He is in Himself as in a space. He creates space. He is and does this so that, in virtue of His own spatiality, He can be Himself even in this created space without this limiting Him or causing Him to have something outside Himself, a space apart from Himself, a space which is not His space too in virtue of His spatiality, the space of His divine presence. Or, to express it positively, God possesses space in Himself and in all other spaces.[5]

The notion of the absolute non-spatiality of God is, Barth claims, "a more than dangerous idea" both because it collapses the infinite, qualitative distinction between the divine and the creaturely, and because it threatens the triune differentiation of God as Father, Son, and Spirit. The personal differentiation of God means, Barth contends, that there is both remoteness and proximity in God. The Son is not the Father and the Father is not the Son. Neither is the Spirit identical with either the Father or the Son. The distinction between the persons entails, Barth contends, that there is distance between them. They have space from and for one another and, just so, they exist in the triune communion of love. The divine omnipresence is in the first instance the particular and unbounded presence of the triune persons one to another in the eternal communion of love.[6]

"The Christian conception of God at least is shattered and dissolved," Barth writes, "if God is described as absolute non-spatiality. Non-spatiality means existence without distance, which means identity."[7] Barth is concerned here with maintaining the distance and thus also the

---

5. *CD* II/1, 470.

6. Omnipresence is treated by Barth under the heading of "The Perfections of the Divine Freedom." See §31 of *CD* II/1.

7. Ibid., 468.

distinction between God and the world, but, as we have seen, he is concerned also with the proper distinction and thus the distance between the persons of the Godhead. Barth again:

> God's omnipresence, to speak in general terms, is the perfection in which he is present, and in which He, the One, who is distinct from and pre-eminent over everything else, possesses a place, His own place, which is distinct from all other places and also pre-eminent over them all. God is the One in such a way that he is present: present to Himself in the triunity of His One essence; present to everything else as the Lord of everything else. In the one case as in the other, inwards as well as outwards, presence does not mean identity, but togetherness at a distance. In the one case, inwards, it is the togetherness of Father, Son, and Holy Spirit at the distance posited by the distinction that exists in the one essence of God. In the other case, outwards, it is the togetherness at a distance of the Creator and the creature.... Presence as togetherness (as distinct from identity) includes distance. But where there is distance there is necessarily one place and another place. To this extent God's presence necessarily means that He possesses a place, His own place, or, we may say safely, His own space.[8]

Barth sets himself here in deliberate opposition to the mainstream Augustinian tradition that proposes, as we have seen, that God is utterly transcendent of space and so non-spatial in himself. The extent to which Barth goes out on a limb here, so to speak, is confirmed perhaps by theologians after Barth who have been willing to follow him in many respects but not in this. I take for notable instance John Webster and also Ian MacKenzie.

In his account of the immensity and ubiquity of God, John Webster insists that we must "empty our thinking about God of the connotations of spatiality, positive and negative."[9] Failure to do so is indicative, Webster contends, of the mistaken tendency to talk of the divine perfections "by maximizing a creaturely conception of immeasurability, or infinite extension."[10] In other words, talk of divine spatiality involves a naïve projection from the creaturely to the divine, an extrapolation

---

8. *CD* II/1, 468.

9. Webster, "Immensity and Ubiquity of God," 94.

10. Ibid. Webster does not direct this criticism explicitly at Barth but neither does he defend Barth against MacKenzie's direct allegation.

from creaturely being to the being of God. Although Webster himself does not do so, Ian MacKenzie directs this criticism explicitly at Barth. "If [Barth] means that there is a direct analogy within the Trinity to created remoteness and proximity . . . then he is guilty of a simplistic application of an *analogia entis*."[11] The use of the terms remoteness and proximity, MacKenzie continues, "suggests that we have not rid ourselves of secretly transferring created values of measurements and dimensions into God."[12]

It is important to note here that in spite of the qualitative distinction between the divine and the creaturely, and despite the fact that we have no language or concepts available to us other than creaturely language and concepts, neither MacKenzie nor Webster dispute the appropriateness in principle of using creaturely language and concepts to speak of God's immanent being and of distinguishing conceptually the immanent from the economic being of God. Indeed their critique of the Barthian approach depends upon this distinction being upheld. The point of difference concerns, rather, the appropriateness or otherwise of spatial language in particular. It is also undisputed among them that in the divine economy God locates himself in creaturely space. In the womb of Mary, in Bethlehem, in Galilee and its environs, the divine Son is spatially located. The omnipresence of God and the divine promise to dwell with his people are realized in the person of Jesus in specific, identifiable locations that are accessible to us. The dispute concerns more specifically, then, the question whether the omnipresence of God is to be regarded as an absolute attribute of God referring to God's being *in se*, apart from his relation to creation, or a relative attribute of God referring only to God's unbounded presence with and for the creature. Barth contends that the omnipresence of God belongs to God's being *in se*, as well as to God's being *pro nobis*. God "possesses and He is in Himself space," Barth writes. "We have no right to limit this statement to God's being in and with creation. God's spatiality cannot therefore, be related to created space alone, while as He is in Himself He is conceived and described as non-spatial."[13] Webster, on the other hand, prefers to say that omnipresence is a relative attribute pertaining only to the economy. That God is omnipresent with respect to creaturely re-

11. MacKenzie, *Dynamism of Space*, 85.
12. Ibid., 86.
13. *CD* II/1, 472.

ality enables us, however, to refer to the *immensity* of God in himself, where immensity means God's qualitative distinction from and utter transcendence of space. Webster does offer important qualifications however: "the conceptual mapping of God's identity in terms of the distinction between absolute and relative may have a certain formal or heuristic justification (parallel to the distinction between God *in se* and God *pro nobis,* of which it is a corollary). But these distinctions must not be pressed in such a way that the 'absolute' acquires greater weight than the 'economic' in determining the *essentia dei*."[14]

Webster is also careful to insist that the immensity of God, an absolute attribute, cannot be expounded without immediate reference to omnipresence, a relative attribute. He notes further that "talk of divine immensity is wholly referred to the enacted identity of God in his sovereign self-presence as Father, Son, and Spirit. Accordingly dogmatics must give precedence to *definition by description* over *definition by analysis*; its account of the being of God and of God's perfections is to be determined at every point by attention to God's given self-identification."[15] Webster has learned that principle from Barth, so the point of difference between the two is narrowed to the question of *what* may be said on the basis of the divine economy concerning the spatiality or the non-spatiality of God in and for himself.

The Triune Spaciousness of God

We have noted Barth's insistence that the confession of God's spaciousness cannot be applied only to the economy while conceiving God in himself as non-spatial. "A distinction of this kind," Barth writes, "would inevitably mean that in the way in which God exists in and with creation (or to put it concretely, in His revelation), God deceives us as to His true being.... If in and with His creation God is the same as He is in Himself, revealing Himself to us in His revelation as not less or other than Himself, then it is characteristic of Him to be here and there and everywhere, and therefore to be always somewhere and not nowhere, to be spatial in His divine essence."[16]

---

14. Webster, "Immensity and Ubiquity of God," 93.
15. Ibid., emphasis in the original.
16. *CD* II/1, 472.

Barth strives to safeguard here the principle that God reveals himself to us as the one he is. It may be argued, however, that in emptying himself, in taking the form of a creature, the Son of God accommodates himself to the conditions of creaturely reality; accepts limitations, that is, that do not belong to his own eternal being, including the limitations of spatial existence. Jesus of Nazareth was not found to be in two places at once, for instance, and when he moved from one place to another he took time to get there. These features of the Word's incarnate life do not entail that God is in himself subject to such limitations, although they do reveal that the divine freedom and love may be exercised in just this way. There are attributes of the incarnate Word, therefore, brought about through the Word's assumption of human nature, that do not pertain to the being of God in himself.

One would have to be careful in following this line of argument to avoid the Nestorian heresy of dividing the divine from the human nature of Christ, but something like this argument seems necessary and defensible in order to uphold the contention of Webster and of MacKenzie that talk of divine spaciousness pertains only to the economy. One could do this, I think, without threat to the principle that God reveals himself as the one he is by arguing that the divine accommodation to creaturely reality reveals truly and reliably God's capacity and his will to be for us in this way. The accommodation to creaturely reality reveals, in other words, the infinite capacity of divine freedom and love but does not license the projection of creaturely reality onto God. The character of God is revealed through his accommodation to creaturely reality but is not determined by it. The attributes of God *in se* would thus be understood as the antecedent conditions of God's being *pro nobis*. In the case of the divine presence in space—through the life of the incarnate Word—we could say that the immensity of God, rather than divine spaciousness *in se*, is the antecedent condition of the Word's incarnate spaciousness. The attribute of immensity is, in Webster's words, "the free, gratuitous, non-necessary character of God's relation to space."[17] Immensity is not itself a spatial concept; it does not signify God's vastness or infinite spaciousness as though God were dispersed through space, but rather God's total freedom from spatial constraint.

Clearly an argument of this kind can be constructed without falling prey to the perils of Nestorianism. But is the Barthian alternative

17. Webster, "Immensity and Ubiquity of God," 94.

legitimate? Can one conclude on the basis of the economy that God has his own space without being guilty, as MacKenzie and Webster allege, of a naïve projection onto God of the conditions of creaturely existence?

The charge against Barth can be refuted, I suggest, by attending once more to the way in which Barth's argument is constructed. He clearly does not proceed from the observation that Jesus exists in creaturely space to the conclusion that there must be some analogy of creaturely spaciousness that belongs to the being of God in himself. There is no *analogia entis* here. The basis upon which Barth speaks of God having his own space is the differentiation of the persons of the Trinity, revealed in the economy as belonging to the being of God in himself. The triune differentiation of God as Father, Son, and Spirit is not an accommodation of God to the demands of revelation, but belongs to the character of the eternal God who is before all things. God is not triune only for the sake of the creature any more than he is love only for the sake of the creature. God is triune and God is love *simpliciter*. Out of the freedom, sufficiency, and fullness of divine love, God determines that there shall be a creature, one who is other than himself. The triune communion of love between Father, Son, and Spirit exists in advance of the creature, therefore, and it is precisely that antecedence that distinguishes the creature from God.

We have noted above Barth's refusal to regard omnipresence as a relative attribute of God, as pertaining that is, only to his relation to creation. "All that God is in His relationship to His creation, and therefore His omnipresence too, is simply an outward manifestation and realisation of what He is previously in Himself apart from this relationship and therefore apart from His creation."[18] Let us recall further, and explore in more detail now, the implications of Barth's contention that God has his own place, or, as Barth also puts it, his own space.[19] Barth's claim rests upon the disclosure in the economy of the dynamism of the divine being. God is not an undifferentiated unity but the dynamic communion in love of the three persons of the Trinity who exist for one another, are present to one another, and who are therefore distinct from one another. This unity in distinction, we have heard, involves both proximity and distance. "Presence does not mean identity, but togetherness at a distance.... Where there is distance," Barth, further contends, "there is

18. *CD* II/1, 462.
19. Ibid., 468.

necessarily one place and another place. If God does not possess space, he can certainly be conceived as that which is one in itself and in all. But he cannot be conceived as the One who is triune."[20]

Barth's account of divine spatiality presses us, I suggest, to a new conception of what space is—the opposite procedure, be it noted, from a projection onto God of what we already hold space to be. Space is, on Barth's account, a condition by which one person is differentiated from another—in God first! But then also for the creature, space is a condition by which persons and also things are differentiated from one another. (It is not the only condition, but it is the one we are concerned with here.) Space, accordingly, is, in the first instance, the outcome of God's determination of his own being as Father, Son, and Spirit. It is the outcome and freely chosen condition of God's self-determination as the perichoretic communion of love that God is. The unity of God does not consist in a monistic, undifferentiated identity, requiring us to conclude in respect of the economy that the names Father, Son, and Spirit identify only the forms of God's appearance and operation, rather than distinct hypostatic identities constitutive of the being of God in himself. It is on account of that Sabellian conception of divine unity that Barth calls the abstract non-spatiality of God a more than dangerous idea.[21]

Because it is the central point of this paper, let me reiterate the procedural move that Barth has made here. Barth's contention that God has his own space, that God is spatial in himself, is not based upon considerations of space in general but upon the particular divine action in space by which God reveals himself as Father, Son, and Spirit. On this basis we may develop a relational and differential account of what space is in accordance with God's disclosure in space and time of his eternal being as Father, Son, and Spirit. Between Father, Son, and Spirit, and constitutive of the being of God, there is both communion (proximity) and distinction (distance). This proximity and distance are essential to the distinction of and the communion between the divine persons.

Although we cannot go along very far with Immanuel Kant's account of what space is, he is right at least in his recognition that space is the condition of our locating objects of experience outside ourselves and of distinguishing them both from ourselves and from one another. Using Robert Jenson's phrase we may push Kant to say that space is

20. Ibid.
21. Ibid.

"the a priori of otherness."[22] Jenson further points out, however, that "when Kant then claims that space simply *is not* 'a determination ... that pertains to objects themselves,' we cannot but turn and sympathize with thinkers who have wondered what Kant can then mean by 'objects.'"[23] Transferring the observation to the theological case we may say, if proximity and distance, and thereby differentiation and relation, are not determinations that pertain to the persons of the Godhead themselves then we must wonder what is meant by persons.

That the nature of persons is at stake in this discussion of the spatiality of God is apparent in Colin Gunton's treatment of the matter in *The Promise of Trinitarian Theology*. Gunton lends support to the spatial conception of the being of God and follows Barth in linking it both to the hypostatic distinction between Father, Son, and Spirit and also to the freedom of God.

> Freedom is to be found in the space in which persons can be themselves in relation with other persons. That is the lesson of the doctrine of the Trinity. Father, Son, and Spirit constitute each other as free persons by virtue of the shape their interrelationship takes in the Trinitarian perichoresis. Otherness is an essential feature of the trinitarian freedom, because without otherness the distinctness, particularity, of a person is lost.... We should say, then, that the essence *of* the being in relation that is the Trinity is the *personal space* that is received and conferred.[24]

This coheres with the principle observed above that space is the freely chosen condition in God of the differentiation of one person from another. As we develop the argument of this paper further, it is this conception of space that we must bear in mind whenever the term "space" now occurs.

Creaturely Space

The next step then is to recognize that divine spaciousness, rather than being a projection of creaturely spatiality, is the presupposition and antecedent condition of the space given to the creature. Barth writes,

---

22. Jenson, *Systematic Theology*, vol. 2, 46.
23. Ibid., 47.
24. Gunton, *Promise of Trinitarian Theology*, 128.

... there exists a divine proximity and remoteness, real in Him from all eternity, as the basis and presupposition of the essence and existence of creation, and therefore of created proximity and remoteness. God can be present to another. This is His freedom. For He is present to Himself. This is His love in its internal and its external range. God in Himself is not only existent. He is co-existent. And so He can co-exist with another also. To grant co-existence with Himself to another is no contradiction of His essence. On the contrary, it corresponds to it.[25]

And further: "God is present to other things, and is able to create and give them space, because He Himself possesses space apart from everything else. The space everything else possesses is the space which is given it out of the fullness of God. The fact is that first of all God has space for Himself and that subsequently, because He is God and is able to create, He has it for everything else as well."[26]

If we follow the argument through and draw on the principles established above, we see that what is given to the creature in the act of creation is distinct being, that is, being in distinction from God. Among the entities that exist in consequence of creation are things and persons other than God, persons who have their own space and their own freedom. It is true only in one sense, therefore, that God creates *ex nihilo*. The sense in which that principle is *true* is that no thing other than God exists prior to creation. There is no energy or matter lying about which God takes to hand in order to fashion the world. Nor is their any power other than God that contributes to creation or against which God has to contend. Other than God, prior to creation, there is simply no thing. That is the truth of the claim that God creates *ex nihilo*. But the claim can mislead. For it is not strictly true that God creates out of nothing. He creates, in fact, out of the fullness of his own being. That is to say, out of the fullness of his freedom and love, God gives to the creature that which is his own, namely, the capacity, the space, and the time for free, loving relationships between persons, including above all, the capacity, the space and the time, for free, loving relationships between created persons and the tri-personal being that he is.

It has sometimes been said in the tradition that in the act of creation God makes room for the creature. There is something to be said

---

25. *CD* II/1, 463.
26. Ibid.

for this formulation so long as we do not follow the kabbalistic idea of *tzimtzum* by which it is asserted that God's making room for the creature involves a contraction of his own being. Such a conception rescinds the relational and differential account of space that we have been concerned with here in favor of a receptacle notion of space, a notion that, as Thomas F. Torrance has shown, is both out of touch with contemporary physics and yields numerous problems for theology.[27] The correct meaning of the claim that God in the act of creation makes room for the creature is that the creature really is other than God. The creature does not occupy God's space; it has its own space and therefore is not identical with God. That the creature is given its own space means that the creature is differentiated both from God and from other creatures and in such a manner as to be able to exist in free, loving relations with them. It is as important here to say that God has his own space as it is to say that the creature has its own space. Colin Gunton again, provides the reason.

> The personal otherness, the self-sufficiency, of God is the basis on which freedom depends because it is the ground for the otherness of the human in relation to God. That freedom derives from the gift in both creation and redemption of the God who has and is personal space, and so can be the creator of such space. If God is not and has not personal space "in advance," in eternity, the danger remains that human freedom will be overwhelmed by a sovereignty of immanence. Our freedom is based in, derives from, God's sovereignty. But unless it is at least in part a sovereignty of transcendence, of personal space, it threatens to overwhelm us.[28]

The creature is given space by God, space that enables it to live freely in relationship with that which is other than itself. It is distinctly our space but—and this too is crucial—what we have and know as our space does not exist apart from the space of the other and, especially, it does not exist apart from God's space.[29] The creature exists in proximity to God. The space of creation is, as Barth puts it, the external basis of the covenant. It is given to the creature precisely so that there may be

---

27. See Torrance, *Space, Time and Incarnation*.
28. Gunton, *Promise of Trinitarian Theology*, 135.
29. The point is taken from *CD* II/1, 476.

a covenant relationship between the creature and God. Creation, is as Barth again puts it, "the realisation of the *divine intention of love*."[30]

In defiance of God's intention, however, there develops in the space given to the creature the tragic history of humanity's attempt to distance itself from God, where distance, in this case no longer means differentiation but separation—distance without proximity, without relationship. Humanity distances itself from the presence of God, or, more accurately, it presumes to do so, for, as the Psalmist confesses, there is no place we can flee from God's presence (Ps 139:7). If it were possible to flee, we would be without a place; we would surely die, for the divine omnipresence means that there is nowhere to go beyond the presence of God. Death is in that respect simply the resumption of the nothingness that obtains apart from the creative, life-giving *ruach* of God. Tragically, that is the destiny humanity chooses for itself, and would succeed in achieving were it not for the fact that God places himself in the way of humanity's deathly determination. The Son of God, takes humanity's place, exposes himself to the reality of godforsakeness and, by defeating death, makes it true that nothing in all creation is able to separate us from the love of God.

If it is true that nothing separates us from the love of God, if it is true that God is present, then we may well ask where the living and loving God is to be found? We may say, first, that God is omnipresent; God is present in all places. "There is no absence, no non-presence, of God in His creation. But," says Barth, "this does not form any obstacle to a whole series of special presences, of concrete cases of God being here or there,"[31] with Jacob at Bethel, with Moses on Mt. Sinai, with Isaiah in the Temple, for example. Barth continues, "[T]hese special cases take place in the context of what God does as He reveals Himself and reconciles the world with Himself. Indeed, we are forced to say that according to the order of biblical thinking and speech it is this special presence of God which always comes first and is estimated and valued as the real and decisive presence."[32]

The living and loving God is especially to be found, is "properly" present, as Barth puts it, in Jesus Christ. Christ is in person the intersection of divine and creaturely space, the locus and actualization of the covenant relationality between God and the creature. It is there,

30. *CD* III/1, 96.
31. *CD* II/1, 477.
32. Ibid.

in Christ, that God makes room for us; it is there that God fulfills his promise to dwell with his people. It is there, in Christ, that the wayward creature is redemptively gathered up from its self-imposed exile and restored to the presence of God.

The question then becomes, where is Christ to be found? How is the place of God's proper presence rendered accessible to us? We know of his birth in Bethlehem, his ministry in Galilee, his death in Jerusalem, but these are places and events remote from us in space and time. Did those who were contemporary with him then enjoy a proximity to the Son of God that is now unavailable to us? The truth is that then, as now, people are united with him through the Spirit. It is through the Spirit that we may know, and love and dwell with him. And the Spirit is at work, most especially, though not exclusively, in the church. The presence of the risen Christ is especially to be found where people are gathered for worship, where the Word of God is heard and preached, and where the sacraments are rightly celebrated. The Lord is especially to be found there on account of his promise that where two or three are gathered in my name I will be in the midst of them (Matt 18:20).

Eschatology

The availability of Christ in Word and Sacrament describes humanity's present reality. In Christ, with whom we are united by the Spirit in baptism, human persons are liberated from their self-imposed confinement and are given space once more to live in communion with God. Yet there is a further reality toward which the church looks forward in hope. We shall let John of Patmos describe it for us: "Then I saw a new heaven and a new earth; for the first heaven and the first earth had passed away, and the sea was no more. And I saw the holy city, the new Jerusalem, coming down out of heaven from God, prepared as a bride adorned for her husband. And I heard a loud voice from the throne saying, 'See the home of God is among mortals. He will dwell with them as their God; they will be his people, and God himself will be with them'" (Rev 21:1–3).

What are we to make of this? Is it "merely" figurative language—a way of conceptualizing spiritual realities having little to do with the creaturely realities of space and time? Or is this a vision of redeemed spatiality, a spatiality in which the proximity between God and his creatures is realized in ways yet unimaginable? It is difficult to make any sense of the creedal statement of belief in the resurrection of the body if there is not in God's presence somewhere for bodies to be. The promise that there are many rooms in my father's house, need not be taken literally as a description of heavenly architecture, in order to accept its assurance that, eschatologically speaking, there will be space for us with God.

Nor is it easy to sustain belief in the bodily resurrection of Christ, towards which the New Testament witness clearly points, if there is now no place for the risen and ascended Christ to be He sits at the right hand of God, it is said, where he sustains all things by his powerful word (Heb 1:3). That location is not somewhere that we can point to, for it is not to be found in our space but in God's. But his presence there, his having a place there, a place he occupies eternally, must be said, on the basis of the divine economy, to be the antecedent condition of our having space at all.

Conclusion

I began this paper with the question, in what way does the spatial expression of the conceptual reality with which theology is concerned correspond to the being of God? Does the spatial language commonly used in theology have some purchase on the reality of God beyond what we might call the *merely* metaphorical? Barth, I think, helps us to see that space is only secondarily a determination of the creature. It is, in the first place, the freely chosen condition of God's threefold differentiation as Father, Son, and Spirit, the condition under which there is both proximity and distance in the being of God and thus personal distinction and communion. Barth says therefore, that God has his own space. Indeed here it is revealed what space truly is. It is possible then to say that spatial language used in theology need not always be a figure of speech. As God has space for himself, for the triune communion that constitutes his own life, so he creates space for us. Our space, distinct from God, is nevertheless the space in which God makes himself present, generally throughout creation, but most especially in Christ. We ought to take this literally. In Christ, as the letter to the Colossians puts it, "the whole fullness of deity dwells bodily" (Col 2:9). God is wholly present *there*. On account of his presence there for us, we are assured that God has space for us eternally, even when our earthly lives have come to an end. The details of that eschatological reality are largely unimaginable, but we can affirm with confidence one of its central features, namely, that we will be with God.

Bibliography

Barth, Karl. *Church Dogmatics*. 4 vols. Edinburgh: T. & T. Clark, 1956–75.

———. *The Epistle to the Romans*. 2nd ed. Translated by Edwyn C. Hoskyns. London: Oxford University Press, 1933.

Gunton, Colin E. *The Promise of Trinitarian Theology*. 2nd ed. Edinburgh: T. & T. Clark, 1997.

Küng, Hans. *The Beginning of All Things*. Translated by John Bowden. Grand Rapids: Eerdmans, 2007.

Jenson, Robert W. *Systematic Theology*, vol. 2. *The Works of God*. New York: Oxford University Press, 1999.

MacKenzie, Ian. *The Dynamism of Space: A Theological Study into the Nature of Space*. Norwich: Canterbury, 1995.

Torrance, Thomas F. *Space, Time, and Incarnation*. Oxford: Oxford University Press, 1969.

Webster, John. *Confessing God*. London: T. & T. Clark, 2005..

4

The Doctrine of the Trinity after Barth

An Attempt to Reconstruct Barth's Doctrine in the Light of His Later Christology

Bruce L. McCormack

SOME YEARS AGO, IN A PRIVATE CONVERSATION WHICH TOOK PLACE in his automobile (while parked outside my flat in the now famous Scotland Street in Edinburgh), I asked Thomas F. Torrance how he himself would characterize the differences between his doctrine of the Trinity and that of Karl Barth. His answer was that his own doctrine owed a great debt to Gregory Nazianzen while Barth's doctrine was "Basilian." I was intrigued by this answer because most of Barth's critics at that time (this was in the late 1980s) characterized his doctrine of the Trinity as typically Western (a combination of elements drawn from Augustine and Hegel).[1] Barth standing with a Cappadocian father? It seemed unthinkable. And yet, I think there is something to Torrance's description—though it needs quite a bit of unpacking to be defended.

Barth's most complete and explicit treatment of the Trinity is to be found in *Church Dogmatics* I/1, as part of his elaboration of the doctrine of the Word of God. The location of this treatment is important. Barth is seeking to answer a single question: who is the subject of revelation?[2] What can be said of this subject on the basis of revelation alone? What is said here about the doctrine of the Trinity is thus controlled by the needs and requirements of Barth's concept of revelation. And given that the concept of revelation he was employing was a distinctively modern concept, one might have expected that the doctrine of the Trinity that

---

1. See Moltmann, *Trinity and the Kingdom*, 10–20, 52–56, 139–44.
2. *CD* I/1, 380.

was constructed on this basis would also be distinctively modern in character. But then we are surprised at just how conventional the results are. Barth's doctrine of the Trinity as it was materially elaborated in §9 especially owes a great debt to the Catholics. At decisive points in his presentation, it is the definitions provided by Thomas and his modern Catholic interpreters (ranging from Matthias Scheeben to Bernhard Bartmann to Franz Diekamp) which provide Barth with the material he needs to expound his own view. He also cites Peter Lombard and Bonaventura and refers to the Councils of Toledo and Florence (as found in Denzinger), the Catholic Catechism, and the *Missale Romanum*. The reason for this is quite simple. Barth was convinced that it was the Catholics alone in the Germany of his time who took any real interest in the doctrine of the Trinity. If he was to have a conversation about these matters with anyone at all, it had to be the Catholics to whom he would turn—a lesson which he had learned during his years in Münster as a member of a Catholic "circle of friends" which included Robert Grosche (who later founded *Catholica*).[3] In any event, references to the ancients (not to mention the Reformers!) are less frequent. And Barth makes no mention whatsoever of Basil of Caesarea. At this time, he seems to have known only the writings of the two Gregory's (among the Cappadocians).

Still, Torrance was not so much arguing for a direct influence of Basil on Barth's thinking as he was pointing to their shared emphasis on the Father as the source of the being of the second and third persons—and, indeed, of triunity.[4] My only comment on this—and it must remain unproven for the moment—is that you would have to elaborate a materially enriched and critically corrected doctrine of the Trinity on the basis of Barth's later Christology in *CD* IV/1 to get a meaningful comparison with Basil off the ground. And then you would also have to take into account the fact that such a reconstructed doctrine would no

---

3. See Neuser, "Karl Barth in Münster, 1925–1930," 38.

4. Cf. Ayres, *Nicaea and its Legacy*, 206: "Basil consistently presents the Father as the source of the Trinitarian persons and of the essence that the three share." It should be noted that Torrance understood Gregory Nazianzen to have rejected the view that the Father is the *arche* of the Trinity. See Torrance, *Trinitarian Perspectives*, 29–32. This, then, is Torrance's point of difference with Barth—and it is a substantial one. For what it requires is an affirmation of two things: 1) that "Father" is not a name for the divine "essence" or *ousia*, but is rather the name of a relation (ibid., 29), and 2) that each person of the Trinity has his being "of himself" (*a se*) (ibid.).

longer be conventional in the least; it would, in fact, be quite modern in character. If one were willing to make allowance for the differences that a shift from an ancient to a modern perspective on issues surrounding divine ontology makes in such comparative work, then the claim that Barth is "Basilian" would begin to make sense. Barth does indeed, on the basis of this reconstructive work, begin to look like a modern version of Basil.

Now it is not my intention to provide a systematic comparison of Barth and Basil in this essay. Such a comparison would require that equal attention be given to Basil, obviously, and the limits proper to even a longish chapter will not allow for that. What I can do is to reconstruct Barth's doctrine in the light of his later Christology, thereby preparing the ground for a possible comparison some time in the future.[5] Even with that de-limitation, however, the aim of this essay remains ambitious. So I will have to beg the reader's indulgence and ask that I be allowed the privilege of speaking in a somewhat magisterial fashion. Think of what I am about to do as a *Problemanzeige*—a modest attempt to "point to a problem" in Barth's dogmatics and to lay down some lines along which I would myself seek to resolve it. The problem has to do with the need to correct certain aspects of Barth's doctrine of the Trinity (in *CD* I/1) in the light of the later Christology (in *CD* (IV/1ff.). Though the basic form or structure of Barth's doctrine of revelation as set forth in his Prolegomena volumes would remain unchanged throughout the *Church Dogmatics*, his material elaboration of the Christology by means of which his doctrine of revelation was grounded *did* change—and that created problems for his earlier doctrine of the Trinity.

---

5. A comparison of Barth's doctrine of the Trinity with that found in the Cappadocians (generally considered) already exists. See Collins, *Trinitarian Theology West and East*. This is a fine study, worthy of much more attention than it has been given to this point. Collins' approach is to use Zizoulas' understanding of the being of God as "an event of communion" as the "controlling" concept by means of which he seeks to find in Barth's writings resources which would enable him to offer a critical correction to Barth's basic model of the Trinity. See ibid., 177. Thus, for Collins, Zizioulas (and the Cappadocians as read by Zizioulas) provides the "fixed" point in the comparison; Barth is adjusted to him. What makes this approach so promising is the fact that Zizioulas is quite open to the elements in modern thinking that also leave their stamp on Barth. Still, if I were to compare the two, I would make Barth the fixed pole and ask how far Zizioulas (and the Cappadocians as read by him) could be adjusted to him—for reasons that will become clear. See below, n.28.

In what follows, I will begin with Barth's concept of revelation and the doctrine of the Trinity to which it gave rise in 1932. In a second section, I will treat Barth's later Christology and the understanding of the Trinity demanded by it. A third section will take up the question of the logical relationship of my reconstruction of Barth's doctrine of the Trinity to the doctrine of election. In my concluding remarks, I shall say a few words about why I think my reconstruction of Barth's doctrine of the Trinity remains within the bounds of ecumenically-established "orthodoxy."

Barth's Concept of Revelation and Its Significance for His Doctrine of the Trinity in CD I/1

Historical Background

One way of describing the seismic changes that the concept of revelation underwent at the dawn of the modern period in Christian theology in the West is to say—in the words of Wolfhart Pannenberg—that the idea of a historical revelation (i.e., a public revelation of God in the form of historical events) was severed from the idea of an inner subjective experience on the part of the biblical writers. "The differentiating and interrelating of an outer revelation, of a public manifestation of God in the events of history, and of inspiration as the effect and interpretation of these events in the subjectivity of the biblical witnesses, were basic to all further discussion of the concept of revelation in Protestant theology during the nineteenth and early twentieth centuries."[6] Such a differentiation allowed for a variety of possibilities where the description of the relation of the objective and the subjective was concerned. One could, for example, lay the greater stress on the external revelation in historical events and make them the object of historical investigation. On this showing, to reconstruct the external events lying behind the New Testament writings was to approximate revelation, at the very least. Or one could affirm the reality of a basic religious awareness which enabled the biblical writers to interpret and evaluate the external events to which they bore witness; a subjective awareness which—precisely because it is also to be found in those who subsequently sought to appropriate their witness—provided the basis for an empathetic understanding of

---

6. Pannenberg, *Systematic Theology*, 222.

what was at stake in that witness. On this understanding, it was not so much what the biblical writers taught as it was their own experience of redemption that was made basic to the concept of revelation.

But there was another development that took place almost simultaneously with the one just described which has an even greater relevance for understanding Karl Barth. Here again, Pannenberg's historical sketch is most helpful. "At this point, the idea of a historical revelation that is distinct from inspiration linked up with the notion that revelation has God not merely as its subject but also as its exclusive content and theme." The idea of a divine self-revelation was not altogether new, Pannenberg notes. It can be found in New Testament texts like John 1:1 and Hebrews 1:1 and also in thinkers like Philo and Plotinus. What was new was the element of exclusivity.

> Only in the philosophy of German idealism do we first find the thought of a self-revelation of God in the sense of the strict identity of subject and content. . . . God is either revealed as himself, just as he is revealed to himself, or he is not revealed at all, at least in the strict sense. Later, perhaps by way of [Philip] Marheineke, Karl Barth took over this linking of the thought of God's self-revelation with that of uniqueness, and he used it in opposition to all ideas of a second source of the knowledge of God.[7]

That Barth received his understanding of self-revelation from Marheinke is, in my view, doubtful. Certainly, he would have been very familiar with the concept from his student days, since its usage was, by that point in time, widespread. What is unquestionably true is that the centrality of the concept of a divine self-revelation in Barth's thinking from *Romans* on through to the end of his life—and the accompanying notion that in revelation, subject, and content are identical—makes Barth's concept of revelation distinctively *modern*.

But we would be missing a crucial element if we did not observe, already at this point, the decisive difference between Barth's elaboration of the concept of a divine self-revelation and that found in Hegel, for example. By November 1923 at the very latest, Barth had begun to explore the possibility of understanding the self-revelation of God in terms of the classical two-natures Christology—and this marked a de-

---

7. Ibid., 222–23.

cisive departure from Hegel and his followers.[8] That meant that a strict identification of the second person of the Trinity with the man Jesus was never a temptation for him. In fact, Hegel's transmutation of God into a human in the incarnation amounted for him to a thinly-disguised apotheosis of the human, to which the door had been opened by the classical Lutheran understanding of the "communication of attributes."[9] In truth, in its initial stages, Barth's concept of revelation had as much— and as little!—in common with Schleiermacher and the romanticists as it did Hegel and the other idealists. For what Barth set forth was a dialectical conception of the divine veiling and unveiling that required, for its completion, an internal activity of the Holy Spirit in the recipient that would enable her to "see" (with the "eyes" of faith) what lay hidden beneath the veil. And that meant that the divine "unveiling" was not merely an objective event (the event in which the second person of the Trinity assumed human flesh) but also a subjective event. And all of this became basic to his derivation of the doctrine of the Trinity in *Church Dogmatics* I/1.

Barth's Derivation of the Doctrine of the Trinity

Given the difference between Barth's understanding of divine self-revelation and that of Hegel, it would be a mistake to try to reduce Barth's derivation of the Trinity to an idealistic understanding of the self-differentiation of an Absolute Subject.[10] What is true is that his Christology, at this stage of his development, is controlled by the needs and requirements of his doctrine of revelation rather than by soteriological considerations, as would be the case later. But his doctrine of revelation is not designed to provide an answer to the subject-object problem bequeathed to the idealists by Kant (as Hegel's was). That was never his problem. His problem was the Godness of God in his self-revelation. He needed to show that while the content of revelation is

---

8. Barth, "Paradoxical Nature of the 'Positive Paradox,'" 152: "What is 'absurd' from the Christian or *theological* point of view is not at all what Tillich so designates the 'once and for all' which it is rather simply our theological duty to affirm. What is 'absurd' is all unreflecting, unclassical, disrespectful deviation from the formula of the Council of Chalcedon, for to hold quietly to this confession would still indicate, *mutatis mutandis*, good insight even today."

9. Barth, *"Unterricht in der christlichen Religion,"* 57.

10. Moltmann, *Trinity and the Kingdom*, 139–44.

"God alone, God Himself, God in His entirety,"[11] revelation takes place in hiddenness; in a hiddenness secured by the ontological distinction between the christological "person of the union" (the Logos) and a human "nature" that does not participate in the divine being and attributes and, therefore, cannot become directly revelatory. At this stage, Barth's Christology is simply a good example of *Reformed* Chalcedonianism. And it is the concept of revelation that includes this Christology that provides the basis for his derivation of the doctrine of the Trinity, not a philosophical problem.

Still, there *is* something very formal about Barth's derivation of the doctrine of the Trinity—and it is here that we must locate the weaknesses in his attempt. Barth believes that the three moments of revelation (unveiling, veiling, and impartation) are contained analytically in the statement "God reveals Himself as Lord."[12] And he believes as well that this statement accurately summarizes the revelation event borne witness to in Holy Scripture. "The statement . . . that God reveals Himself as the Lord, or what this statement is meant to describe, and therefore revelation itself as attested by Scripture, we call the root of the doctrine of the Trinity."[13] The link between the content of the statement on the one hand and the content of revelation itself on the other is to be found in the idea of "lordship." And it is that link which Barth believes, justifies him in deriving the Trinity from a logical analysis of his summary statement.

The formalism of which I speak lies in the lack of positive content given to the concept of lordship. What is in view here is "ontic and noetic autonomy";[14] God's Godness in his revelation is his freedom from human epistemic mastery, a freedom that is secured by his hiddenness in the creaturely medium of his self-revelation. It is that epistemic autonomy which also preserves God's otherness, his freedom in the ontological sense of independent and unique being. So absorbed is Barth by the need to prevent God from being directly identified with his chosen medium of self-revelation that he is content simply to emphasize the distinction between them. Not surprisingly, then, Barth says, "We may unhesitatingly equate the lordship of God . . . with what the vocabulary

---

11. Barth, *"Unterricht in der christlichen Religion,"* 105.
12. *CD* I/1, 306.
13. Ibid., 307.
14. Ibid.

of the early Church calls the essence of God, the *deitas* or *divinitas*, the divine *ousia*, *essentia*, *natura*, or *substantia*."[15] The net result of this equation is that the delineation of the three modes of being in the eternal God that follows will, at each step, give expression to this abstract conception of lordship. I call it "abstract" because it is not controlled, as it would later be in *Church Dogmatics* IV/1, by God's gracious decision to be God "for us" in Jesus Christ.[16] And the power that is contained in this abstract conception of lordship is, in turn, power in the abstract, power that is not defined by the humility, lowliness, and obedience of the Son on his way into the far country.

Once the link between the formal statement and the actual event of revelation has been established, Barth's derivation of the Trinity follows rather smoothly. That "God reveals Himself as the Lord" means that he is and remains the Lord in all the moments of revelation. More expansively expressed: "Revelation in the Bible means the self-unveiling, imparted to men, of the God who by nature cannot be unveiled to men."[17] This statement, repeated three times, becomes the basis for the actual derivation. In each repetition, the accent falls on a different part of the statement.

First, the self-unveiling: God unveils himself, according to Barth, by "taking form." In making this his starting point, Barth makes the first moment in revelation to be the Son. At the same time, he is at least giving a nod to the necessity of rooting what is said about the immanent Trinity in the economic Trinity. What happens in revelation? God makes himself "objective"; he takes up a creaturely medium so that, in it, he might be the "object" of a real human knowing. The event in which God does this—Barth is clearly thinking here of the incarnation—is "something new in God."[18] That God can do this tells us that it is "proper to Him to distinguish Himself from Himself, i.e., to be God in Himself and in concealment, and yet at the same time to be God a second time in a very different way, namely in manifestation, i.e., in the form of something He Himself is not."[19] Thus, the step into incarnate life in hid-

---

15. Ibid., 349.

16. This point is by now well established. See Goebel, "Trinitätslehre und Erwählungslehre," 153–54; and Gundlach, *Selbstbegrenzung Gottes*, 162.

17. *CD* I/1, 315, 320, 324.

18. Ibid., 316.

19. Ibid.

denness is rooted in an eternal differentiation of God from God, a first mode of being and a second. In this, Barth also finds a confirmation of his first statement, that God reveals himself as the Lord.

> ... the lordship discernible in the biblical revelation consists in the freedom of God to differentiate Himself from Himself, to become unlike Himself and yet to remain the same, to be indeed the one God like Himself and to exist as the one sole God in the fact that in this way that is so inconceivably profound, He differentiates Himself from Himself, being not only God the Father but also ... God the Son. That He reveals Himself as the Son is what is primarily meant when we say that He reveals Himself as the Lord. This Sonship is God's lordship in His revelation.[20]

The second moment treats of "the God who by nature cannot be unveiled to men." God, Barth says, is *by nature* inscrutable: "... inscrutability, hiddenness, is the very essence of Him who is called God in the Bible."[21] It is in terms of this hiddenness then, that Barth speaks at some length of the "Father."

Now there is something conceptually odd about this move. Surely it is the Son, not the Father, who is revealed, who remains hidden in revelation. Why associate hiddenness with the Father? Certainly, such a move imperils Barth's attempt to derive an immanent Trinity from the economy, so why do it? The answer, in part at least, must be that Barth identifies the essence of God, in Cappadocian fashion, with the *hypostasis* of the Father. And since, at this time, he defines the divine essence in terms of hiddenness he feels it necessary to speak of hiddenness in relation to the Father. Here again, the abstract character of Barth's definition of the content of revelation—God reveals himself as the Lord—is distracting him from the requirements of his attempt to derive an immanent Trinity from the economy of revelation. Hiddenness in revelation may indeed be necessary. I think that it is, though I would treat the problem in strictly christological terms (making hiddenness a function of the unituitability of the "person of the union"). But you simply cannot derive an immanent Trinity from an economy of revelation that loses sight of the fact that it is the Son who is hidden in revelation.

There is another problem lurking here, an even more significant problem. To identify God's "essence" with hiddenness is to make God

20. Ibid., 320.
21. Ibid.

essentially unknowable. That is not what Barth wants and it is *not* something he would do later. By *Church Dogmatics* II/1 at the latest, Barth is already equating the divine "essence" with that which is given to human beings to be known in his self-revelation.²² When this occurs, the divine "essence" is no longer construed in terms of hiddenness but rather in terms of God's gracious and loving covenant.

The third moment has to do with the "impartation" to men and women. That God remains Lord even in the impartation refers to the fact that the Holy Spirit, who bears witness to the truth of God's self-revelation in Jesus Christ, remains ontologically other than those whom he indwells. That the impartation is nonetheless real and effective means that it makes history. It gives rise, for example, to the New Testament witness. Barth uses this—again somewhat surprisingly—as an occasion to reflect upon the limitations of historical criticism, the difference between saga and myth. Not that such topics could not be addressed in relation to the Spirit's witness, but it is a bit odd to interject it here in a derivation of the immanent Trinity from moments in the economy of revelation.

In any event, Barth thinks that once he has set before us the three moments of "unveiling, veiling and impartation" or "form, freedom and historicity" he has provided himself with a basis for talking about the immanent Trinity. That God reveals *himself* in these three moments—"in unimpaired unity and unimpaired distinction"²³—suggests to him that there is in God one essence and three persons or modes of being.

---

22. See *CD* II/1, 261, 262, 263: "What God is as God, the divine individuality and characteristics, the *essentia* or 'essence' of God, is something we shall encounter either at the place where God deals with us as Lord and Savior or not at all. . . . We are in fact interpreting the being of God when we describe it as God's reality, as 'God's being in act,' namely, in the act of His revelation, in which the being of God declares His reality: not only His reality for us—certainly that—but at the same time His own, inner, proper reality behind which and above which there is no other. . . . And in this very event [of revelation] God is who He is. God is who He is in this event as subject, predicate and object; the revealer, the act of revelation, the revealed; Father, Son and Holy Spirit. . . . We are dealing with the being of God; but with regard to the being of God, the word 'event' or 'act' is *final* and cannot be surpassed or compromised. To its very depths, God's Godhead consists in the fact that it is an event—not any event, not events in general, but the event of His action, in which we have a share in God's revelation." But if we humans have a share in the divine essence through revelation, then God's essence can no longer simply be equated with hiddenness.

23. Ibid., 333.

I have to say that this derivation of the immanent Trinity is far from a rousing success. Barth would have done far better, I think, to have begun (as von Balthasar would later do), with the Sent One in order then to reflect back upon the Sending One and forward to the One who bears witness to the Sent One.[24] The move from the economic Trinity to the immanent Trinity is far more successfully established on this basis than on the basis of a logical analysis of the statement "God reveals himself as Lord." For, as we have seen, Barth has difficulties in distinguishing the first and second persons on this basis, with the result that the Father seems to be both the one revealed in hiddenness and the hiddenness itself—surely a confusion of Father and Son.

Barth's Doctrine of the Trinity

The good news is that Barth's doctrine of the Trinity is much better than his derivation. And since his doctrine of the Trinity is simply mapped onto the derivation, the derivation can be dispensed with and the strengths of the doctrine itself remain standing.

Barth's basic conception is that God is a single Subject in three modes of being. God is the one Subject three times—not "three divine I's," but the "one divine I" three times.[25] "The name of the Father, Son, and Spirit means that God is the one God in threefold repetition, and this in such a way that the repetition itself is grounded in His Godhead.... The so-called 'persons' are a *repetitio aeternitatis in aeternitate*, not then a threeness of eternity *extra se* but a threeness of eternity *in se*."[26] The language of "repetition" is meant to secure the "substantial equality"[27] of the three.[28] It is Barth's way of ensuring that no subordinationism can

---

24. See von Balthasar, *Theo-Drama*, 149–259, 505–23.
25. *CD* I/1., 351.
26. Ibid., 350.
27. Ibid., 352.
28. Paul Collins is quite right, I think, to find in the concept of "repetition" evidence of Barth's belief that the "self-moved being of God" is "the movement of one Person, an 'I.'" See Collins, *Trinitarian Theology West and East*, 26. For Collins, however, this argues *against* Barth's basic model. To this I can only say: Barth's conception of the Trinity bears clear witness to the NT belief that the God whom Christians worship is the God of Israel. In this, it has a distinct advantage over those models that overemphasize a communion of distinct persons, each with its own mind, will, and energy of operation. For that reason, I am not terribly impressed by critiques of Barth's emphasis on

enter in. The concept of repetition, in other words, does the work of the traditional concept of the *homoousios*.²⁹ "The idea we are excluding is that of a mere unity of kind or a mere collective unity, and the truth we are emphasizing is that of the numerical unity of the essence of the 'persons,' when in the first instance we employ the concept of repetition to denote the 'persons.'"³⁰

But the language of "repetition" also ensures that what Barth refers to as God's "modes of being" are wrongly conceived if thought of as impersonal. The one divine Subject is that which defines what it means to be personal;³¹ there is nothing more personal than God is in each of his three modes of being. And God is no more personal in any one mode of being than he is in the other two.³²

It has been suggested that Barth's use of the language of "modes of being" constitutes evidence of the idealistic origins of his doctrine of the Trinity and, specifically, a dependence upon Isaak A. Dorner in particular.³³ But the truth is that his use of this concept entailed a combination of the Cappadocian emphasis on "modes of origination"³⁴ and the Thomistic definition of divine persons as "subsisting relations."³⁵ It was a traditional doctrine he was setting forth here, not a peculiarly modern one.

That point is further underscored by Barth's appropriation of the concept of *perichoresis* to speak of "a definite participation of each mode

---

a single divine Subject. But I also have to say that Collins is not altogether clear as to how he himself understands the persons. What is clear is that he is not satisfied with differentiating the three solely in terms of relations of origin; he wants to add to this, relations of communion. But is he willing to think of each of the three along the lines of the modern concept of personality? On that point, he is less than clear.

29. *CD* I/1, 351.

30. Ibid., 350.

31. *CD* II/1, 271: ". . . if the being of a person is a being in act, and if, in the strict and proper sense, being in act can be ascribed only to God, then it follows that by the concept of person, in the strict and proper sense, we can only understand the being of God."

32. As Robert Jenson puts it, "although the triune identities are not, as such, persons in the modern sense, God is; and if each identity is God, each identity is also personal, and the three a community" (Jenson, *Triune Identity*, 146).

33. Moltmann, *Trinity and the Kingdom*, 139, n.21.

34. *CD* I/1, 363, 365.

35. Ibid., 366. Cf. Thomas Aquinas, *Summa Theologiae* I.Q.29, art.4: ". . .a divine person signifies a relation as subsisting."

of being in the other modes of being, and indeed, since the modes of being are in fact identical with the relations of origin, a complete participation of each mode of being in the other modes of being."[36]

And this leads to another, fascinating aspect of Barth's teaching on the doctrine of the Trinity. Barth holds, again with the Cappadocians, that even numerical predication with respect to God is strictly metaphorical in nature.[37] That is to say, the logic of numbers is something we humans have contrived in order to count the people and things we experience—one of these, a half dozen of those. Such logic breaks down where a *"perichoretic"* spiritual reality is concerned. The real point of the numbers 1 and 3 is negation. Citing the Council of Toledo, Barth says, "It is true of numerical concepts in the doctrine of the Trinity generally that . . . they are to be understood metaphorically, they do not posit quantity in God, and in the last resort they merely imply negations. . . . Thus, the number 1 implies the negation of all plurality of or in God. All further deductions from the use of the concept of number are to be

---

36. Ibid., 370. Paul Collins would like to use this passage as the basis for "a possible interpretation of Barth's concept of the Trinity as an event of communion" (Collins, *Trinitarian Theology West and East*, 32). I would say myself that if any term is used by Barth metaphorically, it would have to be *"perichoresis"*—not "repetition." The concept of *perichoresis* drew its life originally from substance metaphysics. It was the mutual indwelling of three "primary substances" (in the Aristotelian sense) which made *perichoresis* possible. But Barth as Collins rightly notes, set aside the language of "substance" because it seemed in his eyes to tear apart being and act. In the absence of a commitment to substance metaphysics, however, the use of the concept of *perichoresis* can only be metaphorical (i.e., descriptive of the being of the one divine Subject "in" each of his modes of being) The only remaining question is whether one loses contact with the Cappadocians in saying this. My own answer to that problem would be "no." Precisely in the celebrated essay in which he advances the "social analogy" of the Trinity which has commanded so much attention in the theology of the last thirty years or so, Gregory of Nyssa writes, 'Rather does every operation which extends from God to creation and is designated according to our differing conceptions of it have its origin in the Father, proceed through the Son, and reach its completion in the Spirit. It is for this reason that the word for the operation is not divided among the three persons involved. For the action of each in any matter is not separate and individualized. . . . It is not by separate action according to the number of Persons; but there is one motion and disposition of the good will which proceeds from the Father, through the Son, to the Spirit" (Gregory of Nyssa, "An Answer to Ablabius," 262). Even though Barth does not employ the concept of "substance," his understanding of "personality" in God is very close to what is set forth here.

37. Kelly, *Early Christian Doctrines*, 268.

rejected as irrelevant."[38] Likewise, the purpose of using the number 3 is to insist that oneness in God is not the oneness of solitary isolation.[39]

What does all of this mean for "personality" in God? Barth believes that modern theologians mean something quite different by the word "person" than did the ancients. The Boethian definition of "person" (i.e., an individual substance of a rational nature) is an abstraction whose use, by Thomas for example, is to make room for the understanding that divine persons are "subsisting relations."[40] The addition of the concept of self-consciousness to that definition would entail the merging of a nineteenth-century concept of personality with the ancient concept of person.[41] In any event, Barth understands there to be in God one self-consciousness. We might put it this way: there is in God one mind, one will, one energy of operation which "passes" in its entirety from the Father, through the Son, to the Holy Spirit so that it is equally shared by all three. Again, Barth tends to equate divine essence with the Father in the first instance, so it would be a mistake to think here of an Absolute Subject in which all three participate. That, for Barth, would be modalism.

What Barth is rejecting in taking this stance is the idea that there is in God "three independently thinking and willing subjects."[42] This was the view of Roman Catholic philosopher Anton Günther, who was condemned by Pope Pius IX in 1857. Barth sees this teaching as a *novum* in the nineteenth century. In this, I think myself that he was right. Social trinitarians love to speak of Barth's Hegelianism; that is, they love to accuse him of assigning Hegel's concept of the person to an Absolute Subject. What they fail to acknowledge is that they themselves are working with Hegel's concept. It is just that they assign that concept to the threeness of God, rather than the oneness. And, in the end, the view they assign to Barth is precisely the one he rejects under the heading of modalism. No, Barth's understanding of the trinitarian modes of being does not entail a sharing in a divine "personality" that is distinct from all

---

38. *CD* I/1, 354.

39. Ibid.

40. Thomas Aquinas, *Summa Theologiae* I. Q.29, art.4: "a divine person signifies a relation as subsisting."

41. *CD* I/1, 357–58.

42. Ibid., 357.

three (a fourth something), but rather the full possession by God of one and the same personality in each of his modes of being.

Traditional, finally, is Barth's contention that the relation of the economic to the immanent Trinity is analogical in nature. Barth is quite explicit about this—in terms that might even satisfy David Bentley Hart.[43]

> There is an analogy ... between the terms Father Son, and Spirit ... on the one side, and on the other side the three divine modes of being which consist in the different relations of origin and in which we have come to know the truly incomprehensible eternal distinctions in God. . . . [I]f we confused the analogy with the thing itself, if we equated the distinctions that are comprehensible to us with those that are not, in other words, if we thought we had comprehended the essence of God in comprehending His work, we should be plunged at once into the error of tritheism.[44]

What creates the "analogical interval"[45] between the economic Trinity and the immanent Trinity for Barth is the residual "essentialism" present in his distinction between a "divine essence as such" (characterized by a negatively defined "freedom"—as we saw before) and a "divine essence" as it gives itself to be known in God's works.

All we can know of God according to the witness of Scripture are his acts. All we can say of God, all the attributes we can assign to God, relate to these acts of his; not, then, to his essence as such. Though the work of God is the essence of God, it is necessary and important to distinguish his essence as such from his work, remembering that this work is grace, a free divine decision, and also remembering that we can know about God only because and to the extent that he gives himself to us to be known. God's work is, of course, the work of the whole essence of God. God gives himself entirely to man in his revelation, but not in such a way as to make himself man's prisoner. He remains free in his working, in giving himself. This freedom of his is the basis of the

---

43. Hart's critique of Robert Jenson's doctrine of the Trinity focuses on the latter's alleged "collapse of the analogical interval between the immanent and economic Trinity, between timeless eternity and the time in which eternity shows itself . . ." I say "alleged" because it is not my purpose here to examine Jenson's doctrine. See Hart, *Beauty of the Infinite*, 165.

44. *CD* I/1, 372.

45. See Hart, *Beauty of the Infinite*, 165.

distinction of the essence of God as such as the One who works and reveals himself.[46]

Clearly, Barth would like to say (in his words) that "God's essence and work are not twofold but one."[47] But he cannot say it at this point in time with anything like the clarity with which he would do so in the future. The essence of God as comprehended in God's works is not identical with but remains distinct from his essence as such. There is, at most, an analogical relationship between them, but since we cannot know the analogate in this case, we can only guess at the content of the analogy. And that is why Barth must finally say, "The great central difficulties which have always beset the doctrine of the Trinity . . . apply to us too. We too are unable to say how an essence can produce itself and then be in a twofold way its own product. We too are unable to say how an essence's relation of origin can also be the essence itself and indeed how three such relations can be the essence and yet not be the same as the other but indissolubly distinct from one another."[48]

As I say, all of this is quite traditional. Given its largely Thomistic provenance, we could hardly have expected otherwise. But it has to be remembered that these are Barth's years of apprenticeship. He is still learning his craft, studying intensively at the feet of the theological giants of the past. In a very real sense, he has yet to discover his own voice. That would change, however.

Reconstructing Barth's Doctrine of the Trinity—in the Light of His Later Christology

Building-Blocks in Barth's Later Christology

The need to reconstruct Barth's doctrine of the Trinity is rooted in fundamental changes that took place in his doctrine of election and his Christology. That Barth's doctrine of election underwent revision is not a matter of debate. What the ontological implications of that revision might be is, however, a subject of controversy. So I will not start there. I will begin instead with Barth's later Christology and then come back to election.

46. *CD* I/1, 372.
47. Ibid.
48. Ibid., 367.

Barth took up the problem of Christology twice within the bounds of the *Church Dogmatics*—the first time in his Prolegomena, and the second in the context of his doctrine of reconciliation. As was the case with his doctrine of the Trinity, Barth's treatment of Christology in *Church Dogmatics* I/2 was designed to meet the needs of his doctrine of revelation. In truth, this treatment belongs to that phase of Barth's development which was launched by his *Göttingen Dogmatics*. Where motivation, structural design, and basic material decisions are concerned, the Christology of I/2 corresponds quite closely to that found in §6 of the Göttingen lectures. Such differences as exist consist in material expansions; they are not substantive.

If, however, one were to compare §§ 28 and 29 of the Göttingen lectures (Barth's material treatment of the person and work of Christ, respectively) with the Christology of *Church Dogmatics* IV/1ff., one might well be shocked at the changes. That significant change has occurred is already clear from the external arrangement of the material.

§29 opened with a spirited defense of the necessity for treating the person of Christ before his work. The person of Christ, Barth insisted, is the presupposition of his work and the former will be wrongly construed if it is explicated in the light of the latter—as was done in post-Schleiermacherian modern theology.[49] By the same token, the work of Christ too will be misunderstood if a prior knowledge of his person is not in place.[50] At the end of the day, only the ordering of person before work can do justice to the "from above to below" procedure which is needed for a well-ordered understanding of both person and work.[51]

To enter IV/1 is to enter a completely altered landscape. Gone is the division of material between the person and work of Christ. In fact, Barth no longer has a separate locus devoted to the person of Christ. He has so completely historicized the two natures of Christ—and with that,

49. Barth, "*Unterricht in der christlichen Religion*," 75.

50. Ibid., 76.

51. Ibid., 78. While it is true, Barth says, that preaching activity ought—for reasons of clear communication—begin with the work of Christ, in the preacher herself, in her behind-the-scenes labor, must begin with the person of Christ. "The fundamental principle: from above to below, not from below to above! is valid for the preacher as well and in an unchanged form. . . . If the mystery of Christ's person does not stand behind every sentence in the preaching of the *beneficia Christi*, then it is no Christian sermon. And precisely in order to pound that into the heads of preachers, dogmatic science must treat Christ's *person* thoroughly and in the first place."

his understanding of the constitution of the person—that a separate treatment would be superfluous to requirements. Christ's person is now understood to be his work.

Even more significant, however, is the change that has occurred in Barth's understanding of the work of Christ. Central to Barth's theology of the cross in *CD* IV/1 is the suffering of God—a theme that had no place whatsoever in §29 of the *Göttingen Dogmatics* (and was therefore not taken into account in *CD* I/2).[52] And that addition especially made a very obvious difference where the question of God's Godness in his Self-revelation was concerned.

How can God enter into the sphere of human knowing without surrendering himself to human epistemic control, thereby setting aside his sovereign freedom? That was Barth's understanding of his central question in the early days. But by IV/1, the question of the Godness of God in his self-revelation had become deeply ontological. How can God live a human life, suffer, and die—without undergoing change on the level of his being? That was the way Barth now formulated the question.

The traditional answers to the challenge posed to divine immutability by the incarnate life of God lay either in a Nestorian separation of the natures (so that suffering was confined to the human nature alone) or in a Cyrilline instrumentalization of the human nature (so that the pure activity of the Logos vis-à-vis his human nature rendered his divine nature immune to reciprocal influence). Barth's answer would look in a quite different direction than either of these traditional options. We catch sight of his answer in the following passage. If we think that God cannot experience death, he says, then "[O]ur concept of God is too narrow, too arbitrary, too human, all too human. Who God is and what it means to be divine is something we have to learn where God has revealed Himself and, thereby, His nature, the *essence* of the divine.

---

52. Ibid., 111–48. Consideration of the nature of Christ's suffering is limited here to a citation of the Heidelberg Catechism, Q. 37: "That all the time of His life on earth, but especially at the end of it, He bore, in body and soul, the wrath of God against the sin of the whole human race ..." See ibid., 138. The subject of this suffering, moreover, is clearly the man Jesus rather than the Logos. "The whole of the work of Christ is the work of the man who, from the beginning, was headed towards the cross" (ibid., 139). Even humiliation is assigned to the human (ibid., 141). What Barth sets forth in §29 is, from first to last, a thoroughly *classical*—one might even say "pre-modern"—doctrine of the atoning work of Christ.

And when He reveals Himself in Jesus Christ as the God who *does* such things, then it must lie far from us to wish to be wiser than he and to maintain that such things stand in contradiction to the *divine essence*."[53]

Barth's solution to the ontological form of his central question is clear: suffering and death do not change God because they are *essential* to him. Now that can *sound* quite Hegelian, so it is important for us here at the outset to see why Barth's solution to the problem of divine immutability differed from that of the Hegelians.

The Hegelians obtained a suffering God through the most simple and straightforward of devices. The man Jesus as such is, for them, the second person of the Trinity. This was not the path Barth chose to enter. He wanted to retain, at the very least, the *logic* of the two-natures Christology even if he could no longer understand the natures substantially. And to achieve this, he needed an eternal Son of God who pre-existed his assumption of human nature in time. Only one solution remained. To get a suffering God on the soil of a two-natures logic, Barth had to accept the viability of something like a *genus tapeinoticum*[54]—and this too marked a significant advance over against his early Christology. Now given that talk of a *genus tapeinoticum* will be new to many, it requires a bit of explanation.

The origins of the technical terminology of a *genus tapeinoticum* are murky. In all likelihood, they are to be found in early-seventeenth-century Lutheranism, though the conceptuality is somewhat older.[55] *Genus tapeinoticum* means "genus of humility"—and like its logical corollary, the *genus majestaticum* (or "genus of majesty"), it is the name given to a sub-class of the more general conception of a "communication of attributes." Of the two, the *genus majestaticum* alone was used positively, to set forth the Lutheran conviction that the human nature of Jesus Christ participates in the divine attributes as a consequence of the hypostatic union. Of chief interest here were the divine attributes of omnipotence, omniscience, and, most especially, omnipresence. The

---

53. Karl Barth, *Kirchliche Dogmatik* IV/1, 203; ET: *CD* IV/1, 186 (the first and the third emphases are mine).

54. *CD* IV/2, 78, 85.

55. What was made to be orthodox Lutheran teaching on the subject of the communication of attributes in the Formula of Concord was first set forth in a complete form in Martin Chemnitz's great work, *De Duabus Naturis* (first published in 1570, then revised and expanded in 1578). The revised edition has been translated into English. See Chemnitz, *Two Natures in Christ*.

idea was originally advanced in order to explain the real presence of the body and blood of Christ in the elements of bread and wine in the Lord's Supper. If now you were to ask: but wouldn't an inter-penetration of natures allow for two-way traffic? wouldn't it also allow for a participation by the eternal Son of God or Logos in the attributes proper to human nature?—you would have arrived at the content of the *genus tapeinoticum*. But this idea was devised by the early Lutherans as a strictly logical possibility which was then quickly rejected on the grounds of its incompatibility with the divine impassibility. Therefore, on Lutheran soil, the inter-penetration of natures was thought to give rise to one-way traffic only; to a *genus majestaticum* but not to a *genus tapeinoticum*.

Before proceeding, it is worth noting that the old Reformed rejected *both* the *genus majestaticum* and the *genus tapeinoticum*. They refused to accept the idea of an inter-penetration of natures as the basis for a communication of attributes. In its place, they posited a communication of the attributes of both natures to the person of the union, but not to each other. In their view, there could be no direct communion of the natures with each other. Such communion as existed was indirect, mediated in and through the person to whom these natures belonged.

The next step in the history of the idea of a *genus tapeinoticum* came in the nineteenth century. For the first time, positive use of the idea was first made by the members of the so-called Erlangen School as the basis for elaborating a kenotic Christology—which helps to explain why Barth was not inclined to take it up in his early years. Nineteenth-century kenoticists understood the self-emptying of the Logos to consist in the surrender of the omni-attributes as a sort of pre-condition to incarnation; a *kenosis* by subtraction, in other words, through an act of self-deprivation. Barth, on the other hand, understood *kenosis* to take place by addition—that is, through the addition of the human nature. And so, in the *Göttingen Dogmatics*, Barth makes mention of the *genus tapeinoticum* only to raise the question of whether the nineteenth century Lutherans were not more consistent than their seventeenth-century forebears in *accepting* the *genus tapeinoticum*, given their shared commitment to an inter-penetration of natures.[56] Since Barth still followed the Reformed example of rejecting an inter-penetration of natures at this time, he had no use for a *genus tapeinoticum*.

---

56. Barth, "*Unterricht in der christlichen Religion*," 55.

But by the time he wrote *CD* IV/1, the stout opposition to an interpenetration of natures had become something of a dead letter, since he no longer understood the natures substantially. He could now make cautious use of the concept of a *genus tapeinoticum* as a way of suggesting that the history of the self-humiliation of God and the history of the exaltation of the royal man (i.e., Jesus) are one and the same history; that the latter history is so completely "in" the former, that the being of the eternal Word and the being of the man Jesus are both "actualized" in it.[57]

The significance of Barth's acceptance of something like the *genus tapeinoticum* is this: all that the man Jesus does and experiences and, therefore, *is*, is taken up into or appropriated by the Word. It is important to see that this is a positive act. Receptivity is not passivity; it is not a state of inactivity. But receptivity does mean that the Word does not act through his human nature—and he certainly does not act upon it. How does the God-human perform miracles and live without sin? He does this, as the Synoptic Gospels clearly say, in the power of the Holy Spirit. If the Word acted through or upon his human nature, there would be no need for the Spirit's ministry in the life of Jesus; the outpouring of the Spirit would have been rendered superfluous to requirements. But no, the God-human acts *humanly*—as a consequence of the receptive posture adopted by the Word in assuming this human nature.

The last remaining step is to say something about how the person of the one God-man is constituted—now that we have something like the *genus tapeinoticum* up and running. If the divine Word has his being *in the act of receiving* that which comes to him from his assumed humanity, then his person (i.e., the Subject that he is) is compound in nature. The redeeming Subject is neither the Logos *simpliciter* (as Barth seemed to assume in I/2) nor the man Jesus *simpliciter*, but is both—in the unity of a single history in which both are actualized. The redeeming Subject is the God-human in his divine-human unity. Now we can see, I think, how human suffering—and suffering is after all, something that takes place in the man Jesus—can be an event in God's own life. To

---

57. The use of the term "actualization" does not mean that the being of God or even the being of the human is *absolutely* constituted in the temporal history of the one God-human, but only *relatively* (as the outworking of an eternal decision). "Actualization" means that the being of the one God-human which is constituted eternally in an act of divine self-determination is made concretely real in this world—not merely manifested, but made *concretely* real.

ascribe human attributes and experiences to the "person of the union" is to ascribe them to *both* God and Jesus—since it is only as both that the God-human is the person (or Subject) he is. Suffering cannot be restricted to the human nature alone (however true it may be that suffering is a human experience) because it is *as human* (via the *genus tapeinoticum*) that the Word of God is the Word of God.[58]

But then the question becomes: how can the divine Word take up the human experiences of suffering and death into his own lived existence?—if I may put it that way, without undergoing change on the level of his being. How does Barth rescue divine immutability? He does so, as I have already intimated, by making the human experiences of suffering and death to be essential to God. The incarnation (and with that, the experiences of suffering and death) is not a new event in God when it happens in time.[59] It is new to human beings when it takes place; i.e., it can only take place as the revelation of that which had been, to that point in time, a mystery. But it is not new to God because it is the outworking in time of the eternal event in which God gave to himself the being he would have for all eternity. We have before us here another piece of significant evidence demonstrating that an important change has taken place within the bounds of the *Church Dogmatics*. In I/1, as we have already seen, Barth insisted that the incarnation was a new event in God's life.[60] In IV/1, he denies it.

In any event, when the Word suffers humanly in time, he undergoes no essential change because what he is essentially is the God-human. That is what I must now explain, by means of a reconstruction of Barth's doctrine of the Trinity.

Reconstructing Barth's Doctrine of the Trinity

Barth never undertook a complete re-write of his doctrine of the Trinity. It is not inconceivable that he might have done so, had he lived

---

58. It should be noted that a communication from the humanity to the "person" is not something that is directly intuitable. Barth's earlier emphasis upon hiddenness in revelation has been retained, but it is now given a different basis. Hiddenness is a Christological state of affairs, not a trinitarian one. It has to do with the relation of the humanity of Jesus to the "person of the union." It is not a function of a putative hiddenness of the Father.

59. *CD* IV/1, 193.

60. Ibid., 11 n. 18.

to write volume 5 of the *Church Dogmatics*. But alas, he did not. He did however, leave us with a methodological correction and a few hints as the difference that this made where the material content of his doctrine of the Trinity is concerned. The subject of the Trinity is taken up very briefly at the end of Barth's treatment of "The Way of the Son into the Far Country" in IV/1. There, clearly, he is no longer deriving the Trinity simply from analysis of a statement like "God reveals himself as the Lord." He is now thinking about the Trinity strictly on the basis of the narrated *history* of Jesus Christ as attested in Holy Scripture.[61]

Now as we have seen, making divine suffering to stand at the heart of his soteriology has laid upon Barth the obligation of showing how suffering brings no change to God. This he has done by suggesting that suffering is essential to God. Here now, for the first time, we are given an explanation of how suffering could be "essential" to God.

> [I]n equal Godhead the one God is, in fact, the One and also Another, ... a First and a Second, One who rules and commands in majesty and One who obeys in humility. The one God is both the one and the other. ... He is the one and the other without any cleft or differentiation but in perfect unity and equality, He is also a Third, the One who affirms the one and equal Godhead, through and by and in the two modes of being, the One who makes possible and maintains the fellowship with Himself as the one and the other. In virtue of this third mode of being He is in the other two without division or contradiction, the whole God in each.[62]

Notice that Barth is here constructing a doctrine of the Trinity (at least in outline) starting with the obedience of the Son as witnessed to in Holy Scripture. And what he is now saying is that not only humility but obedience too is essential to God.[63] Humility might, of course, be nothing more than a posture or disposition. But obedience must always consist in freely willed activity. To make obedience essential to God is

---

61. It should be noted that I am not the first to suggest that Barth worked with two models of the Trinity within the bounds of the *Church Dogmatics*, rather than just one. Rowan Williams said as much in his essay written in the late 1970s. "Barth on the Triune God," 147–93. But the significant differences between my construction of the second model and that found in Williams' essay should not be overlooked. See below, n. 69.

62. *CD* IV/1, 202–3.

63. Ibid., 193.

to lift freely willed activity—and the suffering that is its goal—into the very being of God. And this has immediate consequences for Barth's material elaboration of the doctrine of the Trinity. "We have not only not to deny but actually to affirm and understand as essential to the being of God the offensive fact that there is in God Himself an above and a below, a *prius* and a *posterius*, a superiority and a subordination. ... His divine unity consists in the fact that in Himself He is both One who is obeyed and Another who obeys."[64] Obedience, we might say, is a "personal property" of God in his second mode of being (as opposed to those "common properties" shared by all members of the Godhead). It is what makes him to be the Son.

The picture of the Trinity that results from these moves is stated in summary form at the very end of this section in IV/1. "[God] is, as the Son, as the One who *submits* in humility, the same as what the Father is, as the One who *decrees* in *majesty*. He is, as the Son, in the *outworking* (in obedience!), the same as what the Father is, in the *Origin*. He is, as the Son, as the *Self-posited* God (or, as the dogma has it, as the Son generated in eternity by the Father), the same as what the Father is, as the *Self-positing* God (as the One who generates the Son from eternity)."[65] In this passage, Barth assimilates eternal generation to the command-obedience structure of the covenant of grace. We would expect no less, given that he has said that obedience is essential to God. But that then also means that he is collapsing the divine processions into the willed activity that takes place in election. In doing so, Barth is treating the divine essence as susceptible to a willed act of self-determination. He is treating the divine essence as *plastic* in nature. "The Godhead of the true God is not a prison whose walls have first to be broken through if He is to elect and so what He has elected and done in becoming man. ... The Godhead of the true God embraces both height and depth, both sovereignty and humility, both lordship and service. It is only the pride of man, making a God in his own image, that will not hear of *a determination of the divine essence* in Jesus Christ."[66] Clearly, the willed act of self-determination, precisely as a determination of the divine essence, *makes essential. That* is the explanation for how Barth can speak of obedience as essential to God.

64. Ibid., 200–201.
65. Barth, *KD* IV/1, 228–29 (translation mine); ET: *CD* IV/1, 209.
66. Barth, *KD* IV/2, 92 (translation mine); ET: *CD* IV/2, 84.

But this then also entails an elimination of the "analogical interval"[67] that the earlier Barth had maintained between the immanent Trinity and the economic Trinity. The immanent Trinity is already, in eternity, what it will become in time. If obedience is proper to God, if it is a personal property of the triune God in his second mode of God, then there is no difference in content between the immanent and the economic Trinity. The immanent Trinity is the economic Trinity and vice versa.

We can also say that the willed receptivity of the Son of God to all that comes to him in and through his human nature is something that is true of him not only in time but also in eternity. If the incarnation is not a new event when it takes place in time, that is because the condition of its possibility is already found in an eternal act of willed receptivity vis-à-vis the humanity to be assumed. To say that the eternal Word has obedience as a personal property is to say that receptivity is proper to this particular mode of being in God.[68] The eternal Word is constituted in eternity with a view towards incarnation in time. On the level of his personal identity, at least, he is already, by way of anticipation, what he will become in time through the assumption of human nature. To put it this way is to suggest that there is no such thing as an "eternal Son" in the abstract. The "eternal Son" has a name and his name is Jesus Christ.

Taking a step back, it has to be said that the basic structure of Barth's doctrine of the Trinity remains unchanged in my reconstruction. One Subject in three modes of being—that remains Barth's view. But materially, the doctrine has changed as a consequence of the fact that Barth's derivation of the doctrine has changed. He no longer equates the divine essence with hiddenness, but with the concrete Subject who is completely given in each of his three modes of being. I call this Subject "concrete" because nothing is said about him beyond that which is made possible by his self-revelation in Jesus Christ, and everything that is said about him is authorized by the historical event. Second, Barth has added to the personal properties of the second person of the Trinity the elements of humility and obedience. And in doing that, he has also added personal properties to the first person and the third. The Father is the one who commands in majesty; the Spirit is the one who binds

---

67. See above, n. 45.

68. *CD* IV/2, 42: "In itself and as such, then, humility is not alien to the nature of the true God, but supremely proper to Him *in His mode of being as the Son*" (emphasis mine).

together Father and Son—but who binds not by being himself the bond of unity but rather by descending upon the man Jesus, by being the power by means of which the God-human obeys *humanly*.

What we have before us now is much closer, in fact, to the Cappadocian understanding, generally speaking, than was the case in *CD* I/1 (however things may turn out with respect to Basil in particular). But it is close to the Cappadocian understanding while remaining recognizably *modern*.[69] The Cappadocian element consists in the recognition that God is triune because the Father has freely willed to be so.[70]

---

69. See *CD* IV/1, 204–5. This is the appropriate place to note my reservations with respect to Rowan Williams' reading of Barth. Williams holds that Barth's second model of the Trinity consists in "a plurality of agency within the Trinity"—which would mean a departure from the single, Subject model of *CD* IV/1. In part, this conclusion rests—as Ben Myers suggests in an essay in this collection—on poor exegesis. Williams understands the way of the Son into the far country as ending, for Barth, in an experience of death that introduces a contradiction into the being of God—a situation of "God against God." But this is a possibility that Barth considers only then to reject. More significant, however, is Williams' inability to understand how Barth can propose "the existence of 'above' and 'below,' *prius* and *posterius*, command and obedience, in the life of God, while still insisting . . . that the divine hypostases are modes of being, and not centers of volition" (Williams, "Barth on the Triune God," 175). The solution offered here—that the eternal Son's obedience consists in the determination for receptivity to the lived existence of the man Jesus—simply does not occur to him. Armed with a Christology that understands receptivity as a personal property of the one divine Subject in his second mode of being, it becomes entirely possible to remain within the bounds of the single, Subject model. On this view, "command" and "obedience" in God are not to be taken as univocally related to what "command" and "obedience" mean on the plane of human to human relations, but analogically—as expressions of an eternal act of self-relating on the part of the one divine Subject which consists in a self-giving to the human covenant partner. It is quite true that Barth introduces more material differentiation into his model of the Trinity in IV/1 than was the case in I/1 (in that more is included in the list of personal properties). But to speak of a plurality of agency within the Trinity is to construct an abstract doctrine of the Trinity that has lost contact with Barth's Christology.

70. John Zizioulas has argued that it was the great contribution of the Cappadocians (and Basil in particular) to have recognized: 1) that the ontological "principle" of the being of God is found not in divine "substance" but in the person of the Father, and 2) that the Father "out of love—that is, freely—begets the Son and brings forth the Spirit." See Zizioulas, *Being as Communion*, 41. To put it this way also means for Zizioulas that God's ontological freedom extends even to his existence. If God's existence were truly necessary, then he wouldn't be absolutely free—as he must be if humans are to experience relative freedom. "The manner in which God exercises his ontological freedom, that precisely which makes him ontologically free, is the way in which he transcends and abolishes the ontological necessity of the substance by being God as *Father*, that is, as he who 'begets' the Son and 'brings forth' the Spirit. This

The modern element consists in the integration of the covenant into the eternal act in which the Father freely constitutes himself as triune.

Barth's Doctrine of Election—Also in the Light of His Later Christology

I have written a great deal on the subject of the logical relationship of election and triunity in God.[71] I do not need to repeat all of that here. I need only to fill out a thought that has already emerged, so as to show that election and triunity are equally primordial in God.

The train of thought I have developed to this point may be summarized as follows. An act of self-determination that makes humility and obedience to be essential to God is clearly a freely willed activity that is constitutive of what and who God is. But now, if the act of self-determination is an act whose consequences "become" essential to God, then we are confronted with two possibilities. *Either* the divine essence was constituted in one way before this "eternal" act and in another way after it *or* this act is ontologically primordial in the sense that there is nothing "before" it—no constitution of the divine essence that is other than or different from what the divine essence is made to be in the act itself.

The first of these options would clearly introduce *change* or mutation into the divine essence—albeit a change that took place in pre-temporal eternity. On this view divine immutability is simply surrendered, with the consequence that we cannot possibly know how God's being was structured before the act of self-determination. If we were then

---

ecstatic character of God, the fact that His being is identical with an act of communion, ensures the transcendence of the ontological necessity which His substance would have demanded—if substance were the primary ontological predicate of God—and replaces this necessity with the free self-affirmation" (ibid., 44). Paul Collins has helpfully described Zizioulas' conception here in terms of an "ontology of the particular"—i.e., an ontology that locates the being of God in a person (the Father pre-eminently) rather than in a substance in which all three members of the Godhead participate. See Collins, *Trinitarian Theology West and East*, 195–97. I should note that it cannot be my concern in this essay to question whether Zizioulas' interpretation of the Cappadocians is correct or not. Zizioulas' subsequent elevation to the office of Metropolitan does suggest, however, that the Greek Church finds his teaching to be, at the very least, an appropriate extension of Orthodox teaching.

71. For a complete list of the essays I have written pertinent to this problem, see McCormack, "Trinity and Election," 30–31, n. 11.

to say that what God was before this act is manifested in God's self-revelation in time, we would be speaking of something we could not possibly know. After all, God would have undergone *essential* change on this view. We could, in this case, know only what he is now, what he has become. And the "becoming" in question would constitute an addition to God's being, making him something either more or less than he had been—and most certainly other than he had been.

The second option, however, would secure divine immutability; for the becoming that it envisions is grounded in an act that is truly primal where God is concerned. There can be nothing antecedent to it—no higher or different mode of existence. So God's becoming in history introduces nothing new into his being. God's becoming in time corresponds to what he has always been, in his eternal becoming.

It should be clear by now that those who would like to read classical orthodoxy into Barth's theology face an impossible task. They would like to ascribe to Barth the view that the immanent Trinity—defined as what God is essentially ("in and for himself") *prior to* the act in which God turns towards the human race in the covenant of grace—remains unaffected by the works of God *ad extra*. What God was before the decision and what God is after the decision are one and the same.[72] But now, once Barth has said that the eternal act of self-determination is *a determination of the divine essence*, that road has been closed to us. Once a determination of the divine essence has been introduced, the options are—as I have said—only two: either essential change in pre-temporal eternity or an ontologically primordial decision that eliminates the possibility of change. The attempt to move from Barth back to classical orthodoxy is no longer a live option.[73]

The logical relationship of election and triunity has already been thematized. For the act in which God determines himself essentially is *election*. If then this act is primordial, then election is primordial. There is no triunity in God apart from election, for the two occur in one and the same event. We might best put it this way: the command of the Father in the covenant of grace generates the Son as a second mode

72. For a fine illustration of this perspective, see Hunsinger, "Election and the Trinity," 179–98.

73. Paul Collins is right to say that "Athanasius' understanding of a community of will which permeates the trinitarian Godhead is considerably different from Barth's understanding of the divine decision which constitutes the Godhead" (Collins, *Trinitarian Theology West and East*, 87).

of being in which the one divine Subject could obey. And the event in which this takes place is also the event in which the Spirit proceeds from both Father and Son as the power by means of which the one God does all things—both *ad intra* and *ad extra*. Thus, election and triunity are given together in one and the same eternal event.[74] Neither has ontological priority over the other. But election has a logical priority over Trinity—because decision has a logical priority over being.

Conclusion: But Is It "Orthodox"?

The Niceno-Constantinopolitan Creed of 381 is the standard by which the ecumenical church ought rightly to judge the orthodoxy of a given piece of trinitarian theology, however new it may be. But the truth is that the Creed is quite minimalist in its claims. It makes a direct equation between the "Lord Jesus Christ" and "the only-begotten Son of God"—which I have done here in my reconstruction of Barth's doctrine. And it says of Jesus Christ, the only-begotten Son, that he was "begotten from His Father before all ages" and that, as a consequence, he is rightly understood to be "Light from Light, true God from true God." Surely these "derivatives" are all consonant with what I have suggested in this essay. Some will probably wonder whether I am able to do justice to the phrase "begotten, not made." They will say that a willed constitution is a "making," not a "begetting." But precisely here, it is important to remember what the church rejected under the label of Arianism.

There are at least three reasons that what I have presented here is not Arian. First, I have no interest in safeguarding the impassibility of what

---

74. On this point, see Williams, "Barth on the Triune God," 178: "the man Jesus *has* already a part in God's eternal being. . . . From all eternity, God's self-differentiation as Son or Word is directed towards the human and worldly object of election, Jesus of Nazareth." And compare with this especially, Collins, *Trinitarian Theology West and East*, 32–33: "The being of God as the event of Father, Son, and Holy Spirit is the result of God's free, conscious, willed, and executed decision. Thus the nature of the divine essence as event and as Trinity arises from the divine decision and act." Or again: "The divine intentionality in the election of Jesus is . . . understood as constitutive of the Godhead both *ad extra* and *ad intra*. Thus the constitution of the Godhead rests eternally upon the Father's intentional act of choosing the Son. . . . The divine intentional agency lies at the very heart of God's relationship with that which is other than himself, and also is that which is constitutive of the divine being, and thus of the divine relationality" (ibid., 84–85). Collins concludes that "the content of the divine will" is "the decision to be the Trinity: Father, Son, and Holy Spirit."

Arius called the "high God." In fact, I do not believe impassibility to be a biblical category for speaking of God at all. Arius, like Nestorius in the next century, had the grip of a Rottweiler on this notion and would not be dissuaded from it, even if that meant a reduction of the ontological status of the Logos to that of an intermediary being between God and the human or, worse, a creature. But I say that all that the Father is, he gives to the Son. If the Son, in obedience to the command of the Father, does not make *direct* use of that which is given to him by the Father—if, instead, he wills to act through the Holy Spirit rather than through his assumed human nature—that constitutes no deprivation, no surrender of the properties common to all members of the Godhead. Second, I do not believe that there was a "time" when the Son was not. The event of the divine self-constitution in the covenant of grace is, for me, the event that *founds* time but it does not take place in time. And there is no "before" and "after" this event. If the event is truly primordial—even for and in God—then there can be nothing before it. Before and after are contained in that event, but only in it—which is why Barth speaks of a *prius* and a *posterius* in the relation of the Father and the Son. But this is not a temporalized *prius* and *posterius*. Third and most importantly, I do not make the Son to be a different Subject than the Father. Such personal properties as I have judged to be rightly ascribed to God in this mode of being do not set aside the basic structure—one Subject in three modes of being.

What then of the term *homoousios*—"of one substance with the Father"? There is no question but that the word "Subject" does for me all the heavy-lifting that is done in the Creed by the word "substance." But if the intention lying behind the creedal word *homoousios* is to insist that God is God in all three of his modes of being, then I have honored that intention in the nomenclature I have adopted. If I am at fault here, then so is Karl Barth.

Finally, the version of the Trinity that I have set forth in my reconstruction is compatible with the Nicene Creed because the Creed does not take up the issue of what constitutes a divine "person." What the "persons" are and how "persons" are related to divine "personality" (self-consciousness, etc.) is left to others to decide. No firm decision has been made in this regard.

For all of these reasons, I would submit that the doctrine I have set forth in this essay stands within the boundaries of what the ecumenical church has judged to be "orthodox."

Bibliography

Ayres, Lewis. *Nicaea and Its Legacy: An Approach to Fourth-Century Trinitarian Theology.* Oxford: Oxford University Press, 2004.
Balthasar, Hans Urs von. *Theo-Drama: Theological Dramatic Theory.* Vol. 3, *Dramatis Personae: Persons in Christ.* Translated by Graham Harrison. San Francisco: Ignatius, 1992.
Barth, Karl. *Church Dogmatics.* 4 vols. Edinburgh: T. & T. Clark, 1956–75.
———. "The Paradoxical Nature of the 'Positive Paradox': Answers and Questions to Paul Tillich." In *The Beginnings of Dialectic Theology,* edited by James M. Robinson, 287–96. Richmond, VA: John Knox, 1968.
———. "*Unterricht in der christlichen Religion.*" *Erster Band: Prolegomena, 1924.* Edited by Hannelotte Reiffen. Zürich: TVZ, 1985.
———. "*Unterricht in der christlichen Religion.*" *Dritter Band: Die Lehre von der Versöhnung / Die Lehre von der Erlösung.* Edited by Hinrich Stoevesandt. Zürich: TVZ, 2003.
Chemnitz, Martin. *The Two Natures in Christ.* Translated by J. A. O. Preus. St. Louis: Concordia, 1971.
Collins, Paul M. *Trinitarian Theology West and East: Karl Barth, the Cappadocians, and John Zizioulas.* Oxford: Oxford University Press, 2001.
Goebel, Hans Theodor. "Trinitätslehre und Erwählungslehre: Eine Problemanzeige." In *Wahrheit und Versöhnung: Theologische und philosophische Beiträge zur Gotteslehre,* edited by Dietrich Korsch and Hartmut Ruddies. Gütersloh: Gerd Mohn, 1989.
Gregory of Nyssa. "An Answer to Ablabius: That We Should Not Think of Saying There are Three Gods." In *Christology of the Later Fathers,* edited by Edward R. Hardy, 256–67. Philadelphia: Westminster, 1954.
Gundlach, Thiess. *Selbstbegrenzung Gottes und die Autonomie des Menschen.* Frankfurt: Lang, 1992.
Hart, David B. *The Beauty of the Infinite: The Aesthetics of Christian Truth.* Grand Rapids: Eerdmans, 2003.
Hunsinger, George. "Election and the Trinity: Twenty-Five Theses on the Theology of Karl Barth." *Modern Theology* 24 (2008) 179–98.
Jenson, Robert. *The Triune Identity: God According to the Gospel.* Philadelphia: Fortress, 1982.
Kelly, John N. D. *Early Christian Doctrines.* Rev. ed. San Francisco: Harper & Row, 1978.
McCormack, Bruce L. "Trinity and Election: A Progress Report." In *Ontmoetingen— Tijdgenoten en getuigen: Festschrift for Gerrit Neven,* edited by Rinse Reeling et al., 30–31. Kampen: Kok, 2009.
Moltmann, Jürgen. *The Trinity and the Kingdom.* Translated by Margaret Kohl. San Francisco: Harper & Row, 1981.

Neuser, Wilhelm. "Karl Barth in Münster, 1925–1930." *Theologische Studien* 130. Zürich: TVZ, 1985.

Pannenberg, Wolfhart. *Systematic Theology*. Vol. 1. Grand Rapids: Eerdmans, 1991.

Torrance, Thomas F. *Trinitarian Perspectives: Toward Doctrinal Agreement*. Edinburgh: T. & T. Clark, 1994.

Williams, Rowan D. "Barth on the Triune God." In *Karl Barth—Studies of His Theological Methods*, edited by S. W. Sykes, 147–93. Oxford: Clarendon, 1979.

Zizioulas, John D. *Being as Communion: Studies in Personhood and the Church*. Crestwood, NY: St. Vladimir's Seminary Press, 1993.

PART TWO

Theology after Barth

5

Election, Trinity, and the History of Jesus
Reading Barth with Rowan Williams

Benjamin Myers

MY AIM IN THIS ESSAY IS TO ADVANCE THE THESIS THAT BARTH'S *Church Dogmatics* includes not one doctrine of the Trinity, but two. In recent years, Bruce McCormack[1] has drawn our attention to the significant distance between Barth's early rendering of the Trinity in terms of the formal structure of revelation in *CD* I/1, and the more actualistic, christologically determined account of the Trinity in *CD* IV/1.[2] McCormack's argument has troubled the placid waters of contemporary Barth studies. His critique of the first volume of Barth's *Dogmatics* in light of the fourth has been condemned by readers like Paul Molnar and George Hunsinger as an intolerable innovation—as an attempt to introduce inconsistencies and ruptures into a text that ought rather to be read as a single, internally coherent whole.

Yet McCormack was not the first to observe a gap between earlier and later conceptions of the Trinity in the *Church Dogmatics*. In fact, some of his core arguments were anticipated as long ago as 1979, in Rowan Williams' remarkable essay on "Barth on the Triune God."[3] Williams advances a stinging critique of Barth's doctrine of the Trinity in I/1, and he argues that this early account is incommensurable with the increasingly christological and historical conception of God's triunity in volume IV. His claim, in a nutshell, is that Barth's early doctrine

---

1. McCormack, *Orthodox and Modern*.
2. All references are to Barth, *Church Dogmatics*. Hereafter *CD*.
3. Williams, "Barth on the Triune God," 106–49.

of the Trinity would have to be subjected to radical revision in light of his later thinking about Jesus and the Trinity.

In the discussion that follows, I want to revisit Williams' arguments and conclusions, noting the striking ways in which his reading converges with McCormack's recent work, before turning to consider the promise of Barth's "second" doctrine of the Trinity for contemporary theology. I will suggest that the trinitarianism of IV/1 allows us to navigate past some of the most problematic developments within recent trinitarian theology: on the one hand, a line of thinking represented by Jürgen Moltmann, where the economy of salvation is understood as a rupture within the being of God; and on the other, a more traditional interpretation represented by Paul Molnar, where the economy is seen merely as one possibility of that freedom which lies behind history in the eternal depths of the immanent Trinity.

Rowan Williams on Barth

In his influential 1995 work, Bruce McCormack showed that Barth is not always a reliable interpreter of his own theology;[4] and the same thesis underpins some of the most important recent German-language work on Barth.[5] Rowan Williams had made the same observation as early as 1979: "No understanding of Barth ... can begin to be adequate if it simply relies upon his own description, however sincere, of his method and intention."[6] Especially in his later years, Barth interpreted his own dogmatics as a work characterized by linear development and internal coherence; he resisted the tendency to identify discontinuities between the earlier and later sections of the *CD*. "In the twenty-three years since I started this work I have found myself so held and directed that, as far as I can see, there have so far been no important breaks or contradictions in the presentation."[7] In contrast, Williams posits a sharp disjunction between the theology of the Word in I/1 and Barth's later christological thought in volume IV.

In Williams' view, the whole frame of reference in I/1 is structured by formalistic epistemological categories. Citing Gustaf Wingren's pro-

---

4. McCormack, *Karl Barth's Critically Realistic Dialectical Theology*.
5. Most notably Pfleiderer, *Karl Barths praktische Theologie*.
6. Williams, "Barth on the Triune God," 115.
7. *CD* IV/2, x.

vocative (if admittedly flawed) critique,⁸ Williams suggests that the Barth of I/1 deploys "a model of two 'beings,'" God and humanity, separated by "an epistemological gulf." If the human predicament is understood thus in epistemological terms, then it follows that God's action is conceived as revelation, the transmission of a message across the gulf: "the human predicament is ignorance."⁹ Here, then, the triune God is envisioned as a single self-communicating subject, as the one who speaks of God. As Barth famously put it, the doctrine of the Trinity is an analytics of the statement: "God reveals himself as the Lord" (I/1, §8).

In contrast to this epistemological doctrine of the Trinity, Williams argues that the logic of IV/1 presses towards "a very much more 'pluralist' conception of the Trinity than is allowed for in I/1."¹⁰ Barth's own attempt to harmonize these two trinitarian models, he suggests, "produces one of the most unhelpful bits of hermetic mystification in the whole of the *Dogmatics*."¹¹ Barth wants to give the impression that his earlier account of the three *Seinsweisen* in a single Subject still coheres with his account of the Son of God "in a far country" (IV/1, 202–5); but his strained argument itself testifies to the difficulty of bringing these very different trinitarian schemata into line with one another. Williams thus argues that the more seriously we take the logic of IV/1, the more we will have to admit that "the kinds of assumption about the freedom and lordship of God with which Barth is working in I/1 will need radical revision."¹² The trinitarianism of IV/1 points to a differentiation of divine subjectivity, and to God's being as a differentiated redemptive movement into human history. This, Williams argues, is a more "pluralist" doctrine of the Trinity, centered not on epistemology but on soteriology and on the history of Jesus. In appealing to plurality within the Trinity, however, Williams is not invoking any comfy notion of a social Trinity. Admittedly, he shares the concern of a critic like Moltmann that "power, lordship, the master-slave relationship, all play an uncomfortably large part in Barth's system"¹³ (though one should note that Williams' essay predates Moltmann's similar critique of Barth

---

8. Wingren, *Theology in Conflict*.
9. Williams, "Barth on the Triune God," 127.
10. Ibid., 129.
11. Ibid.
12. Ibid., 130.
13. Ibid., 140.

in *Trinity and the Kingdom*[14]—both writers are best understood as developing the critique of Barthian subjectivity found in the work of Trutz Rendtorff and the "Munich school").[15] Unlike Moltmann, Williams remains skeptical about the notion of a social Trinity, but he nevertheless agrees that the idea of an individual divine subject is inadequate: "No doubt the so-called 'social' analogy for the life of the Trinity has its grave deficiencies, but at least it insists that the divine life into which the believer is baptized is a relational pattern . . . where the dominant model is not address and obedience (significant though that remains) but mutual sharing."[16] Williams finds in IV/1 a move towards such a trinitarian model—not one of mono-subjectivity and revelation, but of life, reciprocity, and mutual sharing.

In particular, Williams argues that the epistemological formalism of I/1 is displaced by the attention in IV/1 to the place of Jesus' human history within the being of God. "As soon as the *history* of Jesus . . . is allowed a place of genuine salvific import, the unity, clarity, and security of a scheme based upon . . . revelation is put in question."[17] In IV/1, Barth depicts not a single subject communicating itself across an epistemological gulf, but a self-differentiating movement of God's life into history. Again, Williams' argument is not here pointing towards social trinitarianism; his claim is neither that God is a single subject nor that God is three subjects, but that God's being subsists instead as a kenotic movement that brings forth the unity-in-differentiation of *love*.[18] For Williams, the logic of IV/1 is that of a kenotic plurality in which the cross of Christ opens up a distance between God and God, the distance between Father and Son which God traverses in the Spirit. The kenotic obedience of the human Jesus is the movement of God's eternal self-determination, God's self-elected and triune way of being God.

The resulting picture of plurality in God, Williams argues, not only relativizes the importance of revelation in the doctrine of the Trinity; it also demands "a rethinking of the *kind* of revelation . . . and so of the kind

---

14. Moltmann, *The Trinity and the Kingdom*.

15. On the Munich school's complex relation to Barth, see Stefan Holtmann's masterful analysis, *Karl Barth als Theologe der Neuzeit*.

16. Williams, "Barth on the Triune God," 140–41.

17. Ibid., 129.

18. Rowan Williams, "Balthasar and Difference," 81.

of subjectivity from which revelation emerges."[19] It now becomes necessary to think of revelation in more actualistic and apocalyptic terms, so that the concept of revelation takes on a biblical and historical texture, instead of remaining harnessed to the familiar nineteenth-century category of divine subjectivity.[20] Revelation is not a mere making-known of what was already the case, not merely an impartation of God's own knowledge of God. On the contrary, in the New Testament *apokalypsis* denotes the sheer world-altering event of salvation, the incursion of God's life into the world. As Williams observes, Barth's earlier doctrine of the Trinity was driven by an implicit anthropological presupposition: that human beings lack *knowledge* of God. This presupposition "dictates a reading of Scripture almost entirely in terms of 'communication' from God to man"; whereas Scripture itself "points far more consistently to the struggle between God and evil, to a dramatic picture of God engaging in the tragic situation of man."[21] Such a dramatic picture, Williams notes, centers not on *das Wunder der Weihnacht*, "the Christmas miracle, which Barth so much emphasises in . . . I/2," but rather on "the defeat and victory of Good Friday and Easter Sunday."[22] Struggle, engagement, defeat, conquest: this is the language of apocalyptic, of God's personal dramatic involvement in human history for our sake.[23]

At the time of writing his essay on Barth, Williams had been immersed in the great project of translating the volumes of Hans Urs von Balthasar's *Herrlichkeit*, and it is to Balthasar that he now turns to elucidate the significance of IV/1. Balthasar's work on kenosis, he suggests, represents a profound explication of the logic of Barth's trinitarianism. The kenotic movement of God into our history in the events of Good Friday and Holy Saturday: this is not merely some *opus ad extra*, some "arbitrary expression" of God's being; "this is what the life of the Trinity is, translated into the world."[24] Such a kenotic picture takes us a long way

---

19. Williams, "Barth on the Triune God," 130.

20. On the importance of this Hegelian category for Barth's doctrine of the Trinity in I/1, and for a related critique, see Menke-Peitzmeyer, *Subjektivität und Selbstinterpretation des dreifaltigen Gottes*.

21. Williams, "Barth on the Triune God," 128.

22. Ibid.

23. For an interpretation of *apokalypsis* that supports Williams' argument here, see J. Louis Martyn's important commentary, *Galatians*.

24. Williams, "Barth on the Triune God," 130.

from the priority of epistemological questions, or from a preoccupation with revelation and divine subjectivity. Although Barth himself did not go quite as far as Balthasar, Williams nevertheless suggests: "Perhaps it requires a theology like von Balthasar's to show us just how far from the schema of I/1 we are led by the implications of IV/1. The trinitarian scheme which can be developed out of the doctrine of the Son of God in a far country is one which must allow not only for a plurality of agency within the Trinity but also for *the inclusion of the history of man in the being of God.*"[25] Here, then, is the real promise of Barth's later doctrine of the Trinity: it opens the way to a radical rethinking of the relation between God and history, since in this account the human history of Jesus assumes constitutive significance for God's very triune identity.

Contemporary readers can hardly help noticing points of convergence between Williams' analysis and Bruce McCormack's challenging and controversial interpretation of Barth's doctrine of God. Indeed, it is significant that Williams finds in Balthasar's kenotic theology a fulfillment of the promise of IV/1; while McCormack, in his recent T. F. Torrance Lectures, pursues the implications of his own revisionist reading of Barth through the constructive development of a new kenotic Christology.[26] Williams, Balthasar, McCormack: three thinkers who operate in very different registers and are driven by very different questions; yet they share some similar intuitions about what Barth was aiming at in the christological and trinitarian thought that he develops in IV/1. In contemporary Barth studies, critics like Hunsinger and Molnar have objected that the specter of Hegel looms too large behind McCormack's reading of Barth: the divine freedom is jeopardized if human history is thought to be included within the being of God. The criticism is not hard to anticipate; and Rowan Williams' 1979 essay already raises this line of criticism. Does not the trinitarian schema of IV/1 suggest a dangerous "Hegelian blurring of boundaries," he asks, between God and the world?[27] Like McCormack, however, Williams notes that Barth himself was already fully alert to this danger: and it was his doctrine of election

---

25. Ibid., 131; emphasis added.

26. The lectures, presented in December 2007, were entitled "The Humility of the Eternal Son: A Reformed Version of Kenotic Christology." For a preliminary sketch of McCormack's approach, see his article, "Karl Barth's Christology as a Resource for a Reformed Version of Kenoticism."

27. Williams, "Barth on the Triune God," 131.

that enabled Barth to resist Hegel so emphatically, yet without drawing back from a historicization of the doctrine of God. It is election that lets us understand God's self-determination as an act of grace and therefore of true freedom. In Williams' words: "[God] elects, before all ages, to be the God of grace."[28]

Thus Barth does not shrink from the difficult thought that the elected human Jesus is in the beginning with God. From all eternity, God relates to God—God is differentiated as the Father of the Son—through the election of this "human and worldly object," Jesus of Nazareth.[29] And so in IV/2, Barth can understand the death of a particular human being at a particular historical moment as an event that also happens eternally in God. God's being is identical with God's act; so if God acts in the death of a human being, "that death is involved in what [God] *is.*"[30] All this is possible through the freedom of God's gracious election of Jesus: it is the doctrine of election that preserves Barth's understanding of God from any Hegelian blurring of boundaries. Having anticipated and dismissed this criticism, Williams nevertheless presses home the full force of the relation between election and the being of God in Barth's thought. God's eternal will is expressed in the election of Jesus; but this is no accidental act, so that things might perhaps have been otherwise. "He is eternally—how might it be said?—'liable' to elect, 'tending' or 'intending' to elect, and so, in some sense, eternally exposed to the suffering of his creature Jesus, to the 'negation' involved in his own judgement upon the fallen creation. Eternally and in himself he meets and contains and overcomes the possibility of negation."[31] Here too, Williams' reading brings us remarkably close to McCormack's; like McCormack, Williams points to the doctrine of election as the engine that drives Barth's revised understanding of the Trinity. Barth's doctrine of the election of Jesus makes it necessary, eventually, for his doctrine of God to be subjected to drastic revision.

Whereas in I/1 Barth understood the event of revelation as the moment in which a single subject bridges the divine-human chasm in an act of self-utterance, Williams argues—freely deploying some Hegelian terminology—that in IV/1 God's self-communication includes "the ut-

28. Ibid.
29. Ibid.
30. Ibid., 132.
31. Ibid., 132–33.

terance of a contradiction." Here, revelation is not so much the divine–human communication as that event of dialogue between Father and Son which is enacted on the cross. The believer is now not merely asked to hear the Word of revelation, but to be caught up into the very life of revelation, to participate in the system of relations that the cross brings forth.[32] God's eternal being, then, is enacted on Calvary, "but it is also the act whereby *we* are brought into Calvary, Hell, and newness of life" through the inexhaustible resource of the Spirit.[33] On the cross, the Son exists "at the extreme point of distance from the Father." This means, Williams says, that in God's own eternal life there is a "capacity for this 'distance' or 'displacement,'" a capacity for "union with another even across the greatest gulf of contradiction and opposition."[34] There is mutual responsiveness and reciprocity within God's life, not merely an outward-moving act of subjective self-manifestation. In short, God is not "*a* self."[35] For Williams—again implicitly following the critique of Munich school[36]—the aporia of I/1 emerges from its portrayal of God as something akin to an autonomous human subject, "a single self analogous to human selves."[37] And it seems to me that it is this model of autonomous subjectivity which has made so deep an impression on a contemporary reader of Barth like Paul Molnar—a point to which I will return soon.

Rowan Williams' essay is a lengthy, complex, and often untidy cluster of reflections on Barth's trinitarianism, and I have explored here only one strand of its argument, underscoring the distance Williams perceives between the subject-trinitarianism of I/1 and the more historically and christologically shaped trintiarianism of IV/1 as it emerges under the impact of Barth's doctrine of election. For Williams, Barth's real trinitarian legacy is to be found in this "second" doctrine of the Trinity. Taking Williams' reading as a point of departure, I now want to focus more directly on the contemporary theological implications of this second doctrine of the Trinity.

32. Ibid., 133.
33. Ibid., 135.
34. Ibid., 134.
35. Ibid.
36. See especially Rendtorff, "Radikale Autonomie Gottes, 161–81.
37. Williams, "Barth on the Triune God," 134.

The Wounded God

Whereas Barth's doctrine in *CD* I/1 gives an account of the formal dynamics of revelation, the trinitarian theology of IV/1 functions as a critique of the very idea of God. Barth is here embarked on a revision of the whole idea of "divine being"; he is rethinking, in the light of Jesus Christ, what it means for God to be God.

This critical dimension had already emerged sharply in the doctrine of election, where Barth had protested that "there is no deity as such," but only "the deity of the Father, the Son, and the Holy Spirit."[38] Similarly, here in IV/1 Barth insists that "no general idea of 'deity,'" nor any general divine attribute such as freedom or lordship, can be applied to Jesus Christ: "he defines those concepts: they do not define him."[39] The lowliness and humility of Christ belong to the very definition of God; God's deity "is not the deity of a divine being furnished with all kinds of supreme attributes."[40] God's way of being God, the so-called "divine nature," comes to light only in the human history of Jesus. In his humble obedience and death on the cross, Jesus discloses "the mystery of the inner being of God as the being of the Son in relation to the Father."[41]

Jesus thus belongs to the very identity of God. As Barth puts it in his reading of the prologue of the Fourth Gospel, this human being, Jesus of Nazareth, is in the beginning with God.[42] God's "godness" is an event that takes place in the relation between this man and the one whom he calls Father; there is no general divine nature lurking behind the particularities of this history. The "essence of the divine," Barth writes, is something that takes place in Jesus' history.[43] We can think of a divine nature only as our thinking is oriented around the history of this human, the one who is obedient unto death: "It is from this point, and this point alone, that the concept [of the 'divine nature'] is legitimately possible."[44] Barth thus insists that such a thinking of the death of Jesus

---

38. *CD* II/2, 115.
39. *CD* IV/1, 129.
40. Ibid., 177.
41. Ibid.
42. *CD* II/2, 95–99.
43. *CD* IV/1, 186.
44. Ibid., 199.

eliminates the false and idolatrous concept of any "neutral deity," the "pure and empty deity . . . of an abstract 'monotheism.'"[45] As Williams rightly observes, Barth's argument here is driven not by formal categories of revelation or divine lordship (as in I/1), but by the highly specific texture, the historically determinate shape, of Jesus' life. God's identity is bound up with the way of this human, Jesus of Nazareth; God is thinkable only in the thinking of this human history.

I should hasten to add that Barth is not merely advancing an epistemological claim about Jesus. He is not merely suggesting that God would remain remote and unknowable if God had not been accommodated to us in Christ; at this point, Barth is worlds away from Calvin's notion of divine accommodation. Instead, his point is precisely an ontological one: God *has no being* apart from what happens in the human Jesus. The idea of a "divine being" existing outside relation to Jesus is, Barth thinks, the very essence of idolatry. God's being as God is constituted by God's self-determined relation to the human Jesus. Simply put, this means that what happens in Jesus really *matters* for God. Williams underscores this point by speaking of God's risk in Jesus: "God, for our sakes, 'risks' his very identity" in the act of reconciliation.[46] Although this has a not-very-Barthian ring to it, I think it captures vividly the direction in which Barth's thought is moving here. God's being itself is at stake in what happens to Jesus. God has so chosen to identify with Jesus that there is no longer any divine being apart from relation to this human being. Jesus is not merely epistemologically significant, as the one who makes God known; he is ontologically significant, as the one who (so to speak) makes God God.

God's deity, then, is not some entity which calmly precedes (in order to be disclosed in) the history of Jesus. God's deity, rather, consists in God's determination to be the God whose own internal life takes on the form of humiliation, lowliness, and crucifixion. God elects the cross of Jesus as the site of God's own being. The crucified Jesus is the content of God's decision about who God will be from all eternity.

Jürgen Moltmann's 1972 book, *The Crucified God*—a work much more profoundly indebted to IV/1 than the author likes to acknowledge—developed the idea of a breach within the being of God, an in-

---

45. Ibid., 203.
46. Williams, "Barth on the Triune God," 130.

ternal contradiction between God and God.[47] Barth himself anticipates exactly this development—but only in order to resist it. For Barth, the distance that the cross opens up between Father and Son is not an irruption in the prior harmony of the divine being; instead, this distance between Father and Son is precisely God's way of being God. God's being is *eternally* marked by this distance, by the wound of the cross. Barth shares with Moltmann a commitment to the idea that what happens in Jesus really matters for God; but unlike Moltmann, Barth's thought here is framed by a doctrine of election—and that makes all the difference. The doctrine of election makes it clear that the history of Jesus does not introduce a breach in God's deity. The history of Jesus, rather, *is* God's way of being God. Jesus' lowly way into the far country is the path on which God has eternally set God's own being. God is determined to be this kind of God, a God whose being is wholly consistent with what takes place in the history of Jesus. To put it anachronistically, election is Barth's alternative to a Moltmannian theology of the cross. The doctrine of election simply means that God is always *this* God.

Even Moltmann's radical attempt to organize theology around the cry of dereliction is anticipated in IV/1, where Barth writes: "The meaning of the incarnation is plainly revealed in the question of Jesus on the cross: 'My God, my god, why have you forsaken me?'" But, with an eye on Heinrich Vogel's Christology,[48] Barth immediately adds the caution: "the more seriously we take this, the stronger becomes the temptation to approximate to the view of a contradiction and conflict in God."[49] For Barth, the cry of dereliction expresses not a new or alien breach between God and God—as it did for Vogel, and later for Moltmann—but an eternal happening within the being of God, which God has set in motion in the election of Jesus. The cry of dereliction expresses a real distance, a real wound within God; but this is no contradiction of God's deity, since God is eternally the one who chooses this man's crucifixion as the one and only way-of-being-God. This means, I think, that Barth's conception here is more metaphysically radical than anything Moltmann achieved in *The Crucified God*: in spite of all the excellent things Moltmann says about the cross, he still takes it for granted (and

47. Moltmann, *Crucified God*.

48. Vogel, *Christologie*, vol. 1. I thank Bruce McCormack for drawing this reference to my attention.

49. *CD* IV/1, 185.

his entire proposal rests on this assumption) that there is some general "divine being" that precedes and stands behind God's relation to Jesus. Barth, on the other hand, refuses to think any such divine being, any anterior moment at which God's deity was unrelated to what occurs in Jesus' history. God can be God in no other way than the way that God has chosen: the way of the man Jesus. God is thus self-consistent when God allows the cross to open up a breach within the divine being. The Son cries out to the Father across a vast distance, a distance traversed by the Spirit. This is the very shape of God's eternal being: this is what it means for God to subsist as Father, Son, and Spirit.

For Barth, then, God's triunity is always already a cruciform triunity. God elects the death of Jesus as the shape of God's own life. God "is not untrue to himself but true to himself in this condescension."[50] The crucified Christ is the perfect—the beautiful and terrible—realization of what it means for God to be God. The wound of the cross is a real wound; but this wound is already at the heart of that eternal communion, that love which is always in motion between the Father and the Son in the Holy Spirit.

Logos Asarkos?

It will be clear that my reading of Barth here is antagonistic to the notion of a *logos asarkos*, any moment at which God's identity was not already bound up with the human history of Jesus. This reading does not, of course, mitigate the confession of the Son's pre-existence. Barth speaks freely of the Son's eternity and pre-existence. But eternity here is not some anterior divine state that precedes the election of the human Jesus. The Son of God pre-exists precisely as a human being; the human history of Jesus of Nazareth is already the form of God's eternal being: "For Jesus Christ—not an empty *Logos*, but Jesus Christ the incarnate Word, the baby born in Bethlehem, the man put to death at Golgotha and raised again in the garden of Joseph of Arimathea, the man whose history this is—is the unity [of God and humanity]. . . . That he is both . . . is something which belongs to himself as the eternal Son of God for himself and prior to us. In this he is the pre-existent *Deus pro nobis*."[51]

50. Ibid.
51. Ibid., 53.

The Son is pre-existent not as an "empty *Logos*," but as God's *human* Word in Jesus of Nazareth. The second person of the Trinity is a human being—or rather, the divine-human history enacted in Jesus. A *logos asarkos*, or indeed any general "second person of the Trinity," cannot be the *Deus pro nobis* of the gospel. The notion of a Logos-as-such is akin to the idea of a "divine nature": in both cases, we are trying to go back and find in God some reality deeper than the human Jesus. In both cases, therefore, we are involved in idolatry. The *logos asarkos*, for Barth, represents a dark "*Deus absconditus*", which is to say "some image of God which we have made for ourselves."[52] The name of Jesus belongs to God's eternal being, God's way of being God; a God-without-Jesus can only be an idol.

The point of Barth's doctrine of election is that God is eternally predisposed towards the history of Jesus. God's being is a being-towards Jesus of Nazareth. Thus from all eternity, there is really no "second person of the Trinity," but only the divine-human history of Jesus of Nazareth. And this means—here it is really impossible to take IV/1 seriously without adopting something like McCormack's interpretation[53]—that the very trinitarian relations that constitute God's life are already determined by what happens in the human history of Jesus. It is not, therefore, an eternal Logos who is in the beginning with God: it is Jesus of Nazareth. As Barth puts it, "in the history of Jesus we have to do with the reality which underlies and precedes all other reality."[54] God's deity is constituted—through God's own eternal decision—by the way God relates to this particular human history.

Thus Barth can even hint at a kind of self-limitation in God. Not in Moltmann's Kabbalistic and quasi-Pelagian sense (where God and creation are imagined to be jostling for space), but in the sense of God's freedom to restrict God's own possibilities to one particular course of action. The history of Jesus functions as a kind of inner "necessity" for God, in as much as God is freely yet wholly self-determined towards this history. Certainly the Barth of IV/1 knows nothing of Paul Molnar's picture of a sublime divine freedom that stands behind history, with differing possibilities balanced evenly on the scales.[55] In Barth's view, God

52. Ibid., 52
53. McCormack, "Grace and Being," 183–200.
54. *CD* IV/1, 53.
55. Molnar, *Divine Freedom*.

is a God not of *choice*, but of *decision*. God "does not make just any use of the possibilities of his divine nature, but he makes one definite use which is necessary on the basis and in fulfilment of his own decision."[56] God's freedom is not the formal attribute by which the divine nature selects from a variety of options (as though the human history of Jesus were one product alongside others on the supermarket shelf); God's freedom is God's capacity to be God in *this* way, to choose "one definite" way of being God. Freedom is indeed a kind of necessity—but it is simply the necessity of God's own loving self-consistency. God is necessarily faithful to God's own decision about what the divine identity will be like. God is faithful to the election of Jesus. God's will is, we might say, bent eternally on one particular possibility, the history of Jesus. And this means that Jesus is not one possibility among others; he is *the* possibility, the free necessity of God's deity.

To put it more concisely, one might describe Jesus' history as the very shape of what is possible for God. God's freedom is not, as Molnar imagines, a mysterious abyss standing behind this event; rather it is fully realized in the event itself. This history is the form which God's freedom takes. And God's freedom *always already* takes this form, since Jesus is the content of God's eternal decision about who God will be.

In all this, one can see again and again that what is really at stake in IV/1 is the very idea of "God", the very notion of a "divine nature". It's on this basis especially that I think Molnar's understanding of divine freedom ought to be resisted. Molnar is, in his own way, a very faithful disciple of Barth—but it is the Barth of I/1, or perhaps the Barth of I/1 as interpreted by T. F. Torrance, who shapes all Molnar's thinking about divine freedom and the immanent Trinity. Although Molnar's own basic categories are seldom analyzed explicitly, his thinking is structured by a tight sequence of paired opposites: the priority of eternity over history, of the objective over the subjective, of reality over experience, of God *in se* over God-for-us. But the problem with interpreting divine freedom through the lens of these metaphysical categories becomes clear when one considers how slight a place the human history of Jesus assumes in Molnar's thought. Everywhere, the human Jesus stands in the shadow of an antecedent *logos asarkos*; everywhere God's decision is overshadowed by the ominous possibility that God might have chosen otherwise. Against Molnar's best intentions, the real history of Jesus is eclipsed by

---

56. *CD* IV/1, 194.

the sublime divine essence, which stands ineffably behind time and history. Behind the divine decision stands some nameless divine essence—a sentiment vividly captured in Molnar's reply to McCormack: "But if God's election has always taken place, how then can it be construed as a decision?"[57] Here, the Logos-as-such remains the real focal point, the one unshakable presupposition; the history of Jesus is reduced to one possibility alongside others, to be arbitrated by the indeterminate freedom of an unknowable divine essence (unknowable since it goes back behind the history of Jesus, so that we are barred all access to it).

Barth's whole argument in IV/1 amounts to the thesis that there is no such divine essence. A "divine nature"—even if it is described with all the precision of Nicene vocabulary; even if it is the second person of the Trinity—can never be anything except an idol It is Jesus of Nazareth who frees us from the lifeless grip of this idol. God has only one way of being God, and that is the way of God's own decision: the way of the Son into the far country.

Conclusion

In contemporary considerations of the relation between the human Jesus and the eternal being of God, we are, I think, faced with three main alternatives: a mutable divine being who undergoes change as a result of what happens in Jesus (Moltmann); an indeterminate and unknowable divine being who lies behind the election of Jesus (Molnar); or a divine being who is both knowable and immutable, since it is always already determined towards the history of Jesus (McCormack). Taking Rowan Williams' reading of Barth as my point of departure, I have argued that Barth's "second" doctrine of the Trinity points to this third option, a God whose being is eternally shaped by what happens in Jesus' history, and by a self-determined movement towards that history. Williams' reading of Barth might serve as a critical resource for a contemporary trinitarian theology that resists both the internally divided Trinity of Moltmann on the left, and the sublimely free immanent Trinity of Molnar on the right.

Admittedly, I have perhaps been too severe in my criticism of Molnar. For one thing, he is surely right to insist on God's eternal self-consistency: God does not contradict God's being when God enters into

57. Molnar, *Divine Freedom*, 62.

our history; God remains faithful to who God eternally is. This is an insight of vital importance, and on this score I share Molnar's unease with the way a thinker like Moltmann introduces rupture and discontinuity within the being of God. But as I have argued, the trinitarianism of IV/1 does not require any *logos asarkos* or any formalistic notion of divine choice in order to safeguard God's self-consistency. Instead—as both McCormack and Williams have perceived—Barth has an entirely different way of safeguarding the divine self-consistency: namely, the doctrine of election. It is the doctrine of election that allows Barth to say both that the being of God is oriented wholly towards a particular event in history, and that God is eternally what God becomes in this history.

Or to put it more succinctly: God is eternally self-consistent because Jesus Christ is not only the elected human but also the electing God. Jesus *is* God's self-consistency, God's way of being God.

Bibliography

Barth, Karl. *Church Dogmatics*. 4 vols. Edinburgh: T. & T. Clark, 1956–75.
Holtmann, Stefan. *Karl Barth als Theologe der Neuzeit: Studien zur kritischen Deutung seiner Theologie*. Göttingen: Vandenhoeck & Ruprecht, 2007.
McCormack, Bruce L. "Grace and Being: The Role of God's Gracious Election in Karl Barth's Theological Ontology." In *Orthodox and Modern: Studies in the Theology of Karl Barth*. Grand Rapids: Baker, 2008, 183–200.
———. "Karl Barth's Christology as a Resource for a Reformed Version of Kenoticism." *International Journal of Systematic Theology* 8 (2006) 243–51.
———. *Karl Barth's Critically Realistic Dialectical Theology: Its Genesis and Development, 1909–1936*. Oxford: Clarendon, 1995.
———. *Orthodox and Modern: Studies in the Theology of Karl Barth*. Grand Rapids: Baker, 2008.
Martyn, J. Louis. *Galatians*. Anchor Bible 33A. New York: Doubleday, 1997.
Menke-Peitzmeyer, Michael. *Subjektivität und Selbstinterpretation des dreifaltigen Gottes: Eine Studie zur Genese und Explikation des Paradigmas "Selbstoffenbarung Gottes" in der Theologie Karl Barths*. Münster: Aschendorff, 2002.
Molnar, Paul. *Divine Freedom and the Doctrine of the Immanent Trinity: In Dialogue with Karl Barth and Contemporary Theology*. London: T. & T. Clark, 2002.
Moltmann, Jürgen. *The Crucified God: The Cross as the Foundation and Criticism of Christian Theology*. Translated by R. A. Wilson and John Bowden. London: SCM, 1974.
———. *The Trinity and the Kingdom*. Translated by Margaret Kohl. San Francisco: Harper & Row, 1981; German edition 1980.

Pfleiderer, Georg. *Karl Barths praktische Theologie: Zu Genese und Kontext eines paradigmatischen Entwurfs systematischer Theologie im 20. Jahrhundert.* Tübingen: Mohr/Siebeck, 2000.

Rendtorff, Trutz. "Radikale Autonomie Gottes: Zum Verständnis der Theologie Karl Barths und ihre Folgen." In *Theorie des Christentums: Historische-theologische Studien zu seiner neuzeitlichen Verfassung*, edited by Trutz Rendtorff, 161–81. Gütersloh: Gerd Mohn, 1972.

Vogel, Heinrich. *Christologie*, vol. 1. Munich: Kaiser, 1949.

Williams, Rowan. "Balthasar and Difference." In *Wrestling with Angels: Conversations in Modern Theology*, edited by Mike Higton, 77-85. Grand Rapids: Eerdmans, 2008.

———. "Barth on the Triune God." In *Wrestling with Angels: Conversations in Modern Theology*, edited by Mike Higton, 106–49. Grand Rapids: Eerdmans, 2008.

Wingren, Gustaf. *Theology in Conflict: Nygren, Barth, Bultmann.* Translated by Eric H. Wahlstrom. Edinburgh: Oliver & Boyd, 1958.

6

Obedience and Subordination in Barth's Trinity

Phillip Tolliday

Introduction

IN WHAT FOLLOWS I SHALL ATTEMPT TO SHED SOME LIGHT ON THE ISSUE of whether Barth "changed his mind" as a result of his understanding of the doctrine of election that he developed in *CD* II/2. I enter this much-travelled field by way of a discussion that took place in Australia between Kevin Giles and a report written by the Doctrine Commission of the Anglican Diocese of Sydney.[1] I then use this discussion, which raises the question of whether the Son is eternally, functionally—though not ontologically—subordinate to the Father, as a launching platform as it were, into the issue of the impact of *CD* II/2 on Barth's doctrine of God in *CD* IV/1.

Specifically, my focus will be Barth's treatment of reconciliation under the heading of "The Way of the Son of God into the Far Country." Giles read this section of the *Dogmatics* in a way that sought to harmonize it with his doctrine of God as explicated in *CD* I/1. While he claimed to have recognized the revolutionary nature of Barth's understanding of election, it played no fundamental role, and still less a revo-

---

1. Giles, *Trinity & Subordination*. The Doctrine Report, entitled *The Doctrine of the Trinity and Its Bearing on the Relationship of Men and Women* (1999), may be found in Appendix B of Giles' book. I should perhaps note at the outset that in arguing for subordination in Barth's understanding of the Trinity I do not endorse subordination in the gender debate. An assumption held in common by Giles and the Doctrine Commission was that a clear line could be drawn from the nature of the relationship between the intra-divine persons and that of men and women. I believe that this is to push analogical language beyond its proper limits.

lutionary role, so far as Giles could see, in Barth's subsequent doctrine of God. In this Giles claimed to be able to enlist the support of Paul Molnar and, on the basis of more recent scholarship, we might add, George Hunsinger.[2] However, lined up on the other side, and therefore arguing for a fundamental change or at least development, in Barth's doctrine of God subsequent to *CD* II/2 we find Matthias Gockel and Paul Dafydd Jones, led by the pioneering work of Bruce McCormack.[3] Indeed I shall be dependent upon Jones' work for a substantial portion of this essay because I wish to appropriate his understanding of the motif of the Son's obedience. I intend to use the motif of obedience in order to find a way into the debate as to whether the Son is eternally subordinate to the Father—at least in light of Barth's doctrine of reconciliation in *CD* IV/1.

The Sydney Doctrine Commission Report claimed that there existed a "functional subordination" within the Trinity: specifically between the Father and the Son. Giles argued against this position to the effect that any pretence to an "eternal functional subordination" was simply the ancient heresy of subordinationism newly revived. Thus in regard to the relevant section under consideration in *CD* IV/1, Giles argued that the obedience of the Son of God pertained to the economy only, whereas the Doctrine Commission Report read the motif of the Son's obedience back into the eternal, triune life of God.

Scholars have long noted Barth's capacity for subtlety and the way in which his theology is resistant to being "pinned down" as it were, by traditional theological categorizations. Indeed this is one of the characteristics of his theology that makes it so interesting. Nowhere is this more evident than when people come to consider whether or not Barth was a universalist. Superficially at least the answer to the question appears quite straightforward: he was not. He said as much, and also from time to time argued against universalism. Yet the suspicion—indeed in some interpreters, more of a conviction—remains that Barth's theological vision presses inexorably toward a doctrine of universal salvation.

---

2. Molnar, *Divine Freedom*; ibid., "Trinity, Election and God's Ontological Freedom," 294–306; ibid., "Can the Electing God be God without us?" 199–222; and Hunsinger, "Election and the Trinity," 179–98.

3. Gockel, *Barth and Schleiermacher*; Jones, "Karl Barth on Gethsemane," 148–71; Jones, *Humanity of Christ*; McCormack, *Orthodox and Modern*; McCormack, "Karl Barth's Christology as a Resource for a Reformed Version of Kenoticism," 243–51; ibid., "Seek God Where He May be Found," 62–79.

The question therefore arises: which of these positions is the correct one? Could they both be right?

For my money I think both positions are right. Barth does argue against universal*ism* but at the same time adopts a theological position whereby the divine "Yes" always triumphs over the "No." The case is, I believe, structurally similar with the issue of subordination. Barth is certainly no subordinationist and from time to time argues vehemently against it, but he does endorse—particularly in light of his doctrine of election—a strong motif of the Son's obedience, which is not, I shall argue, confined to the economy. Thus in a similar way in which one may speak of an offer of universal salvation though not of universalism, so one may speak of an eternal subordination of the Son—through obedience—though not of an ontological subordinationism.

In this paper I attempt to run together two questions, which are to my mind interconnected. The first question is whether there is subordination in Barth's doctrine of the Trinity, and the second is whether Barth's views underwent a substantive change as a result of his doctrine of election in *CD* II/2. My assumption is that where there is a belief in a change or development of Barth's views after his doctrine of election there is a tendency to be willing to engage with the idea of subordination (though not subordinationism) in his doctrine of the Trinity. Now this is not to suggest that the themes of the Son's subordination and obedience necessarily *require* something akin to McCormack's discontinuity/development thesis—merely that such a thesis is amenable to their exploration.[4]

Giles on Barth

Giles' initial book contained a chapter entitled, "The Retrieval and Refinement of the Nicene Trinitarian Tradition in the Twentieth Century," in which he briefly explored the work of Barth and Rahner. His interpretation of both theologians was the focus of a response

---

4. Thus Jones, *Humanity of Christ*, adopts McCormack's reading of Barth, albeit in a modified form and this comports well with his discussion of history and the Son's obedience. On the other hand, Van Driel, *Incarnation Anyway*, 96–101, has argued "That the incarnate one lives in humiliation and obedience to the Father could also be said to be a perfect expression of who God is in and for Godself, an expression of over-againstness in God which logically and ontologically preceded the act of election" (ibid., 96).

made by Mark Baddeley and was identified as inadequate and misleading. Baddeley was responding to Giles' claim that "conservative evangelicals [had] departed from the mainstream tradition to defend their subordination of women."[5] Giles had claimed that the reason why some evangelicals had embraced functional subordination was not due "to an independent reconsideration of the doctrine of the Trinity," but rather arose "entirely in connection with attempts to preserve . . . male headship."[6] This was a strong charge and one that members of the Doctrine Commission vehemently rejected. Baddeley observed that since the writings of Barth and Rahner preceded the gender debate of the last thirty years it would be important to check whether Giles had interpreted their work correctly. He wrote, "If any party has departed from the mainstream position, then these two theologians will expose this, since they wrote before the debate and were therefore immune to its force."[7]

In what follows I will outline the position taken by Giles in his subsequent book, which, unlike his first book, contained a chapter-length treatment of his analysis of Barth's doctrine of the Trinity with respect to the issue of the subordination and obedience of the Son to the Father.[8] In his explanation of Barth's doctrine of God, Giles focused his attention on three primary areas: the doctrine of the Word of God in *CD* I/1; the doctrine of election in *CD* II/2; and the obedience of the Son to the Father in *CD* IV/1.

Beginning by pointing out Barth's emphasis on the divine unity, Giles noted that God's triunity did not mean that there is a "plurality of individuals or parts within the one Godhead." Instead, "[t]he name of Father, Son, and Spirit means that God is the one God in threefold repetition, and this in such a way that the repetition itself is grounded in His Godhead, so that it implies no alteration in his Godhead, and yet in such a way that he is the one God only in this repetition, so that His one Godhead stands or falls with the fact that He is God in this repetition, but for that very reason He is the one God in each repetition."[9] In this way Barth had argued that "in no sense can Christ and the Spirit be

---

5. Baddeley, "Trinity and Subordinationism," 31.
6. Giles, *Trinity & Subordination*, 109.
7. Baddeley, "Trinity and Subordinationism," 31.
8. Giles, *Jesus and the Father*.
9. Ibid., 281, citing *CD* I/1, 350.

subordinate hypostases.... Only the substantial equality of Christ and the Spirit with the Father is compatible with monotheism."[10] Giles had here outlined Barth's understanding of the unity in Trinity and it would be the base to which he would continually return. He was highly sympathetic to a typically Western approach to the Trinity with its emphasis on the unity or oneness of God.

In *CD* I/1 Barth had clearly rejected subordinationism on the basis that it rested upon "the intention of making the One who reveals Himself there the kind of subject we ourselves are."[11] Subordination proposed that the three moments in God somehow meant a more or a less in God's being as God. But if this were true then Father, Son and Spirit could not be the one, single and equal God. Indeed, Barth had argued:

> According to subordinationist teaching even the Father, who is supposedly thought of as the Creator, is in fact dragged into the creaturely sphere. According to this view His relation to the Son and Spirit is that of idea to manifestation. Standing in this comprehensible relation, He shows Himself to be an entity that can be projected and dominated by the I. Subordination finally means the denial of revelation, the drawing of divine subjectivity into human subjectivity, and by way of polytheism the isolation of man with himself in his own world in which there is finally no Thou and therefore no Lord.[12]

The obvious diminution in being which subordinationism entailed for the Son and the Spirit would, according to Barth (and Giles), entail a similar diminution for the Father. Thus subordinationism must fail. But before turning his attention to Barth's doctrine of election, Giles noted that there was a type of subordination in *CD* I/1 of which Barth did seem to approve.

In referring to the fatherhood of God, Barth had claimed that "He is Father because he is the Father of His only-begotten Son. From the same unity we have at once the further result of the divine sonship of Jesus Christ. There is no abstract person of the Revealer, but the person of the Revealer is the person of Jesus Christ, who is subordinate to the Creator revealed by it, yet who is also indissolubly co-ordinate with

10. *CD* I/1, 353.
11. Ibid., 381.
12. Ibid.

him."[13] Giles admitted that it was not immediately obvious as to how this might be harmonized with what Barth had said earlier. However, one possibility he proposed was that perhaps Barth was "simply saying that *in his person as the Revealer* Jesus is subordinated to the Father, although in himself as God the Son he is 'indissolubly co-ordinate with him.'"[14] But since Barth does not ascribe some things to Jesus' humanity and others to his divinity Giles discounted that option and suggested instead that "what takes place in revelation and reconciliation discloses that the Father and Son are differentiated. Jesus perfectly reveals the Father as he is one with him, yet in reconciliation, 'his *self*-revelation' he is distinguished from the Father because in his work as the Revealer and the Reconciler it is he who takes flesh and is subordinated."[15]

Giles believed that there was a place for subordination here because reconciliation is, so to speak, a second divine act which follows creation. "To this order of creation and reconciliation," Barth had claimed, "[t]here corresponds christologically the order of Father and Son or Father and Word."[16] But this did not imply any inequality between the divine persons. On the contrary, as Giles pointed out, it could only "signify a distinction in mode of being. For reconciliation is no more comprehensible and no less divine than creation."[17] Giles concluded that perhaps Barth was suggesting that "in his characteristic and dialectical style ... God is both high and humble, and Jesus Christ reveals this astonishing fact.... In the work of revelation and reconciliation we see him as subordinated God, God identified with humanity in humiliation and lowliness."[18] Thus for Giles the themes of super- and sub-ordination, or the "high" and "humble," were now to be referred to the Godhead rather than to the relation between the Father and the Son, i.e., the proper distinctions or modes of being within the Godhead.

When he turned his attention to Barth's doctrine of election Giles noted that "Jesus Christ is both the subject of election and its object: he is electing God and the elect human."[19] Sensitive to the tradition that the

13. Giles, *Jesus and the Father*, 285, citing *CD* I/1, 412.
14. Giles, *Jesus and the Father*, 285, emphasis in the original.
15. Ibid., citing *CD* I/1, 412.
16. *CD* I/1, 413.
17. Giles, *Jesus and the Father*, 285, citing *CD* I/1, 413.
18. Ibid., 286.
19. Ibid., 290, citing *CD* II/2, 103.

function of election has characteristically been ascribed to the Father, Giles was alert to the question of whether this might mean that Barth's approach was somehow dividing the Trinity. However he discounted this possibility and claimed instead that "Barth is quite emphatic that . . . Christ's free decision expresses 'the harmony of the triune God.' (For Barth the Father and the Son cannot have separate and distinct wills.) If Christ himself is all-determining God, he is not subordinated in authority to the Father."[20]

In keeping with Barth's understanding of time in which there can be "no clear separation" made between the pre-existent Christ and the incarnate Christ, Giles claimed that "Barth telescopes the two together."[21] Thus there is for Giles a *logos asarkos* but the *logos asarkos* was always a *logos incarnandus*. He made this qualification to guard against the temptation of imagining that it was possible to have some sort of abstract Logos that was not always essentially connected with Jesus Christ. Recognizing and approving of Barth's supralapsarian position, Giles observed that in the incarnation what was always true from the beginning—perhaps even before the beginning—became "concrete reality and actuality."[22] The conclusion of this line of thought was that there could be no absolute separation between Christ in history and Christ in eternity, and Giles quoted with approval Barth's statement to the effect that "we have to say that as Christ is in revelation, so He is antecedently in Himself. . . . [W]e have to take revelation with such utter seriousness that in it as God's act we must directly see God's being too."[23] On the basis of this Giles argued that "what Barth is saying in this and the many other 'antecedent' comments is that just as Jesus Christ is God and man in historical revelation, so he is in eternity. He is not saying, as my evangelical debating opponents seem to think, that just as Jesus Christ is subordinated to the Father in historical revelation so too he is unilaterally subordinated in eternity."[24]

For Giles this was indeed the heart of the issue. In answer to the anticipated question of just why the economy could not be read back into the life of the immanent Trinity, Giles defended the relationship

20. Ibid., 290.
21. Ibid., 291.
22. Ibid., 291, citing *CD* IV/1, 53.
23. Ibid., 291–92, citing *CD* I/1, 428.
24. Ibid., 292.

between the immanent and economic Trinity as one of correspondence but not identity. In agreement with Molnar, he argued that when the economic Trinity is identified with the immanent Trinity creation becomes an act of necessity rather than of grace, and divine freedom is thereby compromised. At stake was the meaning of divine freedom, which, on Giles' understanding, meant that God could be free only if God could have done otherwise than God did.

Despite accepting that Barth's understanding of election "completely overthrows the traditional theological paradigm," and despite acknowledging that we may make "no absolute division between Christ before and after the incarnation," we could, nevertheless, according to Giles, "postulate a division, or perhaps better a dialectical tension, between Jesus Christ as the sovereign and electing God and Christ as man elected to be God."[25] It is Jesus Christ identified with humanity who freely chooses to be obedient to the Father, to suffer and to die. Giles understood this to mean that, "as God who has freely and sovereignly chosen to be man, Christ is obedient to the Father, not by constraint but sovereignly and willingly."[26] It is not altogether clear why Giles labors the point about sovereign choice. He wants to make it clear that divinely willed obedience is not the same as obedience that is compelled or coerced. That, of course, is true; however, we should not draw the conclusion, as it seems to me that Giles does, that divinely willed obedience is somehow attenuated by having been sovereignly chosen.

Giles recognized that historical orthodoxy had "limited Christ's subordination, obedience and suffering to the time of his incarnation."[27] Equally, he was able to appreciate how Barth's interpretation of election had widened this view since Barth now attributed all these things to Jesus Christ, where "Jesus Christ means God identified with man from all eternity."[28] But following Molnar's argument to the effect that there is a correspondence—though not identity—between the immanent and economic Trinity, Giles concluded that the subordination, obedience, and suffering we see in the incarnate Christ are not to be read back into the immanent life of God. This, he claimed, was the contemporary subordinationist strategy. Giles argued that Barth "insists that Christ is

25. Ibid.
26. Ibid.
27. Ibid.
28. Ibid., 293.

eternally sovereign God, he who elects. He is self-determining God. The humiliated, subordinated, suffering Jesus Christ is God who has elected to be man (humankind) in grace and reprobation."[29] From this Giles concluded that there exists a dialectical tension in Barth's theology and it is precisely this tension that is missed by contemporary evangelicals in their support of the eternal subordination of the Son. "They rightly see him [Barth] speaking of the Son of God as subordinate and obedient: what they fail to see is that for Barth Christ is always both the sovereign electing God who rules in majesty and authority, equal with the Father and the Spirit, and God identified with man in obedience, subordination and suffering."[30]

But it is the sub-section of Barth's doctrine of reconciliation entitled "The Way of the Son of God into the Far Country" that poses most sharply the issue of the eternal subordination of the Son. *CD* IV/1, pages 195–203 take us to the core of the issue. When dealing with this section Giles noted Barth's words to the effect that there can be no avoiding of "the offensive fact that there is in God Himself an above and a below, a *prius* and a *posterius*, a superiority and a subordination . . . [and] that it belongs to the inner life of God."[31] Giles admitted that while this might seem "unambiguously to endorse the idea that the Son is eternally subordinated and set under the Father in authority" such a conclusion would be mistaken, since what Barth actually speaks of "is an actual subordination in God himself."[32] Thus: "The One God is both the One obeyed and Another who obeys."[33] "No, not an unequal but equal, not a divided but in the one deity, God is both One and also Another, His own counter-part, co-existent with Himself."[34] "As we look at Jesus Christ we cannot avoid the astounding conclusion of divine obedience . . . in equal God, the one God, is in fact, the One and also Another, that He is indeed a First and a Second, One who rules and commands in majesty and One who obeys in humility. The one God

---

29. Ibid.
30. Ibid.
31. Ibid., 297, citing *CD* IV/1, 200–201.
32. Ibid., 297.
33. *CD* IV/1, 201.
34. Ibid.

is both the one and the other without any cleft or differentiation but in perfect unity and equality."³⁵

From these—selective—citations Giles distilled two conclusions. Firstly, that Barth spoke of subordination in the one "equal God." Secondly, that he spoke also of "a subordination seen in Christ that does not negate his ruling and commanding in majesty."³⁶ Giles then claimed that "Barth is indicating that the subordination seen in Christ actually reveals something about all three divine persons—the one Triune God"—a suggestion that becomes explicit when Barth claims that "it is the Godhead, not Christ alone, who is high and humble."³⁷

Giles observed that "when he [Barth] speaks of the subordination of the Son, he uses elusive, paradoxical and dialectical language that makes it impossible to 'box in' what he is saying," and as an illustration he quoted the following passage from Barth.

> The One who in this obedience is the perfect image of the ruling God is Himself—as distinct from every human and creaturely kind—God by nature, God in His relationship with Himself, i.e., God in His mode of being as the Son in relation to God in His mode of being as the Father, One with the Father and of one essence. In His mode of being as the Son He fulfils the divine subordination, just as the Father in His mode of being as the Father fulfils the divine superiority. In humility as the Son who complies, he is the same as is the Father in majesty as the Father who disposes. He is the same in consequence (and obedience) as the Son as is the Father in origin. He is the same as the Son, i.e., as the self-posited God (the eternally begotten of the Father as the dogma has it) as is the Father as the self-positing God (the Father who eternally begets). Moreover in His humility and compliance as the Son He has a supreme part in the majesty and disposing of the Father.³⁸

---

35. Ibid., 202.

36. Giles, *Jesus and the Father*, 297.

37. Ibid. The actual quote from *CD* IV/2, 84, is as follows in Giles' citation: "The Godhead of the true God is not a prison whose walls have first to be broken through if He is to elect and do what He has elected and done in becoming man. . . . His Godhead embraces both height and depth, both sovereignty and humility, both lordship and service. . . . He does not become another when in Jesus Christ He also becomes and is man."

38. Ibid., 297–98, citing *CD* IV/1, 209.

But to whom is Barth referring when he speaks of the "condescension, self-humbling, and even of suffering and obedience *in God*"?[39] Clearly for Giles the answer is the triune God and the reason for this is that there is only one God in threefold repetition, and if the Son perfectly reveals the Father we must conclude that he has in mind at all times the one triune God revealed in Jesus Christ. Thus Giles concluded, "If Christ is high and humble, so too is the Father and the Holy Spirit."[40] Barth could not, Giles believed, be read as endorsing the conservative evangelical position that Christ is the subordinated obedient Son *simpliciter*.

Some Responses to Giles on Barth

When Mark Baddeley responded to Giles' initial comments on Barth he focused on Giles' implication that Barth's position was that the "Incarnation does not reveal the ordering of intra-trinitarian relationships within eternity, but only general truths about the divine nature. Both submission and command are true of the divine nature and so both are true of each person equally."[41] He then cited at length the quote from Barth that Giles had used, albeit in a much abbreviated form.

> The second idea we have to abandon is that—even supposing we have corrected that unsatisfactory conception of unity—there is necessarily something unworthy of God and incompatible with His being as God in supposing that there is in God a first and a second, and above and a below, since this includes a gradation, a degradation and an inferiority in God, which if conceded excludes the *homoousia* of the different modes of divine being. That all sounds very illuminating. But is it not an all too human—and therefore not a genuinely human—way of thinking? For what is the measure by which it measures and judges? Has there really to be something mean in God for Him to be the second, below? Does subordination in God necessarily involve an inferiority, and therefore a deprivation, a lack? Why not rather a particular being in the glory of the one equal Godhead, in whose inner order there is also, in fact, this dimension, the direction downwards, which has its own dignity? Why

---

39. Ibid., 298, emphasis in the original.
40. Ibid.
41. Baddeley, "Trinity and Subordinationism," 33.

> should not our way of finding a lesser dignity and significance in what takes the second and subordinate place (the wife to her husband) need to be corrected in the light of the *homoousia* of the modes of divine being?
>
> As we look at Jesus Christ we cannot avoid the astounding conclusion of a divine obedience. Therefore we have to draw the no less astounding deduction that in equal Godhead the one God is, in fact, the One and also Another, that He is indeed a First and a Second, One who rules and commands in majesty and One who obeys in humility. The One God is both the one and the other. And, we continue, He is the one and the other without any cleft or differentiation but in perfect unity and equality because in the same perfect unity and equality He is also a Third, the One who affirms the one and equal Godhead through and by and in the two modes of being.[42]

For Baddeley, the references to a "First," "Second," and "Third" indicated that Barth was speaking of realities that applied to each of the persons respectively. There was, he thought, "One who commands and Another who obeys."[43] And it would appear that he could claim Barth's support here when the latter writes:

> In the work of the reconciliation of the world with God the inward divine relationship between the One who rules and commands in majesty and the One who obeys in humility is identical with the very different relationship between God and one of His creatures, a man. God goes into the far country for this to happen. He becomes what He had not previously been. ... But as in His action as Creator, he does not do it apart from its basis in His own being, in His own inner life.... He can enter in Himself, seeing He is in Himself not only the one who rules and commands in majesty, but also in His own divine person, *although in a different mode of being, the One who is obedient in humility.*[44]

On this occasion, at least, it seems that Barth does make a distinction between the persons in such a way as to support Baddeley's interpretation.

Another considered response to Giles came from Robert Letham who argued that the "obedience of Christ as man has a basis in the Son

---

42. *CD* IV/1, 202.
43. Baddeley, "Trinity and Subordinationism," 34.
44. *CD* IV/1, 203–4, emphasis added.

of God himself'"[45] and to suggest otherwise would be to fall into modalism. Barth was acutely sensitive to this point when he wrote that, "if in his proper being as God God can only be unworldly, if he can be the humiliated and lowly and obedient One only in a mode of appearance and not in his proper being, what is the value of the true deity of Christ, what is its value for us?"[46] When we have to do with Jesus Christ we have to do with God. "His [God's] presence in the world is identical with the existence of the humiliated [and] obedient . . . Jesus of Nazareth."[47]

Similarly to Giles, Letham spoke of the unity of God which consists in the fact "that in himself he is both One who is obeyed and Another who obeys."[48] But he included one citation that is absent from Giles: "He is as man what He is as God" for "that is the true deity of Jesus Christ, obedient in humility, in its unity and equality, its *homoousia*, with the deity of the One who sent him and to whom he is obedient."[49] And in regard to the divine freedom he referred to Bromiley's claim that "obedience is not alien to the *Son*." According to Bromiley, whose work was quoted approvingly by Letham, such obedience as Christ gives to the Father even in his eternal deity as the Son implied neither subordinationism nor modalism.[50]

Thus a fundamental difference between Giles and Letham was the latter's assumption that observations about the humiliation, suffering, and obedience of the Son could be read back into the Son's eternal nature, and, with respect to the motif of obedience, the Son's eternal relation to the Father. Giles, on the other hand, had argued that these characteristics of humiliation, suffering, and obedience that we see manifested in Jesus as the Son of God pertain to the incarnate Christ only. And while he did admit, albeit reluctantly, that we can speak of an obedience in God, it is not an eternal obedience of the Son to the Father, but rather a super- and sub-ordination, which, while seemingly referred to the Son, via Barth's understanding of divine repetition, is actually true of the Godhead itself. Hence Giles concluded, "Christ reveals the

45. Letham, *Holy Trinity*, 397.
46. *CD* IV/1, 196–97.
47. Letham, *Holy Trinity*, 397.
48. Ibid., 398, citing *CD* IV/1, 201.
49. Ibid., citing *CD* IV/1, 203–5, [204].
50. Ibid., citing Bromiley, *Introducing the Theology of Karl Barth*, 181. Emphasis added.

triune God. God is not other than he is in Jesus Christ. If Christ is high and humble, so too is the Father and the Spirit."[51]

For Letham the obedience of the Son within the economy could be read back into the life of the immanent Trinity because it had its proper beginning within the inner life of God. "The basis of the determination of the Son to become a human being and thus the basis of his humility and obedience is in the immanent Trinity. The Son is obedient already antecendently in the Trinity."[52] But on what basis might we know this? According to Laats it would be on account of the axiomatic claim that God's being *ad extra* corresponds essentially with God's being *ad intra*.[53] But here we strike the question raised by Molnar and Giles: is the relationship between the immanent and economic Trinity one of correspondence or identity? Let me say at this point that I think Molnar's question is the right one, though I am now less confident than I used to be that his answer, "correspondence, yes; identity, no," is correct. In the final part of this paper I shall argue, contra Molnar (and, by implication, Giles), that Barth's doctrine of election changed the ground rules for how we might "read back" the motif of obedience, and by extension, subordination, into the eternal life of the Son.

An Eternal Subordination?

In an article seeking to defend Barth from modalism Dennis Jowers objected to "Barth's idea of an eternal obedience rendered to the Father by the Son, a hypothesis introduced in *CD* IV/1 which undermines Barth's case against subordinationism set forth in volume 1."[54] Clearly Jowers thought he had detected a significant change in Barth's thought with respect to the obedience and subordination of the Son between *CD* I/1 and *CD* IV/1. There are at least two significant points we can note about this claim. The first is that Jowers obviously thought that the Son's obedience in *CD* IV/1 was not simply restricted to the economy but was instead an "eternal obedience." He worried because he believed it undermined Barth's argument against subordinationism in *CD* I/1. So

---

51. Giles, *Jesus*, 298.

52. Letham, *Holy Trinity*, 402–3, citing Laats, *Doctrines of the Trinity in Eastern and Western Theologies*, 48. The references to Barth include *CD* IV/1, 170, 177, 192–94.

53. Laats, *Trinity*, 35.

54. Jowers, "Reproach of Modalism," 246.

the second point to take away from Jowers' observation is that, at least on his interpretation, an understanding of the Son's eternal obedience to the Father will tend toward subordinationism or, at the very least, undercut earlier arguments against it. If we were to accept this claim then, it seems to me, we would have every reason to resist the motif of the Son's eternal obedience by restricting it to the economy, which is precisely what Giles did. The intriguing question is whether it is what Barth did. From his language of "a hypothesis introduced in *CD* IV/1," it is clear that Jowers believed that Barth had extended the motif of the Son's obedience beyond the economy—equally clear is the fact that he disagreed with Barth on this point.

However, it was possible to accept, as Jowers did, that Barth's mature Christology in *CD* IV/1 was different from his Christology in *CD* I/2 without assuming that this implied a tendency toward subordinationism. Thus recently Paul Dafydd Jones argued that the "Gethsemane excursus . . . holds significance for understanding the Christology of the *Dogmatics* as a whole."[55] This was a strong claim and it indicated his prior commitments as to how the *Dogmatics* ought to be interpreted. Jones claimed that the doctrine of election in *CD* II/2 was "materially decisive" for understanding Barth's later work in volume IV, and so much so that "certain claims in *Church Dogmatics* I [were] significantly qualified."[56] He spoke about how Barth's views in *CD* II/1 were built upon and radicalized by the perspective in *CD* II/2. It was not a case of Barth changing his mind, but rather of developing his thought. As Jones remarks: "[W]ith each successive part-volume, Barth expanded and stabilized his theology, with new layers, categories and claims increasing its overall coherence. . . . [T]he dogmatic coherence of Barth's magnum opus was never a foregone conclusion. . . . [S]ometimes . . . claims in earlier volumes sit awkwardly alongside later conclusions."[57]

---

55. Jones, "Karl Barth on Gethsemane," 149.

56. Jones, *Humanity of Christ*, 8.

57. Jones, "Karl Barth on Gethsemane," 150. If one intends to "tidy-up" Barth and level out the awkwardness, then according to Jones it must not be done in "ways that occlude awareness of transitions within the text" (ibid., 151). His own sketch of how such awkwardness ought be addressed is as follows: "The Christology sketched in *CD* I/2, whole not wholly incompatible with ensuing paragraphs, is superseded—or, better, *aufgehoben*—by a Christology framed by Barth's revolutionary doctrine of election. Given that *CD* II/2 construes God's incarnational action in a way that (positively) applies and deepens Barth's description of God as the 'one who loves in freedom' and

Moreover, he argued that the aim of the prolegomenal volume of the *Dogmatics* was not to offer an expansive description of Christ's person and work, but rather that it was to "establish that God's Word, revelatory of God's triunity and mediated through the Bible, constitutes the exclusive subject matter of theological work."[58] Jones noted that in *Church Dogmatics* Volume I, Barth did not "correlate the economic and immanent trinities in thoroughgoing fashion."[59] Barth certainly agreed that God is not other than the way He appears to be in the event of revelation, thus there was no reason to doubt divine revelation. Nevertheless he did not wish to "annul the distinction between the economy and God's immanent life."[60] Hence in Volume I (at least) Molnar would seem to have Barth's view well-focused in his claim that the relationship between the economic and immanent Trinity was one of correspondence, though not of identity. However, for Jones, this marked a "reservation" on Barth's part, which meant that Volume I did not "cohere fully" with subsequent volumes.[61]

Jones found it highly significant that §59 began with the statement: "The atonement is history."[62] This meant that "(a) the life of Jesus Christ constitutes the identity of Jesus Christ, which, in turn (b) God makes constitutive of the identity of God qua Son."[63] By claiming that the atonement is history, Barth, he believed, was suggesting that "the concrete and particular life of Jesus Christ will govern his dogmatic account of Christ's being and reconciling activity.... [P]ositively it means that the depiction of Christ's life in the narratives of the canonical gospels controls Barth's presentation."[64]

Following McCormack and in particular his essay on the Chalcedonian character of Barth's Christology Jones claimed that in *CD* II/2 Barth began to "close the ontological gap that separates the eter-

---

(negatively) revises the doctrine of God promulgated in *CD* I, one must reckon with the fact that Barth's Christology has a new cast when articulated in the later volumes of the *Dogmatics*."

58. Jones, *Humanity of Christ*, 38.
59. Ibid., 63.
60. Ibid., 64.
61. Ibid. In relation this it is interesting to note within *CD* II/1 Jones still detected a holding apart of the immanent and economic trinities, see p. 76.
62. *CD* IV/1, 157.
63. Jones, *Humanity of Christ*, 191.
64. Jones, "Karl Barth on Gethsemane," 155.

nal Son (the *logos incarnandus* or *logos asarkos*) and the incarnate Son (the *logos incarnatus* or *logos ensarkos*)."⁶⁵ Jones argued that one of the ways in which Barth tried to do this was to turn from the Chalcedonian "two-nature" model towards a "description of God's twofold history." This allowed him to consider what it meant to affirm that God "participated" in Jesus' life *and* also what it meant that Jesus "participated" in God's life. Jones writes: "On the one side, God's 'participation' in Jesus' life means God's self-determination as the incarnate Son. On the other, Jesus' human 'participation' in God's life means involvement in God's 'history through his active obedience to the will of the Father'—an exalting 'obedience, which brings his history into conformity or accord with the history of God's self-humiliation . . . and thereby is made the vehicle of it.'"⁶⁶

Thus for Jones the narrative becomes the clue to the immanent life of the triune God. And it is through the narrative that we apprehend the Son's obedience. The question this poses is whether the Son's obedience is restricted to the economy. Jones argued that because of Barth's assumption of the concrete identity of the divine Son with Jesus Christ the motif of obedience was thereby brought into "the ambit of Barth's trinitarianism."⁶⁷

Jones presented the obedience of the Son from both a divine and human perspective. In the case of the divine obedience, he suggested that Barth approaches it by way of "a consideration of God's 'self-humiliation,' using a discussion of the 'outer moment' of the Son's 'way into the Far Country' to set the stage for his treatment of the 'first and inner moment of the mystery of the deity of Christ' (IV/1, 192)."⁶⁸ The christological category of obedience is understood to be both an "intra-divine event and a human event."⁶⁹

Since my focus here is Barth's doctrine of the Trinity, my primary interest is in the way in which Jones interprets the motif of *divine* obe-

---

65. Jones, *Humanity of Christ*, 66. Citing McCormack, "Karl Barth's Historicized Christology: Just How 'Chalcedonian' Is It?," in McCormack, *Orthodox and Modern*, 201–33.

66. Jones, *Humanity of Christ*, 66, citing McCormack, "Barths grundsätzlicher Chalkedonismus?"

67. Jones, "Karl Barth on Gethsemane," 156.

68. Jones, *Humanity of Christ*, 204.

69. Ibid., 9.

dience, which he does via a "trinitarian amplification of the doctrine of election outlined in *Church Dogmatics* II/2."[70]

Barth, he says,

> wants to avoid the interposition of an ontological gap between the *logos incarnandus* and the *logos incarnatus*. If God qua Son forms the subject of a person whose pre-eminent characteristic is the execution of commands associable with God's first way of being, it follows that obedience is a disposition predicable of the Son as such. Were the theologian to prescind from ascribing this disposition to God in Godself, she would risk suggesting that the eternal Son could be different from the Son revealed in Jesus Christ. She would leave open the possibility that the Son of the immanent Trinity has a character otherwise than that which is revealed economically. And were the theologian to account for the Son's obedience by exclusive reference to Christ's human demeanour, not only would she "split" Christ's person but, worse, she would cast doubt upon the reliability and intelligibility of revelation. For whom or what is being revealed, if Christ is humanly obedient, but God the Son is not?[71]

On the basis of Jones' question it is not difficult to see why he would wish to interpret the motif of obedience in a way that reaches back into the immanent triune life of God. But what does "obedience" actually mean? Surprisingly, perhaps, Jones claimed that obedience did not have to do with "some kind of 'ranking' between Father and Son" though he readily admitted that Barth's patriarchal bias could easily enough lead us to that conclusion.[72] It was, of course, that very notion of an above and a below, a first and a second, that seemed to suggest to Jones a tendency toward subordinationism.[73]

Positively, Jones argued that obedience enabled Barth "to describe God's application of God's loving intentions. It connects what is classi-

---

70. Ibid.

71. Ibid., 206.

72. Ibid., 9.

73. In fact I am not at all sure that Jones has Barth correct on this point. It seems to me that Barth is suggesting that our understanding of patriarchal human relationships between male and female should *not* be the model for talking about subordination in God, but that on the contrary, the *homoousia* of the Trinity should correct our interpretations of human relations. See *CD* IV/1, 202.

cally called the begottenness of the Son with the Son's active—which is to say, incarnational—enactment of divine love."[74]

In *CD* IV/1 Barth emphasized the solidarity and love that God has for humanity in and through God's Son. He makes it clear that this involves that God participates in the being of the world, which means that "His being, His history, is played out as world-history and therefore under the affliction and peril of all world-history."[75]

In seeking to chart a pathway between the rocks of subordinationism and modalism Barth had suggested that

> It is a matter . . . of the one true God being Himself the subject of the act of atonement in such a way that His presence and action as the Reconciler of the world coincide and are indeed identical with the existence of the humiliated and lowly and obedient man Jesus of Nazareth. He acts as the Reconciler in that—as the true God identical with this man—He humbles Himself and becomes lowly and obedient. He becomes and is this without being in contradiction to his divine nature. (He is therefore not exposed to the postulate that He can become and be this only as a creature), but in contradiction to all human ideas about the divine nature.[76]

Jones argues that this suggests something about the overflowing nature of God's love and that "obedience names the Son's willingness to realize God's love in the most radical way imaginable."[77] Indeed for Jones it "identifies [the Son's] willingness to undergo an eternal ontological transformation, to be the conduit by which Christ's humanity and human history is drawn into the time and space of God's being."[78] In short, the Son's obedience explains how it is that God can love in freedom.

Without undoing Barth's trinitarian interpretation in *CD* I/1 of the one God in threefold repetition, Jones argued in §59 that the motif of the Son's obedience enabled Barth to show how the Son responds "eternally and determininatively to the petition of God's first way of being," this in turn serving to reveal and sharpen "a divine triunity in

---

74. Jones, *Humanity of Christ*, 9.
75. *CD* IV/1, 215.
76. Ibid., 199.
77. Jones, *Humanity of Christ*, 207.
78. Ibid.

which the specific actions of God's *Seinsweisen* gain increased clarity and definition, being conspicuously related to distinctive economic and immanent actions [sic]."[79]

Jones, again following McCormack, made a connection between obedience and kenoticism. He noted Barth's references to the second chapter in Philippians in *CD* IV/1, 180–83 and 188–92, but also the fact that by and large Barth did not seek to develop an understanding of kenosis in this volume, preferring instead to use the motifs of obedience and humility. In a paper on the relationship between Barth's Christology and kenosis, McCormack had outlined the differences and similarities between a classical kenoticism as found in the Formula of Concord in the sixteenth century, and that to be extracted from the nineteenth-century kenoticists of whom Gottfried Thomasius is the representative figure.[80] The essential difference between them was that the earlier form of kenoticism "presented itself as a kenosis of the human nature."[81] This meant that kenosis was exclusively an intra-worldly, historical event. It was not a "divestment of certain divine attributes on the part of the pre-incarnate logos in order to make incarnation possible."[82] However, in its later nineteenth-century version it presented itself as "a kenosis of the divine logos."[83] Kenosis, on this account, became a "metaphysical self-emptying" and one that took place in eternity rather than in history. And it was this second version of kenoticism that became prominent during the early part of the twentieth century and which therefore Barth would have been mindful of in his discussions about kenoticism. It is, suggests Jones, one of reasons why Barth declined to give kenosis a significant role in §59, because the restriction of its meaning to "divine self-emptying" would not have conformed to his insistence that God "became flesh without reservation or diminution."[84]

But in spite of their differences the two forms of kenoticism shared something important in common. "Neither was willing to accept a 'communication' of human attributes to the divine—the so-called *genus*

---

79. Jones, *Humanity*, 212.
80. McCormack, "Kenoticism." My following summary is indebted to this article.
81. Ibid., 245.
82. Ibid.
83. Ibid., 246.
84. Jones, *Humanity of Christ*, 215, citing *CD* IV/1, 418.

tapeinoticum (or 'genus of humility')."[85] Thus the two kenotic theories sought to show how and why the divine attributes of the Son could not be attributed to the human Jesus. But they did not consider the possibility that the human attributes might be "communicated" to the divine Son.

Whereas kenosis presumed some divestment of divine attributes—whether after the incarnation, or as a pre-condition for it—Barth's understanding of kenosis in IV/1 was a kenosis by addition rather than by subtraction.[86] According to McCormack: "For the Barth of *CD* IV/1, the 'self-emptying' or 'humiliation' of the Son is not, in the first instance at least, a this-worldly, historical activity on the part of the Logos who has already become incarnate. For the 'humiliation of the Son' in time has its roots in the humility of the Son in eternity—which means that it has its root in the eternal relation of the Son to the Father."[87]

And that which is true of the Son's humility or humiliation holds similarly for the motif of the Son's obedience. What unfolds in time "corresponds to" what happens in eternity. Here we once more reach the text that proved a point of contention between Giles and the members of the Sydney Doctrine Commission: "there is in God Himself an above and a below, a *prius* and a *posterius*, a superiority and a subordination."[88] How might we interpret these juxtaposed terms? McCormack suggests that one way Barth interpreted them was via the motifs of command and obedience. He writes

> The Father "commands" and the Son "obeys." . . . Now this is still a somewhat improper way of speaking. The eternal relation in which the Father "commands" and the Son "obeys" is the very relation by means of which the one God freely constitutes his own being in eternity. God as "Father" . . . is the self-positing God; God as "Son" is the self-posited God. . . . But if the relation in which God "commands" and God "obeys" is identical with the relation which constitutes the very being of God as triune, then it is very clear that what the Son does and therefore is in time finds its ground in what he does and therefore is in eternity.[89]

---

85. McCormack, "Kenoticism," 247.
86. Jones, *Humanity of Christ*, 214. See also McCormack, "Kenoticism," 248.
87. McCormack, "Kenoticism," 248–49.
88. *CD* IV/1, 200–201.
89. McCormack, "Kenoticism," 249.

The consequence of this line of thought is, I think, that we need to make a clear distinction between the *ordo essendi* and the *ordo cognoscendi*. In apprehending the obedience and humility of the Son to the Father and thus of the subordination of the Son to the Father, we ought to avoid the temptation of imagining that what *appears* to us as being first, is in *truth* first. On the basis of the arguments put forward by McCormack and Jones we would do well to ask whether it is rather derived from the immanent trinitarian relations between God's first and second ways of being. If the latter is true then it would mean that humility, obedience, and subordination are proper to the intra-trinitarian relations between the Father and the Son and are therefore essential to God.[90]

Conclusion

I have suggested in this essay that the question of whether Barth's doctrine of the Trinity endorses a subordination of the Son to the Father is connected to the issue of whether Barth changed his mind, or at least developed his views significantly, as a result of writing his doctrine of election. I think there is evidence to indicate a development in Barth's theology subsequent to and as a consequence of his doctrine of election. Further, contra Giles, I believe that it is reasonable to posit a subordination of the Son to the Father that is not confined simply to the economy.

It is clear that Barth was no subordinationist, yet as he relinquished a tight hold on a "two natures" Christology and turned instead to an analysis of history from within his perspective of an "actualistic ontology" he was led to follow where the narrative took him: into the "far country." As the narrative unfolded, so the characteristics of the human Jesus, suffering, humiliation, obedience, and subordination were readily displayed. It was not so much that these could be read back into the immanent life of the triune God, as that it was recognized by Barth that it was from within the immanent life of the triune God that they had their genesis.

90. See McCormack's essay in this collection (p. 109) where he argues: "If obedience is proper to God, if it is a personal property of the triune God in his second mode of God, then there is no difference in content between the immanent and the economic Trinity. The immanent Trinity is the economic Trinity and *vice versa*."

Bibliography

Baddeley, Mark. "The Trinity and Subordinationism: A Response to Kevin Giles." *Reformed Theological Review* 63 (2004) 29-42.

Barth, Karl. *Church Dogmatics.* 4 vols. Edinburgh: T. & T. Clark, 1956-75.

Giles, Kevin. *The Trinity & Subordination: The Doctrine of God and the Contemporary Gender Debate.* Downers Grove, IL: InterVarsity, 2002.

———. *Jesus and the Father: Modern Evangelicals Reinvent the Doctrine of the Trinity.* Grand Rapids: Zondervan, 2006.

Gockel, Matthias. *Barth and Schleiermacher on the Doctrine of Election: A Systematic-Theological Comparison.* Oxford: Oxford University Press, 2006.

Hunsinger, George. "Election and the Trinity: Twenty-Five Theses on the Theology of Karl Barth." *Modern Theology* 24 (2008) 179-98.

Jones, Paul Dafydd. *The Humanity of Christ: Christology in Karl Barth's Church Dogmatics.* London: T. & T. Clark, 2008.

———. "Karl Barth on Gethsemane." *International Journal of Systematic Theology* 9 (2007) 148-71.

Jowers, Dennis. "The Reproach of Modalism: A Difficulty with Karl Barth's Doctrine of the Trinity." *Scottish Journal of Theology* 56 (2003) 231-46.

Laats, Alar. *Doctrines of the Trinity in Eastern and Western Theologies: A Study with Special Reference to K. Barth and V. Lossky.* Frankfurt: Lang, 1999.

Letham, Robert. *The Holy Trinity in Scripture, History, Theology, & Worship.* New Jersey: P. & R., 2004.

McCormack, Bruce. "Karl Barth's Christology as a Resource for a Reformed Version of Kenoticism." *International Journal of Systematic Theology* 8 (2006) 243-51.

———. *Orthodox and Modern: Studies in the Theology of Karl Barth.* Grand Rapids: Baker, 2008.

———. "Seek God Where He May be Found: A Response to Edwin Chr. Van Driel." *Scottish Journal of Theology* 60 (2007) 62-79.

Molnar, Paul. *Divine Freedom and the Doctrine of the Immanent Trinity: In Dialogue with Karl Barth and Contemporary Theology.* Edinburgh: T. & T. Clark, 2002.

———. "The Trinity, Election and God's Ontological Freedom: A Response to Kevin W. Hector." *International Journal of Systematic Theology* 8 (2006) 294-306.

———. "Can the Electing God be God without us? Some Implications of Bruce McCormack's Understanding of Barth's Doctrine of Election for the Doctrine of the Trinity." *Neue Zeitschrift für Systematische Theologie und Religionsphilosophie* 49 (2007) 199-222.

Van Driel, Edwin Chr. *Incarnation Anyway: Arguments for Supralapsarian Christology.* Oxford: Oxford University Press, 2008.

7

Filioque? Nein
A Proposal for Coherent Coinherence

Myk Habets

Introduction

MY FAMILIARITY WITH BARTH COMES CHIEFLY THROUGH HIS STUDENT, friend, colleague, and advocate, Thomas Torrance, someone whose work I am well-versed in. I am fully aware that when Torrance reads Barth, or for that matter Calvin, Athanasius, John of Philoponos, or any other figure in the Great Tradition with whom he agrees, he reads them as allies of his own project, glossing over those parts of their theology that do not align themselves with his own, or, at worst but sadly sometimes, reinterpreting what they said on the assumption that Torrance knew what they wanted to say better than they knew themselves. This reinterpretation of the Tradition is well known with Torrance and I do not seek to defend it here. Suffice it to say that perhaps his excesses are simply illustrative of our own attempts at reading the Tradition and looking for allies for one's own position.

Be that as it may, it is all the more surprising and significant on those occasions when Torrance reads Barth and, instead of warmly and uncritically adopting his theology, takes a stand against him and offers a challenge. One area that Torrance challenges Barth is in his reading of the *filioque* doctrine. Barth, as is well known, was an outspoken advocate of the *filioque*, while Torrance, perhaps just as well known, was highly critical of it and sought, in his own theology, to find a way beyond the ecumenical impasse it has created for over a thousand years.

In Torrance's theology we see a lively example of what it looks like to do theology "after Barth," the theme of the present volume. Concerning the *filioque*, it provides a further illustration of what a trinitarian theology after Barth may look like when it has learnt from Barth and then proceeds to a constructive theology by working through his thought and not simply bypassing or ignoring it altogether.

What follows is a brief but probing analysis of Barth's defense of the *filioque*, Torrance's objections to it, the trinitarian theology that drives such analyses of this ecumenical "problem," and then his proposed "solution" to the problem in dialogue with Eastern Orthodoxy. I shall conclude with an update on the current status of the *filioque*, not only after Barth, but also "after Torrance," and make some tentative recommendations for today. An integral aspect of these recommendations will be the reconception of the divine processions such that the *filioque* becomes, not incorrect, but unnecessary. And so to Barth's defense of the *filioquist* grammar we now turn our attention.

Barth on the Filioque: "Common" vs. "Double" Procession

Barth's treatment of the *filioque* is most comprehensive in *Church Dogmatics* I/1, 477–89. Here he takes up the theme and defends it exegetically and theologically. He also takes the time to consider alternate proposals and potential challenges to his theology before dismissing each as inadequate. Barth then proceeds to consistently work out his *filioquist* theology in subsequent volumes of the *Church Dogmatics*, however, these later comments are merely illustrative of his stated position in *CD* I/1. Barth's theology here is consistent both with his shorter comments in his *Göttingen Dogmatics* and with his trinitarian theology in the earlier *Der Romerbrief* II. A brief rehearsal of Barth's doctrine of the *filioque* and various attempts to understand it is all that is required here.

Central to Barth's constructive argument in favor of the *filioque* is his rejection of any doctrine of "double procession."[1] His argument is explicitly not that of "standard" post-Augustinian Western theology but rather, and as is typical and so appealing with Barth, his is a creative

---

1. *CD* I/1, 486–87. Cf., *CD* III/1, 45, 49, 59; *CD* IV/1, 209, 308.

re-expression of the doctrine. Throughout this section of *CD* I/1, Barth is thoroughly Augustinian in both his doctrine of the Trinity and the subsequent and requisite doctrine of the *filioque*. According to his reading of Augustine, and a correct one we might add, the Father and the Son are the sole source of the procession of the Spirit, but the Father foremost ("*principaliter*" in Augustine).[2] The subsequent history of Western *filioquism* was to ignore the *principaliter* clause altogether and thus espouse the very theology the Eastern churches thought the *filioque* would inevitably sponsor. It is the retention of Augustine's *principaliter* clause that most commentators and critics of Barth miss altogether.[3] Guretzki concludes that Barth's doctrine of the *filioque*, while clearly standing within the Western trinitarian tradition, is atypical in that he refuses to speak of a "double-procession" in favor of a "common procession" of the Spirit—a position that has more affinity with the Eastern position than many of Barth's critics may have thought.[4]

In *Der Romerbrief* II of 1921,[5] the *filioque* is not mentioned and yet the work is an important foundation for Barth's later *filioquism*. Here, as Guretzki highlights,[6] a "Christocentric dialectical pneumatology" is at work in which the Spirit is understood to be the one who simultaneously highlights the infinite qualitative distinction between God and humanity, eternity and time, and yet he binds God and humanity together in union with Christ. This ontic union with Christ is a reflection of the union within God in which the Holy Spirit upholds the Father and Son in a "union-in-distinction" and a "distinction-in-union." Thus the Spirit is the Spirit of the Father and the Son, the *bond and boundary* between them. It is this emerging dialectical pneumatology that provides the groundwork for an understanding of the *filioque* in Barth's subsequent works.

In the *Göttingen Dogmatics* of 1924, the *filioque* first formally appears in relation to an explication of the threefold form of the Word of God: preaching proceeds from revelation and Scripture as the Holy

---

2. See *CD* I/1, 482, where he appeals to Augustine, *De trinitate*, 15.26.47; ET: *On the Holy Trinity*, NPNF (Grand Rapids: Eerdmans, 1994), vol. 3, 225.

3. One reliable commentator who does read Barth correctly here is Hunsinger, "The Mediator of Communion," 155 n.10.

4. Guretzki, *Karl Barth on the Filioque*, ch. 3.

5. Barth, *Der Römerbrief* (1926); ET: *The Epistle to the Romans* (1968).

6. Guretzki, *Karl Barth on the Filioque*, ch. 1.

Spirit proceeds from the Father and the Son.[7] In this work Barth lays a foundation for his theology—to conceive of the immanent Trinity only on the basis of the economic Trinity. His *Church Dogmatics* may be seen as an attempt to apply these principles consistently. It is this broad context within which the *filioque* takes shape.

In line with the pneumatology of *Der Römerbrief* and the trinitarianism of *Göttingen*, Barth turns, eight years later in 1932, to an explicit discussion of the *filioque* in *CD* I/1, par. 12 "God the Holy Spirit." The thesis with which he opens and subsequently exegetes is as follows: "The one God reveals Himself according to Scripture as the Redeemer, i.e., as the Lord who sets us free. As such He is the Holy Spirit, by receiving whom we become the children of God, because, as the Spirit of the love of God the Father and the Son, He is so antecedently in Himself."[8] Following this thesis Barth expounds the Niceno-Constantinopolitan Creed in four moves, the *filioque* being the third of these.

Several features immediately stand out from this thesis and are developed in Barth's subsequent discussion. First, a rigorously Augustinian doctrine of the Trinity is adopted with little development. In this area Barth is unoriginal. The Holy Spirit is the bond of love between Father and Son; he is the essence of relationship between these two. And so: "This togetherness or communion of the Father and the Son is the Holy Spirit. The specific element in the divine mode of being of the Holy Spirit thus consists, paradoxically enough, in the fact that He is the common factor in the mode of being of God the Father and that of God the Son. He is what is common to them, not in so far as they are the one God, but in so far as they are the Father and the Son."[9]

Barth then declares: "Thus, even if the Father and the Son might be called 'person' (in the modern sense of the term), the Holy Spirit could not possibly be regarded as the third 'person.' In a particularly clear way the Holy Spirit is what the Father and the Son also are. He is not a third spiritual Subject, a third I, a third Lord side by side with two others. He is a third mode of being of the one divine Subject or Lord."[10]

---

7. Barth, *Göttingen Dogmatics*.

8. *CD* I/1, 448.

9. Ibid., 469. There follows a quotation from Augustine, *De trin.*, 6.5.7; and John of Damascus, *Ekdos.*, 1.13.

10. Ibid.

Even more explicitly reliant upon Augustine, Barth asserts of the Holy Spirit that he is "The *vinculum pacis* (Eph 4³), the *amor,* the *caritas,* the mutual *donum* between the Father and the Son. . . . He is thus the love in which God . . . as the Father loves the Son and as the Son loves the Father. . . . He is the 'result' of their common 'breathing.'"[11] To reiterate, Barth is so far unoriginal in his Augustinian trinitarianism.

A second general observation is that the Holy Spirit is distinct but not separate from the Father and the Son, being of the same substance or essence. In discussing the processions of the divine persons, Barth makes it clear that procession is not from the essence of God but from another mode or modes of being of this essence (*CD* I/1, 474). Thus the *filioque* is first of all a negation of any sense of the Holy Spirit as an emanation of the divine essence. Further, the three modes of being are distinct but never separate, something the Augustinian notion of appropriations means to describe. The Word's procession and the Holy Spirit's, which is also a spiration, may be denoted but cannot be comprehended (*CD* I/1, 476). These themes are then expanded in Barth's *filioquist* grammar.

When Barth comes to the creedal clause on the Spirit's procession from the Father *and the Son* he continues to develop his theology of the threefold form of the Word of God. Here he speaks of a "schedule of relations" that exists between the three forms. As Guretzki's study highlights, "The geometric characterization of the interrelationships of the *GD* in which revelation has priority over Scripture and preaching gave way in the *CD* to speaking of the complete coinherence of preaching, Scripture and revelation."[12] The subsequent result in the *CD* was to downplay the threefold Word as an analogy for the intratrinitarian relations. However, Barth continued to uphold the *filioque* throughout the *CD* despite the fact that "he appeared to have left behind the very ground upon which he originally adopted the *filioque*."[13] This causes tensions in Barth's *filioquism* and ultimately draws the charge of an inconsistent trinitarianism in his thought; both of which we shall consider presently.

Distinguishing his view of the "common origin" of the Spirit from the typical Western construal of the "double procession," Barth

11. Ibid., 470, citing Augustine, *De trin.*, 15.27.50.
12. Guretzki, *Karl Barth on the Filioque,* 290.
13. Ibid.

sought to uphold the *homoousion* of the Spirit with the Father and the Son while still maintaining a clear distinction between the three. According to Guretzki: "Barth indicated a procession of the Spirit neither from the being (*Sein,* or *ousia*) of God alone, nor from the distinct modes of being (*Seinsweisen,* or *hypostases*) of the Father and the Son. Rather, in order to avoid giving ontological precedence to either the being (*Sein*) or the modes of being (*Seinsweisen*), Barth sought to maintain a delicate dialectical unity of the *Sein* and the *Seinsweisen* as the common origin of the Spirit. Barth . . . understands the *filioque* to affirm that the Spirit proceeds *from-the-common-being-of-the-modes-of-being-of-Father-and-Son*."[14]

Guretzki is correct, but only in part. That the Spirit proceeds "*from-the-common-being-of-the-modes-of-being-of-Father-and-Son*" seems an entirely correct reading of Barth. However, this is quite a different claim from the contention that Barth refuses to privilege either the being/essence of God or the persons/modes of being. Barth, in conformity with Augustinian trinitarianism, privileges two modes of being, that of the Father and the Son, over the essence of God or the three modes of being. It is thus hard to see what Guretzki's conclusions are based on. It is equally easy to see how Barth's theology is not acceptable to either the post-Augustinian Western tradition with its stress on *De Deo Uno* and the substance of God, or that of Eastern theology with its stress on the *De Deo Trino* and specifically the sole *monarchia* of the person of the Father.

Throughout his *filioquism* Barth sought to uphold what he saw as the unique dialectical relationship that exists between the Father and the Son. He derives this from the economy, certainly, but his theological construal is primarily derived from Augustine at this point of the *Church Dogmatics*. It was thus necessary for Barth to maintain the *filioque*, lest one fail to recognize the unique dialectical relationship existing between the Father and the Son. Once more, Guretzki notes that "To speak rightly of God in his self-revelation is to affirm the eternal union-in-distinction and distinction-in-union of the Father and the Son in the Holy Spirit, who is the mediation of communion. This, according to Barth, is what it means for the Spirit to proceed from the common essence or being of the two modes of being, Father and Son."[15]

14. Ibid.
15. Ibid., 291.

Barth's differences with Eastern monopatrist theology were primarily over his principle of the identity of the economic and immanent Trinity. He charged Eastern theology as being speculative and philosophical as it severed *theologia* from *oikonomia*. Barth follows what he terms a strict "rule" in which "statements about the divine modes of being antecedently in themselves cannot be different in content from those that are to be made about their reality in revelation."[16] And again, "the reality of God which encounters us in His revelation is His reality in all the depths of eternity."[17] The direct application of this rule is that the *filioque* must not only be read off the economy, but, importantly and fundamentally, it must also be used to affirm an immanent *filioque*, otherwise "the fellowship of the Spirit between God and man is without objective ground or content."[18]

So insistent is Barth on this point that he rejects any attempt to restrict the *filioque* to the economy and not also see it paralleled in the immanent Trinity. He also rules out all attempts to interpret the *filioque* in terms of διa του υ'ου ("*through* the Son") as a possible interpretation of ἐκ του πατρος ("*from* the Father").[19] According to Barth this sidesteps the real issues and undermines an understanding of the unique relationship between the Father and the Son. In response this is, however, simply to assert a thoroughgoing Augustinianism and to critique contrary views *a priori* on that basis. Turning the tables on the Eastern monopatrist tradition, Barth maintains that only the *filioque* properly maintains the monarchy of the Father in that the Spirit proceeds from the Father and the Son but from the Father *principaliter*.[20] If διa του υιου is accepted then, in Barth's opinion, the Son becomes a mediating principle only. According to Barth, this in turn leads to a full blown Origenist subordinationism. The ultimate problem Barth sees, however, is that, "above all it is the unity of the Trinity which we must see to be endangered at every point by the denial of the *Filioque*."[21] Thus the *filioque* is an integral part of Barth's Augustinian trinitarianism and

---

16. *CD* I/1, 479. See *CD* I/1, 483 where he repeats and summarizes his argument.
17. Ibid., 479.
18. Ibid., 481.
19. Ibid.
20. Ibid., 482.
21. Ibid., 483.

cannot be dispensed with without also bringing into critique Barth's doctrine of the Trinity as a whole, at least as it is construed in *CD* I/1.

On the basis of his Augustinian theology Barth maintains that economically and immanently the Father is always and can be none other than first, the Son second, and the Holy Spirit third. Barth argues this on the basis of the primacy of the relationship between the Father and the Son from which, out of which, and on the basis of which, the Holy Spirit proceeds or is the bond of love or their mutual essence. To further his argument Barth clarifies the *relations of opposition* between Father and Son as follows:

> As the Son of the Father He, too, is thus *spirator Spiritus*. He is this, of course, as the Son of the Father. To that extent the *per Filium* is true. But here *per Filium* cannot mean *per causum instrumentalem*. This Son of this Father is and has all that His Father is and has. He is and has it as the Son. But He is and has it. Thus He, too, is *spirator Spiritus*. He too, has the possibility of being this. This is how we explain and prove the *qui procedit ex patre Filioque*.[22]

To support his argument Barth entertains a brief biblical survey of the mission of the Holy Spirit in relation to the life of Christ. However, against Barth's exegetical arguments in *CD* I/1 is the fact that he reads the entire history of Christ from a post-resurrection, post-ascension perspective so that all the pneumatologically related events of Christ's life, canonically recited, are viewed as the Spirit who proceeds from the Father and is sent by the Son. Thus to view the ministry of Christ, indeed the Christ event, as an aspect of the Spirit's mission is ruled out of court *a priori*, rather than being an *a posteriori* conclusion. Barth rigidly adheres to such a methodology in working from the economic to the immanent Trinity. His exegetical comments are thus less convincing than he thinks they are. Indeed, by removing the retrospective *a priori* the validity of regarding the Son's mission as an aspect of the Spirit's has been convincingly argued elsewhere.[23]

Barth then asks certain perceptive questions before answering each one in the negative. Significant for my study, Barth asks if, on the basis of a doctrine of *perichoresis*, one could posit a completed circle of mutual relations whereby the three divine modes of being proceed mutually as

---

22. Ibid., 484.

23. See, amongst others, Habets, *Anointed Son*; and Pinnock, *Flame of Love*, 79–111.

modes of being from the one God. Thus the Son could proceed from the Father and the Spirit (*spirituque*). Barth summarily dismisses the notion on the basis that, "It is a further description of the *homoousia* of Father, Son, and Spirit, but has nothing to do with begetting and breathing as such, and therefore needs no supplementation in this direction, so that the postulate cannot be said to have, formally, a legitimate basis."[24] But what if such a *perichoretic* construal could account for begetting and spirating as well as mutual processions, even of a form of origin and action of the Father from the Son and the Spirit (*Credo in Patrem qui ex Filio Spirituque procedit*)? What if such a basis could be legitimized? Would it then be permissible and maybe even orthodox and worthy of consideration at least as a *theologumenon*? Would such an attempt be an example of doing trinitarian theology *after* Barth? We shall attempt to answer these questions further below.

Beyond *CD* I/1 Barth continues to assert his *filioquist* theology but does so on a different basis as indicated earlier. In *CD* I/2 a *filioquist* grammar is deployed in order to maintain the unity and indivisibility of the work of the Son and the Spirit. Here the Spirit is the Teacher of the Word and thus pneumatology needs to be understood as an aspect of Christology. In *CD* III/1 a *filioquist* grammar is maintained within Barth's doctrine of creation. Because the Spirit is the ontic ground of communion between the Father and the Son he is also the ontic ground for a real connection between God and the creature, and precisely so on the basis of his being the ontic ground of communion between the divine and human in Jesus. "The Creator Father unites himself with creation in Jesus Christ in the history of creation by the Holy Spirit—the Holy Spirit who proceeds eternally from the Father and the Son,"[25] writes Guretzki. In *CD* IV/3.2 Barth's *filioquism* is applied to the doctrine of reconciliation where the grammar is used to assert the mediative nature of confrontation and communion between Jesus and the church which, again, is an economic echo of the immanent trinitarian relations. Amidst this discussion Barth articulates the role of the Spirit as both "bond and boundary" in relation to Christ and the church, and, significantly, the "bond and boundary" within the immanent being of

---

24. *CD* I/1, 485.

25. Guretzki, *Karl Barth on the Filioque*, 292. Guretzki's is the only complete study on Barth's doctrine of the *filioque* and as such provides a rich resource for further engagement.

God. Barth's originality and movement beyond Augustine becomes apparent at this point. In summarizing Barth's doctrine of the *filioque* Guretzki concludes: "Thus, for Barth, to affirm the *filioque* is to affirm the eternally fruitful dialectic that exists between the Father and the Son in the Holy Spirit. Or, to put it yet another way, the *filioque* for Barth is dialectical shorthand for speaking after God as he has revealed himself to be in his eternal dialectical structure (*Realdialektik*)."[26]

What May We Learn from Barth?

After this brief surview of Barth's *filioquism* it is clear that his is not the last word on the issue, no matter how much he may have thought it was. Before moving beyond Barth we may ask what use Barth's doctrine of the *filioque* has. One answer is that it provides an insightful pointer to some of the persisting theological issues that cluster around the *filioque* and offers a creative and thorough account of how one of the masters sought to construct their own accents in this area. From Barth we may learn a good deal, both about the issues involving the *filioque* and, possibly, pitfalls to be avoided by those following after him. A second answer is that Barth's attempt sought to "preserve in this matter a delicate dialectic between the essence (*Sein*) and the persons (*Seinsweisen*) of the Trinity without giving ontological priority to one or the other."[27] How far Barth succeeded in doing so is a matter of debate, but in his attempt, at least, to hold the two together he stands in continuity with two of the more significant attempts at addressing the issue of the *filioque*, those of Thomas Torrance on the one hand and the 1995 Roman Clarification on the other.[28] In this, Barth seems entirely on the right track and to be

26. Ibid., 294. He also comments on the charge that Barth's *filioquism* results in a subordination of the Spirit and directly refutes that claiming there are no grounds upon which a pneumatological subordination can be a justified reading of Barth's theology. What critics often claim, however, is that Barth's *filioquism* results in denying an independent ontic role to the Spirit in the work of salvation as opposed to a merely noetic role. Guretzki claims that merely reading *CD* I/1 could yield this impression but when read in the context of the complete *CD* this cannot be substantiated. In fact, according to Guretzki, if anything Barth tends towards a superordinationist pneumatology, especially in *CD* IV. The accuracy of Guretzki's claim will not be assessed in this essay.

27. Ibid., 297–98.

28. In 1995 the Roman Catholic Church, at the instigation of Pope John Paul II, issued, via the Pontifical Council for Promoting Unity, the official text of the Roman Clarification as, "The Greek and Latin Traditions about the Procession of the Holy

followed. A third lesson we may learn from Barth's *filioquism* relates to the Athanasian parallels in Barth's thought which are latent and require further examination. This is, arguably, exactly what Torrance and the Roman Clarification provide. Thus, there are lessons to learn from Barth which point to a healthy life "after Barth."

More critically, we also note several weaknesses in Barth's theology. As his study concludes, Guretzki correctly notes the ambiguity in Barth's thought concerning the *filioque* in relationship to origin in God and in the doctrine of *perichoresis*. Guretzki's specific critique is that Barth increasingly links the *filioque* to the doctrine of *perichoresis* without delineating how *perichoresis* and origin are themselves related.[29] But this is where trinitarian theology after Barth may draw its most fecund energy, as we see in the subsequent theology of, to name but two figures, the trinitarianism of Thomas Torrance and Thomas Weinandy. Barth and Torrance speak of the procession of the Holy Spirit in terms of *perichoresis*, despite the fact that both Eastern and Western traditions have normally spoken of the procession in terms of origin. Guretzki asks that "more work be done to disentangle these concepts."[30] The present study is an attempt to make a contribution to just such a disentanglement.

While Guretzki ends up affirming the central propositions Barth makes on the *filioque*, others are not so complimentary.[31] According to Hendry's critique, for Barth's theology to be consistent it would have to insist on a double procession (he should have said a "common procession") of the *Son* from the Father and the Spirit, a *spirituque*, on the

Spirit," in the weekly English language newspaper *L'Osservatore Romano* N.38 no.1408 (20 September 1995) 3, 6. Hereafter, "The Roman Clarification." This represents the results of sustained Roman Catholic–Eastern Orthodox dialogue over the issue of the *filioque*. It removes the *filioque* from creed and liturgy. Significant responses include those of Zizioulas, "One Single Source"; Tavard, "Clarification on the Filioque?" 507–14; and Coffey, "Roman 'Clarification' of the Doctrine of the Filioque," 3–21. The "Roman Clarification" presents a monopatrist theology in line with the East by adopting Augustine's language of the *principium* of the Father.

29. Guretzki, *Karl Barth on the Filioque*, 298.

30. Ibid., and in personal correspondence (11/3/2009)

31. Important critiques of Barth's *filioquism* include: Hendry, "'From the Father and the Son,'" 449–59; ibid., *Holy Spirit in Christian Theology*; Heron, "'Who Proceedeth From the Father and the Son,'" 149–66; Smail, *Giving Gift*; ibid., "Holy Spirit in the Holy Trinity," 149–65; Smail, "Doctrine of the Holy Spirit," 87–110; and Jenson, "You Wonder Where the Spirit Went," 296–304. A useful comparison between Barth and Jüngel can be found in Chung, "An Introduction to the Pneumatologies of Karl Barth and Eberhard Jüngel," Parts 1 and 2.

basis of an adherence to the correspondence of the economic and immanent Trinity.[32] We have already noted Barth's rejection of this suggestion based on the argument that this conflates the otherwise distinct concepts of divine origin of the persons and the concept of *perichoresis*, coupled with his insistence on reading the life of Jesus back from the resurrection and thus rejecting the prior mission of the Spirit. According to another critic, Tom Smail, the fundamental issue with Barth's *filioquism* is twofold: first, it does not give due weight to the Father as the *fons et origio totius divinitatis* ("fount and origin of the complete divinity"); and second, it fails to identify the relational reciprocity between the Son and the Spirit, resulting in an inevitable *filioquism* that tends to subordinate the Spirit to the Son.[33] These are simply representative critiques of Barth's *filioquism* and highlight some of the central issues to be addressed in those who wish to genuinely attempt trinitarian theology after Barth.

A final critique I note here of Barth's doctrine of the Trinity and accompanying *filioquism* is provided by Robert Letham. In assessing Barth's trinitarianism, Letham concludes that while Barth is not a modalist, he is guilty of suggesting, if not outright supporting, a unipersonal view of God.[34] He comes to this conclusion on the basis of a number of factors. In Barth's proposition and subsequent exegesis that "God reveals himself as the Lord,"[35] God's lordship is seen as in some sense prior to the Trinity. "Immediately, the question arises as to the subject of the Trinity. Barth's stress is on the oneness of God,"[36] writes Letham. With obvious roots in Augustinian theology, Barth locates the divine subject in the oneness of God or his essence, now defined as lordship.[37] Alar Laats argues in similar fashion that it is thus a linear,

---

32. Hendry, "From the Father and the Son," 454. Guretzki, *Karl Barth on the Filioque*, 29, notes Moltmann's similar critique in *Spirit of Life*, 71, and that neither Hendry nor Moltmann are actually in favor of a *spirituque*. Someone who does argue for a *spirituque* is Boff, *Trinity and Society*, 204–6. I shall return to aspects of Boff's position below.

33. Smail, "Doctrine of the Holy Spirit," 107–8. Barth's response to such a charge is that the reception of the Spirit by the Son is restricted to his humanity, not to the intratrinitarian *Seinsweisen*.

34. Letham, *Holy Trinity*, 271–90, especially, 275, 277, 287, 289.

35. *CD* I/1, 306–7; 349.

36. Letham, *Holy Trinity*, 274.

37. John Zizioulas is well known for his criticism of Augustine's trinitarianism, which he calls a form of essentialism. We read, "The one God is the Father. Substance

unipersonal model that Barth adopts, rather than an orthodox trinitarianism.[38] The divine subject is thus ambiguous in Barth's *Dogmatics*. Laats considers it to be the Father alone while Moltmann believes it is the divine essence.[39] Moltmann should, I believe get the nod here for Barth seemingly considers the divine subject to be the *common-being-of-the-modes-of-being-of-Father-and-Son*. However, Laats is correct also in that the Father is equivalent to the divine essence. Personality, as Barth uses the term and as it is used typically today, is not determined decisively by the idea of consciousness or a single will, although these are involved, but rather, by the social nexus. Thus an essential moment in personality is its social location, that is, its relatedness to other personalities.[40] Given the Augustinian emphasis on the oneness of God and the priority of the Father, it is a logical and a consistent conclusion that at the heart of Barth's trinitarianism lurks a rather lively unipersonality that undermines all mention of genuine triunity.[41] When Barth goes on to state that the Trinity is God in threefold repetition and a concept of *Seinsweise* is adopted, that is, the preference for modes of being over persons, then the unipersonality of God seems to be more than accidental.

After *CD* I/1 where Barth defines the essence of God as lordship he asserts that the essence or nature of God is twofold: freedom/lordship and love: "God's being consists in the fact that He is the One who loves in freedom."[42] Despite the inclusion of love in the essence of God, Barth's doctrine of God is still unipersonal, as the Father is the one who loves, the Son is the one who receives this love, and the Spirit is the bond of love between them According to Laats, and on the basis of Barth's unipersonality, the Father is the subject or personality and the Son is a

---

is something common to all three persons of the Trinity, but it is not ontologically primary until Augustine makes it so" (Zizioulas, "On Being a Person," 40).

38. Laats, *Doctrines of the Trinity in Eastern and Western Theologies*, 37, cited in Letham, *Holy Trinity*, 275.

39. Moltmann, *Trinity and the Kingdom*, 143.

40. This is chronicled in Laats, *Doctrines of the Trinity in Eastern and Western Theologies*, 37–39.

41. This thesis is strengthened again when we note that in the *CD* Barth departs from his Göttingen Lectures of April 1925 where he was able to affirm the existence of three divine subjects. See McCormack, *Karl Barth's Critically Realistic Dialectical Theology*, 355–56.

42. *CD* II/1, 322.

subject only because he is the repetition of the first subject. The Spirit is then a third repetition. Thus the Trinity is a threefold intradivine repetition of the Father who alone is truly a person.[43] As noted earlier, this is consistent with Barth's contention that "The Holy Spirit in particular, then, even were that possible in the case of the Father and Son, could under no circumstances be regarded as a third 'person,' in the modern sense of the concept."[44]

Here Guretzki's charge, that Barth's theology becomes somewhat ambiguous when he moves from an appeal to the threefold Word of God to *perichoresis*, must be strengthened to the charge that it is manifestly inconsistent. To define *Seinsweise*, Barth appeals to Calvin's notion of subsistent relations.[45] Thus, *Seinsweise* is "the mode of being of an existent."[46] These three modes of being or subsistences are the Father, Son, and Spirit and are distinguished by their distinctive relations to one another, or what he calls "dissimilar relations of origin to one another."[47] But this is not what his commitment to divine unipersonality, derived from Augustine, actually allows. As Letham concludes, "Although he avoids modalism, Barth cannot be entirely exonerated from the charge of unipersonality. His obvious intention is to follow in the line of ecclesiastical orthodoxy.... But he is wedded to the Western and Augustinian model, in which the persons are problematic."[48] More specifically, with Letham, Moltmann, and Williams it may be concluded that once the *filioque* is adopted then the implicit subordination of the Spirit, now conceived as the rather impersonal bond of love between the Father and the Son, seems inevitable.[49]

---

43. See Laats, *Doctrines of the Trinity in Eastern and Western Theologies*, 43–54.
44. *CD* I/1, 537.
45. Calvin, *Institutes of the Christian Religion*, 1.13.6.
46. *CD* I/1, 360.
47. Ibid., 363.
48. Letham, *Holy Trinity*, 278. See the similar criticisms made by Smail, "Doctrine of the Holy Spirit," 106.
49. This criticism is made by Letham, *Holy Trinity*, 287–88; Moltmann, *Trinity and the Kingdom*, 142–43; and Williams, "Barth on the Triune God," 170–78.

Can We Go beyond Barth?

In an earlier study Guretzki outlines five common approaches to the issue of the *filioque* before arguing that, in fact, none are satisfactory.[50] Guretzki's taxonomy provides a useful way to assess the question whether we can go beyond Barth in this area and, if so, how. The five approaches are: First, the *filioque* is a metaphysical speculation and thus to be ignored as irrelevant.[51] Second, the *filioque* is biblical, but theologically insignificant.[52] Third, the *filioque* is theologically necessary and must be retained.[53] Fourth, there is a mediating or synthetic position between *filioquist* and non-*filioquist* positions.[54] Fifth and finally, the *filioque* is to be rejected for ecumenical and theological reasons.[55]

Options three and five are the only valid ones in Guretzki's opinion: either the *filioque* is to be retained, or it is to be rejected on ecumenical and theological grounds. Further, in his evaluation of these positions, Guretzki concludes there are *four* possible responses to the *filioque* rather than the obvious two. The *filioque* is to be accepted or rejected and a prior methodological issue has to be answered: the economy reveals the immanent Trinity or it does not. "On this basis," writes Guretzki, "one might conclude that the Spirit 1) does or 2) does not proceed from the Son in the economic Trinity as in the immanent Trinity, or, the Spirit 3) does or 4) does not proceed from the Son in the economic Trinity alone."[56]

Guretzki argues further that one cannot simply accept or reject the *filioque* as if this had no consequences upon other doctrines, the "intra-

---

50. Guretzki, "*Filioque*," 182–206.

51. Exemplars cited are Reymond, *New Systematic Theology*; and Stackhouse, *Evangelical Landscapes*.

52. Exemplars cited are Erickson, *Christian Theology*, 952, 952–53; and Grider, *Wesleyan-Holiness Theology*.

53. Exemplars cited are Bray, "Double Procession of the Holy Spirit in Evangelical Theology Today," 415–26; and Bloesch, *Holy Spirit*, 271.

54. The exemplar cited is Grenz, *Theology for the Community of God*, 89.

55. Exemplars cited are Pinnock, *Flame of Love*; Moltmann, *Trinity and the Kingdom*, 178–87; ibid., "Theological Proposals Towards the Resolution of the Filioque Controversy," 164–73; Pannenberg, *Systematic Theology*, vol. 1, 317–19; and Jenson, "You Wonder Where the Spirit Went?"

56. Guretzki, "*Filioque*," 198.

systemic issues," as he puts it.⁵⁷ For instance, if one rejects the *filioque* in line with the East, does this also commit one to the Eastern doctrine of uncreated divine energies? If not, why? Many attempts to resolve the *filioque* issue suffer, according to his reading of which I am highly sympathetic, because they evince of sort of pick-'n'-mix approach to theology whereby this doctrine is accepted, that one rejected, and the systematic structure of the whole becomes incongruent. What Guretzki appears to be highlighting is the fact that the *filioque* is consistent with certain doctrines of the Trinity, but is inconsistent with others. If one rejects Barth's *filioquism* does this automatically and necessarily entail a rejection of Augustinian trinitarianism as well? Further, does a rejection of the *filioque* commit one to an Eastern trinitarianism?

All of this brings us to the theology of Thomas Torrance. Torrance addresses Guretzki's call for an awareness of all the issues involved in this discussion, not least of which is one's position on the relation of the economic to the immanent Trinity, alongside a reconsideration of the trinitarian framework within which one chooses to operate (compelled by God's self-revelation in the incarnate Son of course). Torrance attributes to Barth (and Rahner) a rejection of the Western tradition which divides the doctrine of the One God from the doctrine of the Triune God.⁵⁸ In so doing, Barth (and Rahner) returned the church to "the trinitarian doctrine of God which was decisively formulated in the Nicene-Constantinopolitan Creed in the fourth century upon which the whole church rests."⁵⁹ Working after Barth, Torrance sets the doctrine of the Trinity back into its place of centrality and thereby seeks to highlight how the doctrine of the Holy Trinity constitutes the fundamental ground and grammar of Christian theology. He does so, however, by adopting a radically different doctrine of the Trinity than Barth's Augustinianism, and thus finally rejects the *filioque*.

In this regard, the work of Torrance on the *filioque* takes on special significance as he did not simplistically accept or reject the doctrine, nor was he unaware of the so-called intrasystemic issues involved in the adoption of any dogma. Rather, as a result of these commitments it

---

57. This point, in fact, provides the rationale for Guretzki's major study, *Karl Barth on the Filioque*.

58. See the programmatic essay by Torrance, "Toward an Ecumenical Consensus on the Trinity," 77–102, where he discusses Rahner's *Grundaxiom* at length.

59. Torrance, *Trinitarian Perspectives*, 4.

is Torrance's long held conviction that the doctrine of the Trinity provides the best basis "for deep doctrinal agreement that cuts beneath and behind the historical divisions in the Church between East and West, Catholic and Evangelical, and to point the way forward for firmly based ecumenical agreement in other areas of traditional disagreement."[60] Hence an examination of Torrance's ultimate rejection of the *filioque* and his trinitarian theology after Barth may pay rich dividends for those of us working not only after Barth but now after Torrance as well.

Torrance on Barth and the *Filioque*

Throughout his career Torrance considered the *filioque*, and given his theological interest and ecumenical efforts with Eastern Orthodoxy, brokered a "solution" to the controversy which the World Alliance of Reformed Churches and the Eastern Orthodox Church came to accept in an Agreed Statement in 1991.[61] Torrance regarded the Agreed Statement as one of the most significant events in his entire ministry. It is Gary Deddo's conviction that Torrance's contributions to resolving the long-standing division over the insertion of the *filioque* clause into the Nicene Creed will "stand as perhaps Torrance's greatest contribution to the life of the church."[62] While we may agree with the intent of Deddo's comments, it is hard to share his enthusiasm, especially considering the fact that since the publication of Torrance's proposal relatively few theologians from East or West have taken the time to consider it let alone adopt it in any formal way.[63] Whether this may happen in the future remains to be seen.

---

60. Ibid., 5.

61. See Torrance, *Trinitarian Faith*, 231–47; Torrance, *Christian Doctrine of God*, 168–92, Torrance's final position on the *filioque*. For the official text of "The Agreed Statement on the Trinity," see *Theological Dialogue between Orthodox and Reformed Churches*, vol. 2, 219–26. The Agreed Statement and various other explanations on it can be found in Torrance, *Trinitarian Perspectives*.

62. Deddo, "Holy Spirit in T. F. Torrance's Theology," 107.

63. One theologian who has taken notice of it is Colyer, *How To Read T. F. Torrance*, 233–41. Guretzki's, *Karl Barth on the Filioque*, an otherwise fine study, ignores the Agreed Statement altogether, even when Guretzki includes a specific analysis of Torrance's *filioquism* (see ibid., 40–44; 197–213), despite showing an awareness of it in an earlier article, ibid., "Filioque," 184 n. 7.

Torrance began his 1963 essay, "The Relevance of the Doctrine of the Spirit for Ecumenical Theology," as follows: "It is one of the curious features of church history that the Western Church which had officially championed the addition of the *filioque* clause to the Nicene-Constantinopolitan Creed has tended in practice to ignore it, whereas the Eastern Church which decidedly rejected it has tended to uphold the emphases which it was designed to safeguard—without of course ever agreeing to the formal statement that the Spirit proceeds from the Son as well as the Father."[64] This statement provides us with a suitable window into Torrance's position *vis-à-vis* the *filioque*. While Torrance rejects the insertion of the *filioque* clause into the Creed he clearly believes the theology it seeks to safeguard is acceptable, not only to the West but importantly to the East.[65] According to Torrance, acceptance of the theology behind the *filioque* serves certain key functions. First, it retains a sense of the Spirit's holiness and majesty as one of the persons of the Godhead but at the same time asserts that the Holy Spirit is the Spirit of Sonship, the personal Spirit. Second, it reminds us that the Spirit has an essentially christocentric relation. A direct corollary of this christocentric relation is a denial of natural theology. In a terse statement we read, "The *filioque* is another way of saying *solo Christo, solo verbo, sola gratia, sola fide*."[66] In this way the *filioque*, in its first period of usage, was a guard against the threat of Arianism.

Of course, as has been well documented, the rejection of the *filioque* in the East is attributable to at least two reasons. First, on political grounds it was unconstitutionally inserted into the Creed; only an ecumenical council may alter an ecumenical creed. Second, on historical grounds, in the face of Arian, Macedonian, and Tropici assertions that the Spirit was a creature of the Son, the East sought to uphold and insist on the procession of the Spirit from the Father, the one source (*arche*) and fount (*pege*) of the Godhead, and to avoid a procession from the Son. Given the fact that the political and historical climate has shifted drastically, what should the church's position on the *filioque* be now?[67]

---

64. Torrance, *Theology in Reconstruction*, 229.

65. Torrance, "Introduction," xcvii–c. It is also clear by his mention of Eastern Orthodoxy that his acceptance of the *filioque* at this point was not due to a lack of awareness of the Orthodox position (xcix).

66. Ibid., 229–30.

67. This is a question Congar asks and answers in the following way: "The Roman Catholic Church could, under the conditions that I have outlined, suppress the Filioque

In lapidary fashion Torrance maintained in 1965, "perhaps it does not matter very much today whether the formal statement that the Spirit proceeds from the Son as well as from the Father is adopted or not."[68] What does matter is that the *homoousion* of the Son and the Spirit is maintained. Later in his career, when he came into more sustained and direct contact with Eastern theology, Torrance alters his stance on the *filioque* and positively rejects it outright not as heretical, but as misleading and insufficient, and in its place he offers an alternative proposition.

In *Theology in Reconstruction* Torrance maintains that Athanasius' theology of the Spirit implied what Augustine meant by the *filioque* and yet Athanasius never actually used that language.[69] For Athanasius the Spirit always proceeds *from* the Father and *through* the Son.[70] However, due to the analogies he adopted, source-river and light-radiance, when extended to include the Spirit in the form of source-river-water, and light-radiance-enlightenment, could not be pressed beyond their proper scope without implying two sources in a way the Arians would have seized upon. But Athanasius did not say the Spirit proceeds from the Father alone, for that would have contradicted his entire theology. When Athanasian analogies are understood within the ambit of his thoroughgoing *homoousial* doctrines of the Son and Spirit one can see that no subordination of the Spirit was intended, nor was a double procession,

---

in the creed, into which it was introduced in a canonically irregular way. That would be an ecumenical action of humility and solidarity which, if it was welcomed in its really 'genuine' sense by the Orthodox Church, could create a new situation which would be favourable to the re-establishment of full communion" (Congar, *I Believe in the Holy Spirit*, 3.214).

68. Torrance, *Theology in Reconstruction*, 230.

69. In addition to Athanasius, Torrance also looks to Epiphanius and Cyril of Alexandria for a solution to the *filioque*; Torrance, *Christian Doctrine of God*, 185. McIntyre, *Shape of Pneumatology*, 151, notes that in one place only Augustine says the Spirit proceeds from God who is Father, Son, and Holy Spirit (*De Trin* 15.31–36), not specifically or simply from the Father. I.e., the Spirit is "the Gift of God." McIntyre notes that Thomas F. Torrance argues that this is exactly Calvin's view of the *filioque* and is in line with Gregory of Nazianzus on the *filioque* (*Trinitarian Perspectives*, 35). This leads McIntyre to muse: "It would be an interesting thought, maybe no more, if Augustine were found to stand alongside Gregory of Nazianzus and Calvin on the subjection of the procession of the Spirit." See Calvin, *Institutes*, 1.13.2, 19; 1.13.20, 24; and Torrance, *Trinitarian Perspectives*, 19–20, 29. McIntyre's intuitions certainly seem correct although he may have miscalculated Torrance's position regarding Augustine's trinitarianism.

70. Torrance, *Theology in Reconstruction*, 218.

if by that is meant two equal sources or *archai*. This is, in Torrance's estimation, the same theology as that expressed in the original wording of the Creed at the Council of Nicaea (325): "Confessing that: We believe in one God ... And in one Lord Jesus Christ, the Son of God, begotten of the Father as only begotten, that is, from the essence of the Father, [*ek tes ousias tou Patros*]."⁷¹ Hence, the Son does not proceed from the *person* of the Father but from the *being* (*ousia*) of the Father, argues Torrance.⁷² From this early theology Torrance then engaged Eastern theological thought in depth resulting in his nuanced and developed theology that came to fruition in the 1990s, particularly through the ecumenical "Agreed Statement," which we shall now consider.

Throughout the years 1977 to 1991 the World Alliance of Reformed Churches (WARC) engaged with the Eastern Orthodox Churches in dialogue over the doctrine of the Trinity, and specifically the *filioque* as part of those discussions. Torrance took the lead in these discussions, which were initially with the WARC and the Greek Orthodox Churches through a series of consultations that took place between 1979 and 1983. By 1990 the conversation was widened to include the Pan-Orthodox Communion, meeting in Minsk, Russia, in September 1990. This group met again in Geneva and on March 13, 1991, and produced the "Agreed Statement on the Holy Trinity,"⁷³ which removed the *filioque* and spoke of the *monarchia* of the Father and of the Godhead, emphasized the *homoousial* relations of the three divine persons, and stressed a doctrine of *perichoresis* built around Torrance's idea of onto-relations. As a result the Agreed Statement spoke of the sending of the Spirit from the Father *through* the Son. Over several publications Torrance has narrated the content of the consultations and sought to popularize the Agreed Statement and the requisite rejection of the *filioque*.⁷⁴

In an essay detailing the main features of the Agreed Statement Torrance identifies four significant points. First, the Statement affirms the personal status of the Father, the Son, and the Holy Spirit but also

---

71. In 325 the Creed was altered and "from the essence of the Father" was replaced with "from the Father" [*ek tou patros*].

72. Torrance, *Christian Doctrine of God*, 141.

73. "Agreed Statement on the Holy Trinity."

74. The most important publications include: *Theological Dialogue between Orthodox and Reformed Churches*, vol. 1; *Theological Dialogue between Orthodox and Reformed Churches*, vol. 2; and *Christian Doctrine of God*. See Deddo, "Holy Spirit in T. F. Torrance's Theology," 89.

affirms as orthodox the personal status of the one Being of God. Thus in the doctrine of the Holy Trinity the one Being of God does not refer to static essence or abstract *ousia* but to the intrinsically personal "I Am" of God.[75] Second, the Statement lays stress on the *monarchy* of God, "or the one ultimate Principle of Godhead, in which all three divine Persons share equally, for the whole indivisible Being of God belongs to each of them as it belongs to all of them."[76] The *monarchy* is thus the triune Godhead *and* the person of the Father, but, strictly speaking, it is the *being* of the Father, the one triune Godhead, that *monarchy* actually refers to.[77] Third, and consequently, the Spirit proceeds from the Father, but given the previous definition of *monarchy*, "the Holy Spirit proceeds ultimately from the Triune Being of the Godhead."[78] Thus the Spirit proceeds out of the mutual relations within the one being of the Holy Trinity "in which the Father indwells the Spirit and is Himself indwelt by the Spirit."[79] And finally, the Agreed Statement recommends an approach to the Trinity that is neither from the three persons to the one God (Eastern), nor from the one being of God to the three Persons (Western), but rather, starts with the "*dynamic Triunity* of God as Trinity in Unity and Unity in Trinity."[80] As other essays highlight, the doctrine of *perichoresis* is being recommended here along Athanasian and Cyrillian lines.

Several years later in his *magnum opus*, *The Christian Doctrine of God*, Torrance's final position on the *filioque* is defined. Consistent with the theology within the Agreed Statement, Torrance writes: "It is when we apply the concept of *perichoresis* rigorously to this doctrine of the Holy Trinity together with the concept of the triune *monarchia* that it

75. Torrance, *Trinitarian Perspectives*, 112. It is on this point that "Torrance and Zizioulas are on the same page" (Del Colle, "'Person' and 'Being' in John Zizioulas' Trinitarian Theology," 73).

76. Torrance, *Trinitarian Perspectives*, 112.

77. Torrance and the architects of the Agreed Statement accepted the doctrine of the *monarchy* according to Athanasius, Gregory Nazianzen, and Cyril of Alexandria over that of the other Cappadocians and in so doing they rejected what may be termed standard, Palamite Eastern theology represented so ably by John Zizioulas. For critical engagement see Del Colle, "'Person' and 'Being' in John Zizioulas' Trinitarian Theology," 70–86.

78. Torrance, *Trinitarian Perspectives*, 113. At this point Torrance and Zizioulas find themselves diametrically opposed.

79. Ibid.

80. Ibid., 114, italics in original.

becomes possible for us to think through and restate the doctrine of the procession of the Holy Spirit from the Father in a way that cuts behind and sets aside the problems that divided the Church over the *filioque*."[81]

Hence Torrance's simple but profound solution is to assert that the procession of the Spirit must be *from* the Father *through* the Son[82] as they each mutually indwell each other as the one being of God.[83] Thus the Holy Spirit proceeds from the one *monarchia* of the triune God,[84] and as such, "from the Father and the Son" and "from the Father through the Son" are both correct statements; but not if they are understood in accordance with the view that *monarchia* is limited to the person of the Father; and not if they are understood in accordance with the view that there is a distinction between the underived deity of the Father and the derived deity of the Son and Spirit; and not if they are understood in accordance with the view that the Holy Spirit does not belong equally and completely *homoousially* with the Father and the Son in their two-way relation with one another in the divine Triunity.[85]

Agreeing on the language that "the Spirit proceeds *from* the Father *through* the Son," Athanasius, amongst others, was looked to in favor of certain of the Cappadocians, whose emphasis on the *monarchia* of the Father alone tended to threaten the status of the Son and the Spirit. Following Athanasius primarily, the Agreed Statement locates the unity of the Trinity not in the person of the Father but in the *perichoretic* Triunity of the being of God. This is what encourages Torrance to con-

---

81. Torrance, *Christian Doctrine of God*, 190.

82. Ibid.

83. Less attractive but no less profound is Moltmann's "solution" to the *filioque* found in his *Trinity and the Kingdom*, 185: "The Holy Spirit who proceeds from the Father of the Son." Under his proposal the *monarchy* of the Father is left intact but the Son is incorporated in a meaningful way. The Father is only Father in relation to the Son (not the Spirit); hence if the Spirit proceeds from the Father this presupposes the generation of the Son. Also the existence of the Son is presupposed along with the mutual relationship of the Father and the Son. So the Father is the natural origin of the Spirit not the Son, but not in a way that does not involve the Son. The works of the Trinity are indivisible. The Son is connected relationally. So the Spirit proceeds from the fatherhood of God, i.e., from the Father's relationship to the Son. This makes the inner-trinitarian relationship between Word and Spirit clearer. The two processions are simultaneous and in common. So the Spirit proceeds from the Father in the eternal presence of the Son, and so the Son is not uninvolved in it.

84. Torrance, *Christian Doctrine of God*, 190.

85. Ibid.

clude as early as 1965: "This being so we can forget about the *filioque* clause—it was entirely wrong to introduce it into the Ecumenical Creed without the authority of an ecumenical council—but we cannot allow to slip away from us the Athanasian teaching of the *homoousion* of the Spirit."[86] And so we read in *Trinitarian Perspectives*, written nearly thirty years later:

> The firm conviction that the Holy Spirit like the Son is perfectly consubstantial with the Father brought the doctrine of the Holy Trinity to its completion in the mind of the Catholic church, but at the same time it made clear the awesome truth that God has opened up for us a way of communion with himself, whereby he may be known in the inner trinitarian relations of his eternal Being. This is the understanding of the Holy Trinity which called forth from Gregory the Theologian and Calvin the Theologian alike ceaseless wonder, meditation, and worship.[87]

The way in which Torrance seeks to resolve the *filioque* dispute is what interests us here. Torrance's simple but profound solution that the procession of the Spirit must be *from* the Father *through* the Son as they each mutually indwell each other as the one being of God, could equally be expressed differently. Torrance could have said, but did not, that the procession of the Holy Spirit is *from* the Father, *through* the Son and *in* or *by* the being of the Spirit (*spirituque*). Or alternatively, he could have simply said, the Spirit is from the being of the Father, or just as simply, the (*hypostasis* of the) Spirit is from the Being of the Spirit. Each statement is synonymous within Torrance's trinitarian logic.[88] "Thus the procession of the Spirit is to be thought of not in any partitive way but only in a holistic way, as procession from the completely mutual relations within the one indivisible being of the Lord God who is Trinity in Unity and Unity in Trinity."[89]

In his appeal to the *homoousion* of the Son and the Spirit in an Athanasian sense, to the doctrine of *perichoresis,* and to the *monarchia* of

---

86. Torrance, *Theology in Reconstruction*, 219.

87. Torrance, *Trinitarian Perspectives*, 40.

88. Why Torrance did not make these synonymous statements is not known, but it may be due to the fact that he was recommending the Agreed Statement as widely as possible and so did not want to risk undue offence, leaving to those theologians working "after Torrance" the task of teasing out the implications of this theology. That is, at least, what I would like to think is the case.

89. Torrance, *Trinitarian Perspectives*, 113.

God residing both in the person of the Father—by appropriation only—but ultimately in the one triune Godhead, Torrance rejects Augustine's doctrine of the Trinity (Torrance never was enamored with Augustine's theology), and by implication Barth's also. In a work on Karl Barth's theology, Torrance expresses his fundamental rejection of Augustinian trinitarianism—and thus of this aspect of Barth's own theology: "So far as the earlier volumes of *Church Dogmatics* are concerned, my chief difference with Barth relates to the element of 'subordinationism' in his doctrine of the Holy Trinity, which I regard as a hang-over from Latin [Augustinian] theology. . . . This inevitably affects an approach to the *filioque* clause in the Western Creed."[90]

As a direct consequence of both the *homoousion* and *perichoresis* Torrance developed what he termed an *onto-relational* concept of the divine persons. By "onto-relational" Torrance implies an understanding of the three divine persons in the one God in which the ontic relations between them belong to what they essentially are in themselves in their distinctive *hypostases*. In short, onto-relations are being-constituting-relations. The differing relations between the Father, Son, and Spirit belong to what they are as Father, Son, and Spirit, so the *homoousial* relations between the three divine Persons belong to what they are in themselves as persons and in their communion with one another.[91] The divine Being and the divine communion are to be understood wholly in terms of one another. This onto-relational understanding of Person defined as person-in-relationship is also applicable to inter-human relations, but in a created way reflecting the uncreated way in which it applies to the trinitarian relations in God.[92] Thus onto-relations are not modes of existence for Torrance; "They are persons in the fullest sense, constituted by relationality that is homoousial and perichoretic, one with each other in their relational being and mutually inhering in each

---

90. Torrance, *Karl Barth, Biblical and Evangelical Theologian*, 131. In the same passage Torrance traces the same problem back through Cappadocian trinitarianism.

91. Torrance, *Christian Doctrine of God*, 102–3.

92. We can also see in this redefinition of "person" how the scientific method that Torrance has borrowed from Maxwell, Einstein, and Polanyi in terms of field theory and relativity is having a direct bearing on theological science, especially here in the realm of anthropology as it relates to being and personal being (Heidegger). Torrance sees the Fathers as working under the same scientific method and coming to the same theological conclusions. See his discussion of "person," and "being" in ibid., 103–5.

other," as Del Colle reminds us.⁹³ As a direct result Torrance affirms the traditional *taxis* or order of the divine persons with the stipulation that the generation of the Son and the procession of the Spirit from the Father applies only to the mode of their enhypostatic differentiation and not to the causation of their being.⁹⁴

As we have seen, one must not start with the unity or start with the Trinity but with the Triunity. That is, neither the general (essence) nor the personal (hypostases) should be emphasized to the relative neglect of the other. An adequate doctrine of the Trinity must put *essence* and *hypostasis* on the same level of reality and importance.⁹⁵ This is emphasized in the work of Paul Molnar, who reminds us that a doctrine of the Trinity must not start with plurality nor with unity, "but with the triune God who is simultaneously one and three."⁹⁶

In two places in his study on Barth's *filioquism* Guretzki turns his attention to Torrance's rejection of the *filioque* and seeks to bring Torrance into dialogue with Barth.⁹⁷ According to Guretzki, Torrance's is an exegetical-theological critique of Barth's theology. He also notes the fact that Torrance actually paid scant attention to Barth's doctrine of the *filioque*, choosing instead to focus upon his own proposals. Guertzki thus believes Torrance bypasses Barth altogether on this question. In a correct assessment of Torrance and Moltmann, however, Guretzki concludes that "by virtue of their alternative proposals, they are critical of Barth's doctrine of the *filioque* and see it as being a dogmatic hindrance."⁹⁸

Guretzki believes Torrance critiques Barth on the basis of a Western doctrine of double procession, rather than Barth's doctrine of common procession. He thus implicitly suggests that Torrance has misunderstood Barth's position at this basic level. On the basis of this

---

93. Del Colle, "'Person' and 'Being' in John Zizioulas' Trinitarian Theology," 79.

94. See ibid., 80, who cites Torrance, *Christian Doctrine of God*, 179; and Torrance, *Trinitarian Perspectives*, 135.

95. This point is made by Price, "Some Notes on Filioque," 515–35. Price argues to retain the *filioque* in an Augustinian sense (which he mistakenly describes as "double procession") in which the Spirit proceeds from the Father *principaliter* (as from an *arche*), and from the Father and the Son together *communiter*, since Father and Son are consubstantial (ibid., 535).

96. Molnar, *Divine Freedom*, 232.

97. See Guretzki, *Karl Barth on the Filioque*, 40–44, and 197–213.

98. Ibid., 40. Moltmann is also included in this section of Guretzki's study.

assumption Guretzki believes Torrance is objecting to the procession of the hypostatic origin of the Spirit from the *hypostasis* of the Father (East), or the *hypostases* of the Father and the Son (West). This allows Guretzki to conclude that Torrance's critique of both East and West is largely accurate; however, unbeknown to Torrance, this critique is actually shared by Barth.[99] Much of Guretzki's critique defends Barth's doctrine of the common procession of the Spirit from the Father and Son but not as if this is from two persons or modes of being in abstraction from the shared divine being, that is, the Spirit proceeds from God's triunity. According to Guretzki, "this is a significant point that nearly every scholarly commentary on Barth's doctrine of the *filioque* has missed, including Torrance himself."[100] This is a bold claim and one that simply cannot be sustained in relation to Torrance. Given the lack of direct statements in Torrance's theology of Barth's *filioquism* coupled with the fact that Torrance's trinitarianism posits just such a procession of the Spirit from the being of God, it would appear that a more likely explanation is that Torrance did understand Barth's theology precisely at this point, but understood that if upheld, as Torrance sought to do, it undermines an Augustinian doctrine of the Trinity and necessitates another trinitarianism, namely a pro-Nicene-Athanasian doctrine of God's triunity. It is not Barth's doctrine of common procession Torrance rejects, but the Augustinian unipersonalism inherent in it in the early parts of the *Church Dogmatics*. In such a trinitarianism there is no place, logically, for the *filioque* as it is commonly conceived. Where Torrance does advance on Barth's theology of the procession of the Spirit is that not only does the Spirit proceed from the "common-being-of-Father-and-Son's-modes-of-being," as per Barth,[101] but from the actual Triunity, the common being of the three persons, the Father, the Son, and the Holy Spirit, a point Guretzki himself notes but fails to explain.[102] In short, "the Holy Spirit proceeds from the One Being which belongs to the Son and to the Spirit as well as to the Father, and which belongs to all of them together as well as to each of them. . . . Strictly speaking, then, it must be said that the Holy Spirit proceeds from the one

---

99. Guretzki, *Karl Barth on the Filioque*, 198–204.

100. Ibid., 202.

101. The phrase is that of Guretzki's, ibid., 204.

102. Ibid.. See Torrance, *Christian Doctrine of God*, 186–88.

Monarchy of the Triune God."[103] On the basis of this fundamental but subtle difference Torrance accuses Barth's trinitarianism of an implicit subordinationism. As a result, Torrance contends again that this makes it possible "to think through and restate the doctrine of the procession of the Holy Spirit from the Father in a way that cuts behind and sets aside the problems that divided the Church over the *filioque*."[104]

Guretzki's examination of Torrance's difference with Barth concludes rather abruptly without any real explanation. The root difference between the two thinkers comes down to Barth's insistence on safeguarding the unique relationship between the Father and the Son both *ad intra* and *ad extra* in a way that Torrance did not find necessary. Barth thus sought to stay closer to what he thought was revealed in the economy while Torrance, Guretzki would have us believe, was more content to develop certain theo-*logical* conceptions and thus, presumably, move away from God's self-revelation in and through Jesus Christ.[105] The problem with this conclusion is, of course, a divergence over how to proceed from the economic to the immanent Trinity, an issue we have already had occasion to examine in both Barth and Torrance. Barth, as you will remember, refused to read back into the immanent Trinity the presence of the Spirit in Jesus' incarnation, limiting this to the humanity of Jesus alone, whereas Torrance, as with many others in the tradition, is not compelled to reserve the pneumatological *kairoi* of the Son's incarnation to the economy alone but sees an echo of the missions of the Triunity in the processions of the divine persons.[106] Thus the Spirit is as personally active in the immanent Trinity as he is amongst the economic Trinity in Torrance's doctrine of the Triunity.

As a final challenge Guretzki concludes his excursus on Torrance's doctrine of the *filioque* in the following way:

> Though Torrance's view of the Spirit's procession from the Monarchy of the Trinity might be dogmatically deduced, it is not clear that it is intelligible or coherent (i.e., What might it possibly mean for one divine hypostasis to proceed from all three hypostases, including itself?), nor whether Torrance's account faithfully reflects how the Gospel of John, for example,

---

103. Ibid., 190.
104. Ibid.
105. Guretzki, *Karl Barth on the Filioque*, 209–12.
106. See further in Habets, *Anointed Son*, 118–87.

can affirm the oneness of the Father and the Son in a way that it does not affirm a congruous oneness between the Father, Son, and Spirit. In this regard, Barth's dialectical view of the filioque, while certainly not without its own problems, might be a more satisfying way of responding to the Johannine witness in such a way that the Spirit is brought to bear upon the unique Father-Son relationship.[107]

As important as Guretzki's critique is, it is ultimately unconvincing. Torrance's doctrine of the Trinity has the lion's share of the early church on its side, is a largely correct reading of the pro-Nicene theology, and provides the basis for genuine ecumenical agreement while calling for further development. What Torrance did not provide, however, was a constructive trinitarianism that built upon the foundational doctrines he established. As with so much of his theological career, it fell to Torrance to clear away the epistemological and theological ground in order to establish a robust theological foundation upon which others may build. For these reasons we must look beyond Barth and now Torrance if we wish to achieve a doctrine of the Triunity that is able to encompass and uphold the doctrinal rungs of this orthodox ladder. The best such attempt to do this is, in our opinion, the reconceived doctrine of the Trinity offered by Thomas Weinandy.[108]

Reconceiving the Trinity with Thomas Weinandy

In light of the perceived inadequacies of the received trinitarian tradition (East and West), Thomas Weinandy, Executive Director of the Secretariat for Doctrine and Pastoral Practices, United States Conference of Catholic Bishops, presents a reconceived doctrine of the Trinity in *The Father's Spirit of Sonship: Reconceiving the Trinity*.[109] He considers

---

107. Guretzki, *Karl Barth on the Filioque*, 215.

108. The irony that it would take a Roman Catholic, and a Franciscan at that, to offer such a reconceived doctrine of the Trinity would surely not be lost on Torrance!

109. Weinandy, *Father's Spirit of Sonship*. Critical interaction with Weinandy's work is severely limited but includes Habets, "Little Trinitarian Reflection," 80–81; Habets, "Spirit Christology," 199–235; Habets, *Anointed Son*, esp. 222–27; and Robichaux and Pester, "*Father's Spirit of Sonship*," 53–58. Ormerod, "What Is the Goal of Systematic Theology?" 38–52, does make passing mention of it but only to suggest that "the proposals of Coffey and Weinandy in relation to the role of the Holy Spirit in the procession of the Son are hardly remarkable in contemporary Trinitarian theology" (ibid., 49). He then goes on to say they are "remarkably constrained" compared to those of

the weaknesses of the trinitarian constructions of both East and West to be situated in an inadequate, even flawed, conception of the role and function of the Holy Spirit within the trinitarian life. In this he shares a common conviction with Torrance. In the West the Father and Son play active roles while the Spirit assumes a passive function as merely the Love or Gift shared by the Father and the Son. Under this presentation how is the distinct personality of the Holy Spirit identified? In the East the *monarchy* of the Father is so pervasive that the notion of *perichoresis* is undermined. Each of these criticisms we have leveled at Barth's defense of the *filioque* in *CD* I/1, so Weinandy's work becomes all the more insightful here.

Without denying a biblical sense of the Father's *monarchy*, Weinandy argues that a proper understanding of the Trinity can only be attained if all three persons, logically and ontologically, spring forth in one *simultaneous, nonsequential*, eternal act in which each person of the Trinity subsistently defines, and equally is subsistently defined, by the other persons.[110] This drives Weinandy to present a thesis that, "may seem subtle, yet [is] one that I believe radically transforms and revolutionizes the Christian understanding of the Trinity."[111] His thesis is simply that "The Father begets the Son in or by the Holy Spirit. The Son is begotten by the Father in the Spirit and thus the Spirit simultaneously proceeds from the Father as the one in whom the Son is begotten. The Son, being begotten in the Spirit, simultaneously loves the Father in the same Spirit by which he himself is begotten (is Loved)."[112]

In this sense the Spirit proceeds from the Father and is identified as the one *in whom* the Father begets the Son. In this double movement the Father is defined (personed) as the Father of the Son and the Son too is defined (personed) as the Son of the Father. In short, all three persons of the Trinity, within their relationships, help constitute one another. With this trinitarian construction Weinandy's thesis is in

---

Leonardo Boff (*Trinity and Society*) and Gavin D'Costa (*Sexing the Trinity*). By contrast Farrow, "In the Spirit," 220, suggests that Weinandy's thesis is "relatively new to the dogmatic tradition."

110. Weinandy, *Father's Spirit of Sonship*, 15. Note the affinities with Calvin's formulation of the doctrine of the Trinity. See Warfield, "Calvin's Doctrine of the Trinity," 187–284; Torrance, "Calvin's Doctrine of the Trinity," 41–76; and Letham, *Holy Trinity*, 252–68.

111. Weinandy, *Father's Spirit of Sonship*, 17.

112. Ibid.

accord with that of Torrance, especially his view of trinitarian onto-relations. However, Weinandy adds some constructive elements missing in Torrance's work.

The presuppositions of the trinitarian argument are founded on several related points. First, the three persons of the Trinity as they reveal themselves in the economy of salvation manifest their inner trinitarian life and relationships. This is in accord with the general Rahnerian axiom that "the economic is the immanent Trinity." Second, the economic Trinity is primarily expressed in functional terms in the Bible, yet inherent in these functional categories lies a trinitarian ontology; "The *pro nobis* manifestation of the Father, the Son, and the Holy Spirit innately contains and naturally unveils *in se* ontological reality," writes Weinandy.[113] This trinitarian construct highlights the Father's *monarchy* without any subordinationist tendencies. To do this a mutual coinherence or *perichoresis* of action within the Trinity must take place whereby the persons are who they are because of the action of *all three*. While the Son and the Holy Spirit come forth from the Father this is not some prior ontological action but rather in the coming forth all three persons are who they are, and they are so precisely in reciprocally interacting upon one another, *simultaneously* fashioning one another as themselves.

What makes *perichoresis* intelligible is the active role of the Holy Spirit within the Trinity, both economically and immanently.[114] The Father begets the Son in the *spiration* of the Spirit so the Spirit makes the Father to be the Father of the Son and the Son to be the Son of the Father. The Spirit thus proceeds from both Father to Son and Son to Father and so becomes distinct in his mutual relation to them as the love by which they come to be who they are for one another. This conception moves beyond both Western and Eastern models. In the West

113. Ibid., 22. Weinandy devotes two chapters (2 and 3) to explicating the New Testament witness to the role of the Spirit in the life of Christ, especially focusing on his conception, baptism, death, and resurrection, before going on to examine the Pauline and Johannine literature. He thus follows Torrance over Barth in understanding Jesus relationship to the Spirit in more than anthropological and economic terms.

114. Weinandy adopts the premise that actions of the economic Trinity manifest the being of the immanent Trinity, thus the Spirit defines and confirms the incarnate Sonship of Jesus and the relationship with his "Abba" Father in the economy and likewise eternally defines the sonship of the Son and the fatherhood of the Father and in the same moment the Spirit is personed as the Spirit of fatherhood and the Spirit of sonship. Ibid., 53–85.

the Holy Spirit is Love shared between the Father and the Son. As such he is passive and impersonal. In the East the Son and Spirit proceed out from the *hypostasis* of the Father in a linear fashion. In this reconceived model the Holy Spirit is now given an active role within the Triunity that guarantees him a personal distinction. Within the Triunity the distinction of the persons is ordered upon *both action and origin*. From these are established the mutual relations by which the persons of the Trinity subsist and are distinguished.

The *monarchy* of the Father must be maintained within the one being of the Triunity and not prior to or outside it. In the East the tendency has been to see the Godhead as residing in the Person of the Father alone and he mediates divinity to the Son and Spirit. In the West there is the distinct impression that the Godhead is distinct from the three persons as an independent but apophatic *ousia* of oneness. Both are incompatible with the biblical revelation. The Godhead is neither the Father *alone* nor a solitary *substance* separate from the three persons. The Godhead is the Triunity. The one Godhead is the action of the Father begetting the Son and spirating the Spirit, thus sharing with them the whole of his deity constituting them as equally divine. In this way the *monarchy* of the Father is maintained but within the Triunity of persons.

Because the Son is begotten from the Father he is the Son and proceeds by way of generation. For this reason *filiation* is ascribed to the Son. Each of the terms "Father" and "Son" presuppose the other and the relationship between them. But this action, traditionally understood, is a passive one, whereby the Son is Son due to his begetting from the Father. Is there a sense in which he also has an active role of a reciprocal nature that equally constitutes his being the Son in relationship to the Father? This question can only be answered in light of the role of the Holy Spirit.

In order to differentiate the Spirit from the Son the early church spoke of the Son's *generation* and the Spirit's *spiration*. But exactly what the difference was the early church was at odds to adequately explain. Working with existing trinitarian paradigms we have no adequate explanation as to why the Spirit is not another Son or at the very least a *grandson* to the Father. The reason provided by our new paradigm is that "[the] Father is the Father in that he begets the Son in the Spirit. The Father spirates the Spirit in the same act by which he begets the Son, for the Spirit proceeds from the Father as the fatherly Love in whom or by whom the Son is begotten."[115]

This understanding of the Trinity maintains the *monarchy* of the Father as the *fons divinitatis* (fount of divinity) from whom came both the Son and the Spirit, without also positing any subordination within the Trinity (an Eastern tendency) or dividing *De Deo Uno* (the oneness of God) from the treatise *De Deo Trino* (the threeness of God) (a Western tendency). As the Word of God, the Father breathes forth the Son, which implies impulse and motion. This impulse or motion is the Breath of God, the *Pneuma*. Hence, Word and Spirit go together out from the Father in a mutual, coinhering relationship with each other. In the economy as in the immanent Trinity God is revealed as the Father who begets the Son in or by the Holy Spirit. The Son responds to the Father in reciprocal fashion as the obedient Son in or by the Holy Spirit.

What is distinctive about Weinandy's thesis is that the truly subsistent relation of the Holy Spirit is one related not only to the joint source of Father and Son (*filioque*) or Father only (*monarchy*) but rather that the Spirit actually defines or "persons" both Father and Son as much as the Father and the Son define his subsistent relation (*spirituque*). When we ask, "What is the personal role of the Holy Spirit comparable to that of fatherhood of the Father and sonship of the Son?" we can say, with Weinandy, the Holy Spirit is the completer of fatherhood and sonship within the persons of the Father and the Son. We read: "The Spirit (of love) then, who proceeds from the Father as the one in whom the Father begets the Son, both conforms or defines (persons) the Son to be the Son and simultaneously conforms or defines (persons) the Father to be the Father. The Holy Spirit, in proceeding from the Father as the one in whom the Father begets the Son, conforms the Father to be Father for the Son and conforms the Son to be Son for (of) the Father."[116]

Working with Rahner's *Grundaxiom* we can see in Scripture a number of pointers to this very thesis which may help us to fully grasp the dynamic. In Scripture the Spirit is called both the *Spirit of God* (Father) and the *Spirit of the Son*. We can take these two terms to mean the Spirit is the one who forms or conforms God as Father and the Son as Son. In turn we read that salvation consists in God making us his children (lit. *sons*) and so he becomes our Father in, by, or through the

115. Ibid., 69.
116. Ibid., 17.

Holy Spirit. Here God's work *ad extra* parallels those of his Being *in se*. As Weinandy puts it:

> The Spirit then not only allows us to call the Father "Abba," but it is the same Spirit that reveals the Father as "Abba" for us. Without this "Abba"—Spirit neither would God be "Abba." Analogously then, we can conclude that as the Holy Spirit makes God "Abba" for us *ad extra* so he conforms the Father as "Abba" to the Son within the immanent Trinity as well. As the Spirit of sonship conforms the Son to be the Son (love for the Father is the essence of sonship), so the Spirit of the Father conforms the Father to be Father (love for the Son is the essence of fatherhood).[117]

The church universal agrees that the distinction of the persons within the Trinity are ordered upon action and origin. From these are established the mutual relations by which the persons of the Trinity subsist and are distinguished. Exactly how we understand this is the cause of debate, however.

Reconceiving Divine Processions

In the West the Father is defined by paternity because he is the unbegotten or ingenerate source of the Son and the Holy Spirit. The East, in strongly defending the *monarchy* of the Father, has overemphasized the proceeding of the Son and Spirit from the Father *alone*. The person of the Father is then the *fons divinitatis* in an exclusive sense. The error of this Eastern development is to place the entire Godhead in the *hypostasis* of the Father alone.

Weinandy's thesis replaces both misconceptions and suggests that the one being of the Godhead is the Father giving the whole of his divinity to the Son and to the Holy Spirit and in so doing receiving from Son and Spirit his identity, if we may use such a term. However, both action and origin must be thought of in a strictly simultaneous, not chronological, fashion. The one Godhead, the one being of God, is the action of the Father begetting the Son and spirating the Spirit, and so sharing with them the whole of his deity, constituting them as equal persons and receiving from them his own being-constituting-relation. Thus the *monarchy* of the Father is maintained, but within the one being of God who is a trinity of persons. This upholds Torrance's crucial

117. Ibid., 37.

insights developed earlier, but goes further in clarifying the distinction of the persons within the Trinity ordered as they are upon action and origin. On this basis of the above we may affirm the following conclusion of Weinandy's:

> The person of the Father indeed constitutes the ontological being and personhood of the Son and the Holy Spirit, but he does so in the one being of God. The substance of God is not the Father. The being of God . . . is the Trinity which is the one act of the Father begetting the Son and spirating the Spirit. The eternal constituting of the persons takes place within . . . the one being of God, and therefore is the one being of God. There is neither a priority of oneness nor of threeness. Three persons are one God or one God is three persons.[118]

Advancing on Weinandy's thesis we can say that indeed the Father as a subsistent relation himself, is defined (personed) by the Son in the Spirit as much as the Son is defined (personed) by the Father in the Spirit, albeit in different ways. Hence the Father can also be said to proceed from the Godhead—the one dynamic, *simultaneous* being-constituting relations (onto-relations) of the three persons. His existence, even as the *monarchy*, is an in-existence, a *perichoretic* union with the Son and Spirit by which he is personed. Hence we may, with Boff, suggest that "If this is so, it follows that everything in God is triadic, everything is *Patreque, Filioque,* and *Spirituque.*"[119]

By way of summary we may affirm: The Son is Son because he is begotten from the Father and proceeds from the Father by way of generation. Filiation is ascribed then to the Son. The Son *eternally* comes forth from the Father as the Father's perfect image and offspring. Each of the terms "Father" and "Son" presupposes the other and the relationship between them. In terms of the received tradition the procession of the Son from the Father is inherently passive. It is a receiving only. Under this new model the Son is also given an active role in defining or personing the Father (and the Spirit). The same goes for the Father. The Father is Father in the act of begetting the Son in or by the Holy Spirit. A third time, the Spirit is the Spirit in proceeding from the Father through the Son and in personing the Father through the Son and in personing the Son from the Father. While Boff's suggestion has difficulties and

---

118. Ibid., 64.
119. Boff, *Trinity and Society*, 146.

risks flattening out the *axis* of the three divine persons, if not negating them completely, he is right to conclude that "Each person receives everything from the others and at the same time gives everything to the others. As they are Three Uniques, there are in fact never binary relations of opposites between them (Father to Son, or Father-Son to Holy Spirit) but only triadic ones of communication and communion."[120]

We have seen that the church fathers could not actually differentiate the *processions* of the Son and the Holy Spirit except to say the Son is *begotten* and the Spirit *proceeds* (is *spirated*). Why there were not two sons or why the Spirit was not a grandson could not be fully or finally explained. Many simply appealed to mystery. Weinandy's thesis seeks to probe both Eastern and Western traditions to come up with this more developed understanding: "The Father is the Father in that he begets the Son in the Spirit. The Father spirates the Spirit in the same act by which he begets the Son, for the Spirit proceeds from the Father as the fatherly Love in whom or by whom the Son is begotten."[121]

In God, knowing and loving are simultaneous acts—the begetting and spirating come forth from the Father as distinct, but concurrent, acts. *The Father does not, even logically, first beget the Son and then love the Son in the Spirit.* The begetting and the proceeding mutually inhere in one another. When we add to this, beyond what Weinandy explicitly does, the eternal coming *to be* of the person of the Father (who cannot *be* without the Son and the Spirit), then we have a coherent doctrine of coinherence: three simultaneous instances of action and origin from the one triune Godhead.

Let me summarize then how begetting and spirating may be differentiated. According to Weinandy:

> The Son is Son because, having been begotten by the Father in the Spirit of sonship, he loves the Father as Son. This act of filial love, enacted in the Spirit of sonship, is what makes him the Son. This means that the Father is the Father not only because he begets the Son, but also because, in the begetting of the Son, the Son loves the Father, and so as Son helps constitute the Father as Father. The Father would not be Father unless he had a Son who loved him as Son. Now the cornerstone which holds together this fatherly act of lovingly begetting the Son and this

---

120. Ibid., 147.
121. Weinandy, *Father's Spirit of Sonship*, 69.

filial act of the Son loving the Father is provided by the action of the Spirit.[122]

In even stronger terms Weinandy offers the following: "It is by the Spirit that the Father substantiates or 'persons' himself as Father because it is by the Spirit that he begets the Son. In so doing the Father substantiates or 'persons,' by the same Spirit, the Son and the Son personally re-acts, and so is 'personed' in the Spirit of sonship, as Son of the Father."[123]

Two biblical illustrations are used by Weinandy to support this thesis, that of the use of *Abba* and the divine Word/speech. We shall only note the first. The word "Abba" contains within it the new trinitarian ontology Weinandy is presenting. The term "Abba" testifies to the *monarchy* of the Father. The Father is "Abba" in that he begets the Son, and the Son is Son by crying out "Abba" to the Father. Moreover, this "Abba," as pertaining to the Father and to the Son, is suffused with the Holy Spirit. The Spirit makes this mutual and reciprocal "Abba"-love to be "Abba"-love. It is the Spirit who conforms the Father as "Abba" to the Son and conforms the Son to cry "Abba!" to the Father. The Spirit makes the Father and the Son to be what they are to one another because he proceeds from both as their mutual love for one another.

Why, then, is the Holy Spirit a person? He is so because of his unique subsisting relation. The Holy Spirit subsists precisely as the one in whom the Father and the Son are named and thus personed and simultaneously the Spirit is named or personed. The Father subsists in relation to the Son *only in the Holy Spirit* by whom he begat the Son. The Son subsists in relation to the Father *only in the Spirit* who conformed him to be Son. The Spirit subsists as pure relation (person) together with the Father and the Son in that he defines and sustains their relationship and so imparts or manifests their names. This is why the Spirit lacks a proper name (like Father or Son). His personhood is no less than that of the Father and the Son but it is, nevertheless, defined or personed in a different manner; spiration as opposed to begotten. "The Holy Spirit is the hidden or unnamed person or 'who' because the very nature of his subjectivity as a subsistent relation is to illuminate or, more deeply, to substantiate or person the Father and the Son for one another."[124]

---

122. Ibid., 73.
123. Ibid.
124. Ibid., 83–84.

The external *missions* of the divine persons are related to their internal *processions* and the internal *processions* are the basis for the external *missions*, just as Torrance indicated earlier. So we cannot do away with the eternal processions as many today would want. With Aquinas I want to stress that "Since procession always supposes action, and as there is an outward procession corresponding to the act tending to external matter, so there must be an inward procession corresponding to the act of remaining within the agent."[125]

Already within Scripture there is too much evidence for a concrete and specific doctrine of the immanent Trinity to simply write this study off as a piece of esoteric speculation or impractical theologizing. With the aid of Weinandy's reconceived trinitarian ontology we can build upon it in the following way.

Rather than the traditional models of two processions, that of the Son and the Spirit, in which the Spirit is essentially passive, Weinandy's thesis must be developed further in order to elaborate more consistently the *perichoretic* relations of the three persons of the Triunity.[126] As Weinandy writes: "While, both in the East and the West, the *perichoresis* or *circumincession* has been seen as the result of the begetting and the spirating, I have emphasized the *perichoresis* of the actions themselves; . . . the acts of begetting and spirating co-inhere in one another and thus account for why the persons themselves co-inhere. Actually, the persons themselves are the co-inhering acts. This *perichoresis* of the trinitarian act gives an unprecedented dynamism to the persons and to their life within the Trinity."[127]

Weinandy stops short of positing three eternal processions and probably for good reason. However, if three processions are not appropriate what may be the next best thing? The doctrine of *perichoresis* presented by Torrance and developed by Weinandy suggests an onto-relational understanding of the divine persons, without the exception of

125. Aquinas, *Summa Theologiae I*, q.27, 1.
126. Hence the critique of the thesis of LaCugna, *God with Us*. Her central axiom is that "*theologia* is fully revealed and bestowed in *oikonomia*, and *oikonomia* truly expresses the ineffable mystery of *theologia*" (ibid., 221.) This collapses the Trinity into the economy to the point where the Trinity does not exist ontologically apart from the economy. Thus the Trinity is not the three persons of Father, Son, and Holy Spirit but rather an impersonal theological principle of revelation. For a full critique see Molnar, *Divine Freedom*, 1–25.
127. Weinandy, *Father's Spirit of Sonship*, 79–80.

the Father. So while it may be imprudent to suggest the Father *proceeds* from the one being of the Godhead, may I suggest the following:

1. The Father is Father because he is the unbegotten *monarchy* and because he is personed and derives his *monarchy* from begetting the Son (and spirating the Spirit) and being loved by the Son as his Father.

2. The Son is Son because he is the eternally begotten of the Father, and he is the one who loves the Father as the eternal Son.

3. The Spirit is the Spirit because he eternally proceeds from the Father through the Son and because he is the Spirit of fatherhood and the Spirit of sonship.

Weinandy refers to a proposal of Leonardo Boff's which I believe carries us forward significantly when Boff argues for the following, briefly referred to earlier:

> Using the descriptive terminology of tradition, we would say: the Father "begets" the Son in the bosom of the Spirit (*Filius a Patre Spirituque*), or the Father "breathes out" the Spirit together with the Son (*Spiritus a Patre Filioque*). . . . In this way we should have a trinitarian equilibrium since all is triadic and perichoretically implied; all is shared, circulated, reciprocally received, united through communion. . . . [T]his perichoretic communion does not result from the Persons, but is simultaneously with them, originates with them. They are what they are because of their intrinsic, essential communion. If this is so, if follows that everything in God is triadic, everything is *Patreque*, *Filioque*, and *Spirituque*. The coordinate conjunction "and" applies absolutely to the three Persons: "and" is always and everywhere. . . . The Son is "begotten" by the Father in the Holy Spirit. . . . In trinitarian terms, The Father "begets" the Son Spirituque, that is, in communion with the Holy Spirit.[128]

While the Latin terms Boff employs are disposable, his general thesis has considerable merit. When Boff's proposal is shorn of its sexual imagery (which I did not reproduce) and tritheistic leanings, that is, when it is chastened by Weinandy's proposal and informed by Torrance's robust accounts of *perichoresis*, it offers a way forward.

---

128. Boff, *Trinity and Society*, 6, 146–47; see also 84, 204–5, 236. Cited in Weinandy, *Father's Spirit of Sonship*, 80–81. Weinandy himself rejects a third procession and is reticent about using the proposed term of Boff's, "*Patreque*."

The Father, the Son, and the Holy Spirit are simultaneously personed in distinctive ways, ways that maintain a divine order (*taxis*) that maintains the *monarchy* of the Father, and the "shyness" or translucent-but-no-less-personal quality of the Spirit, along with the unique *filial* relationship of the Son.

Trinitarian theology after Barth does not and will not progress in one direction. There is no single path for those working *after* him to follow. Indeed, many will choose divergent, even mutually exclusive paths to follow and still claim Barth as their motivation. Who knows what Barth would have thought of that? What is clear is that trinitarian theology after Barth shows great energy and offers great promise.[29]

---

129. I am grateful to Thomas Weinandy, David Guretzki, and Gannon Murphy for reading this chapter in draft form and providing many helpful comments. David Guretzki also provided me with an advance copy of his work on Barth's *filioquism*, for which I am extremely grateful. All page numbers to this final work refer to an early proof copy.

Bibliography

Aquinas, Thomas. *Summa Theologiae.* Westminster, MD: Christian Classics, 1920.
Barth, Karl. *Church Dogmatics.* 4 vols. Edinburgh: T. & T. Clark, 1956–75.
———. *Göttingen Dogmatics.* Grand Rapids: Eerdmans, 1991.
———. *Der Römerbrief.* Munich: 1926. English translation: *The Epistle to the Romans.* Translated by Edwyn C. Hoskyns. 6th ed. London: Oxford University Press, 1968.
Bloesch, Donald G. *The Holy Spirit.* Downers Grove, IL: InterVarsity, 2000.
Boff, Leonardo. *Trinity and Society.* Kent: Burns & Oats, 1988.
Bray, Gerald. "The Double Procession of the Holy Spirit in Evangelical Theology Today: Do We Still Need It?" *Journal of the Evangelical Theological Association* 41 (1998) 415–26.
Calvin, John. *Institutes of the Christian Religion.* Edited by J. T. McNeill. Translated by F. L. Battles. Philadelphia: Westminster, 1960.
Chung, Miyon. "An Introduction to the Pneumatologies of Karl Barth and Eberhard Jüngel," Part 1. *Torch Trinity Journal* 7 (2004) 106–21.
———. "An Introduction to the Pneumatologies of Karl Barth and Eberhard Jüngel," Part 2. *Torch Trinity Journal* 8 (2005) 60–72.
Coffey, David. "The Roman 'Clarification' of the Doctrine of the Filioque." *International Journal of Systematic Theology* 5 (2003) 3–21.
Colyer, Elmer. *How to Read T. F. Torrance: Understanding His Trinitarian and Scientific Theology.* Downers Grove: IVP, 2001.
Congar, Yves M. J. *I Believe in the Holy Spirit.* Translated by D. Smith. 3 vols. New York: Seabury, 1983.
D'Costa, Gavin. *Sexing the Trinity: Gender, Culture, and the Divine.* London: SCM, 2000.
Deddo, Gary W. "The Holy Spirit in T. F. Torrance's Theology." In *The Promise of Trinitarian Theology: Theologians in Dialogue with T. F. Torrance*, edited by E. M. Colyer, 81–114. Lanham, MD: Rowman & Littlefield, 2001.
Del Colle, Ralph. "'Person' and 'Being' in John Zizioulas' Trinitarian Theology: Conversations with Thomas Torrance and Thomas Aquinas." *Scottish Journal of Theology* 54 (2001) 70–86.
Erickson, Millard J. *Christian Theology.* Grand Rapids: Baker, 1985.
Farrow, Douglas. "In the Spirit: A Review Article." *Expository Times* 107 (1996) 220.
Grenz, Stanley J. *Theology for the Community of God.* Nashville: Broadman & Holman, 1994.
Grider, J. Kenneth. *A Wesleyan-Holiness Theology.* Kansas City: Beacon Hill, 1994.
Guretzki, David. "The Filioque: Assessing Evangelical Approaches to a Knotty Problem." In *Semper Reformandum: Studies in Honour of Clark H. Pinnock*, edited by S. E. Porter and A. R. Cross, 182–206. Carlisle, UK: Paternoster, 2003.
———. *Karl Barth on the Filioque.* Surrey: Ashgate, 2009. All page numbers to this work in this chapter refer to an early proof copy supplied to me by the author.
Habets, Myk. *The Anointed Son: A Trinitarian Spirit Christology.* Princeton Theological Monograph Series 129. Eugene, OR.: Pickwick, 2010.
———. "A Little Trinitarian Reflection." *Evangel* 19:3 (2002) 80–81;
———. "Spirit Christology: Seeing in Stereo." *Journal of Pentecostal Theology* 11:2 (2003) 199–235.

Hendry, George. "'From the Father and the Son': The *Filioque* after Nine Hundred Years." *Theology Today* (1955) 449–59.

———. *The Holy Spirit in Christian Theology*. London: SCM, 1957.

Heron, Alasdair I. C. "'Who Proceedeth from the Father and the Son': The Problem of the Filioque." *Scottish Journal of Theology* 24 (1971) 149–66.

Hunsinger, George. "The Mediator of Communion: Karl Barth's Doctrine of the Holy Spirit." In *Disruptive Grace: Studies in the Theology of Karl Barth*. Grand Rapids: Eerdmans, 2000.

Jenson, Robert W. "You Wonder Where the Spirit Went." *Pro Ecclesia* 2 (1993) 296–304.

Laats, Alar. *Doctrines of the Trinity in Eastern and Western Theologies: A Study with Special Reference to K. Barth and V. Lossky*. Frankfurt: Lang, 1999.

LaCugna, Catherine M. *God with Us: The Trinity and the Christian Life*. San Francisco: Harper, 1991.

Letham, Robert. *The Holy Trinity: In Scripture, History, Theology, and Worship*. Philipsburg: Presbyterian and Reformed, 2004.

McCormack, Bruce L. *Karl Barth's Critically Realistic Dialectical Theology: Its Genesis and Development, 1909–1936*. Oxford: Clarendon, 1995.

McIntyre, James. *The Shape of Pneumatology: Studies in the Doctrine of the Holy Spirit*. Edinburgh: T. & T. Clark, 1997.

Molnar, Paul D. *Divine Freedom and the Doctrine of the Immanent Trinity*. New York: T. & T. Clark, 2002.

Moltmann, Jürgen. *The Spirit of Life: A Universal Affirmation*. Translated by Margaret Kohl. Minneapolis: Fortress, 1992.

———. "Theological Proposals Towards the Resolution of the Filioque Controversy." In *Spirit of God, Spirit of Christ*, edited by Lukas Vischer, 164–73. London: SPCK, 1981.

———. *The Trinity and the Kingdom: The Doctrine of God*. Translated by Margaret Kohl. Minneapolis: Fortress, 1993.

Ormerod, Neil. "What Is the Goal of Systematic Theology?" *Irish Theological Quarterly* 74 (2009) 38–52.

Pannenberg, Wolfhart. *Systematic Theology*. Vol. 1. Grand Rapids: Eerdmans, 1991.

Pinnock, Clark H. *Flame of Love: A Theology of the Holy Spirit*. Downers Grove, IL: InterVarsity, 1996.

Pontifical Council for Promoting Unity. "The Greek and Latin Traditions about the Procession of the Holy Spirit." In *L'Osservatore Romano* N.38 no.1408 (20 September 1995) 3, 6.

Price, Charles P. "Some Notes on the Filioque." *Anglican Theological Review* 83.3 (2001) 515–35.

Reymond, Robert L. *A New Systematic Theology of the Christian Faith*. Nashville: Nelson, 1998.

Robichaux, Kerry S., and John Pester. "*The Father's Spirit of Sonship*: A Review Article." *Affirmation and Critique* 1 (1996) 53–58.

Smail, Thomas. "The Doctrine of the Holy Spirit." In *Theology beyond Christendom*, edited by J. Thompson, 87–110. Allison Park, PA: Pickwick, 1986.

———. *The Giving Gift*. London: Darton Longman & Todd, 1994.

———. "The Holy Spirit in the Holy Trinity." In *Nicene Christianity: The Future for a New Ecumenism*, edited by C. Seitz, 149–65. Grand Rapids: Brazos, 2001.

Stackhouse, John G. *Evangelical Landscapes: Facing Critical Issues of the Day.* Grand Rapids: Brazos, 2002.

Tavard, George H. "A Clarification on the Filioque?" *Anglican Theological Review* 83 (2001) 507–14.

Torrance, Thomas F. "The Agreed Statement on the Trinity." In *Theological Dialogue between Orthodox and Reformed Churches*, vol. 2, edited by T. F. Torrance, 219–26. Edinburgh: Scottish Academic Press, 1993.

———. *The Christian Doctrine of God.* Edinburgh: T. & T. Clark, 1996.

———. "Introduction." In *The School of Faith: The Catechisms of the Reformed Church*, translated and edited by T. F. Torrance, xcvii–c. London: James Clarke, 1959.

———. *Karl Barth, Biblical and Evangelical Theologian.* Edinburgh: T. & T. Clark, 1990.

———. *The School of Faith: The Catechisms of the Reformed Church.* Translated and edited by T. F. Torrance. London: James Clarke, 1959.

———. *Theological Dialogue between Orthodox and Reformed Churches.* Vol. 1. Edited by T. F. Torrance. Edinburgh: Scottish Academic, 1985.

———. *Theology in Reconstruction.* Grand Rapids: Eerdmans, 1965.

———. "Toward an Ecumenical Consensus on the Trinity." In *Trinitarian Perspectives: Toward Doctrinal Agreement*, by Thomas F. Torrance, 77–102. Edinburgh: T. & T. Clark, 1994.

———. *The Trinitarian Faith: The Evangelical Theology of the Ancient Catholic Church.* Edinburgh: T. & T. Clark, 1988.

Warfield, Benjamin B. "Calvin's Doctrine of the Trinity." In *Calvin and Augustine*, edited by Samuel G. Crig, 187–284. Philadelphia: Presbyterian and Reformed, 1974.

Weinandy, Thomas G. *The Father's Spirit of Sonship: Reconceiving the Trinity.* Edinburgh: T. & T. Clark, 1995.

Williams, Rowan. "Barth on the Triune God." In *Karl Barth: Essays in His Theological Method*, edited by S. W. Sykes, 147–93. Oxford: Clarendon, 1979.

Zizioulas, John. "On Being a Person: Towards an Ontology of Personhood." In *Persons, Divine and Human*, edited by Christoph Schwöbel and Colin Gunton, 33–46. Edinburgh: T. & T. Clark, 1991.

———. "One Single Source: An Orthodox Response to the Clarification on the Filioque." www.orthodoxresearchinstitute.org/articles/dogamtics/john_zizioulas_single_source.htm (accessed 11.3.2009).

8

The Triune Savior of the World

Andrew Burgess

Introduction

This essay will explore the nature of salvation as a work of the triune God. A key claim is that failure to develop a theology of salvation within a properly triune framework leads to theological distortion, with the potential to damage the self-understanding of the church in relation to partnership in God's mission. This also involves the assertion that a proper understanding of the *telos* of salvation is essentially a trinitarian matter as we are led to examine the saving purpose of God for all creation and for humans in particular.

To begin with some necessary commonplaces, Colin Gunton wrote that everything "looks different when theologised with and through the doctrine of the Trinity,"[1] and he was absolutely right. Robert Jenson put it this way: trinitarian theology "is not initially a sort of reflective enterprise; . . . initially it is rather the first level act of calling on God by the triune name, and of making prayers and sacrifices that follow the triune logic and use the triune rhetoric. And in this mode, trinitarian theology does not have a point, it *is* the point."[2] If the doctrine of the Trinity is orthodoxy—if it is right belief—then it is not merely "doctrine" in the sense that modernity, and it seems much of postmodernity also, mischaracterizes ideas as abstractions without anchor or meaning in the world of being and doing. If the Trinity is right doctrine then God *is*

---

1. Gunton, *Father, Son, and Holy Spirit*, 22.
2. Jenson, "What Is the Point of Trinitarian Theology?" 31.

Trinity, and all reality, all thinking, being and doing are to be illumined by that truth.

That a Christian theology of salvation must be trinitarian in form and understanding is therefore somewhat redundant. Soteriology as it wrestles with the reality of the saving God and saved creation cannot but begin with the assumption that the God who saves is the Holy Trinity, and yet from the beginning the direction of thought has rightly moved in the opposite direction; the saving work of God in Jesus of Nazareth is the source of the understanding of God as the Triune One.[3] The movement of our understanding in both directions must in fact be maintained. There is a virtuous circularity here. Belief in the triunity of God must condition and shape any attempt to describe the salvation God gives, and equally the reality of the saving birth, life, death, resurrection, *and* the ongoing ascended life of Jesus of Nazareth must be the primary ground of our description of the Trinity.

This means that attempts to describe what it is that God does in saving must be faithful to the relevant data—the reality of Jesus as he reveals God's triunity—and that this faithfulness must apply just as fully to those parts of our soteriology which speak of the *telos* of salvation. What follows therefore falls broadly into three sections: a very brief sketch of the movement from understanding Jesus to worshipping God as Trinity, involving a claim that failure to move from Jesus of Nazareth to description of the ontological Trinity is failure to take him seriously; secondly, an attempt to offer insights around a trinitarian depiction of salvation, with particular reference to questions such as "What is done?," "By whom?," "For whom?" and "To whom?"; thirdly, the goal of salvation comes into view with its own set of trinitarian dynamics.

The Necessary Move from Soteriology to Christology and Trinity

Much has been written on this matter, and nothing of worth will be added to it here, but we may note, even now, the reluctance of some contemporary theologians to allow the move from the story of Jesus of Nazareth, a story of human particularity and historicity, to ontological

---

3. Within the variety of starting points for grounding the doctrine of the Trinity almost all begin with the reality of Jesus, whether in revelation *per se*, or the cross, to name two strong contenders.

claims for the eternal being of God. Reasons for such reluctance are rather obvious, with discomfort at the sheer scale of the claims not least among them. Yet these claims, with their entire enormity, are inherent within the New Testament itself and have always occasioned shock and discomfort—"Paul, great learning is driving you mad!" The occasion can be removed by doing away with claims of Jesus and his disciples—"God was in Christ reconciling the world" can be discarded as an over-the-top gloss—but once we have discarded all the bits of the New Testament that shock our sensibilities we have nothing of value left!

To focus directly on Barth for a moment, clearly we must be aware of the ontological implications in the claim that God is revealed in Jesus of Nazareth and that God is both subject and object of this self-revelation. The assertion that this is precisely where Barth anchors his doctrine of the Trinity may be upheld as an "accurate oversimplification."[4] The God who is truly present in the Incarnate Son is undeniably the God of all eternity—the alternative is some form of Sabellianism in which the real God remains somewhere hidden behind this history, and the connection between the reality of Jesus and the ultimate reality of God is lost.[5]

However, the argument for maintaining that the God we meet in Jesus is in fact the Eternal God, truly revealing Godself and creating in us the capacity for reception of and response to that revelation, cannot be and is not upheld merely because we fear that we will have less (or nothing) to say if we surrender it. Our theological faithfulness is not a matter of some sort of utilitarianism, where we hold to certain views with an ever increasing desperation and shrill sound to our voices because we fear to lose the only piece of ground from which we can hope to speak. The fundamental question of theology is not "Will I have something to say?" but "Is this faithful to God?" Revelation demands as a faithful response our assent that the Lamb of God who takes away the sin of the world is none other than God the Son who from all eternity is

---

4. Dalferth follows Jüngel in describing the earlier emphasis in *Church Dogmatics* as more upon revelation as the ground of trinitarian thought and the later as more upon Christology, especially the distinction between Father and Son in the event of the cross. See Dalferth, "Eschatological Roots," 155–56.

5. The technical matter here is the affirmation that the identity of the Son is found in the union of God and human *both ensarkos* and *asarkos*, i.e., that this is the identity of God from all eternity, the Father of *this* Son, the Son of *this* Father, and the Spirit of *these* two.

to be worshipped and glorified with the Father and the Spirit as the one God of Abraham, Isaac, and Jacob.

Historically, of course, this revelation of God is dominated by the economy of salvation. Jesus Christ, the particular man from Galilee, is God the Redeemer, and God's self-revealing is itself at the core of salvation. The eternal triunity of God is therefore understood to interrupt, disrupt, and even overcome the march of history and human notions of progress in the particular history of Jesus of Nazareth as the history *par excellence* of God's saving work in God's own creation.[6] The Christ cannot be abstracted from this work and neither therefore can the doctrine of God, which is to say that "the doctrine of the Trinity must not be abstracted from the doctrine of the atonement."[7]

We must therefore state with full force and vigor, and with all humility and self-awareness in our limitation, that God the eternal Trinity is in fact the triune Savior of the world, for the history of God's saving work is identical with the self-revelation of this God. But this, of course, itself opens up the necessity of thought moving in the opposite direction—not as an act of capricious intellectualism outworking in self-sustaining circularity, but as another step of obedience, as the nature of the object of reflection necessarily shapes the act of thought and reflection itself. Rightly established on the ground of the Father's self-revelation, in the Son and by the Spirit, the doctrine of the Trinity must also offer insights back into, and even regulate the description of, its own ground in this same work of salvation God undertakes in the person of the Son.

The Triune Work of Salvation

One of the regulative features of doctrines is, obviously, what we may describe as the negative function—when a doctrine simply rules out certain modes of thought and description. A clear instance of this is the way that once established the doctrine of the Trinity rules out any

---

6. We may note in passing the absolute necessity that God be understood in distinction from the world, and from the march of history *per se*. This does not imply or require an understanding of God as somehow divorced from the ongoing life of the creation or absent from human history, in fact quite the reverse, but it does involve the free agency of God in distinction from and *therefore* in relationship with the whole creation and the whole of history.

7. Gunton, *Father, Son, and Holy Spirit*, 25.

description of atonement or reconciliation which is not itself susceptible of trinitarian development or which implies any sort of rift in the activity or intention of the persons of God.

Salvation—of the creation, of human creatures—must be understood as the singular gracious work of God, the revelation of God opened up for us from Genesis to Revelation demands nothing less. This means, of necessity, the singular work of God in God's triunity. So we say that Jesus the Son is at work in his incarnation and that this work is redemptive, but we must also say that this is also the Father's act and the activity also of the Spirit. As the classic formula maintains: *opera trinitatis ad extra sunt indivisa*. This is nothing more or less than the gospel, the good news that the face of God is revealed in the life death and resurrection of Jesus. What does it mean to say with John that "God is love"? No more and certainly no less than that God has come in the flesh, and that we too have seen that glory, the glory of the Father's only Son, full of grace and truth. If the walk of the Son incarnate is a walk of obedience and worship, with the Father as the object, then the work done is the work of the Father. Christians therefore worship God who is the very agent of salvation.

This has clear implications for the interconnection and relationship of what are often called "judgment" and "grace"—a subject on which I have written elsewhere, and remain fascinated by—suffice it to say here that any elucidation of the economy of salvation which parcels out God's judgment to one person of the Trinity and locates the movement of grace in the activity of another simply will not do.[8] The implications for certain explications of substitutionary atonement are obvious, and although it has become rather too easy to sneeringly deprecate all forms of substitution as slavishly conservative and morally deficient, nonetheless the point is well made.

Leaving such matters to one side for the moment, we may inquire regarding the positive function of the doctrine of the Trinity in soteriology. The first answer to be given returns us immediately to the realm of

8. For the beginnings of a treatment of some key issues around the interpenetration of judgment and grace within the saving work of God, although without deeper engagement with the doctrine of the Trinity see my "Salvation as Judgement and Grace." In trinitarian faithfulness Barth is surely correct when he locates the "Yes" and the "No" of God to fallen human creatures (and, we might say, to the whole fallen creation) in the same event of Jesus and especially his cross, but without parceling out those two words into separate moments or to Son and Father respectively. See further below.

revelation, and brings us (as all theology should) to praise and worship of God, for the primary word we must speak is this: God is our Savior. Not merely that God wills salvation, true and wonderful as this is, and not only that this will of God's is fully effected in our truly being saved, and in the reconciliation of all creaturely reality, but that *it is God who saves*. The implications are vast, and two very brief points are all that space and time allow here:

First: what fundamental assurance and encouragement is inherent in the revelation of the God who saves! If God is for us who can be against us? Such statements are basic to the faith, but that should not imply that we avoid or ignore them.

Second: the achievement of Jesus is therefore fully adequate to save. There can be no question whether what Jesus does is what it actually takes to save sinners, or whether what he is about is sufficient for the salvation of the worst of sinners. There can be no mathematical equation in play, as in those historic discussions of the equation between the number of sins Jesus bore and the sins of those he saves. Is what Jesus does adequate to reconcile sinners with the righteous God of Sinai and of Isaiah, Amos, and Micah? Of course! He *is* this God. Is Jesus' offering of himself effective to return an entire creation to the Creator. Indeed, he *is* the Creator. The enormity of the incarnation, and therefore of the revelation of God as the saving Trinity cannot but humble even the most self-assured theologian and drive all Christians to pray and to work.

That brings us to examine the core questions for this essay: if it is the Triune God who saves, then "What is done?," "By whom?," "For whom?," and "To whom?"

What Is Done?

If we take this question to mean "what is achieved" the simple answer is "reconciliation" of the creation with God. Moreover, à la Barth and others, we may describe this reconciliation initially in terms of the union of God and humanity in the person of the Redeemer himself. Some go further and describe the operation of the eternal Son upon fallen human nature as the source of Jesus' obedient life. There are attendant dangers in talking this way, although it is not unusual to do so, as a sort of Apollinarianism lurks in the notion that the Logos is the operative force. Barth however does not fall into this trap, due to the way he conceives of the incarnation as the Logos becoming the God-human Jesus of Nazareth, rather than the Logos assuming and acting upon Jesus humanity—it is the fully human person who *is* the Logos and who is active, rather than the Logos acting *upon* that human person. As God *in the flesh* Jesus is already the reconciliation of *flesh* (and therefore creatureliness) with God in himself.

This is not, however, enough. Jesus' life death and resurrection involve more than the historical reality of the union of God and humanity in human form—or to put it better, the union itself involves more than static notions of ontological union. It involves the movement and action of God toward humanity, in the person of the eternal Son, but at the same time we must recognize the activity of this human toward and for the Father, and thus also toward and for other humans. Gunton describes the relationship of the Father and incarnate Son in this way: "There is a relation, taking place in time, which is and is not identical with the relation of the Son to the Father in the Spirit in eternity. It is identical, because what Jesus does in the flesh is the work of God the Father. It is not [identical] because this is an authentically human action. . . ."[9]

It is this genuine human action on the part of the God-human that is at one and the same time the true origin of the doctrine of the Trinity, for it is in the incarnation that distinction and otherness are revealed within the very being of God. Beyond this, the drama of God's human action in Jesus of Nazareth (no less divine in its being human action) provides the core of the answer to the question "What is it that is done to bring salvation?" Both poles of the trinitarian reality must be upheld: the work of Jesus is a genuine human work; and the work of Jesus is the work of God, Father, Son, and Holy Spirit. Radically, we are forced to maintain—against the instincts of much western philosophy, and much even of the Christian tradition—that the work of Jesus of Nazareth is truly human precisely in that it is the work of God. The incarnation allows us no space in which to radically oppose the being of God in eternal triunity and the possibility of God taking human flesh, or undertaking genuine human action. Thus, when we describe this work of God (or explicate God's activity in terms of attributes or "perfections") we do nothing less than name who God is. As Barth has it: "For as the triune God, both in regard to His revelation and to His being in itself,

9. Gunton, *Father, Son, and Holy Spirit*, 28.

He exists in these perfections, and these perfections again exist in Him and only in Him as the One who, both in His revelation and in eternity, is the same."[10]

Although various atonement models and theories shed light on the reality of God's reconciliation of the world within the act and being of Jesus, his faithfulness in relation to his Father in worship and obedience—as the human work of God incarnate—must remain central, and exercise some level of control over the variety of metaphors and models that can be offered. Some metaphors offer little and some simply fail, and an inescapable question is to be addressed in each case: is this way of thinking through salvation fundamentally trinitarian, or does it fail at the most basic level?

Who Is It Done By?

In anticipation of returning to "What is done?" let us move on to the question "Who by?" Recognizing that a considerable answer has already been offered in an examination of the agency of Jesus of Nazareth, and the claim that God is here at work, we now need to add to that description of agency.

An explanation of trinitarian agency in the work of the man Jesus does not flow without recognition of the role of the Spirit, and much has been said about this by theologians such as Gunton and Torrance. If the work of God in the man Jesus is *not* ascribed to the agency of his divine nature at the expense of his human nature—if we are to acknowledge the fully human work of the incarnate Son—then the role of the Spirit in enabling and empowering his worshipful human obedience comes to the fore. This is in no sense to be understood as a *replacement* of God's agency *in* the incarnate Son with an agency in the Spirit acting *upon* the incarnate Son, and especially not if that implies some sort of work of the Spirit in "possessing" the man Jesus for the purpose of God. What is best described is a full consonance between the personhood of the incarnate Son and the filling and empowerment of the Spirit so that the economy of each is maintained, but the absolute unity of trinitarian purpose and action is illuminated also. It is not the Spirit who walks the pathways of Galilee and Judea, and sets forth ineluctably toward Golgotha, just as it is not the Father who does so either. Yet it is the case that the Spirit

10. *CD* II/1, 324.

indwells and is at work in Jesus the incarnate Son as he does these things, and that, as the Spirit indwells and the Son walks, the Father is at work in both. The whole is a work of the one God in Trinity. What this yields, of course, is an opportunity to rethink a great deal about the truth of humanity, and the nature of genuine human agency in relation to God and in the power of the Spirit, and a far stronger pneumatology than the Western tradition is normally credited with achieving. We find ourselves in the realm of the divine appropriations and of the question of the simplicity of God. A brief glance at what remains a complex and controversial area of theology is required.

The tradition has placed a high priority on the simplicity of God, and rightly so. By simplicity has been meant that God's manifold activities and multiplicity of attributes do not in any wise involve contradiction or conflict in the being of God, and moreover that God does not have "parts." This is to say that mercy, for example, is not additional to God's essential being—an accident—but that God's merciful action is the same as God's *being* merciful: God *is* mercy. Further, the divine appropriations mean that any action applicable to one particular person of the Godhead must at the same time be described as the action of all three and therefore of the One God. However, the way in which the tradition has anchored God's simplicity has often been at the expense of triunity. So Augustine's classic treatment of appropriations maintains God's simplicity by smoothing out any differences or distinctions in the activity of the persons of the Trinity. Augustine can say that the heavenly voice heard at Jesus' baptism may equally said to be that of the Father, or the Spirit, or the Son himself, or of the Trinity as a whole.[11] What is altogether absent here is any notion that the Father, Son, and Spirit can be held to be equal in Godhead while being differentiated in relations, or utterly united in Trinity while having economies that are in some sense distinct (mutual). The formula *opera trinitatis ad extra sunt indivisa* comes to mean that the activities *ad extra* bear no direct relation to the being of God *ad intra*.

So Barth criticizes what he calls the "semi-nominalism" of the tradition in claiming that the multiplicity of attributes are merely a feature of human attempts to describe the simple (unitary) being of God.[12] Rather

---

11. Augustine of Hippo, *De Trinitate*, 1.8. On this see Jenson, *Systematic Theology*, vol. 1, 111.

12. See *CD* II/1, 335.

Barth offers a reworking in which the reality of incarnation and the actuality of revelation demand that theology recognize the multiplicity of attributes and variety of activities of God *ad extra* as inherent in the eternal being of God *in se, without contradicting the simplicity of God.*

The key here, as earlier is the willingness to make the move required by the gospel—the move that the doctrine of simplicity is at least intended to make and safeguard—to recognize that God's mercy toward us is none other than an act in which God has God's own being. So Barth can say of God's grace that it is inherent in God's own being.

> There is no higher divine being than that of the gracious God, and no higher divine holiness than that which He shows in being merciful and forgiving sins.[13]

> This is how God loves. This is how He seeks and creates fellowship between Himself and us. By this distinctive mark we recognize the divinity of His love. For it is in this way, graciously, that God not only acts outwardly towards His creature, but is in Himself from eternity to eternity.[14]

Of course, the question must arise, without any creature toward whom to be gracious how can God be eternally gracious? Barth's answer is simply this: we cannot know, but we must maintain that God's being is identical with God's act toward us, and thus God cannot but be described as eternally gracious. "The form in which grace exists in God Himself and is actual as God is in point of fact hidden from us and incomprehensible to us."[15]

All this enables us to bring the earlier trinitarian answer to the question "Who is it that acts in saving?" God the Holy Trinity acts, in a threefold economy. This is an economy of election, salvation, and sanctification as the expression of God's particular holiness in consecrating Godself, not in isolation or mere distance from fallen humanity, but in confronting and overcoming evil, sin and death, and doing so by taking up the creature's cause and need. "God's holiness figures itself in the will of the Father for the creature which is embodied in the Son's work of sin-bearing and reconciliation, and it is extended to us by the Holy

---

13. Ibid., 356.
14. Ibid., 357.
15. Ibid., 357.

Spirit's sanctification of the reconciled."[16] Clearly the human career of life, death, resurrection and ascension of God incarnate—the particular man Jesus of Nazareth—remains at the center, but this very career is itself the field of action of the triune God, Father, Son, and Spirit, in mutual economy and being.

Who Is It Done To?

So, next, the question arises "To whom is it done?" Is there some way in which we ought to speak of something being done "to" someone? Once again, a classical Western way of doing so involves the description of Jesus' obedient death as acting upon the Father in such a way as to turn wrath away and yield mercy and grace instead. As earlier, this is an already much criticized aspect of certain forms of substitution theory, but a brief glance is in order. The problem is that the will and intention of Father and Son are all too easily split, so that the Father requires the payment of a penalty for sins committed but, once the Son pays the penalty, then becomes gracious. Certainly it is not normally put this way, and the caricature is very rough. Perhaps to avoid the obvious problems in the caricature, what is more often described is the Father's desire to show mercy as constrained by the holy and just requirement that wrongdoing be punished. Jesus is therefore the solution to a divine conundrum, as he makes a way for unavoidable punishment to be meted out, and at the same time for grace to triumph. In one sense this is a wonderful description of the Father's desire to forgive, and provides a clear enough explanation of a mechanism of salvation as the Son acts upon the Father in such a way as to secure forgiveness. However the problems are clear—as above either the will and agency of the Father and Son are somewhat bifurcated, as the Son brings grace out from beneath the Father's intent to punish, *or* the Father too desires to forgive but is constrained by holiness, with the sense arising that the Father is either subject to an internal split between grace and judgment/love and holiness or is somehow constrained by an *external* standard of righteousness holiness. Certainly neither of these will do, and it will absolutely not do to accept a mechanism which splits the agency of the Father and Son in such wise as to be only questionably trinitarian.[17]

16. Webster, *Confessing God*, 124.
17. See, for example, Webster, *Confessing God*, 118–19.

But, continuing for the moment with the matter of the Son in some way doing something to or toward the Father, does this exhaust the question? In the first instance we may say that within God something takes place that takes the form of sacrifice—as the Letter to the Hebrews has it, the Son offers himself in an obedience that fulfills and transcends the preceding sacrificial system and can be understood as in some sense a sacrifice pleasing to God, on the basis of which his death is itself transcended in resurrection and his ongoing life taken up into the very presence of the Father. In this way we may even speak of Jesus' death as substitutionary—in fact a thorough going trinitarian description of atonement requires that we do so.[18] Jesus' human obedience is substituted for normal human disobedience, and he takes up his role as Messiah and head over a new eschatological people.

This set of events need not, and should not imply that this self-offering changes the Father in the sense of a shift from wrath to mercy, but within all this something does occur, surely, in God. The eternal Son, now risen, does not renounce human form and being, but instead takes that transformed and perfected new humanity into the ongoing life of the Trinity. God must surely be said to be changed by the incarnation and that change is cemented in the resurrection of the Son, although the *telos* remains finally hidden in the eschaton. It seems that we ought to say something like this: God the Trinity takes on human flesh through the *agon* of Jesus' life and death, and in doing so transforms the being and the future of the whole creation, but at the same time God changes Godself, and incorporates humanity into God's own being and therefore into a shared future. No one has attempted a fuller development of these thoughts than Robert Jenson, but in the end his project fails.[19]

Great care must be taken at this point, for the tradition has expressed a deep aversion to speaking of change of this sort in the being of God, and quite understandably so. The immutability of God stands as one of the bedrock attributes of traditional theism. However, it is true, as writers such as Jenson and Gunton have made plain, that often the interpretation of God's "unchangability" owes more to platonic notions than Judaeo-Christian understandings. Can we speak appropriately of the activity of God in the history of Israel, culminating and overflowing

---

18. See McCormack, "Ontological Presuppositions," 346–66.
19. For one significant angle of critique see my "Community of Love?" 289–300.

to the whole creation in the history of the Israelite Jesus—the story of the incarnation—somehow involving change in God?

If we are to do so then the care taken must surely be to insist that the "change" is actioned by God and God alone. God is not changed by circumstance, or affected by reality outside of Godself (the creation) such that God is altered. To insist that God's perfections evidenced economically are in fact the eternal perfections of the triune One is in fact to insist that whatever narrative plot we may identify in God's economy reflects the eternal being of God. As with Barth above, we may be forced to say that we cannot fathom what this eternal being of God might be, but that we nonetheless hold to the revelation of God's identity *in se* as expressed in God's economy *ad extra*. This, of course, provides the foundation for Barth's doctrine of election, wherein the being of God in eternity is identified as the being of the God who elects humanity in electing Godself in the person of the Son. In this wise we finally reject any notion of God being changed even by the incarnation, while yet maintaining the reality of the plot of God's "history." God as God "becomes" even by the adoption of undying, redeemed humanity seated at the Father's right hand in glory is still the eternal God *in se*, from everlasting to everlasting.

Of course, there now remains the second necessary aspect of the question "Toward whom is the work of salvation oriented?" This is what Barth habitually called the subjective pole, or moment, of reconciliation—the change wrought in humans and therefore in the realm of creation—and this in turn fills out the answer to the inquiry "What is done?" Once again trinitarian insight must lead us, for whatever change is brought about in humans is brought about through the agency of the Trinity as a whole, but with a particular focus on the activity of the Spirit. Although the New Testament itself speaks in a number of ways to this, a key term is that of "incorporation" into Christ—that somehow the Spirit unifies the faithful with Jesus himself, and this is best understood as both a function of the genuine gift of human faith and of the faithfulness of Jesus himself. (The two in inseparable unity.) Substitution of Jesus' righteousness for the unrighteousness of sinful humanity, as above, ought to be understood in such a fashion that while a Christian may say "Jesus' righteousness has obscured my unrighteousness" this cannot be taken to mean that the work of Jesus remains merely objective for me and that I may lay claim to his righteousness without any sense of God acting upon me such that in Christ I too become a subject of salvation through the power of the Holy Spirit. God creates a new humanity, and therefore the firstfruits of the new creation, in the outpouring of the Spirit upon all flesh and the ordination of a holy priesthood of saints, apostles, martyrs, and prophets, and this new people is moment by moment called to cooperate with the Spirit, being transformed into the "likeness of Christ." The work of salvation as a work of the Trinity is not comprehensible or susceptible of description apart from this outpouring of the Spirit. Without such description the whole *telos* and function of the work is lost, and arid attempts to speak of the saving God reach their limit in naming the objective achievement of Jesus, but make no particular sense of his ascension and ongoing role as Savior, or of the work of the Spirit.

For What Purpose Is It Done?

All this is already an answer to the question "To what end is salvation?" The *telos* of salvation is the reconciliation of all creation with its gracious triune Creator, and this end is achieved in the united differentiation of work undertaken by that Creator. Here eschatology feeds off soteriology as both respond to the story of Jesus. Incorporation into Jesus involves being carried forward in him in an orientation toward the future He is bringing—the final reconciliation of all things in the new creation. This is (now and therefore was ever) the *telos* of all things, and one of the keys to understanding judgment must surely be to see that *apart* from this purposed goal there can be no future for any part of the creation. In this sense judgment serves the purpose of grace, but exactly in so doing defies any attempt to elide or reject its necessity. God the Trinity is moving all things toward a future in which the cry will be uttered "Behold the dwelling place of God is with humans," but this is also therefore the future which no liar or idolater may enter.

Even here the trinitarian reality of God demands a revision of much popular conception of the matter, for the new creation is not to be envisaged as static eternity based on platonic notions of perfection as stasis. Rather the adoption of human flesh into eternity achieved in the incarnation and revealed in the resurrection and ascension of the incarnate Son, along with the implications for understanding the immutability and eternity of the Trinity, drive an eschatology that foresees an eternal history stretching before God and God's creation rather than a stasis of timelessness. The pattern of creaturely worship and obedience evidenced in Jesus provides the template for the prophetic imagination to stretch forward toward the *telos* of all things in reconciled relationship and utter partnership after the manner of and even incorporated into the life of God the three-in-one. God turns out to be such that the Trinity "makes space" within its own life and fellowship for humanity somehow gathered up into the Son.

Failure at this point to allow a trinitarian soteriology to control eschatological thought does such violence to teleology that the various visions of the future are unrecognizable as images of the same reality. On the one hand Hegelian-style modernist theology can see only "more of the same"—the march of human history into an infinity of realizing selfhood—while functionally unitarian eschatology can only overcome the paucity of fallen history with an absence of history grounded in the static being of a monadic deity. Of course, any number of eschatologies do not fall fully into either trap, but nonetheless are not adequately trinitarian. In regard to the poles described, the point is, undoubtedly, that these are not in fact visions of the same end, and that both fail miserably to do justice to the future of the creation in and with God the Trinity.

So, to make explicit what has been present all along, the eschatological reality of Jesus is breaking into the old and dying age at every moment and every point. In many ways faithful Christian theology simply is eschatology (as Barth so famously said it must be[20]) as the church wrestles with the task of reflection upon the invasion of the realm of sin and death by the salvation that God has wrought. To return to the beginning for a moment, with a fresh lens to our eye, the doctrine of the Trinity flows itself from just this place. As Dalferth states: "[The] self-disclosing and self-communicating presence of God's creative love is the complex eschatological reality to which Christian theology refers. It is eschatological in the sense of being the final and ultimately true reality in which and through which we all have our being. Three features are essential to its eschatological character: it is *divinely constituted*; it is *christologically determined*; and it is experienced as the *break-in of*

---

20. Barth, *Epistle to the Romans*, 314.

radical newness in our life. Individually and together these three features give rise to a trinitarian account of God."[21]

Finally therefore we come to the crux: the eschatological in-breaking of salvation in "the kingdom of God," and in the incorporation into Jesus of that people called and named for him, can only be expressed in a community that embodies that in-breaking. The church is therefore a community of God the Trinity, and as such a community created to serve the mission of the triune Savior of the world.

Such an eschatological community seeks to live in the present the reality of the *eschaton*, but of course only does so within the tension created by Jesus' ascension. The *eschaton* is finally about the *eschatos*—the presence of Jesus himself, in whom the new creation is already embodied, and whose immediacy at the end will make that end the new beginning. In the meantime—the time between ascension and *Parousia* the church lives out the eschatological call of Jesus in the power of the Spirit, orienting all of life to the *telos* of the fulfillment of the Father's will for all creation. Worship and obedience occupy the central place in the life of this church, but notions of obedience and worship are themselves interpreted through the framework of trinitarian eschatology. Just as Jesus embodied and enacted faithful worship and obedience in drinking the cup to the dregs, and did so in service of the mission of God, so must the church conceive of worship as inseparable from obedience to the same mission—a point made plain enough throughout the story of Jesus, from Genesis to Revelation. With the seven churches of Asia Minor the contemporary church stands ever in need of reminder that the Trinity is at work, and that while Jesus' embodiment of the new creation is held at "the Father's side" the world remains permeable to the Spirit whose kingdom cannot be finally defeated by the empires of this age. Thus the church has courage to charge the darkness—to pursue justice to our own cost, to neglect the pursuit of the vainglory of this age, for our hope is in heaven, where Christ our Lord and brother is—reigning with the Father—and our life is mediated in the Spirit. We declare the mighty works of God because we hope in the Spirit for the revelation of the lordship of Jesus at the end of the age and we trust in the goodness of the Father's will. The church simply exists as the being and act of this people because the Trinity is God over the church and the fruit of God's being and act.

21. Dalferth, "Eschatological Roots," 160.

So What?

What happens when non-trinitarian models of atonement and images of God's work of salvation are admitted? At the most basic level we are left with little more than ourselves. This is most obvious in that classic modernist theology stemming from Kant, in which the doctrine of the Trinity is either rejected utterly, or is really of no significance, and the incarnation is either denied or at best affirmed merely in talk of symbol and myth. Within such schemes it is clear that God is seen as the great enabler of salvation, but there is a real sense in which humans are to be the agents of their own ascent to God.[22] What is happening here is precisely that fault with which this essay began—the refusal to move from Jesus of Nazareth, his cross and rising again, to the ontological considerations his reality requires we wrestle with, and which in turn yield the doctrine of the Trinity. In relation to the salvation he mediates we can now say that if that salvation is not anchored in trinitarian formulations then the gospel is truncated to a symbol for human hope, faithfulness and power, but the activity of God in that story becomes reduced to an external referent for that hope, but nonetheless essentially external. The tendency is then toward a conscious or sub-conscious Hegelian move, and to see God's work in the movement of history and the evolution of the world and human societies. Within such thinking the anchors in contemporary concerns are usually plain, but the level of unfaithfulness to the biblical story of Jesus is simply staggering.

On the other hand, the gospel stands as the gospel of the triune Savior of the world—the power of salvation let loose upon the world in the dynamic inter-relation and work of the God who is Father, Son, and Holy Spirit, one God to be glorified and worshipped forever. Amen and amen.

---

22. Even such intelligent and sophisticated work as Sallie McFague's recommendation of models such as "God as the lover of the world," and "the world as God's body" are flawed by their failure to maintain a necessary attendance to the Trinity as the truth of God's being. See McFague, *Models of God*.

Bibliography

Barth, Karl. *Church Dogmatics*. 4 vols. Edinburgh: T. & T. Clark, 1956–75.

———. *Der Römerbrief* (1922). ET: *The Epistle to the Romans*. 2nd ed. Translated by E. C. Hoskyns. London: Oxford University Press, 1933.

Burgess, Andrew. "A Community of Love? Jesus as the Body of God and Robert Jenson's Trinitarian Thought." *International Journal for Systematic Theology* 6 (2004) 289–300.

———. "Salvation as Judgement and Grace." In *God of Salvation: Essays in Systematic Theology*, edited by Ivor J. Davidson and Murray A. Rae. Aldershot, UK: Ashgate, forthcoming.

Dalferth, Ingolf U. "The Eschatological Roots of the Doctrine of the Trinity." In *Trinitarian Theology Today: Essays on Divine Being and Act*, edited by Christoph Schwöbel, 147–70. Edinburgh: T. & T. Clark, 1995.

Gunton, Colin E. *Father, Son, and Holy Spirit: Toward a Fully Trinitarian Theology*. London: T. & T. Clark, 2003.

Jenson, Robert W. *Systematic Theology*, vol. 1: *The Triune God*. Oxford: Oxford University Press, 1997.

———. "What Is the Point of Trinitarian Theology?" In *Trinitarian Theology Today: Essays on Divine Being and Act*, edited by Christoph Schwöbel, 31–43. Edinburgh: T. & T. Clark, 1995.

McCormack, Bruce L. "The Ontological Presuppositions of Barth's Doctrine of the Atonement." In *The Glory of the Atonement: Biblical, Historical and Practical Perspectives*, edited by Charles E. Hill and Frank A. James III, 346–66. Downers Grove, IL: IVP, 2004.

McFague, Sallie. *Models of God: Theology for an Ecological, Nuclear Age*. Minneapolis: Fortress, 1987.

Webster, John. *Confessing God: Essays in Christian Dogmatics II*. London: T. & T. Clark, 2005.

9

The Contribution of Karl Barth's Doctrine of Appropriation to a Trinitarian Ecclesiology

Adam McIntosh

Introduction

KARL BARTH'S DOCTRINE OF THE TRINITY IS THE FOUNDATION OF HIS *Church Dogmatics* in that it is his answer to the three questions of revelation: Who is God? How do we come to know this God? And, how does this affect the life of human beings? Barth answers these questions in relation to the triune identity of God and thereby makes the doctrine of the Trinity constitutive for the whole of his *Church Dogmatics*. Given this, what does it mean to speak about Barth's trinitarian theology? Moreover, what does this contribute to a constructive trinitarian ecclesiology? This paper will focus on these questions by way of an examination of Barth's doctrine of appropriation. The first two sections focus on the place of Barth's doctrine of appropriation within his doctrine of the Trinity and his distinctive understanding of this doctrine. The third section considers the way that Barth directly and indirectly makes use of this doctrine in his special ethics and ecclesiology. The final section draws conclusions about its contributions to a constructive trinitarian ecclesiology.

Barth's Doctrine of Appropriation

We begin by considering Barth's doctrine of the Trinity. Barth explains the doctrine of the Trinity in terms of the dialectical concepts of "unity in Trinity" and "Trinity in unity" (oneness in threeness and threeness in oneness). He employs the term "triunity" as the combination of these two formulae.[1] When the "unity in Trinity" or "Trinity in unity" is discussed independently there is an inevitable one-sidedness. The "*unity* in Trinity" is best conceptualized in terms of the doctrine of *perichoresis*. He understands the "*Trinity* in unity" in terms of the doctrine of appropriation. The doctrines of *perichoresis* and appropriation are the two hermeneutical principles of the concept of triunity. For Barth, both are proper perspectives of God insofar as they are interpretations of God's self-revelation in the witness of Scripture, although in themselves they are incomplete and must continue to be complemented by their dialectical counterpart. This one-sidedness of the doctrine of the Trinity is unavoidable in thinking about the triune God. The theologian can only describe these dialectical aspects of the doctrine of the Trinity in response to God's self-interpretation in the witness of Scripture, without attempting to simultaneously conceive the oneness and threeness of God. In other words, the concept of triunity is both an affirmation and negation; yes each perspective is proper, but it remains incomplete speech about God and must be complemented by the other side of God's triunity.

For Barth, the dialectical concept of *perichoresis* explains God's unity in terms of the communion of the three modes of being.[2] The persons "mutually condition and permeate one another so completely that one is always in the other two and the other two in the one."[3] Barth understands God's unity to be in the threeness of the persons; in their *perichoretic* relations. God's being is understood by Barth as an active relationship between the Father, Son, and Holy Spirit, and he concep-

---

1. *CD* I/1, 368.

2. Barth argues that the concept of "personality" in the nineteenth century complicates the patristic term *persona* by the addition of the attribute of self-consciousness. This resulted in neo-Protestant theology applying the modern concept of personality to the Father, Son, and Holy Spirit, without this concept applying ontologically to the Father, Son, and Holy Spirit, which would result in tritheism. He argues that neo-Protestantism "limited itself to a purely phenomenological doctrine of the three persons, an economic Trinity of revelation, three persons in the sense that God Himself was still in the background as absolute personality." To avoid the connotations of the modern concept of personality being applied to the concept of person, Barth utilizes the term "mode of being." His intention was to express more precisely that God is God in a special way as Father, Son, and Holy Spirit. Ibid., 353–60.

3. Ibid., 370.

tualizes this in terms of the doctrine of *perichoresis*. The existence of all three divine modes of being is made relative by the necessity of their coexistence with the other two since "none exists as a special individual, but all three in-exist or exist only in concert as modes of being of the one God and Lord who posits Himself from eternity to eternity."[4] The *perichoresis* of the three divine modes of being does not diminish the "Trinity in unity" of God. Rather, the three modes of being of God all work in the order suitable to them, in which all three "reciprocally interpenetrate each other and inexist in one another."[5]

The doctrine of appropriation is the conceptual framework by which Barth deals with the "*Trinity* in unity." In its most simple form, its task is to bring to speech the distinguishing features of the operations of the triune God, while simultaneously recognizing the *perichoretic* unity of the one God. In Scripture, there are particular works that we appropriate to one person of the Trinity that we cannot ascribe to the other two persons. For instance, it would not make sense to say that the Son came upon the disciples with tongues of fire on the day of Pentecost, that the Holy Spirit suffered under Pontius Pilate, or that the Father was born of the Virgin Mary. The doctrine of appropriation brings to speech these distinctive works, according to the biblical witness in which God characterizes himself in distinctive modes of existence, while recognizing that these works are the indivisible work of the triune God. For Barth, God's self-interpretation in the witness of Scripture is the foundation for speaking about the distinctive works of the persons of the Trinity and he frames this doctrinally within the doctrine of appropriation. In Scripture, God is made known in different modes of existence whether as God the Creator, God the Reconciler, or God the Redeemer. God's unity is to be understood in this variety. A quick glance at the architecture of the *Church Dogmatics* indicates the way in which Barth systematically works out the economy of God according to the doctrine of appropriation. The doctrine of creation is an explication of God's works from the perspective of God as Father; the doctrine of reconciliation is God's works from the perspective of God as Son; and the doctrine of redemption was planned by Barth to be God's works from the perspective of God as Spirit. For Barth, these are not arbitrary

4. Ibid., 370.
5. Ibid., 396.

appropriations, but are derived from the distinctive acts of God in the witness of Scripture.

Qualifications to the Doctrine of Appropriation

Of course things are never that simple with Barth, even though this remains an accurate description of his overall procedure for the doctrine of appropriation. There are five qualifications to Barth's doctrine of appropriation and its function within the *Church Dogmatics* that will make clear his distinctive use of this doctrine. These will also partly pre-empt and respond to at least some of the common criticisms directed towards this doctrine. The first is in relation to the underlying ontology of this doctrine. One criticism of the doctrine of appropriation is that it is a compensating strategy for an unbalanced essentialist trinitarian ontology in which essence precedes the communion of the three persons.[6] This may be a justifiable criticism of some uses of this doctrine, but Barth does not employ it in this way. His doctrine of appropriation is not based on an essentialist ontology, but if anything it is based on an actualistic ontology in which God's being is actualized in God's distinctive activities in time, as God eternally elects to be for creation. God's being is an act and the doctrine of appropriation is a way of *bringing to speech* God's being as *distinctive* acts, as it acknowledges God's self-interpretation in the witness of Scripture. Of course Barth does not advocate an ontological distinction between God's distinctive acts resulting in three separate actualized beings, but uses the doctrine of appropriation as a way of bringing to speech God's actualistic being. The main point is that the doctrine of appropriation is a hermeneutical tool that provides the language for speech about the distinctive divine

---

6. This is what Catherine LaCugna suggests about Augustine's use of the doctrine of appropriation. "The doctrine of appropriation is a compensating strategy within Latin theology that tries to reconnect the specific details of salvation history to specific persons" (LaCugna, *God for Us*, 100). Thomas Torrance argues that the laws of appropriation "brought in by Latin Theology to redress an unbalanced essentialist approach to the doctrine of the Trinity from the One being of God, which obscured the evangelical approach from the economic Trinity, falls completely away as an idea that is both otiose and damaging to the intrinsic truth of Christ who, as the Word and only begotten Son of God, constitutes the *one* revelation of the Father and the *one* way by which we can go to the Father." Torrance does, however, acknowledge that Barth does have a different approach in his employment of this doctrine. Torrance, *Christian Doctrine of God*, 200.

persons without necessarily committing to particular ontological claims about the triune God.[7]

This leads us to the second qualification that all three persons are in some way involved in each distinctive work. Barth says that God cannot be conceptualized in terms of "a dramatic entry and exit of now one and now another of the divine Persons, of the surging up and down of half or totally individualised powers or forms or ideas."[8] Rather, what is implied in an appropriation is the indivisible co-presence of the other two persons in the work of the one.[9] "By the specific assigning of a word or deed to this or that person of the Godhead, there should be brought to our awareness . . . the truth of the triunity which is in fact undivided in its work and which still exists in three persons."[10] Barth frames this according to the rule *opera trinitatis ad extra sunt indivisa* ("the external works of the Trinity are undivided"). For Barth, this does not mean that no distinguishing work can be ascribed to God as Father, Son, and Holy Spirit. Rather, it means that the works of creation, reconciliation, and redemption are never exclusive to one person, even though they are distinguishable works and spoken about primarily in relation to one person of the Trinity.[11] For Barth, the identity of the distinctive works of the triune God is dependent on their *perichoretic* relations and not as either isolated persons or as an undifferentiated deity.

This point is further indicated in the correspondence between the appropriation and the eternal relations of origin. The relations of origin refer to the intra-trinitarian relations of the divine persons. For Barth, the divine persons are differentiated, not in isolation from one another, but in their eternal self-relatedness with the relations of origin shaping the divine action. To appropriate a particular work to God as Father, Son, or Holy Spirit will be in accordance with the intra-trinitarian rela-

---

7. The doctrine of appropriation does, however, make ontological claims about the triune God insofar as *through* this *tool* Barth intends to refer to the three persons of God's being and that is an ontological claim insofar as it refers to the being of the Trinity.

8. CD 1/1, 374–75.

9. Ibid., 370.

10. Ibid., 373.

11. Barth avoids the common criticism of Augustine's use of the rule *opera trinitatis ad extra sunt indivisa* that the unity of God's essence results in no distinguishing action being ascribed to the particular persons of the Trinity. See Chia, "Trinity and Ontology," 452–68.

tional structure of God's being. One example will suffice to indicate how he understands this. Barth defines the relation of origin of the Father to the Son and the Spirit in terms of God's fatherhood (*paternitas*). He maintains that the Father is only able to be meaningfully described as the creator because there is an analogy between the work of creation and God's eternal fatherhood.

> As the Father, God procreates Himself from eternity in His Son, and with His Son He is also from eternity the origin of Himself in the Holy Spirit; and as the Creator He posits the reality to all the things that are distinct from Himself. The two things are not identical. Neither the Son nor the Holy Spirit is the world; each is God as the Father Himself is God. But between the relationship in God Himself and God's relationship to the world, there is an obvious proportion. In view of this it is meaningful and right to designate God the Father in particular (*per appropriationem*) as Creator, and God the Creator in particular (*per appropriationem*) as the Father.[12]

Barth describes the Father as the holy creator because of the Father's intra-trinitarian role as *arche* in relation to the Son and Spirit. This is why it is appropriate to think of the Father in particular as the creator, while maintaining that the works of God are indivisible.

The fourth qualification to the doctrine of appropriation is its limitation. In Barth's understanding, knowledge of the persons of the Trinity in their distinctiveness is not to be confused with the distinction in God, even though there is proportional similarity, otherwise it would be meaningless to talk of distinctions at all. The distinctions of the persons of the Trinity brought to speech in appropriations analogically hint at the eternal distinctions, although these distinctions remain incomprehensible to human beings and cannot be completely applied to the triune God without tritheism. Knowledge of God follows and is determined by the object of revelation, God, while not corresponding directly to God. For this reason Barth describes appropriation as "improper" speech about God. "Improper" means that "it is not an exhaustive understanding, that it is one-sided, that it needs to be supplemented, that we cannot and should not proclaim its exclusive validity, that it must imply what is not actually contained in it as such."[13]

12. *CD* III/1, 49.
13. *CD* I/1, 395. See also III/1, 49–57; and III/4, 33–40.

This does not mean that the doctrine of appropriation is to be abandoned as an untrue understanding of the triune God. As Barth states:

> It is only an appropriation to the degree that it does not also express the truth of perichoresis, of the intercommunity of Father, Son and Spirit in their essence and work. But it expresses the truth and imparts true knowledge to the degree that with the equation it touches upon and denotes the distinction which there is also in the *opus ad extra,* the order and sense in which God as the triune is the subject of the *opus ad extra indivisum.* It expresses the truth to the degree that with its specific emphasis on the Father or Creator it points to the affinity between the order of God's three modes of being on the one hand and that of the three sides of His work as Creator, Reconciler and Redeemer on the other.[14]

In other words, our knowledge of God is inadequate in this conceiving of God's works alongside one another. "In the fragment, mirror and riddle of the detailed, it is knowledge of the one and the whole which is for us here and now the one and the whole only in the manifoldness and sequence of the detailed."[15] Theological speech can only follow and articulate the object itself according to the object's self-interpretation, referring to the being of God in the untruth appropriate to human beings. Scripture witnesses to these distinctions in God's modes of existence and therefore it is proper, within this stated limitation, to speak of these distinctions.

The final qualification to Barth's doctrine of appropriation is that he grounds it on a christocentric epistemology. Jesus Christ is the center of God's revelation from which the other spheres of God's works are to be understood. According to Barth, the doctrine of the Trinity is the unfolding of the confession that Jesus Christ is Lord. This means that a trinitarian theology does not *ipso facto* mean that there is an equal emphasis or importance given to the three divine modes of being. He argues that historically considered the Father, Son, and Holy Spirit do not have the same importance in the doctrine of the Trinity.[16] The Son is the revelatory center of the doctrine of the Trinity from which the distinctive works of God as Father and Spirit are also brought to speech. Thus,

14. *CD* I/1, 396.
15. *CD* III/4, 35.
16. *CD* I/1, 314–15.

Barth's constructive trinitarian theology, explicated using the hermeneutical tool of the doctrine of appropriation, is applied consistently using a christocentric epistemological center. In the order of knowledge Jesus Christ is first, even in consideration of the distinctive works of God as Father or Spirit. For instance, knowledge of the Father as the Creator of heaven and earth follows the belief in Jesus Christ; the latter is the epistemological basis of knowledge of the former and the former is the presupposition of the latter. In Jesus Christ, we come to know God the eternal Father and Creator of all that exists. This is also the case with the work of the Spirit. There is no work of the Spirit in isolation from Jesus Christ because the Spirit witnesses to the Son. Barth makes this clear in the following: "The witness of the Holy Spirit does not have itself either as its origin or goal. It has no content of its own. It has no autonomous power. It does not shine or illuminate in virtue of its own inherent light."[17] The witness of the Spirit to Jesus Christ is, for Barth, the self-attestation of Jesus Christ. Barth uses a christocentric *trinitarian* theology, since Jesus Christ is the revelatory center of knowledge of the triune God. Barth's point is simple: that Jesus Christ is normative for our understanding of the distinctive works of the triune God. The different perspectives of God's works have a christological center from which the other angles of God's works are to be seen. Although there are multiple perspectives of the one God, there is only one epistemological center: Jesus Christ.

Barth's Use of the Doctrine of Appropriation

Special Ethics

We are now in a position to consider Barth's *use* of the doctrine of appropriation with the intention of drawing out its implications for ecclesiology. As noted earlier in this essay, Barth structures the *Church Dogmatics* according to the doctrine of appropriation. Apart from the architecture of the *Church Dogmatics*, the clearest and most explicit use of this doctrine is found in Barth's special ethics. Barth clearly sees a connection between this doctrine and its usefulness for ethics. The good action of human beings is to be viewed from the perspective of the action of God and God's goodness. Special ethics deals with the

17. *CD* IV/2, 130.

divine command and human action from the concrete standpoint of God's distinctive works. Its task is "to accompany this history of God and man from creation to reconciliation and redemption, indicating the mystery of the encounter at each point on the path according to its own distinctive character."[18] In his discussion of *Ethics as a Task of the Doctrine of Creation*, at the opening of volume three, part four of the *Church Dogmatics*, Barth explicitly connects his special ethics with the doctrine of appropriation. This is indicated in the following:

> But what may and must be seen together must not be confused, intermingled or even identified. And where we must not split and separate, we may and must distinguish. The *perichoresis* of God's three modes of being does not destroy their independence. And if the one whole God is the Subject and Author of creation, reconciliation and redemption, this is not to deny that His actions in each of these three spheres is a particular one, so that it is permissible and even imperative, as in older trinitarian dogmatics, to ascribe the work of creation *per appropriationem* to the Father, that of reconciliation to the Son and—always *per appropriationem*—that of redemption and consummation to the Holy Spirit, thus making a genuine distinction. And a similar distinction is allowed and required in relation to the divine command: allowed because the variety of spheres in which God commands in some sense invites it; and commanded because it is really impossible to see how a concrete understanding of the one command of the one God is to be reached if we make no use of the invitation to view it in the manifold form given by the variety of these spheres.[19]

This makes clear Barth's use of the doctrine of appropriation for the purpose of providing the language for thinking about ethics in relation to the distinctive works of the triune God. From this we can see that Barth is convinced that the object of theology, the triune God, compels the theologian to first speak of God from the perspective of God's distinctive works and then to speak of the correlates to these works in the ethical life of human beings. "In this event, as we have seen, it is always a question of God in His articulated and differentiated action, and of man in his corresponding articulated and differentiated being

---

18. *CD* III/4, 26.
19. Ibid., 33.

in relation to this God."[20] In other words, Barth's concern with special ethics is not to look at three separate commands of God, but to consider the *one* command of God from *different* perspectives.

Special ethics embraces a plenitude of particular demands that correspond to the three differentiated planes of God's works. Each distinctive work calls forth a corresponding ethical response from human beings. Barth describes this in terms of divine act towards humanity followed by a corresponding demand of distinctive obedience. These differentiated works describe the triune identity of the commanding God. Because they are works *for* human beings, they also characterize humanity in our existence as ethical creatures. For Barth, God's free actions create the conditions for the human response to God as God enters into history as Creator, Reconciler, and Redeemer, creating and demanding the possibility of obedience as an acknowledgement of who God is and who humanity is. As God enters into history in his distinctive works this demands practices that correspond to the account of humanity defined by the distinctive divine actions. The following quotation makes this clear:

> [Humanity] is the creature of God, namely, the one whom God had in view when He created heaven and earth, determining him as His covenant partner and finally for participation in His eternal life. He is the sinner to whom God in His wonderful freedom is gracious. That is, he is the being who has disobeyed God, broken the covenant, denied his own nature and missed his vocation, yet to whom God is faithful quite apart from and in defiance of his deserts, so that without being worthy of it he may hold fast to His promise in faith, live by His forgiveness and hope in Him. And he is the child of the Father led by the Spirit, who as the time of contradiction, conflict and suffering moves to its end already lives in hope in the presence of God's future and final revelation which will fully reveal him as that which he is even now.[21]

In this neat summary of the direction of the three spheres of God's works, Barth indicates the triadic perspective of humanity that follows the manifold works of God *for* humanity. The task of special ethics is to articulate the differentiated identity of humanity as it corresponds to the differentiated action of God, all aimed at the transformation of

20. Ibid., 29.
21. Ibid., 25.

command to obedience in the concrete practices of human beings. Special ethics accompanies the history of God, with the doctrine of appropriation providing a hermeneutic for the perspectival character of this history.

This model of distinctive divine action and human participation in Barth's special ethics is also applied by Barth in his ecclesiology. The *ecclesia* is defined by its *becoming* in time a preliminary representation of what God has created in his *distinctive* acts as Creator, Reconciler, and Redeemer. This means that the church can be seen from the different perspectives of God as Creator, Reconciler, and Redeemer,[22] instead of only from a christological perspective,[23] even though Barth operates from a christocentric epistemology and thus Christology is the dominant mode for ecclesiology in the *Church Dogmatics*. Because of this, the most obvious example of this use of the doctrine of appropriation in relation to ecclesiology is the distinctive work of Jesus Christ. Barth puts it this way: "All ecclesiology is grounded, critically limited, but also positively determined by Christology."[24] It is important to note that Barth says this within his discussion of the economy of reconciliation. This is built into the very architecture of the doctrine of reconciliation, with the different perspectives of the work of

---

22. See my doctoral dissertation entitled, "The Doctrine of Appropriation as an Interpretative Framework for Karl Barth's Ecclesiology of the Church Dogmatics."

23. There have been several attempts to define the logic of Barth's ecclesiology. These studies tend to be dominated by totalizing Christological interpretations. The first major study of Barth's ecclesiology was Colm O'Grady's two part study of the church in Barth's theology, O'Grady, *Church in the Theology of Karl Barth*; and O'Grady, *Church in Catholic Theology*. O'Grady acknowledges the trinitarian structure to Barth's ecclesiology, but he does not examine how Barth constructs a trinitarian ecclesiology. This tendency towards a dominant Christological interpretation has continued to be the norm in studies of Barth's ecclesiology. The second important study, almost four decades after O'Grady, is Kimlyn Bender's book that again focuses on Barth's "Christological" ecclesiology, although in a more sophisticated way than O'Grady. Bender, *Karl Barth's Christological Ecclesiology*. Bender argues that Barth's ecclesiology is based on a Chalcedonian pattern, the logic of the hypostatic union and an *anhypostatic* and *enhypostatic* Christology. Bender avers that this Christological framework provides Barth with a paradigm for understanding the relationship between God and human beings and therefore the church. Nicholas Healy also has a shorter study of Barth's ecclesiology, which again employs a dominant Christological interpretative framework. Healy argues that Barth establishes a single definition of the church, as the body of Christ, and then Barth uses this definition as the basis for developing his systematic ecclesiology. Healy, "Logic of Karl Barth's Ecclesiology," 253–70.

24. *CD* IV/3.2, 786.

reconciliation demanding a corresponding response in the life of the church. A quick outline of this familiar structure will make this clear. In volume 4, part 1, Jesus Christ is considered by Barth as "very God." In this discussion, Barth emphasizes the priestly work of the Lord as servant. The reconciling work of the Lord as servant is the justification of human beings. This work of Jesus Christ defines the church in terms of the gathering of the church in faith by the Holy Spirit. In volume 4, part 2, the accent is on Jesus Christ as "very man" and his kingly work as the servant as Lord. The reconciling work of the Son of Man is the sanctification of human beings. The sanctifying work of Jesus Christ defines the church in terms of the upbuilding of the church in love by the Holy Spirit. Finally, part 3 focuses on Jesus Christ in the unity of "very God" and "very man" and his prophetic work as the true witness. This discussion focuses on the *revelation* of reconciliation. The vocation of the Christian corresponds to the revelation of reconciliation. The prophetic work of the Son defines the church as the sending of the Christian community in hope. In all three christological discussions the divine action creates justification, sanctification and vocation for humanity in Jesus Christ, and this results in a command in which the *ecclesia* is called to be a preliminary representation of the human condition defined by the distinctive divine acts.

Justification and Ecclesiology

There are many instances of this in Barth's ecclesiology, but one example will suffice to indicate the way in which Barth makes use of the doctrine of appropriation. We will briefly consider Barth's account of the justifying work of Jesus Christ and relate it to his ecclesiology. Jesus Christ, the Lord as servant, entered into the "far country" for the purpose of undertaking that which human beings cannot effect themselves. In this downward movement of the Son of God, in his humiliating death on the cross, humanity is justified. Barth understands Jesus Christ to be the *judge*, the *judged*, and the *judgment*. Jesus Christ is the fulfillment of the righteous judgment of God on all people because he takes the place of sinful humanity by becoming the judge judged.[25] Justification is the transposition of the human predicament of being wrong before God, because of sin, into a new relationship of being right before God.

---

25. *CD* IV/1, 222.

The death of Jesus Christ has the double meaning of being the *rejection* as well as the *pardoning* of human beings. By sin human beings have aligned themselves with the nothingness that is the antithesis of God's good creation, and in so doing have become the enemies of God. This is what Barth eloquently describes as human beings' "senseless alliance with the darkness which God the Creator has marked off from light and rejected, as the great and inconceivable, but for all its inconceivability very real, invasion of that which is, because God has willed and created it, by that which in itself is not."[26] Justification is therefore the human wrong made right in the right one judged wrong. Colin Gunton describes this as "a substitutionary bearing by God in Christ of God's rejection of human sin."[27]

The justifying work of Jesus Christ has definitively and irrevocably reconstituted the original covenantal relationship between God and human beings. This is a fundamental aspect of Barth's doctrine of justification. Human beings are no longer wrong before God, even though they continue to do wrong against God in sin. They have "crossed the threshold from wrong to right, and therefore from death to life."[28] In the reconciling work of the Lord as servant, the wrong of human beings stands in the *past* as the death of the sinner, and the right of human beings is *already* their future in the judgment of God. "It is our wrong and death which is behind us, our right and life which is before us. The transition from that past to this future is the present."[29] This means that sinful humanity has literally become a situation that is *past* in Jesus Christ. "It is present only as something which has been eternally removed and destroyed."[30] In the same way, the righteousness of humanity in Jesus Christ has become the future of humanity that already is actual. "In Him I am already the one who will be this righteous man [sic] and live as such, just as in Him I am still only the unrighteous man, to the extent that I once was this man."[31] Thus, the door of the future is already open and the door of the past has inexorably closed. "It is to-day, to-day that its content, the great hope, can and should be lived—the power of

26. Ibid., 533.
27. Gunton, "Salvation," 145.
28. *CD* IV/1, 557.
29. Ibid., 547.
30. Ibid., 553.
31. Ibid., 555.

the world to come as the power of this world. The righteous sentence of God opens wide to sinful man even in this world the gate of the world to come."[32] It is of fundamental importance to Barth's doctrine of justification that in the death and resurrection of Jesus Christ, *all* human beings have had their sins forgiven, and have been established as right before God. George Hunsinger describes this as Barth's doctrine of "universal objective participation," which means that "our objective participation in Christ precedes our active participation through faith. Jesus Christ is the one great inclusive human being."[33]

From this understanding of the justifying work of Jesus Christ Barth formulates his ecclesiology as the *becoming* in time a preliminary representation of what God has created for human beings in his *distinctive* act as Reconciler. Thus, Barth opens his christological ecclesiology by stating that the "problem" that is the concern of ecclesiology is the "subjective realization of the atonement."[34] This ecclesiological problem is the outworking of the logic described above. He defines the problem of ecclesiology as the subjective realization of the atonement, because the reconciling work of Jesus Christ is the *objective* being of all people that is to be realized in time, in the concrete historical existence of the church. In relation to God's works seen from the distinctive perspective of reconciliation, and within reconciliation the justifying work of Jesus Christ, this means that the *ecclesia* is called to become in a preliminary way the *justified* existence of humanity. Barth states that the church is "the gathering of those men whom already before all others He has made willing and ready for life under the divine verdict executed in His death and revealed in His resurrection from the dead."[35] In Barth's ecclesiology, the life under the divine verdict is a life lived as justified humanity actualized in Jesus Christ, but lived in a preliminary way before all others in the life of the *ecclesia*. The church is the *particular* people who live in an anticipatory and preliminary form what *all* human beings are already in Jesus Christ. The *ecclesia* is therefore understood by Barth as a being-in-becoming; its becoming in time corresponds to the human reality actualized in the differentiated divine action centered in the reconciling work of Jesus Christ. This is what I take to be the meaning

32. Ibid., 605.
33. Hunsinger, "Tale of Two Simultaneities," 77.
34. *CD* IV/1, 643.
35. Ibid., 661.

of the "subjective realization of the atonement."[36] The genius of Barth is that this is only *one* very rich perspective *within* the reconciling work of Jesus Christ, with reconciliation being a perspective of the manifold works of the triune God, articulated within the framework of the doctrine of appropriation.

A Trinitarian Ecclesiology

We are now in a position to consider the contribution of Barth's doctrine of appropriation to a constructive trinitarian ecclesiology. In its most simple form, the doctrine of appropriation is an interpretative process that makes intelligible speech about that which is distinctive about the persons of the Trinity. We see this in its use in the theology of Barth, but also in theologians such as Augustine and Aquinas. For example, Augustine uses this doctrine to stretch the possibility of language to speak about God as distinctive persons in order to affirm the meanings found in Scripture. The doctrine of appropriation allows Augustine to acknowledge that which the Scriptures say about particular persons, while stating that this is incomplete speech about God. For the Father and Son together are not one Word, the Son and the Father together are not the Father, and the Spirit and the Son and Father are not together Spirit. For Augustine, there is something distinctive about God as Father, Son, and Holy Spirit that requires speech, even though this is relative speech about God.[37] Aquinas similarly understands the doctrine of appropriation as speech appropriate to human beings in our limited understanding of God. Its purpose is the manifestation of our faith, in a way familiar and suitable for human beings.[38]

Building on the understanding of these theologians, we can conceptualize the doctrine of appropriation as providing the language for the unspeakable and giving intelligibility to the unintelligible. It extends trinitarian language and therefore allows more to be said about God by way of the theologian thinking in radically particular ways about the persons of the Trinity. To speak about the distinctive perspectives is

---

36. Ibid., 643.

37. St. Augustine, *The Trinity*, 7.1.2. Neil Ormerod puts it well by saying that for Augustine the doctrine of appropriation allows him "to affirm meanings as found in Scripture while at the same time acknowledging their limitations" (*The Trinity*, 101).

38. Aquinas, *Summa Theologica*, 1, Q39 a7, a8.

improper speech about God, insofar as each work of God presupposes the *perichoretic* relations of the triune God, and yet the hermeneutical process of the doctrine of appropriation gives intelligibility to this speech. Language is precariously pushed to its limits holding together the trinitarian dialectic of the Trinity in unity and unity in Trinity. It does this by giving attention to the particular so that we have access to the absolute Trinity, while the absolute remains beyond the particular accounts of God for us. For the one God is in the particular and the particular are the various angles of the whole. There is one indivisible triune God, brought to speech in the rich variety of the persons of the Trinity. The persons are all wholly God, and the triune God is of course not composed of separate parts, but the divine persons are not God in the same way. In this way, the doctrine of appropriation provides what we may call a hermeneutic of incompleteness, in which the divine persons are brought to speech in a way that acknowledges that which is beyond the radicalized accounts of the distinctive persons, while not detracting from the incomplete particularized accounts.[39] It does not articulate separate accounts of God, but the one account of God seen from an irreducible multiplicity. Again, this is not undertaken by whim, but is an interpretation of the distinctions in God's modes of existence in the witness of Scripture.

Implications for a Trinitarian Ecclesiology

The implications of this account of the doctrine of appropriation for ecclesiology are considerable. Basically, the doctrine of appropriation can also be used as a hermeneutic for the *ecclesia* as the church corresponds to the distinctive works of the triune God. It provides intelligibility and the language for a radically particularized ecclesiology, with manifold perspectives of the church. This means that a trinitarian ecclesiology does not need to give equal emphasis to all three persons of the Trinity in every discussion, or to the communion of the three persons, thereby creating a triadic equanimity and an authentically "trinitarian" ecclesiology. This hermeneutic of incompleteness offers

---

39. In his seminal work *God's Being Is in Becoming*, Eberhard Jüngel describes Barth's doctrine of appropriation as a "hermeneutical process" for defining the being of God. It is such a process because it is "the possibility of bringing God to speech" in the particularity of the persons of the Trinity. Ibid., 49–50.

a variegated ecclesiology by presenting intensified perspectives of the church as it corresponds to God's works. These perspectives will articulate the differentiated identity of humanity and the cosmos as it corresponds to the distinctive divine works as Father, Son, and Holy Spirit, with the mission of the church being to witness to these acts of God. All these accounts in their singularity will be intentionally one-sided[40] and therefore incomplete speech about the church, as it will be only one angle of the variety of God's works. However, these singular accounts are the indivisible work of the one God seen from different angles and are therefore proper speech about God.

This suggests that we should move away from the attempt to define one basic ecclesiology. The doctrine of appropriation rejects what Nicholas Healy describes as "blueprint ecclesiologies," which is the attempt to encapsulate the dominant characteristics of the church through a singular image or term such as communion, sacrament, or body of Christ.[41] For instance, in many recent ecclesiologies the concept of communion is touted as the basic model for ecclesiology from which there might emerge differences within a set parameter. Those who advocate for a communion ecclesiology tend to argue that the church should be in a temporal form what God as Trinity is as persons in relation. Colin Gunton is a good example of this. He says that "the being of the church should echo the dynamic of the relations between the three persons who together constitute the deity. The church is called to be the kind of reality at a finite level that God is in eternity."[42] The problem with "blueprint ecclesiologies," such as communion ecclesiologies, is that they tend to result in very different accounts of the church by using the same concept, and they reduce the diversity of perspectives available for ecclesiology to a singular concept. For example, the term *communion* offers many differing and sometimes conflicting accounts of ministry, lay-clergy distinction, ecclesial orders, and so on. Healy makes the point that, "To say that 'communion' is a necessary model of the church is to say remarkably little, since the model can be used in conflicting ways

---

40. It is interesting that one of the most frequent criticisms of Barth's ecclesiology is his purported inadequate account of the Spirit. I have examined this criticism in a previous article; McIntosh, "Doctrine of Appropriation," 278–91.

41. Healy, *Church, Word and the Christian Life*, 25–51.

42. Gunton, *Promise of Trinitarian Theology*, 80.

and have conflicting theological meanings, depending on its context."[43] A trinitarian ecclesiology should not be understood as the attempt to capture the essence of the church within a singular concept derived from the doctrine of the Trinity. The doctrine of appropriation works against all "blueprint ecclesiologies" and instead it presents intensified perspectives of the church by engaging the singular narratives of God's self-interpretation in the witness of Scripture, centered in the history of Jesus Christ.

What I'm suggesting is that ecclesiology follows, to slightly adapt a term used by George Hunsinger,[44] a *perspectival strategy of juxtaposition*. This allows the variegated works of the persons of the Trinity to be seen in intensified forms, with a constant juxtaposing of the unimpaired variety of God's works *as* Father, Son, and Holy Spirit and their correspondence in the life of the church. This gives permission for intensified accounts of the variety of God's works in the biblical narratives. There are many permutations that this ecclesiology can take. For instance, we can consider the church from the perspective of broad categories such as creation, reconciliation, and redemption, and within each category we can focus on different angles such as Barth's focus on justification, sanctification, and vocation within the reconciling work of Jesus Christ. Then within each account there may be dominant images of the church employed such as the body of Christ within the reconciling work of Jesus Christ. Likewise, the theologian can reflect on the distinctive narratives of God's self-characterization such as the story of Pentecost, the Exodus story, and so on. The key point is that the theologian can present intensified accounts of the church as it corresponds to the multiplicity of God's self-characterization without the charge of imbalance or the disappearance of a person of the Trinity. The task of the theologian is not to locate a singular concept for the church, but to juxtapose the variety of perspectives of the church as it corresponds to the variety of God's works as Father, Son, and Holy Spirit.

---

43. Healy, "Communion Ecclesiology," 450.

44. Hunsinger convincingly argues that Barth employs a "dialectic strategy of juxtaposition" to describe the inconceivability of the incarnation. This refers to Barth's dialectical Christology in which he maintains that it is impossible to simultaneously think of the divine and human natures of Jesus Christ. Hunsinger avers that Barth deliberately switches between an "Alexandrian idiom" and an "Antiochian idiom" without dissolving the antithesis. Hunsinger, "Karl Barth's Christology," 127–42.

Finally, the task of the theologian is to articulate the practices of the church as they correspond to the variety of God's works for us. This is the way that I described Barth's use of the doctrine of appropriation within his special ethics. For Barth, the various spheres of God's works *for* human beings characterize humanity in our existence as ethical creatures. The doctrine of appropriation can be applied to a constructive trinitarian ecclesiology in a similar way. Like Barth's special ethics, the task of the theologian is to articulate the differentiated identity of humanity as it corresponds to the differentiated action of God, and this new creation is historicized in the life of the *ecclesia* as it corresponds to the divine action in a preliminary way. Correspondence is fundamentally an ethical and missional category as it expresses the call of the Christian community to witness to the triune God through its conformity to that which God accomplishes in his works for all of creation. What the doctrine of appropriation contributes to this is radically particularized accounts of the church. Each distinctive account of God for us as Father, Son and Holy Spirit give rise to ethical injunctions, with the vocation of the church being to witness to God in its distinctive and manifold practices.

Conclusion

In this essay, I have examined Barth's doctrine of appropriation and its contribution to a trinitarian ecclesiology. This doctrine can be understood as an interpretative process that makes intelligible radicalized perspectives of God for us as distinctive persons. In relation to ecclesiology, it can also be used as a hermeneutic for the *ecclesia* as it also gives intelligibility and the language for a radically particularized ecclesiology. I described this as a perspectival strategy of juxtaposition, which offers a variegated ecclesiology by presenting intensified perspectives of the church as it corresponds to God's works, without the need for thinking simultaneously about the works of God or the different perspectives of the church. A trinitarian ecclesiology, making use of the doctrine of appropriation, would reject all "blueprint ecclesiologies" which attempt to use a singular image or definition of the church to encapsulate its dominant characteristics. Instead, the doctrine presents intensified perspectives of the church by engaging the singular narratives of God's self-interpretation in the witness of Scripture. The mission of the church is its becoming in time a preliminary representation of the differentiated identity of humanity as it corresponds to the differentiated action of God.

Bibliography

Aquinas, Thomas. *The Summa Theologica of St. Thomas Aquinas.* Revised Edition 1920, Online Edition 2000, by Kevin Knight. http://www.newadvent.org/summa.
Augustine. *The Trinity.* Boston: Daughters of St. Paul, 1965.
Barth, Karl. *Church Dogmatics.* 4 vols. Edinburgh: T. & T. Clark, 1956–75.
Bender, Kimlyn. *Karl Barth's Christological Ecclesiology.* Aldershot, UK: Ashgate, 2005.
Chia, Roland. "Trinity and Ontology: Colin Gunton's Ecclesiology." *International Journal of Systematic Theology* 9 (2007) 452–68.
Gunton, Colin. *The Promise of Trinitarian Theology.* Edinburgh: T. & T. Clark, 1997.
———. "Salvation." In *The Cambridge Companion to Karl Barth*, edited by John Webster, 143–58. Cambridge: Cambridge University Press, 2000.
Healy, Nicholas. *Church, World and the Christian Life: Practical-Prophetic Ecclesiology.* New York: Cambridge University Press, 2000.
———. "Communion Ecclesiology: A Cautionary Note." *Pro Ecclesia* 4 (1995) 442–53.
———. "The Logic of Karl Barth's Ecclesiology: Analysis, Assessment and Proposed Modifications." *Modern Theology* 10 (1994) 253–70.
Hunsinger, George. "Karl Barth's Christology: Its Basic Chalcedonian Character." In *The Cambridge Companion to Karl Barth*, edited by John Webster, 127–42. Cambridge: Cambridge University Press, 2000.
———. "A Tale of Two Simultaneities: Justification and Sanctification in Calvin and Barth." In *Conversing with Barth*, edited by John McDowell and Mike Higton, 68–89. Aldershot, UK: Ashgate, 2004.
Jüngel, Eberhard. *God's Being Is in Becoming: The Trinitarian Being of God in the Theology of Karl Barth. A Paraphrase.* Edinburgh: T. & T. Clark, 2001.
LaCugna, Catherine M. *God for Us: The Trinity and Christian Life.* New York: HarperCollins, 1991.
McIntosh, Adam. "The Doctrine of Appropriation as an Interpretative Framework for Karl Barth's Ecclesiology of the Church Dogmatics." Dissertation, D.Theol, Melbourne College of Divinity, 2006.
———. "The Doctrine of Appropriation as an Interpretative Framework for Karl Barth's Pneumatology of the *Church Dogmatics*." *Pacifica* 20 (2007) 278–91.
O'Grady, Colm. *The Church in the Theology of Karl Barth.* London: Geoffrey Chapman, 1968.
———. *The Church in Catholic Theology: Dialogue with Karl Barth.* London: Geoffrey Chapman, 1969.
Ormerod, Neil. *The Trinity: Retrieving the Western Tradition.* Wisconsin: Marquette University Press, 2005.
Torrance, Thomas F. *The Christian Doctrine of God: One Being, Three Persons.* Edinburgh: T. & T. Clark, 1996.

10

Why Do Humans Die?

An Exploration of the Necessity of Death in the Theology of Robert Jenson with Reference to Karl Barth's Discussion of "Ending Time"

Andrew Nicol

IT IS SURELY NO SURPRISE THAT ROBERT JENSON BE INVOKED IN A VOLume of essays on Karl Barth and trinitarian theology, but why death? It has often been suggested, not least by Jenson himself, that the doctrine of the resurrection is at the center of his dogmatics. Less apparent however, is the degree to which his proposals are shaped by the resurrection's necessary corollary—death. Furthermore, Jenson's understanding of the nature of death is located within a conception of human personhood that is thoroughly founded in and enabled by the triune God.

Following the lead of Augustine much Christian thought has tended to see death as a result of the fall, as an intrusion in the natural order of things.[1] Much like Augustine's fuller perspective, Jenson argues Thomas Aquinas taught that even though matter was corruptible, God's favor had preserved humans from death. The decay of death was allowed after God withdrew preservation of bodily existence after the fall.[2] However, some influential theologians, including in recent years Paul Althaus, Karl Rahner, and Eberhard Jüngel, have suggested that death is also part of God's original intention for human beings. Perhaps

---

1. Although, Jenson suggests that Augustine's fuller thought contends that originally humans could die, but did not because they were sustained by the tree of life. See Jenson, *Systematic Theology*, 2:330.

2. Aquinas, *Summa Theologiae*, i–ii.85.5–6, cited in Jenson, *Systematic Theology*, 2:330.

the most influential of all however, has been Karl Barth. Consciously following his lead in this regard, Robert Jenson has also argued that death as such is an appropriate boundary to finitude. This essay explores the necessity of death in Jenson's theology and its critical location in an ontology of human personhood thoroughly sourced in triune personal relations. This theme emerges early in Jenson's thought and is consistently characterized by conversation with Barth—one of his earliest and most influential dialogue partners. For this reason the essay begins with a synopsis of Barth's construal of death as "Ending Time," and moves to an analysis of Jenson's thought that observes his ongoing affinity with Barth and his almost inevitable departures.

Barth and the Necessity of Death

For Barth death is intrinsically linked to temporality. Humans exist in time allotted by God and this time is the "divinely given space for human life."[3] This time has a beginning, certain duration, and an emphatic end. In Barth's view finitude, or temporal limitation, necessitates mortality.[4] Protest against this limitation is understandable for it is proper that life holds onto life.[5] However, his crucial point is that long life, even infinite life, has no guarantee of fulfillment—*life needs the reality of limited duration*. Barth's logic unfolds in three propositions:

1. Life in an allotted span is appropriate as such is our difference from God.

2. It is not a *disadvantage* to live a definite span.

3. It would in fact be dangerous for humans to have to live an indefinite span.[6]

---

3. *CD* III/2 554.

4. Wolfhart Pannenberg on the other hand, argues that finitude does not imply mortality. See especially Pannenberg, *Systematic Theology*, 3:560f.

5. Barth argues that it is proper to protest the barrier of allotted time, for "human life is ignorant of its own true nature when it accepts the fall as its original and authentic destiny, and therefore when it is not troubled by the demand for duration and finds no problem in the allotment of its time" (*CD* III/2, 555).

6. Ibid., 562f.

Fundamentally, life needs the negation of everything that negates it, and everlasting human time cannot achieve this.[7] Barth notes that "In an infinite life restless craving would remain unrest."[8] Human beings must therefore end this life—they must die. This, argues Barth, is a natural and inherently good aspect of their creation. There is thus divine intention in the necessity of our death.

One day we shall have had our life then. But, what we shall have and be on the far side of our life in time is what death calls into question. For Barth, death returns us to the same non-being as we began. That we emerged from non-being is not necessarily negative, nevertheless implicit in our return to non-being is a pervasive threat, in Barth's words, a "gloomy shadow." This threat, properly understood, is not merely non-existence, but negation—in other words, judgment. Barth states in vivid imagery that this judgment hangs over life like a "tree marked for felling. . . . [This life] is devoted and delivered to this judgment, like a bracket with a minus before it which changes every plus in the bracket into a minus. The bracket is still there, but the minus stands in front of it canceling every other prospect but this fatal change."[9] Beginning and ending bound a life of irreparable guilt. Most importantly, therefore, as we approach our end, we approach God.[10]

Thus Barth also wants to say that death as we *actually* experience it is not as God intended. Even so, because humans are indeed guilty, we find ourselves under the sign of judgment justly. While this sign of judgment does *not* belong to God's good intention, it is all the same used and ordained by him. If there is a true, natural, and good nature to death, Barth reflects, it is thoroughly concealed under this guise. Barth therefore develops an important distinction between a natural death, which constrains our temporality, and a fearful death, which we experience in the light of our guilt. It is in this latter sense that death is evil. Barth states, "As man's eternal corruption, but also as its sign, death is not a part of man's nature as God created it. But it entered the world as an alien lord—it is the wages of sin."[11]

---

7. Ibid., 561.
8. Ibid., 562.
9. Ibid., 597.
10. Ibid., 596.
11. Ibid., 600, Cf. Rom 5:12, 14, 17; Rom 6:23, 8:6; and 1 Cor 15:22, 56.

At this point Barth asks whether one should not stop and simply admit that death is an experienced evil. What warrants the enquiry however, is the critical mitigating factor—the possibility that we have been spared this plunge into rejection and negation because another has suffered this death for us. The very ministry of Jesus demonstrates God's onslaught against the evil invasion of death in the world of life. Barth reminds us that it is the demons who are first to recognize Jesus' true identity. God's permission of this oppositional force is proven provisional. God will not allow death to run its course forever. This "last enemy" of humanity is declared God's enemy too in the death and resurrection of Jesus. The New Testament therefore measures humanity by what God has done for it. Before and apart from what God has done in Jesus Christ, man is dead even while he lives. As Barth states: "our behavior makes our life *eo ipso* ['by that very fact'] a forfeited life given over to death."[12] Death is thus not a tyrant in its own right. *In the rule of death we have to do with the rule of God.* So, it is not only death, but God who awaits us. It is therefore God not death that is to be feared.[13]

The appropriate fear of God then, is to hold fast to the cross of Christ. God is really the boundary of death, as death is the boundary of man. God is therefore the Lord of death, but does not affirm it. Barth argues that the Old Testament question concerning deliverance from death is secretly pregnant with a positive answer: "His [Christ's] death, resurrection and coming again are the basis of absolutely everything that is to be said about man and his future, end and goal in God."[14] Those who believe in Jesus can longer look at their death as though it were in front of them. It is behind them. Their old man has been crucified with Christ. In the event of the cross time is fulfilled. The meaning of the cosmos has happened in this event. The sign remains and while we still suffer the threats of the enemy, we do *not* have to suffer the judgment.[15] Consequently, our death must be understood christologically. The life of Jesus Christ, as God's life with and for unworthy man, is the only goal of

12. *CD* III/2, 601.

13. Summarized from ibid., 608.

14. Ibid., 624.

15. Barth states, "No other man stands at this center, and therefore no other really stands under the judgment of God. Other men, Christians consciously and the rest unconsciously, find themselves somewhere on the periphery around this center, and therefore . . . under the sign of judgment" (*CD* III/2, 605).

history. Christ's death is our justification, *not as a death instead of ours*, but in the most literal sense our death by which we pass through God's judgment.

In what sense is human death necessary then? If Christ was in fact blameless, is there a sense in which death in terms of judgment was not his inevitable end? Must we not have to be able to die if what Christ has done is not in vain? Well, Barth contends, infinite life brings the potential to multiply guilt on an infinite scale and the tendency to postpone the ordering of relationship. Barth affirms that, "We have to be finite, to be able to die, for the ἐφάπαξ ['once for all'] of the redemption accomplished in Christ to take effect for us."[16] In Barth's judgment therefore finitude is not intrinsically evil: "It belongs to the revelation of his glory in us, to the final proclamation of our justification in the judgment, to the removal of the overhanging sign of God's judgment, to the settled and incontestable factuality of our participation in God's eternal life, that one day we should merely and definitively have been."[17]

Ultimately, the fact that death has good and evil aspects can only be understood with reference to the triune God. Why do humans die? According to Barth, "Nature as well as unnature, good as well as evil, God's creation as well as the disastrous collision between the holy God and fallible man, are all present in man's end, in his dying and death."[18] Ultimately however, death is itself not the judgment, nor is it as such the sign of the judgment of God. It is only so *de facto*. God is humanity's beyond as Barth decisively concludes: "If hope in Christ is a real liberation for natural death, this rests on the fact that by divine appointment death as such belongs to the life of the creature and is thus necessary to it.... If we did not have to do with the definitive end of human life, we should not have to do with its resurrection and definitive co-existence with that of God."[19]

The Thinking of Robert Jenson

There are several ways in which one could approach the question of death in the thinking of Robert Jenson. One such point in which Jenson

16. Ibid., 631.
17. Ibid.
18. Ibid., 632.
19. Ibid., 639.

is in clear agreement with Barth is the utter actuality of Christ. On a related note, George Hunsinger once suggested that "Robert Jenson greatly advances the discussion [of Barth] by fully rising to the level of a 'strong misreading.'" Referring to Jenson's book *God after God*, he states, it is "perhaps the most provocative, incisive and wrong-headed reading of Barth available in English."[20] Yet, despite these concerns, Hunsinger goes on to acknowledge that Jenson clearly comprehends Barth's "real pulse"—the absolute priority of Jesus' existence. For Jenson too, it is this absolute priority that is the very possibility and meaning of our life and death. He insists that, "A human end that was not what we know as death is a might-have-been."[21] That God could have done things differently is simply counter-factual. Jenson is fond of Luther's dictum that "God has created us precisely to redeem us." In this sense there is no room for a hypothetically unfallen humanity for which the Son would have come. Thus the dialectic of death as an intended natural end and an intrusive evil force can be held together for both Barth and Jenson because of their commitment to the priority of God's redemptive purposes. In this way evil, while not enacted by God, is in Jesus Christ turned to God's purposes. He adds, "There would have been an undying humanity only in a created history that did not contain the cross, and under a God whose second identity was not the crucified Jesus."[22]

Human ending must therefore be understood in christological and consequently trinitarian terms. As Jenson sees it, God makes room for us within God's own triune life. We are brought into this triune conversation by virtue of our relation to Christ, as part of the *totus Christus*. For Jenson then, human being as such is constituted by inclusion in the triune conversation. Human personhood is created in accordance with God's triune personal life[23] and the image of God in creatures refers to our location in that God-relation itself.[24] Death is an intrinsic dimension of this conversation. The following section will focus on three interrelated spheres which illustrate how in Jenson's system the death or end of the person can be an intended natural end *and* the last enemy. The three key notions are: relationality, identity, and temporality.

20. Hunsinger, *How to Read Karl Barth*, 15.
21. Jenson, *Systematic Theology*, 2:331.
22. Ibid.
23. Ibid., 96.
24. Ibid., 65.

Relationality

Humans are determined in being-together. Jenson following a similar line to Barth summarizes this way: "God's address to us is the Son, who is the human person Jesus of Nazareth. To receive myself from God and be directed toward him is therefore to receive myself from and be directed toward a fellow human. And it is to receive myself from and be directed toward a human person who precisely to be himself brings others with him."[25]

Humans are unique among creatures because they are "praying animals."[26] A prayerful response is only enabled insofar as the triune God has addressed the creature and establishes human polity in mutually obligating discourse. Humanity's uniqueness is therefore the specific relation God takes up with us which overcomes our alienation from each other, and supremely from him. Jenson maintains that if personhood is intrinsically relational because it is founded in the creature's inclusion in triune personal life, eschatological inclusion in that life requires death. Deification requires resurrection and correspondingly death. That our supernatural end is in God means we must die, because as Jenson emphatically states: "The redeemed histories are complete in their deaths. And they are brought into the history of God as those for whom the Son died; they appear in God's life because and as Jesus' love infinitely interprets them. They are brought into God as the *interpretandum* of the inner dialogue of the Son's actual triune life."[27] This brings us to the second key notion. Death settles our identity.

Identity

Central to Jenson's understanding of personhood is self-transcendence. This refers to that human ability to take up a vantage point outside ourselves, to make ourselves our own objects. Jenson argues that self-transcendence is the most fitting conception of a *vestigia trinitatis*. He states, "We transcend ourselves toward God and each other. . . . We are counterparts of the Father as we find ourselves in the

---

25. Ibid., 73.
26. See especially Jenson, "Praying Animal," 311–25.
27. Jenson, *Systematic Theology*, 2:348.

Son in whom the Father finds himself."[28] As Francis Watson puts it, in Jenson's system the "doctrine of the Trinity provides a social model for human as well as divine personhood.... And the ground of this socially realized personhood, in which apperception, ego and freedom are united, is the triune God."[29]

Accordingly, drama and coherence appropriate to the story, are vital factors in Jenson's overall construal of reality. To be self-transcendent is to recognize ourselves in a story that awaits a proclaimed conclusion. Because people are stories, they have a plot. While we live, our story is of course unfinished. Each of us lives our lives as the hero of a drama missing its last act. "What am I here for?" remains an open question. This is why humans posit a suitable end to their story. For the most part this end does not, according to Jenson, successfully conceive of the extinguishment of consciousness. He maintains that to the concept of truly vanished consciousness, no projected experience or representation can correspond.[30] So often our projected cessation of being involves some conception of a continued ability to apprehend it. In a sense the termination of my consciousness turns out to be impossible to think. The religious quest is thus the human attempt to take care of our own ending. This is the essence of religion according to Jenson—it is the invention of eternity in the flight from temporality and death.

This means that death is the key. Jenson insists that only death makes our life a bounded whole. But, of course this is not a whole that one can apprehend. We do not live the now of our death—I am never therefore this whole for myself. There is however, one sense in which we may apprehend ourselves as a bounded whole. This occurs when another communicates their anticipation of my finished self. As Jenson outlines, "We are persons in that I am something for you and you are something for me. What I am for you is the player of a role assigned neither by you only, nor by me only, but by an inherited pattern of life together, into which history inserts each of us at his unique place."[31] We may thus obtain a glimpse of our possible coherent story through the communicated reflection of others.

28. Ibid., 65.

29. Watson, "'America's Theologian,'" 210.

30. For an extended discussion of this point see the first chapter on death in Jenson, *On Thinking the Human*.

31. Jenson, *Story and Promise*, 71.

Nevertheless, this address which enables a proleptic view of our final self can also be threatening. It may be a word that binds or manipulates, as we too bind and manipulate others in our address to them. This is the dilemma of original sin. If to be is to be addressed, the selfish nature of our address will bind. Death even dictates that the promissory nature of our love will ultimately be interrupted. As Jenson reflects, "What makes death the Lord's enemy, and fearful for us, is that it separates lovers.... Having no more being would be no evil were being not mutual."[32] Death breaks relationship and death is often so painful and tragic because we are mutual.

Supremely however, Jenson, like Barth, insists that the brokenness of our actual experience of death must be seen in the light of the cross and resurrection of Christ. Death, even as an enemy of God in one sense, settles our identity in time, because it is *that life* which is eschatologically interpreted by the triune God who transcends and conquers death itself. Jenson states: "If we were to simply continue after death, in whatever fashion, those raised would not be identified by their lives lived toward death and made whole entities by it. And that is to say their death would not have been their death, and their new life would not be God's victory over death.... The life that will be appropriated into God is the life that ends in death...."[33] Death is necessary because it appropriately bounds our temporal existence. This leads us to the third key notion—temporality.

Temporality

The explication of death and personhood in Jenson's work is undergirded with an idiosyncratic conception of temporality and futurity. To further understand how death plays its part we must return to what Hunsinger sees as Jenson's "wrongheadedness." For Jenson this represents a fundamental and determinative move away from Barth.[34] He relates this development in a 1972 autobiographical article. As previously mentioned Jenson had learnt from Barth to "confess the earthly history

---

32. Jenson, *Systematic Theology*, 2:331.
33. Ibid., 346.
34. One may clearly observe this move in Jenson's first book and adaptation of his doctoral thesis, *Alpha and Omega*.

of Jesus as itself the 'crisis' of all other time."[35] But, he fears that in the equation of eternity with Jesus' time there is a danger of drawing "Christ off and back into a Calvinist place 'before all time.'"[36] Eternity, maintains Jenson, cannot be a timelessly available other realm. He sees in Barth's view of eternity a form of "supra-temporality" which only partly corresponds to what time is for us. For Jenson there is no archetypal temporality outside of history. Paul Cumin has observed that for Jenson archetypal temporality *is* the Trinity itself as three interacting yet unified poles of historical time.[37] This "move" is essential to our discussion of death, because in Jenson's proposal God has to work out his identity in temporal history—*God too must face death*. The working out of the triune God's self-identity in time clearly has critical theological implications. While this paper does not have the scope to explore these implications, their sheer weight, even audacity, require acknowledgement. These issues notwithstanding, one might ask whether Jenson has fully acknowledged the nuances of Barth's perspective on eternity and time. Has he misunderstood Barth or chosen to read Barth a certain way in order to go "beyond" him? Whatever the case (and I suspect the latter), Jenson sees himself departing from Barth at this point. His definitive standpoint is that God does not exist in abstract timelessness.

Death then is a brute existential fact of finitude. Jenson wants to agree with Heidegger that we get a sense of "totality" by facing the death that lies temporally ahead of us. For Heidegger however, what defines humanity is immersion in the historicity of human Being-in-time. However, this radical sense of human temporality makes nothingness the far side of being. Fulfillment no longer points beyond death. Sartre on the other hand had objected that death actually breaks off life and robs it of meaning. Either way, death equals non-being, and as Jenson maintains you can't be there for your own non-being.[38] The fabric of reality in Jenson's thought is unreservedly temporal, however for him the far side of being is not nihilism, but inclusion in the triune life.

---

35. Jenson, "About Dialog," 40.

36. Ibid.

37. This insight is taken from the analysis of Paul Cumin in, "Robert Jenson and the Spirit of It All," 164.

38. Jenson emphasizes this point in several places including *On Thinking the Human*, 2–4; and *Systematic Theology*, 2:327–28.

Whilst God is not timeless, our time is however encompassed in God's triune life. In this sense, God is the Beginning and End of time. In and through time God reconciles the world to its goal.[39] Jenson states, "[And] if the triune God is the real God, then time is the *accommodation* this life makes in itself for the particular History that the Son in fact and freely is, Jesus' history with what is not God."[40] This temporal life for Creator and creatures is orientated to the future. To be is to be a relation to the future. Early in his career Jenson says he learnt from Rudolf Bultmann "to see time as the horizon of the Bible's explication of human life; and to understand God's transcendence as 'the Insecurity of the future.'"[41] Futurity has remained an important aspect of Jenson's theology. However, he insists that Bultmann failed to "narrate the crisis in which God will be the End."[42] So, Jenson's thought emphasizes that the gospel is a promise with content; the word of a narratable future, and of God as the power of that specific future. The specificity comes from the story of Jesus. Thus for Jenson the biblical God is not the Persistence of the Past but the Power of the Future. It is from the future that he creates and commands us to himself. Reality is essentially eschatological and it is that "we *will* be what we will be with him, that we *are* at all."[43]

Death however, is a fundamental condition on any human promise. Only a promise that had death behind it could be unconditional. Jenson states, "Only love that has undergone death for the other and just thereby lives anew can be sure in itself."[44] Therefore, "Only the success of death, only resurrection, can be the act of life from the future free from and for the past. . . . If Jesus is risen, this life is enacted."[45] For Jenson it is the triune transcendence of death through resurrection which is the key to the conquering of death. This is both the *defeat of an enemy* and an intended means by which *identity is settled*. An implication of this triumph is not that the creature evades death but that through it they meet the living God. Jenson states this clearly when he says: "God's overcoming of death is not, therefore, only his overcoming of some-

39. Jenson, "Creation as a Triune Act," 40.
40. Ibid. Emphasis in the original.
41. Jenson, "About Dialog," 40.
42. Ibid.
43. Jenson, "Creation as a Triune Act," 42. Emphasis in the original.
44. Jenson, *Systematic Theology*, 2:332.
45. Jenson, *God after God*, 17.

thing intruding into his creation. It is simultaneously his transformation of creature's natural temporal finitude, and just so his achieving of his original end for the creation in one of its defining aspects."[46]

Ultimately, Jenson proposes that our death cannot be thought in any other way than as Christian trinitarian theology. Otherwise we cheat; we must always produce a concept of death paired with a representation of not-quite death.[47] Humans die as a means by which the creature's life in time is brought to a necessary conclusion. Both Barth and Jenson emphasize however that this is far from the final word—the triune God is on the far side of death.

Conclusion

Jenson's depiction of personhood and the necessity of death is richly sourced in the life of the triune God. The contention that death has a basis in God's original intent for humanity is provocative and faces squarely the angst of temporal existence. This is something Barth and Jenson elucidate insightfully. Humans must die because it makes their temporal existence a whole. The good news says Jenson, is that the bounded life we have led, whether broken, cut short, or long and fulfilled, will be divinely interpreted by love in the infinite eschatological community of the triune God.

There are also many questions that arise from this construal. In conclusion however, two important issues are offered for brief critical reflection. Firstly, does Jenson's phenomenology of death make salvation *too* eschatological an event? In Jenson's system it is the motive force of the Spirit that pulls events powerfully and coherently toward realization. Just how the Spirit determines the dramatic coherence of God's life in history, without "approaching" from the future, relies on a "helix-like" conception of time with the risen Christ at its center.[48] Jenson is aware that this is difficult to conceive, and imagination notwithstanding, one is inclined to question its overall coherence.[49] Douglas Farrow has

---

46. Jenson, *Systematic Theology*, 2:331.

47. Jenson, *On Thinking the Human*, 15.

48. Jenson, "Scripture's Authority in the Church," 35.

49. Whilst criticized by some for not showing a "suitable" degree of metaphysical imagination, Oliver Crisp clearly raises issues of logical coherency in Jenson's notions of time and pre-existence. See Crisp, "Robert Jenson on the Pre-existence of Christ," 27–45.

argued that such a dominant futurity actually conflates ontology and soteriology, whereby rising from the dead constitutes *true* being.[50] In his attempt to eschew a protological determination of reality, has Jenson somehow diminished temporal existence in preference for eschatological openness?

Secondly, the explication of sin and judgment is notably light in Jenson's theology of death. Again, Farrow observes that Jenson, by construing death as "native to humankind," has adopted a piece of natural theology that "even Barth failed to excise."[51] Whilst both Barth and Jenson may be defended on this charge, this criticism emphasizes the lack of emphasis on death as the "wages of sin," particularly in Jenson. This is no new criticism. Jenson, in characteristic candidness, recounts in the preface to the reprint of *Story and Promise* how the critical appraisal of the book by his revered *Doktorvater* Peter Brunner struck deeply. He relates Brunner's words: 'There was simply something missing he said . . . or at best only present 'in disguise' under the notion of 'alienation': the sheer reality of sin and judgment. 'That my death nakedly and inescapably . . . confronts me with the holiness of God; . . . a confrontation in which the issue is my eternal lostness . . . and merciful rescue, for Christ's sake, from this deserved and established fate—this function of death is hardly worked out in your discussions. Has not Barth triumphed over Luther here?'"[52] Yet despite this passionate admonition, Jenson has made a choice. He is most certainly aware of the weight of sin, but in his judgment the church's message in the second person is always and only that, "because the Lord Jesus has risen, you are God's beloved child, and our saying this to you is your last judgment, let out ahead of time."[53] It is in this sense that the necessity of death loses its sting. But, does it leave something unsaid? Indeed, has Barth triumphed over Luther?

---

50. Farrow, Demson, and Di Noia, "Robert Jenson's Systematic Theology," 93.
51. Ibid., 92.
52. Jenson, *Story and Promise*, 2.
53. Ibid., 4.

Bibliography

Barth, Karl. *Church Dogmatics*. 4 vols. Edinburgh: T. & T. Clark, 1956–75.

Crisp, Oliver. "Robert Jenson on the Pre-existence of Christ." *Modern Theology* 23.1 (2007) 27–45

Cumin, Paul. "Robert Jenson and the Spirit of It All: Or, You (Sometimes) Wonder Where Everything Else Went." *Scottish Journal of Theology* 60 (2007) 161–79.

Farrow, Douglas, David Demson, and J. Augustine Di Noia. "Robert Jenson's Systematic Theology: Three Responses." *International Journal of Systematic Theology* 1.1 (1999) 89–104.

Hunsinger, George. *How to Read Karl Barth: The Shape of His Theology*. Oxford: Oxford University Press, 1991.

Jenson, Robert W. "About Dialog, and the Church, and Some Bits of the Theological Autobiography of Robert W. Jenson." *Dialog* 11 (Spring 1972) 38–42.

———. *Alpha and Omega: A Study in the Theology of Karl Barth*. New York: Nelson, 1963.

———. "Creation as a Triune Act." *Word & World* II (1982) 34–42.

———. *God after God: The God of the Past and the God of the Future, Seen in the Work of Karl Barth*. New York: Bobs-Merrill, 1969.

———. *On Thinking the Human: Resolutions of Difficult Notions*. Grand Rapids: Eerdmans, 2003.

———. "The Praying Animal." *Zygon* 18 (1983) 311–25.

———. "Scripture's Authority in the Church." In *The Art of Reading Scripture*, edited by Ellen F. Davis and Richard Hayes, 27–53. Grand Rapids: Eerdmans, 2003.

———. *Story and Promise: A Brief Theology of the Gospel about Jesus*. Philadelphia: Fortress, 1973.

———. *Story and Promise*. 1973. Reprint, Ramsey, NJ: Sigler, 1989.

———. *Systematic Theology*. Vol. 2, *The Works of God*. New York: Oxford University Press, 1999.

Pannenberg, Wolfhart. *Systematic Theology*. Vol. 3. Grand Rapids: Eerdmans, 1998.

Watson, Francis. "'America's Theologian': An Appreciation of Robert Jenson's Systematic Theology, with Some Remarks about the Bible." *Scottish Journal of Theology* 55 (2002) 201–23.

11

Prayer, Particularity, and the Subject of Divine Personhood

Who Are Brümmer and Barth Invoking When They Pray?

John C. McDowell

Introduction

THE TITLE "TRINITARIAN THEOLOGY AFTER BARTH" IS A DECEPTIVELY simple one. With the reference to trinitarian *theology* it appears to have learned from Barth that the doctrine of the Trinity is no mere dogmatic addendum, merely another thing confessed. Instead, it is, in some way or another, regulative of what counts as Christian. Of course, all Christian doctrines overlap and interpenetrate one another, but as doctrines they have their *raison d'être* in the confession of *God*. However, a claim by Daniel Migliore that "Rightly understood, the doctrine of the Trinity is not an arcane, speculative doctrine" implies that something terribly wrong has occurred in theological reflection.[1] Problematic is not only the modern feeling that the doctrine of the Trinity is "esoteric and speculative," but also the separation between the doctrine and Christian practice. Consequently, Migliore feels compelled to counter by arguing that "the route that we take and the conclusions that we reach in the doctrine of God will profoundly influence everything else that we say about Christian faith and life."[2]

---

1. Migliore, *Faith Seeking Understanding*, 59.
2. Ibid., 56.

Migliore's worries echo Karl Rahner's celebrated complaints made a few decades earlier. Whatever the merits and demerits of Rahner's claim as an *historical* observation on Western theologies—and significant work challenges the connections between Augustinian trinitarianism and individualism, hierarchicalism, and so on, connections largely dependent upon Théodore de Régnon's now-classic thesis—the theological claims remain significant.[3] There are two such broad arguments here: firstly, the positive one that the doctrine of the Trinity has theologically regulative significance for everything Christian; and the negative one, that in practice it does not have the force it should have.[4] Not only do many critiques of the doctrine fail to understand the doctrine as itself theological reflection on early Christian doxologies and thus practices of worship, but also disregard that it in turn came to be the lens through which worship was offered by expressing who the One worshipped is.[5]

But what does "*after* Barth" mean? It can be taken in a chronological sense that has theological significance for the regulation of trinitarian theology, a trinitarian theology that has learned to ask who God is in some manner through Barth's trinitarian reflections. On the other hand, there is a chronological sense that refuses to do its trinitarian theology through him. Worries about whether Barth has truly engaged with the pluriformity, or the very *trinitarianness*, of God in his account of the Trinity could understand the "after Barth" as a way of returning

---

3. Régnon, *Études de théologie positive sur la sainte Trinité*. Régnon's now highly contested study "discovered" the distinction between Western and Eastern theological tendencies: the Latins proceeded from general nature to concrete person, thereby prioritising divine unity; and the Greeks proceeded from person to nature, so emphasizing the plurality of divine persons.

4. On the latter, see Jüngel, "Trinitarian Prayers," 244.

5. Soskice, "Trinity and Feminism," 136: "The doctrine is best seen not as an additional conviction, but rather as providing the frame in which central convictions rest." But here is a tension, one often associated with George Lindbeck's cultural-linguistic account of doctrine. Is the doctrine of the Trinity not *also* an additional conviction, even if not merely or perhaps even primarily so? After all, the doctrine aims to say something about God, however fragilely, in order to express what is most appropriate regarding the question "who is to be worshipped?" While this is not to suggest that the doctrine is *explanatory*, it does belong to a kind of "realism" that refuses to reduce God to human self-description (which is not to say that the grammatical account of doctrine does, but it perhaps does not make clear where "God" does not become reduced to linguistic-rules).

threefold difference to theology over against Barth's perceived indulgence in singularising divine subjectivity.

Even so, it is important not to reduce the plurality of accounts of "Trinitarian Theology after Barth." This book's title, then, cannot demand anything less than an attentiveness to, and honesty in assessing, a whole host of complex issues.

Mentioning honesty here leads conveniently to the theme of prayer, since, as Rowan Williams indicates, prayer is significant "for an honest theology."[6] Barth's own claims in this regard in his *Evangelical Theology* lectures emerges from earlier arguments such as that which ties prayer and obedience: "The prayer of the Christian to God is the basic act of the obedience engendered in faith."[7] Prayer is offered to God and, given that the doctrine of the Trinity is irreducibly the measure of what counts as the Christian confession of God, it is intimately connected to the triunity of God's being God. Taking seriously the critical observations of Rahner and Migliore demands that there be ways in which a theological account of prayer necessitates a theological engagement that pre-eminently involves reflection on the doctrine of the Trinity.

When discussing the early modern intellectual context Amos Funkenstein identifies "changes of connotation that some divine attributes underwent in a new intellectual climate."[8] The changes were so materially significant, and thus not sealed in some innocuous sphere called "apologetics" as several who criticize Barth on "natural theology" imagine, that he feels compelled to critically exclaim, "How much more deadly to theology were such helpers than its enemies!"[9] Vincent Brümmer's well-known account of prayer, it will be suggested, is an instance not so much of prayer shaped by a trinitarian account of divine self-identification but of a theistic tradition that is at best tangentially comprehensible within a trinitarian dogmatic framework, but at worst essentially disfiguring of it in important ways.[10]

The paper will not attend to thematically genetic issues with reference to Brümmer, nor test the genealogy of the changes suggested by

---

6. Williams, *On Christian Theology*, 13.
7. *CD* III/3, 283.
8. Funkenstein, *Theology and the Scientific Imagination*, 9.
9. Ibid., 8. LaCugna somewhat trivialises the differences in "Philosophers and Theologians on the Trinity," 169, 171.
10. Brümmer, *What Are We Doing When We Pray?*

Funkenstein or others, but rather begin to propose very broadly a non-departicularizing theological description of prayer developed largely through a critical reading of *What Are We Doing When We Pray?* and Barth's doctrine of the Trinity in *CD* I/1.[11]

Generality, Abstraction, and the Theistic What Is "Prayer"?

Words take their meaning from the company they keep and the differences they then perform from the other words in these contexts. While this is particularly clear with homonyms, it is true of all other words as well. Consequently, we need to see what words are doing in any given linguistic situation, and in observing this it becomes clear that language-use is a skill that involves intensive training within communities of linguistically communicative agents. What kind of "company" does talk of "prayer" keep, and in particular that of Brümmer's account?

His book title initially suggests the importance of reflection on concrete practices or performative contexts through making a connection between prayer and *acts* of praying. But it is immediately apparent that he never defines the "we" in his study's focus. Without careful attention to the demands of this particularizing matter there will come, largely by default even if not by design, an assumption that the "we" refers to all those who pray. This again raises the question of what is meant by "prayer," and so we come full circle—we need to have some sense of what prayer is in order to ask what we are doing when we pray; but in order to have this sense attention must be paid to concrete practices of people who do pray. One way out of the difficulty is to start from what so-called "religious communities" call "prayer" and reflect philosophically upon that. According to D. Z. Phillips, "to understand what prayer is one must refer to the religious community from which prayer derives its intelligibility."[12]

On one level it could be argued that one does not have to *begin* by claiming some knowledge of what prayer is; but merely commence by observing practices that various religious groups name "prayer." So

---

11. My focus will not be on Barth's texts that explicitly theologically address prayer, but rather on something broader, the trinitarian *ethos* of his dogmatics developing in the early 1930s.

12. Phillips, *Concept of Prayer*, 36.

William Swatos argues, "People pray, and that is all a sociologist needs to know to begin work."[13] Nevertheless, on another level, this strategy finds it difficult to avoid imposing just such a pre-understanding. After all, what counts as similarity and difference in the practices and with what assumptions do we measure and evaluate these? How can we evaluate talk of Christian life *as*, and thus not merely *involving*, prayer? What can we do with Bruce Marshall's observation that "the Christian community presents us with a confusing welter of beliefs and practices"?[14] Simply, what counts as "prayer"?

Recently there have been studies attempting to test "the efficacy of prayer" that have set groups of Christians, Jews, Muslims, Buddhists, and others certain tasks the results of which could generate empirically measurable data. The assumption is that all these groups are doing something essentially the same, and further that their various "prayer" practices can be formulated with a scientifically measurable outcome.[15] Is this an example of a thorough and careful attentiveness to different practices that, in the end, turn out to be doing the same thing, or an imposed singular categorization? Understood in the former fashion, the study of prayer would begin by describing the multiplicity of practices in order to seek similarities that would enable ways of continuing to talk of the diversity under the umbrella term "prayer."

It is noticeable that Brümmer largely fails to consider these difficulties and consequently follows a common but nonetheless cavalier attitude to particularity, tending to lapse into a substantial, and thus not innocuous, mistake of abstracting prayer talk from concrete practices.

Clearly prayer as human performance can be studied by a plethora of human and social studies: in particular, psychology, anthropology, sociology, history, cultural studies, religious studies, and so on. Even the natural sciences have more recently attempted to get in on the act. Nevertheless, what Christians at least, for all their differences, think they are doing when they pray is something that cannot be reduced without remainder to these disciplines of the phenomenal. What I mean by this is hinted at by Miroslav Volf when he argues that "beliefs are already

---

13. Swatos, "Power of Prayer," 103.

14. Marshall, *Trinity and Truth*, 19.

15. See Poloma and Gallup, *Varieties of Prayer*, 8–9; Gallup and Jones, *One Hundred Questions and Answers*, 36; Byrd, "Positive Therapeutic Effects of Intercessory Prayer," 826–29; Benson, *Beyond the Relaxation Response*, 146.

entailed in practices."¹⁶ Yet it is equally the case that belief can *affect and effect practice*. According to L. Gregory Jones, speaking particularly about Christian initiation, practice is bound up with not only action but desire and belief in a complex and dynamic interchange.¹⁷

The implication, beyond any naïve and habitual bifurcation of beliefs and practices familiar in modernity, is that differences in practice of "prayer" so-called have to do in significant ways with differences in belief, in how pray-ers understand what they are doing, and particularly how they understand the one prayed to. As Phillips recognizes, "One only has to compare accounts of religious experience to appreciate how diverse they are, and how different are the conceptions of God which underlie them."¹⁸

To return to Brümmer's account, there seems to be more going on with his study than simple inattentiveness to difference and particularity, or the strategy working *remoto christo*, as Anselm might say, for a non-Christian audience. He assumes that prayer is offered to God, and yet no attempt is made to demonstrate the difficulty of using this theological term. Consequently, among other things, he masks the sense of different, and often incompatible, practices of usage. Michael Buckley's study is particularly suggestive for understanding what is happening here theologically. Modern thinking developed in directions where it disabled the particularity of theological regulation so that "more specifically the person and teaching of Jesus or the experience and history of the Christian Church, did not enter the discussion."¹⁹ Brümmer appears caught in a web of theistic signification that abstracts "God" from the operations of the triune economy, and thus confuses God with something else. Not only is this a mistake from a theological perspective, it distorts what is meant by Christian life and practice, mistakenly assuming it is little more than an instance or expression of something more basic and common, what the early British deists called "natural religion."²⁰

---

16. Volf, "Theology for a Way of Life," 256.

17. Jones, "Beliefs, Desires, Practices," 194.

18. Phillips, Concept of Prayer, 7.

19. Buckley, *At the Origins of Modern Atheism*, 33, 55. Cf. Burrell, *Faith and Freedom*, 3–4; Lash, "Considering the Trinity," 185.

20. There is a further crucial abstraction in Brümmer's study. For it prayer is something *we* do rather than that *into which we are drawn*, particularly as it is performed

One Person, Many Persons? Adding Up the Personality Disorder

Brümmer promisingly argues that "It would be a category mistake to interpret the believer's claim that God answers prayer as an experimental hypothesis."[21] The promise lies in the distinction between prayer and observable natural phenomena, the latter being "governed by causal necessity," and the former being related to Personal agency which is always the result of the agent's free choice between alternative courses of action.[22] Since prayer involves personal agencies that entails, among other things, that prayer and its effects cannot be observed in any simply measurable sense. Equally promising, and consequent to this, is Brümmer's refusal to equate prayer with manipulatability. Machines, being "governed by causal necessity," "can be manipulated."[23] In contrast, persons can be persuaded but their "decision to act remains up to" them.

Yet the logic of his claims here is not entirely sound, and one must consider a distinct limitation in the analogy of persons as it is employed without further qualification—persons can indeed be manipulated. It takes little reflection on the work of ideology critics, among many others, to realize that persons are not indeterministically placed, existentially "footloose and fancy free," despite the more indeterminist accounts of the human person that have characterized modern ethical and epistemological constructivisms. Whether they *should* be manipulated is a question on a different level. Brümmer's account broadly could be supported by, among other things, a strategic claim that persons are *ontologically* non-manipulable since the truth of their being is in their relation with God. This, though, would be still a form of determination since it involves an ontic *receptivity* or *dependence upon* God, and that is not an option Brümmer, with his more indeterminist sensibility, seems able to suggest.

One might respond further by saying that God is not a human person and therefore not manipulable in the way human persons are. Yet

---

for us or *in our place* by Jesus, the Logos incarnate. See McDowell, "'Openness to the World,'" 253–83. Of course, there is a pneumatological dynamic to this (that prayer involves the Spirit of Christ praying *in* us) that Brümmer equally neglects.

21. Brümmer, "What Are We Doing When We Pray?" 2.
22. Ibid., 5.
23. Ibid., 6.

this would be to admit that the concept of persons be limited in its appropriate attribution to God. Brümmer, it would seem, is deploying the analogy of persons in some less than analogical ways. Of course he, with a personalist version of what Peter Geach calls "two-way contingency,"[24] properly distinguishes persons and machines, and the biblical imagery of divine personhood draws theology closer to analogies of persons-in-conversation than active agents acting on machinery or even the impersonal operations of fate. But there is a danger in overplaying the *analogy* and thus of subverting the difficulty of explicating divine personhood by categories fitted for the universe. Take the notion of prayer as "conversation." What is happening here? In conversation, the personal disposition of the conversants toward one another is determinative for both the shape and the results of the conversation. Brümmer sees something of this in prayer, and even argues that "sincere or wholehearted" requests do prayers' "efficacy" offered "to a personal God."[25] This is a suggestive assertion, which might all seem well and good since one's disposition generally determines what one is doing, and the shape of its consequences are largely dependent upon that. Moreover, the claim in some sense can resist the reduction of prayer to emergency situations, a kind of last resort measure that, intended or not, renders "God" something to be used for our own ends. Much prayer (prayer for loved ones who are ill, national days of prayer during periods of national crisis, and so on) does take the form of something like conjuration. This, according to Rahner, signals the human's attempt "to subject God to himself."[26] Brümmer's concept of divine "personal-ness," then, seems to deny the reduction of God to the object of manipulative requests, and his conception of prayer as conversation can remind us that the "personal" God is not an object of our demanding.

What happens then to prayers of impetration? A conversational approach implies at least that prayer is *much more than petition*. So Peter Baelz argues that "Prayer is more than asking God to give us this or that."[27] Asking, here, becomes one aspect of a more "rounded" sense of the activity of prayer, and in this way is less in danger of reducing God

---

24. Geach, *God and the Soul*, 89; cf. Brümmer, *What Are We Doing When We Pray?* 30.

25. Brümmer, *What Are We Doing When We Pray?* 7.

26. Rahner, *Practice of Faith*, 71.

27. Baelz, *Does God Answer Prayer?* 7.

to the objectified provider of our needs. Prayer has to do with personal relations, and thereby prayer as thanksgiving, confession, contemplation, and so on needs to be emphasized.

Nevertheless, the question remains whether these dialogical terms appropriately prevent the drawing of "God," and talk of God's personhood and agency, into the most unsophisticated anthropomorphism: "He is a person and therefore free in what he does."[28] Here are all kinds of questions one might want to put to Brümmer with regards to his connecting of prayer, efficacy, and faith. For now it is important to see the kind of "onto-theology" that undergirds his presentation. The problem lies partly in the way the prayerful asking to God is construed, but even more fundamentally in terms of the way *God as conversant* is conceived. Unless the analogy of persons in conversation is developed with considerably more hesitancy, recalling the partiality in the function of any and all metaphors and analogies, what we find driving the notion of prayer as "conversation," at least in Brümmer's sense, is a certain understanding of persons and of the I-Thou relation of two "others"[29] (Baelz's preferred term "communion" may have other, and more satisfactory, connotations).[30]

His account echoes post-Enlightenment accounts of the self in which relations are free relatings of undetermined agents or persons. This is the reason why he categorically rejects Thomas's considerably more careful and suggestive account of "double agency" for describing divine-human relations, castigating it as ultimately a deterministic conception of the universe that renders human freedom and independence superfluous, and that thereby raises the specter of passive resignation to the way things are. Brümmer's opposition to such renderings of the God-human relation is largely the product of a theology that is locked into compatibalist moves of likening prayer to the kind of bipolar exchange involved in conversation ("God does what he is asked *because* he is asked."),[31] therein also raising the specter of divine capriciousness: "if

28. Brümmer, *What Are We Doing When We Pray?* 53.

29. Stump, "Petitionary Prayer," 582, for instance, speaks of prayer in terms of a protective "buffer" against two vastly unequal "persons."

30. Baelz, *Prayer and Providence*, 101.

31. Brümmer, *What Are We Doing When We Pray?* 33. The divine-human relationship becomes inverted with God responding in some way or another (either by granting, or refusing to grant) to the pray-er's requests, and thus placing the initiative with the pray-er. Certainly one way of mitigating the force of that is to understand prayer

he is to be acknowledged as a person, there is nothing automatic about what he does, and we should not *presume upon* him."[32] Consequently, it is revealing to hear him claim that his critical distinction "does not imply that they [viz., prayers] cannot be tested at all."[33] The effect of the personal disposition of the pray-er "does increase the *probability* [of the success of prayer requests] in a way that could be shown statistically. One could inquire, therefore, whether devout prayers to a personal God would not increase the chances of the events prayed for in a statistically significant way."[34] Even if he does come to claim the difficulty of statistically measuring under experimental conditions the efficacy of prayer, Brümmer feels that the nature of the connection between prayer/prayer/efficacy is such that there may well be just such "evidence." This is quite an admission and indicates that his account does not sufficiently theologically challenge the evidentialist reduction, we might say with Jean-Luc Marion, of "God into being" or, with Thomas Aquinas, into a genus. In this he is far from alone among philosophers. As David Burrell observes, "the endemic tendency of philosophers treating divinity is to assign God a place in the universe, albeit the largest or the first or the most significant."[35] While he does acknowledge that God is not a cause like other causes, Brümmer's God is too neatly construed as an agent in a world of agents, even if his privileging of the personal metaphors in God-talk subvert some of the more unpalatable consequences of talk of God in terms of being an impersonal cause in a world of causes.

This entails that the trinitarian theological problem lies deeper than simply the matter of the number of persons, as happens in the kind of social trinitarian account offered by Richard Swinburne, among others. A conceptuality of the "I-Thou" retains the sense of independent subjects *over and against each other* no more than the thought of one I and three Thous. In fact, in an earlier article Swinburne unashamedly argues that the doctrine of the Trinity has to do with three individuals,

---

as divine gift and invitation. Yet God remains responsive here, and the conversation is momentary. Moreover, we have to ask just how far "prayer" is conversation when its heart is *petition*, asking. What meaning would the term "conversation" have if one of the conversants was continually asking for things of the other?

32. Ibid., 54.
33. Ibid., 7.
34. Ibid.
35. Burrell, "Divine Action and Human Freedom," 104.

three "gods" in fact.³⁶ Aside from the obvious tritheism and the question over what the doctrine of the Trinity was doing with the, in its Latin form, *una substantia*, the point that Sarah Coakley's incisive critique makes of Swinburne is that this doctrine of God is modeled on the basis of "three Cartesian 'individuals'" theologically projected.³⁷ Of course, "even if projection always [to some degree or another] has a role to play in theology," Karen Kilby observes, "it is here playing a distinctive, and distinctively problematic one."³⁸ The social trinitarians like Swinburne, and even Moltmann, want to say some very precise things about God, and the character of these things prompts Kilby to argue, "much of the detail . . . [appears to be] derived either from the individual author's or the larger society's latest ideals of how human beings should live in community."³⁹

What resources do theologies of "prayer as conversation" have to prevent one "from mistaking the image for God, from thinking of God as subject to the limitations of our imagery"?⁴⁰ Conversation requires two linguistic subjects who share a linguistic context, and manifestly God does not share such a context with God's creatures, and thus talk of God's speech, Word, and revelation should be handled in appropriate ways. This is in tension with a theological perspective that insists that "God," as von Balthasar declares, "is not a Thou in this sense of being simply another I," an object, even if that be the objectivity of a rational subject who stands over against us and can encounter us as an other.⁴¹ Instead, God is, von Balthasar argues, "the profoundest mystery within our own being," even as God remains distinguishable from us so that the immanence of this being "within" is not to be construed "as so interior to us that we confuse it with our own being, with a natural wisdom

---

36. Swinburne, "Could There Be More than One God," 225–41.

37. Coakley, "'Persons' in the 'Social' Doctrine of the Trinity," 128. Understanding the doctrine of the Trinity as being essentially about numbers has been a thought plaguing modern critical treatments of it, from John Hick's application of the image of the square-circle to James P. Mackey's charge that it is "at worst, an intellectual conundrum comprising some strange celestial mathematics" (*Christian Experience of God as Trinity*, 3).

38. Kilby, "Perichoresis and Projection," 439.

39. Ibid., 441.

40. McCabe, *God Still Matters*, 27. Cf. Phillips, *Concept of Prayer*, 50; Tillich, *Systematic Theology*, 1:127. However, see McIntyre, *Theology after the Storm*, 198, 205.

41. Balthasar, *Prayer*, 19.

given us once and for all, and ours to use as we will."[42] That entails that "we cannot hold conversation with God," although when used with proper caution the conversational metaphor may well remain useful.[43]

This dogmatic context is not even considered by Brümmer. His "God" is abstracted from the economy of God's graceful performance with God's creatures. The problem is not so much one of semantics and method used, as if his account would be more satisfactory if only he spoke of the *triune* God and not "God" *simpliciter*, or if he reflected more on the biblical account of prayer than provide abstract, *sounding* philosophical reflections on practices of prayer. The problem irreducibly is that of a *substantial* or *material* abstraction.

At the very least, a "conversational" model for prayer is distinctly limited. After all, language of "conversation" may be too bland. As Barth observes, to clasp the hands in prayer is the beginning of an uprising against the disorder of the world. In a modest approval of the controversial metaphor, then, Barth declares that "In the first three petitions [of the Lord's Prayer] our prayer is *a sort of* conversation with the heavenly. It is like a sigh."[44] At its best, "conversation" remains a metaphor needing to be supplemented, especially with a sense of ethical urgency. At its worst, however, it is distracting and even theologically inappropriate. Put starkly, Bümmer has, in the words of Lash on modern "theisms," "lost sight of the difficulty of speaking of God."[45] Likewise he has lost sight of the difficulty of speaking to God.[46]

Less Object-ion to the Pluriformity of the Divine Subjectivity

Barth's doctrine of the Trinity as developed in *CD* I/1 would not seem to be particularly promising for generating theological proposals for redirecting theologies of prayer. Barth is well known at this point in his *oeuvre* for rejecting the appropriateness of discourse of personhood in

42. Ibid., 23.
43. Ibid., 11f.
44. Barth, *Prayer*, 43, my emphasis.
45. Lash, "Considering the Trinity," 190.
46. Among other things, conversation can suggest linguistic fluency of invocatory address, whereas being before God has more to do with confession, purgation and transformation, with "being-in-becoming."

relation to the threefoldness of God's being God.[47] In response, the term "person" is given its place as an indication of the personality of God, while the divine differentiations are controversially renamed "modes."[48] Critics suggest that in responding to modern anthropological atomization Barth unwittingly assumes and repeats it, only now drawing it into the very discourse about the being of God. In this respect, the use of the phrase "three modes of being" is the least of the worries in many ways, and only the most superficial readings attribute Sabellianism to this when it is quite clear, as we will see below, that the language functions not to make the divine pluriformity something successive, and therefore limited to the economy, but simultaneous.[49] The difficulty is deeper, it is commonly suggested. Consequently, it would appear that any thought of developing a trinitarian theology of prayer "after Barth" would need to reject his account of the doctrine of the Trinity.

Briefly to return to Brümmer, his problem was not so much the one of numbers, of having only one, as much as the kind of one he assumed that could be spoken of without hesitation as "God." As Barth claims, what is important is "not any knowledge of any unity of any God," but of the unity appropriate to *God*.[50] Brümmer's "one" is an objectification of God largely through projecting post-Enlightenment understandings of persons as selves. Even if he does resist some of the more fashionable immanentist moves that isolate or atomize selfhood, and does so by conceiving of a relation with God as Self, Brümmer's way of doing this amounts to a slightly different but nonetheless real reductionist immanentism—God as categorically present to human understanding as being "person" and thus distinctively like items in the intramundane.

Barth too uses discourse of personhood of God and even frequently employs the category of I-Thou relations, in relation to "the divine I which confronts man in this [revelatory] act in which it says Thou to him."[51] In fact, God, Barth declares of the act of prayer itself,

---

47. *CD* I/1, 355–59. This is somewhat different to his earlier use. Cf. Barth, *The Göttingen Dogmatics*, 100.

48. *CD* I/1, 359.

49. For example, LaCugna's, *God for Us*, 252, is a simplistic reading.

50. *CD* I/1, 353.

51. Ibid., 304.

is addressed as "Thou."⁵² Nevertheless, what Barth is doing here is quite different from Bümmer in certain significant theological ways. In order to explore this claim there are a considerable number of observations that need to be made, and the following discussion therefore will be an involved and lengthy one.

It is worth beginning with unpacking the significance of the theological architectonic that develops the doctrine of the Trinity in dogmatic *prolegomena*. This, of course, was a bold and radical move in its time, which provokes Barth to admit that "we are adopting a very isolated position from the standpoint of dogmatic history."⁵³ The opening of the *Church Dogmatics* with prolegomena, Barth maintains, is something of a concession to modernity, but nonetheless it is one that calls significant conceptual features of familiar strands of modernity into question. For instance, Barth rejects beginning-from-first-principles, and instead begins-within-the-midst. Moreover, his move is not one of epistemic construction but of discovery. Thus Barth's work here is critical, suspicious of certain modern epistemic categories, among other things, and transformative of them.

But transformative of what in particular? Critics like Richard H. Roberts often laud his "redirection of theological interest to the doctrine of the Trinity" so that God is distinguished from the theistic *One* as the living Father, Son, and Spirit.⁵⁴ Equally extolled is his claim concerning the doctrine's regulative significance. But Barth, they argue, is inconsistent in claiming to be *responsive* to revelation since he imposes modern categories on revelation.⁵⁵ He, this account continues, reduces the doctrine of the Trinity to the grammatical logic of revelation discourse. So Moltmann, for example, asserts that "Barth developed the doctrine of the Trinity out of the logic of the concept of God's self-revelation."⁵⁶

Roberts and those who follow him, as well as Moltmann and Pannenberg independently and earlier, claim that Barth is directed by "the unfolding of a certain 'obscure metaphysics.'"⁵⁷ This, Roberts claims,

---

52. Ibid., 316.
53. Ibid., 300.
54. Roberts, *Theology on Its Way?* 81.
55. So, e.g., Volf, "Theology for a Way of Life," 6; and Grenz, *Rediscovering the Triune God*, 51.
56. Moltmann, *Trinity and the Kingdom*, 140.
57. Kerr, *Christ, History, and Apocalyptic*, 89. Kerr, however, fails to explore his

is the metaphysics of German idealism. It is Barth's residual idealism that forces him to provide an account of eternity that generates a christologically constrained conception of time that in turn renders revelation somewhat isolated from the contingencies of history, and reduces the expressiveness of the Trinity to the singularity of the temporally compressive "single act" of revelation.[58]

Roberts' suggestions are subtle and too involved for anything less than brief considerations here. Nonetheless, one possible response to them observes that Barth at least claims to work in an *a posteriori* manner, exploring and explicating the dogmatic implications of the biblical witness.[59] He speaks emphatically of God's revelation as the "Lord" being the ground, foundation, or root of the doctrine of the Trinity, and thus of "a genuine finding" from the Scriptures. By this he does not mean revelation taken in some grammatico-logical sense, but that which is encountered through the scriptural witness. This is clear not only from statements he makes concerning the connection of the doctrine and *biblical exposition*, "for to abandon exposition would be to abandon the text too," but from his small-print *practice of biblical commentary*.[60] In fact, it is only after several reflections or "commentary" on biblical texts that Barth unpacks revelation as "the self-unveiling of God."[61]

This is a useful but conceptually superficial response to Roberts since it does not address the assumption that certain idealist conceptions determine Barth's reading of the biblical witness. The deliberatively chosen language of "subjectivity" and the divine "I" does indeed involve an allusion to German idealism (and more indirectly again, to Cartesian subjectivity). Yet what is regularly missed is the way Barth deploys these terms in order to subvert the sense of atomized and individuated selfhood familiar to these modern anthropologies. In the first place, God is spoken of as the Subject, and by specific implication our being subjects is not either something autonomously self-grounded, or even some-

---

"Barth-the-Idealist" thesis in sufficient detail, too readily making sweeping judgments. This necessary expansion could, for example, take the form of providing a more concrete and textually specific tracing of Barth's relation to, and use of, Hegel. Fuller consideration of Roberts is presented in McDowell, *Hope in Barth's Eschatology*.

58. See especially Roberts, *Theology on Its Way?* 90, 93.

59. *CD* I/1, 332. Alan Torrance cites *CD* I/1, 296, in response in "The Trinity," 76–77.

60. *CD* I/1, 311.

61. Ibid., 315.

thing of primary significance in the business of being-as-knowers or being-as-agents. The anthropocentric direction of modern epistemology is hereby interrogated (albeit implicitly since Barth's explicit targets are those who expressly are *theologically* shaped by modernity).[62]

In the second place, Barth's notion of the "revealed unity" of the divine I-ness is pluriform, a density of non-identical self-identification that "is not to be confused with singularity or isolation."[63] It is this that subverts modalist readings of Barth. So, he declares, "Singularity and isolation are limitations necessarily connected with the concept of numerical unity in general. The numerical unity of the revealed God does not have these limitations."[64] From this he refuses to countenance the oneness of God as a being "alone . . . without a counterpart." Instead, "In Himself His unity is neither singularity nor isolation. Herewith, i.e., with the doctrine of the Trinity, we step on to the soil of Christian monotheism."[65] It is precisely to depict the *relationality* of divine difference *ad intra*, then, that Barth utilizes modalist language. This is clear from the opening of §9 "The Triunity of God." The "three distinctive modes of being" subsist "in their mutual relations: Father, Son, and Holy Spirit."[66] Importantly, Barth claims that while he prefers "not to use the term 'person' but rather 'mode (or way) of being,'" his "intention" is "to express by this term, not absolutely, but relatively better and more simply and clearly the same thing as is meant by 'person.'"[67]

In this context, talk of God's threefold reiteration or "a repetition of God" (*eine Wiederholung Gottes*)[68] importantly stresses that each "mode of being" (*Seinsweise*) is not anything other than God's self-repetition, or three ways of being God in the *simultaneous* modes of Father, Son, and Spirit.[69] What Barth objects to is the way the earlier use of *substance* language has come to be understood, particularly in the conception

62. I am not, therefore, in obvious disagreement with Bruce McCormack's essay in this collection, although I am more convinced that Barth has a theological eye on Cartesian and Fichtean-type philosophies of identity and is presenting something of a theological challenge to them.

63. *CD* I/1, 354.
64. Ibid., 354.
65. Ibid.
66. Ibid., 348.
67. Ibid., 359.
68. Ibid., 229; *KD* I/1, 315.
69. Ibid., 360.

of an unmoved mover.[70] Hence Collins' further problem with Barth's untrinitarian, and Augustinian, sounding presentation of the doctrine of the Trinity as *self*-moved fails to appreciate the function of the language in *CD* I/1. For Barth, there are not three "objects" called God, as if "God" is an umbrella term for these three beings, but one God and only one God whose plural life as Father, Son, and Spirit is united.[71] The concept of "repetition" is Barth's way here of describing divine unity-in-distinction, the threefoldness of God, without succumbing to modern notions of three objects, subjects or personalities.[72] Nonetheless, in the repetition there is "a self-distinction of God from Himself."[73] It is this "becoming," this threefold repetition of self-in-distinction, that is referred to as God's "being."[74]

Pannenberg is a good example of those who badly miss Barth's point here.[75] He rightly notices that Hegel lies in the background, but goes too far in claiming *identity* in structure between Barth's doctrine of the Trinity and Hegel's idea of the unfolding self-consciousness of the Absolute. The mistake lies in seeing Barth as repeating in a new context Hegel rather than, in important ways, subverting him by, among other things, refusing to "imprison" the being of the triunity of God to history, as if the creature is necessary to the realization of God's self-identifiability; refusing to develop the idea of divine subjectivity in the post-Cartesian direction of self-*consciousness*; and in undermining the successiveness of the Hegelian process.[76] For this reason Pannenberg

---

70. For this reason it is not accurate to explain, as Paul M. Collins does in *Trinitarian Theology West and East*, 26, that Barth simply replaces traditional essence or substance talk with eventful concepts in a way that misses the fact that "The traditional language of essence or substance did not entirely exclude a concept of motion or movement (*kinēsis*)," as is evident in the Platonist tradition.

71. *CD* I/1, 349.

72. Ibid., 350–51.

73. Ibid., 316.

74. Collins does in *Trinitarian Theology West and East*, 28–29, make a crucial mistake over "the becoming which occurs in the incarnation and revelation of God *ad extra*," glaringly missing the fact that if the being *is in becoming* then there is *no being prior to becoming*, and thus no two-stage deity in Barth. There is *neither temporality nor ontological distinction* in the notion of the reiteration, just as there was not for the fourth-century Nicenes when adopting the concept of the "eternal generation" of the Son.

75. See Pannenberg, *Systematic Theology*, 1:296.

76. Of course this does not mean, for Barth, a blanket ban on all things idealist. See Busch, *Karl Barth*, 387.

fails to hear Barth's pluralizing account of the Godhead and consequently mistakenly asserts that Barth leaves "no room for a plurality of persons in the one God but only for different modes of being in the one divine subjectivity." While Barth's account cannot provide what Moltmann's "social trinitarianism" or Pannenberg's "historical trinitarianism" thinks is necessary for a trinitarian account of God, what results is nonetheless a sense that this divine Subject is utterly unlike any subject we can otherwise conceive of. Barth is opposed to developing analogies on grounds prior to learning from the scriptural witness to the event of divine self-revelation (*Sich-Offenbaren*) itself.

It is for this reason that Barth, following Augustine in *De Trinitate*, admits the *necessary* limitations of analogy and language. "[T]here are no analogies. This is the unique divine trinity in the unique divine unity."[77] "There can be no question of rationalising because rationalising is neither theologically nor philosophically possible here. . . . But all rational wrestling with this mystery, the more serious it is, can lead only to its fresh and authentic interpretation and manifestation as a mystery."[78] While language of "modes of relation" does not carry the sense of relations that critics value with the term "persons," it is quite clear that Barth's is a non-individuated divine Subject, with neither the reduction of the plurality to successiveness or moments of a neutral fourth or an essence underlying them. Hunsinger's warning, then, is a good one: "modalism can be charged against Barth only out of ignorance, incompetence, or (willful) misunderstanding."[79]

Indeed, in order to emphasize the themes of divine prevenience and grounding of the creature in dependence on God Barth reverses the normal direction of analogy, and makes the ontological claim which deliberately utilizes and applies certain modern anthropological ideas as being primarily attributable to God: "The real person is not man but God," and we are persons "by extension."[80]

Discourse of subjectivity belongs in modern epistemologies to crucial distinctions between subject and object. Barth's transcription of such language does something considerably different, and his evidently

77. *CD* I/1, 364.

78. Ibid., 368.

79. Hunsinger, *Disruptive Grace*, 191. Cf. Jüngel, *Doctrine of the Trinity*, 23, citing *CD* I/1, 382.

80. *CD* II/1, 272.

modest use of I-Thou conceptuality, possibly taken from Isaak August Dorner, aids in the process. I-Thou terminology is particularly significant in preventing the reduction of God to the conditions of impersonality, to "It-ness," even if it is not used to offer a simple conception of God as "personal" ("He-ness")—language is theologically stretched to the breaking point here. In other words, discourse of divine subjectivity refuses the reduction of God to an object that the modern subject is set over against and can master, control, possess, or manipulate, as modern epistemologies' subject-object scheme do invariably. Even in the event of God's self-objectification God remains Subject, and therefore unpossessable and unmasterable.

This non-objectification of God is sustained by the correlation with three further categories in *CD* I/1—those of divine eventfulness or being-in-act, divine freedom, and divine hiddenness. The first of these, divine *being-in-act*, is well constructed to emphasize that revelation is God's own *self*-presentation, the unveiling(-in-veiling) of God's own subjectivity or personhood to "others."[81] But it does three important further but interrelated things. It thwarts any static arrangement of the life of God, thereby diminishing the divine Subject into the position of an object. Yet the negation of hiddenness and creaturely control is not the primary role of the discourse, since it functions to locate God's givingness, as God's own Revealer, Revelation, and Revealedness. God's being is act, and that being is therefore *in* God's act.

Whatever else is going on, the point of the doctrine of the Trinity in I/1 is to stress the plural movement of *God's* revealing, and for that reason, as much as any other, Barth has to stress the unity of the event, the singularity-in-multiplicity of revelation. In this context, then, charges that Barth is beginning from unity and only then, with some difficulty, considering the relationality of divine difference are inattentive to the contextual function of the doctrine in I/1. Barth develops a particular conceptual ethos (ethos rather than "model") for a specific purpose: to dogmatically challenge modern theological accounts that

---

81. Revelation *is* God's self-presentation, divine availability. Collins, *Trinitarian Theology West and East*, 4, speaks of "the category of event as the means of the self-revelation of God." Following a brief discussion of John Macmurray and T. F. Torrance, he has distinguished between "act" (that appropriate to God's being) and "event" (that means of the act's being presented). However, rather than focus on God's being-in-act, or God's eventfulness, Collins problematically worries that Barth's actualism "relates to an understanding of 'history'" (ibid., 14).

assume the validity of certain epistemic arrangements emerging from individualized and epistemic subject-centered accounts of selfhood or personhood. At any rate, judging from the observations made earlier concerning Barth's strategy of moving *from* biblical reflection on the Christic revelation in the pneumatic revealedness *to* consideration of the divine unity-in-plurality and plurality-in-unity, it is not at all clear that he has *begun* from the unity of divine being at all.[82] And a further decisive implication is that it is not clear that Barth is even developing a "model" of the Trinity as such. He certainly denies that he is providing anything as closed as a "system of Trinitarian doctrine."[83] At this point it is worth indicating that several commentators feel something different emerges from the later volumes of the *CD*. While I do not want to dispute this, at least not without further detailed investigation, I would offer a couple of observations—principally, claims that *CD* I/1 and IV are substantially different need to consider the context of I/1 better before such a grandiose assertion can be suggested.[84] But it is imperative also to recognize that even if there are significant presentational differences, what Williams describes as later "clarifications and refinements," that this would not necessarily be a problem (unless, of course, the differences are *materially* significant) since the doctrine will have a different feel when considered in a different context.[85] After all, this is the procedure Barth's dogmatics develop so that God can be considered from the perspective of questions of prolegomena (*CD* I), from the divine being as perfection (*CD* II), from the perspective of creatureliness (*CD* III), the event of reconciliation (*CD* IV), and the finality of consummation (*CD* V). So, in his *Evangelical Theology* Barth develops the telling meta-

---

82. Much of the criticism of Barth here emerges from the sensibility inspired by Régnon, and popularized in relation to Barth by Moltmann. From here it has problematically ossified into standard textbook fare.

83. *CD* I/2, 879.

84. Laats, *Doctrines of the Trinity in Eastern and Western Theologies*, overdetermines the differences while failing to see both the context of I/1 and real continuities. McCormack's essay in this volume claims that *CD* I/1 is composed during Barth's years of apprenticeship, derivatively construing the doctrine of the Trinity before finding his own voice. While this is not untrue, as such, it underestimates the rich achievements of these earlier sections of the *CD*. Saying this, however, is not to suggest that Barth's thought does not shift and develop in noticeable ways.

85. Williams, *Wrestling with Angels*, 119.

phor of the theologian's constant moving around the mountain of the divine which produces compatible but different perspectives.[86]

Concomitantly the being-in-act thematic, perhaps most notably, undermines the great ugly ditch of the Kantian noumena-phenomena dualism, at least in respect of the knowing of God. Revelation involves not merely God as God appears to us in God's economy, but equally the very *ding-an-sich* sc that the event of revelation has to do with the availability of *God* and nothing less than God in the divine Subject's self-presentation. It is this which modalism is unable to provide since it seeks a God behind so-called "revelation," and thus a solitary monad that is not self-revealed.

Finally, and consequently, the being-in-act thematic prevents the construal of revelation as that which is past, whether that be simply the Jesus who was, divinely authored texts, or any aspect of history. Revelation is a "performative" or "self-involving" concept in Barth which therefore does not imprison God "in a past revelatory event which can be the subject only of human recollection."[87] The threefold movement of revelation cannot be conceived without the contemporaneousness of revealedness (even if that revealedness is focused intensively on the event of incarnation).[88] Yet the flipside criticism focuses on the worry that Barth's eventful or actualist account of revelation is too occasionalist, a disapproval that operates from the loosening of the revealedness from the revelation, something that I/1's trinitarian account is equally a refusal of. Of course, it remains feasible to entertain the possibility that Barth was not entirely successful in staving off these theo-temporal dislocations, subsuming revelation and revealedness within one another when dealing with theological themes such as election, creation, ethics, and so on. Yet, more concrete reflection is needed either to sustain or contest these further charges.

---

86. Barth, *Evangelical Theology*, 34.

87. Citation from Williams, *Wrestling with Angels*, 109. See Hunsinger, *Disruptive Grace*, chs. 9 and 13.

88. Given that that is sc for Barth it appears distinctly odd that a number of critics claim that Barth's account is past-centered, "retrospective rather than prospective" as David L. Mueller protests in *Karl Barth* (Waco: Word, 1972), 153. Moltmann's charge that Barth's thought is insufficiently eschatological derives not so much from revelatory pastness but from the moment of the revelatory present, the eternal present in time. See his *Theology of Hope*, 55–58.

The second of the three categories, divine freedom, is crucial for understanding God's acts as *grace*. Freedom denotes a non-necessitarianness. The point is not to disable the *involvement* of God, and thus to detract from the givingness of God (as if, with Moltmann's critique, Barth's theology lapses into arbitrariness). Nor does it hide God behind God's acts. Instead, it functions precisely as a clarification of the theological rule of God's being with and for the creature by qualifying that as talk of *grace*.[89]

The third category, that of the divine mystery, is not designed to reserve God's being as the conceptuality of the *deus absconditus* does, to express the absence of ontic revealability from the revealedness *sub contrariis*. Even at this stage in his theological development, Barth's reflections suggest that hiddenness has less to do with God's *essence*, in contrast to God's revealedness, but more to do with the depths of the divine eventfulness in revelation.[90] Consequently, Barth's is not an account of divine mystery in the manner provided by post-Kantian accounts (a certain type of "the way of negation") that trace the limits of rationality for the epistemic subject. Failure to recognize this is a failure to understand how the mystery operates for Barth as theological protection of the non-objectivization of God and thus the denial of natural theology (this post-Kantian version is "mystery via a negative natural theology"). God is not construed as the passive Kantian noumena, the inactivity of the Limit, and thus the noumenal removed from phenomenality. Rather, for Barth, mystery, or "hiddenness" as he often prefers to term it in an allusion to Luther's *theologia crucis* and with less conceptually flat resonance, is given, revealed. God is the Subject of God's own hiddenness, hiddenness *in* revealedness, and this entails that the mystery appropriately spoken of God is *not in contradistinction* with God's revealedness.[91] The triune God is always infinitely richer than what is known, heard, and depended upon by creatures in their creaturely limitations and particularly as these are further hampered under the conditions of the creatures' sin.

---

89. "Lordship" is not a reference to "absolute freedom" for Barth. God's freedom is not an absolute *freedom*, a freedom that is separated from the freedom of God for us, but rather the absolute freedom of *God*.

90. Cf. *CD* II/1, 261.

91. Helm, "Karl Barth and the Visibility of God," 277–78, has missed this in *CD* I and II/1, claiming of II/2 that "God's hiddenness is fully eliminated."

Roberts declares Barth's "treatment of the Trinity [to be] . . . grandiose."[92] What this section, among other things has suggested, is that there is, in fact, significant modesty in Barth's account. This is particularly clear with his hesitancy concerning talk of the inner life of God, a reticence all too lacking in many other trinitarian accounts that can detail the consciousness and events of the divine life, invariably in ways that are culturally reflective. Barth's properly limited and limiting account performs a specific task: he observes the significance of the broad lines of some of what is revealed, and redirects modern subjects to their grounding in the self-revelation of the triune God. Consequently, the focus in I/1 is on more noetic matters, the identifiability (or better, self-identifiability) of God in Jesus Christ and in the event of the Spirit's revealing. It is *God* who is known. It is, then, proper that the matter of unity should be paramount, although it is contestable that this *is* so in I/1 or that it needs to be so. Thus the context of I/1 indicates something of why noetic categories dominate Barth's envisioning of the Trinity. At least here, one can contest Alan Torrance's criticism over Barth's "failure" to root the doctrine in worship.[93]

But there is something else in Barth's use of noetic categories that has to be understood: there is the suggestion that *knowledge* is not a category referring to simple cogitation, ideas, concepts or cerebrality, in other words what goes on in heads, even if that "knowledge" has practical import.[94] This is clear from hints provided by two features of Barth's reasoning. Firstly, that the subjectivity of God, God's self-knowledge, is often depicted in terms of God's relations. Secondly, that what is meant by the knowledge of God involves the creature being drawn into God's relations. Echoing some of what was claimed earlier regarding the inter-

92. Roberts, *Theology on Its Way?* 93.

93. See Torrance, *Persons in Communion*. Interestingly, however, Torrance's perspective seems to shift, see "The Trinity," 79. Cf. Hunsinger, *Disruptive Grace*, 144 n. 20.

94. Following several less well-read commentators, and particularly the broad thesis of Gustav Wingren, Alister McGrath complains that Barth relegates the article on justification to secondary status because of his epistemologicalization of theology, "Karl Barth's Doctrine of Justification," 172–90; cf. Wingren, *Theology in Conflict*, 28f. Yet Barth refuses the doctrine's centrality for several reasons, significantly because it functions only under the conditions of fallenness, whereas post-II/2 the organizing ontological "center" is the doctrine of election. While Barth does tend to use noetic concepts soteriologically, "knowledge" is broader than what goes on in the mind. Even the normally considerably more sophisticated and careful reading of Williams seems to miss this, see *On Christian Theology*, ch. 9; and *Wrestling with Angels*, ch. 7.

rogative and transformational use of categories familiar in epistemic matters, John Webster declares, "It is not so much that doctrines are transposed into epistemology as that epistemology is transposed into doctrine."[95]

As persons in the knowledge of, or communion with God, Barth's account demands that God's freedom not be abstracted from the freedom to be for us, and this is important to I/1 even if it only becomes particularly clear with II/2. Moreover, attention to issues of sociality or social mediatedness entails that God's freedom does not impose itself upon us.[96] The knowledge of God is not a private matter of spiritual individuals, but the knowledge of the community of God's people among whom the event of revelation is mediated through the reading of the Scriptures and the proclamatory witness to the divine event.

What emerges from all this is a sense of God being ever-eventful; a properly theological anthropology of human dependency; and the agency of hearing mediatorially and being made responsibly responseable. It is surprisingly a very modest and under-determined account of God's inner life. There is, then, considerable sense in Jüngel's likening the function of Barth's doctrine of the Trinity of 1932 to Bultmann's anti-objectivizing demythologisation.[97]

Conclusion: Prayer and the Triune God

Using the term "God" is darkly difficult. As Lash claims, "there are no limits to the possibilities of idolatry, to the scope we have for absolutizing people, events, forces, projects, ideas, nations, and institutions."[98] Theological discourse about God, the unpossessable "Absolute," however, precisely has to resist such "absolutizing" of the creaturely, otherwise it misidentifies the mystery of God's eternal richness, fails to check our propensities for idolatry, and domesticates the divine in patterns more expressive of human being. Simply multiplying the numbers does not solve the problem. There may be those who cry "Lord, Lord, Lord" but

95. Webster, *Karl Barth*, 82.

96. It is this sense of the *multiplicity of mediations*, all witnessing to the *event* of revelation in its *revealedness*, that is missed in Roberts' critique of christomonism in Barth, Roberts, *Theology on Its Way?* 87.

97. Jüngel, *Doctrine of the Trinity*, 22.

98. Lash, "Considering the Trinity," 187.

who are less than faithful to the nature of divine plurality. One of the contentions of this paper has been that Barth's *CD* I/1 may be more suggestive of good trinitarian description than is often supposed. It does not fall as foul of the criticisms, now deeply embedded in the textbook culture, as is often supposed. This is certainly not to say that there are not things in Barth's account worth being concerned about, nor to flatten Barth's later theological renegotiations. Nor is it to admit that a sufficiently rich theology of prayer can be developed out of its *modest* work.

Yet the implications of I/1 for theologically reconceiving prayer are pronounced, even if at this stage in our reflections they can be posited only as a few fairly broad hints concerning, or at most heuristic devices or even theologico-grammatical rules for, what counts as "prayer" when spoken of Christianly. In fact, there is a sense in which at every stage the suggestions of significance will have to be consciously broad. That, however, has less to do with any possible generalization involved in speaking of God than with the *specific* nature of theological language or talk of *this* that is called "God", and the performative dynamic of a "practice." Such theological hesitations would prevent easy moves from, for instance, a theology of obedience to God as sovereign to unconditional obedience to the monarch or the state, or from the wrath of God to vengeful practices of justice, and so on.[99]

Firstly, "God" cannot be abstracted from the relations of divine self-expression in Jesus Christ, as revealed in the Spirit. That means that there can be no meaningful dogmatic sense of a theology of that is of "prayer in general" since prayer is what is appropriate in *response* to God, directed and shaped by he in whom God is "free for us."

Secondly, God is not manipulable or instrumentalizable, and this is not because God is spoken of simply as "personal," but rather because what is meant by "God" makes no sense of practices attempting to manipulate God. God is event and thus the Subject of God's own non-objectifiable objectification. Consequently, the idea of prayer as gaining or getting from God by acting upon God, perhaps by utilizing an incantatory formula in order to be efficacious, is a dogmatic mistake.[100]

---

99. Cf. Volf, "'The Trinity Is Our Social Programme," 403–23.

100. At a later date I will consider the texts in which Barth seems to suggest prayer's influencing God and of God's repentance, e.g., *Prayer*, 13; *CD* II/1, 498.

Thirdly, God is always event and therefore never "object" in any simple sense. In that regard, questions have to be asked concerning the successiveness involved in relay-race type images of the event of praying—that the pray-er acts (prays) and God does not (the passivity of listening), *then* God acts (grants that prayed for) and the pray-er does not (the passivity of reception of the gift). Instead, what is meant by divine and human agencies in the practice and event of prayer is considerably more complex and less conflictual, and hence non-successive in any simple sense.

Fourthly, persons, in knowing the divine Subject, know themselves to be grounded in dependence and therefore to be in *receipt* of their lives in grace as gift, and consequently as ecstatically living in dependent response as those who are neither self-grounded nor self-defining autonomous subjects. In this sense, because it is response to God's prevenient agency, prayer is not primarily something we offer to God but rather that which involves our agency as an agency of *responsiveness*.

Fifthly, the context of the knowing of God is communal in the sense that the divine grace is ever giving through the community of worship. Therefore persons are not hearers either in individuated immediateness (since the directedness of God's giving is always mediated) or as atomised spiritual individuals. In this context, the notion of individuals at (private) prayer involves a vital dogmatic oversight. It is the church that is at prayer even when the one engaged in the performance is on her own.

Finally, as the subjectivity of the relations of grace that are communicative (or in communion) in and through the primary mediatorial form of divine incarnation, God is transformative of human subjectivity. Prayer, here, looks distinctly odd from an incarnationalist perspective when it bypasses considerations of needs not covered by common discourse of "the spiritual."

Brümmer's account of prayer, in contrast, lives and breathes a different air. It appears to run aground on the very thing that LaCugna, among others, claims is inappropriate when confessing the doctrine of the Trinity to be "the Christian doctrine of God": that there is "a God 'in general.'"[101]

---

101. LaCugna, "The Trinitarian Mystery of God," 154.

Bibliography

Baelz, Peter, R. *Does God Answer Prayer?* London: Darton, Longman & Todd, 1982.
———. *Prayer and Providence: A Background Study.* London: SCM, 1968.
Balthasar, Hans Urs von. *Prayer.* Translated by A.V. Littledale. London: Chapman, 1961.
Barth, Karl. *Church Dogmatics.* 4 vols. Edinburgh: T. & T. Clark, 1956–75.
———. *Evangelical Theology: An Introduction.* Translated by Grover Foley. London and Glasgow: Collins, 1963.
———. *The Göttingen Dogmatics: Instruction in the Christian Religion,* vol. 1. Translated by Geoffrey W. Bromiley. Grand Rapids: Eerdmans, 1990.
———. *Prayer.* Translated by Sara F. Terrien. Louisville: Westminster John Knox, 2002.
Benson, Herbert. *Beyond the Relaxation Response.* New York: Times Books, 1984.
Brümmer, Vincent. *What Are We Doing When We Pray? A Philosophical Inquiry.* London: SCM, 1984.
Buckley, Michael J. *At the Origins of Modern Atheism.* New Haven: Yale University Press, 1987.
Burrell, David B. "Divine Action and Human Freedom in the Context of Creation." In *The God Who Acts: Philosophical and Theological Explorations,* edited by Thomas F. Tracy, 101–9. University Park: Pennsylvania State University Press, 1994.
———. *Faith and Freedom: An Interfaith Perspective.* Oxford: Blackwell, 2004.
Busch, Eberhard. *Karl Barth: His Life from Letters and Autobiographical Texts.* Translated by John Bowden. London: SCM, 1976.
Byrd, Randolf C. "Positive Therapeutic Effects of Intercessory Prayer in a Coronary Care Unit Population." *Southern Medical Journal* 81 (1988) 826–29.
Coakley, Sarah. "'Persons' in the 'Social' Doctrine of the Trinity: A Critique of Current Analytic Discussion." In *The Trinity: An Interdisciplinary Symposium,* edited by Stephen T. Davis, Daniel Kendall, and Gerald O'Collins, 123–44. Oxford: Oxford University Press, 1999.
Collins, Paul M. *Trinitarian Theology West and East: Karl Barth, the Cappadocian Fathers, and John Zizioulas.* Oxford: Oxford University Press, 2001.
Funkenstein, Amos. *Theology and the Scientific Imagination: From the Middle Ages to the Seventeenth Century.* Princeton: Princeton University Press, 1986.
Gallup, George, Jr., and Sarah Jones, *One Hundred Questions and Answers: Religion in America.* Princeton: Princeton Research Center, 1989.
Geach, Peter. *God and the Soul.* London: Routledge, 1969.
Grenz, Stanley J. *Rediscovering the Triune God: The Trinity in Contemporary Theology.* Minneapolis: Fortress, 2004.
Helm, Paul. "Karl Barth and the Visibility of God." In *Engaging with Barth: Contemporary Evangelical Critiques,* edited by David Gibson and Daniel Strange, 273–99. Nottingham Apollos, 2008.
Hunsinger, George. *Disruptive Grace: Studies in the Theology of Karl Barth.* Grand Rapids: Eerdmans, 2000.
Jones, L. Gregory. "Beliefs, Desires, Practices, and the Ends of Theological Education." In *Practicing Theology: Beliefs and Practices in Christian Life,* edited by Miroslav Volf and Dorothy C. Bass, 185–205. Grand Rapids: Eerdmans, 2002.

Jüngel, Eberhard. *The Doctrine of the Trinity: God's Being Is in Becoming.* Translated by Horton Harris. Edinburgh: Scottish Academic, 1976.

———. "Trinitarian Prayers for Christian Worship." Translated by Frederick J. Gaiser. *Word and World* 18 (1998) 244–53.

Kerr, Nathan R. *Christ, History, and Apocalyptic: The Politics of Christian Mission.* London: SCM, 2008.

Kilby, Karen. "Perichoresis and Projection: Problems with Social Doctrines of the Trinity." *New Blackfriars* 81 (2000) 432–45.

Laats, Alar. *Doctrines of the Trinity in Eastern and Western Theologies: A Study with Special Reference to K. Barth and V. Lossky.* Frankfurt: Lang, 1999.

LaCugna, Catherine M. *God for Us: The Trinity and the Christian Life.* San Francisco: HarperCollins, 1992.

———. "Philosophers and Theologians on the Trinity." *Modern Theology* 2:3 (1986) 169-81.

———. "The Trinitarian Mystery of God." In *Systematic Theology: Roman Catholic Perspectives,* vol. 1, edited by Francis Schüssler Fiorenza and John P. Galvin, 152–94. Minneapolis: Fortress, 1991.

Lash, Nicholas. "Considering the Trinity." *Modern Theology* 2:3 (1986) 183–96.

McCabe, Herbert. *God Still Matters.* London and New York: Continuum, 2002.

McDowell, John C. *Hope in Barth's Eschatology: Interrogations and Transformations beyond Tragedy.* Surrey, UK: Ashgate, 2000.

———. "'Openness to the World': Karl Barth's Evangelical Theology of Christ as the Pray-er." *Modern Theology* 25 (2009) 253–83.

McGrath, Alister E. "Karl Barth's Doctrine of Justification from an Evangelical Perspective." In *Karl Barth and Evangelical Theology,* edited by Sung Wook Chung, 172–90. Milton Keynes: Paternoster, 2006.

McIntyre, John. *Theology after the Storm: Reflections on the Upheavals in Modern Theology and Culture.* Grand Rapids: Eerdmans, 1997.

Mackey, James P. *The Christian Experience of God as Trinity.* London: SCM, 1983.

Marshall, Bruce. *Trinity and Truth.* Cambridge: Cambridge University Press, 2000.

Migliore, Daniel L. *Faith Seeking Understanding: An Introduction to Christian Theology.* 2nd ed. Grand Rapids: Eerdmans, 2004.

Moltmann, Jürgen. *Theology of Hope: On the Ground and Implications of a Christian Eschatology.* Translated by James W. Leitch. London: SCM, 1967.

———. *The Trinity and the Kingdom: The Doctrine of God.* Translated by Margaret Kohl. London: SCM, 1981.

Pannenberg, Wolfhart. *Systematic Theology,* vol. 1. Translated by Geoffrey W. Bromiley. Grand Rapids: Eerdmans, 1991.

Phillips, Dewi Z. *The Concept of Prayer.* London: Routledge & Kegan Paul, 1965.

Poloma, Margaret M., and George H. Gallup Jr. *Varieties of Prayer: A Survey Report.* Philadelphia: Trinity, 1991.

Rahner, Karl. *The Practice of Faith: A Handbook of Contemporary Spirituality.* Edited by Karl Lehmann and Albert Raffelt. London: SCM, 1985.

Régnon, Théodore de. *Études de théologie positive sur la sainte Trinité.* Vol. 1. Paris: Retaux, 1892.

Roberts, Richard H. *A Theology on Its Way? Essays on Karl Barth.* Edinburgh: T. & T. Clark, 1991.

Soskice, Janet. "Trinity and Feminism." In *The Cambridge Companion to Feminist Theology*, edited by Susan Frank Parsons, 135–50. Cambridge: Cambridge University Press, 2002.

Stump, Eleonore. "Petitionary Prayer." In *A Companion to Philosophy of Religion*, edited by Phillip L. Quinn and Charles Taliaferro, 577–83. Oxford: Blackwell, 1997.

Swatos, William H., Jr. "The Power of Prayer: Observations and Possibilities." In *Religious Sociology: Interfaces and Boundaries*, edited by William H. Swatos, 103–4. New York: Greenwood, 1987.

Swinburne, Richard. "Could There Be More than One God?" *Faith and Philosophy* 5:3 (1988) 225–41.

Tillich, Paul. *Systematic Theology*, vol. I. Chicago: University of Chicago Press, 1951.

Torrance, Alan. *Persons in Communion: An Essay on Trinitarian Description as Human Participation*. Edinburgh: T. & T. Clark, 1996.

———. "The Trinity." In *The Cambridge Companion to Karl Barth*, edited by John Webster, 72–91. Cambridge: Cambridge University Press, 2000.

Volf, Miroslav. "'The Trinity Is Our Social Programme': The Doctrine of the Trinity and the Shape of Social Engagement." *Modern Theology* 14:3 (1998) 403–23.

———. "Theology for a Way of Life." In *Practicing Theology: Beliefs and Practices in Christian Life*, edited by Miroslav Volf and Dorothy C. Bass, 245–63. Grand Rapids: Eerdmans, 2002.

Webster, John. *Karl Barth*. New York: Continuum, 2000.

Williams, Rowan. *On Christian Theology*. Oxford: Blackwell, 2000.

———. *Wrestling with Angels: Conversations in Modern Theology*. London: SCM, 2007.

Wingren, Gustav. *Theology in Conflict: Nygren, Barth, Bultmann*. Translated by Eric H. Wahlstrom. Edinburgh: Oliver & Boyd, 1958.

PART THREE

Theology beyond Barth

12

The Doctrine of the Trinity—The Major Stumbling Block in Inter-Religious Dialogue?

Reflections on the Methodological Function of Theological Concepts

Ulrike Link-Wieczorek

Translated by Duncan Reid

Introduction

AS A POINT OF ENTRY INTO INTER-RELIGIOUS DIALOGUE, THE DOCTRINE of the Trinity does not seem to offer much help. In any case not if we start from the presupposition that such a point of entry can be based on commonalities. We could for example think of speech about revelation as the appropriate entry point for Christian-Muslim dialogue, since talk about revelation is to be found in both religions. But it is wise to be cautious with words that sound the same. Pim Valkenberg for example warns us that superficial commonality of concepts can quickly lead onto thin ice, as behind such commonalities can lurk significant differences.[1] We are already familiar with this problem on a smaller scale from inter-Christian ecumenical dialogue. Above all it shows us that our terms do not necessarily function as we would expect outside of our contexts, both local and extended. Pim Valkenberg points out that even within intra-Christian dialogue a propositional understanding of revelation is by no means unproblematic. We can go a step further: it is not only the

---

1. Valkenberg, *Sharing Lights on the Way to God*.

linguistic expression that is only superficially the same when talking about revelation—it could be the experience as well. We are familiar with this problem in the discussion of "mystical" experience, which supposedly underlies all religions. Representatives of the American analytical philosophy of religions especially, like for example, Steven T. Katz, are very critical of this concept.[2] In different religious "language-games" the experiences themselves are necessarily different—only superficially do they sound the same. In fact each tradition means something quite different by this term: GOD.

We tend to regard the doctrine of the Trinity as a point that stands firmly against such false homogenization. Here we have to do, according to this presupposition, first and last with a great difference. We do not need to scratch on a seemingly unified surface here to discover the differences. They are immediately apparent, in fact as typologically sharp-edged as the differences that Pim Valkenberg can trace underneath the surface of unity. Concerning the doctrine of the Trinity, the differences from Judaism and Islam stick out above the surface: on the one hand, in Judaism and Islam, a clearly monotheistic picture of God, on the other, a complicated trinitarian one, that constantly runs the risk of no longer being regarded as monotheistic. The typology is to be seen even more clearly in the language of Christian confessional statements: there, a distanced monotheism, a God who is inaccessibly transcendent; here, a God who comes near in many and varied ways. There, in Judaism and Islam, a distant God; here, in Christianity, an intimate, approachable God. If you enter into inter-religious dialogue, according to the advice of confessional Christianity, you had better not forget the doctrine of the Trinity, for only then will you be able to show your true face as a Christian believer, and—last but not least—the true face of God. In inverse relation to its comprehensibility—and who really does understand it?—in intra-Christian discourse, for example on a confessional level, the doctrine of the Trinity becomes for inter-religious dialogue the badge of Christian identity as such. This is a paradoxical picture. Within Christianity the doctrine of the Trinity—in any case outside of academic discourse—is felt to be too complicated to be helpful to reflect one's own belief. On the other hand it will be pressed upon us by Christian dogmatists as a necessary travel pack if we want to enter into inter-religious dialogue.

2. Katz, *Mysticism and Religious Traditions*.

In what follows I would like to attempt a passage of this Scylla and Charybdis. For this reason I will develop an interpretation of the Trinity as contemplative speech. To support this claim I shall begin with a thesis outlining the relevance and significance of the economic Trinity. This will be complemented by an excursus about the Jewish theology of the name of God by which we will then be led to an understanding of trinitarian theology as a way of contemplating the vitality of God. The third section will reflect upon the consequences of this approach for interreligious dialogue.

The Trinity as a "Thick" Experience of God

Christian discourse about a trinitarian God has to be understood above all to refer to belief in the identity of the God of Israel and Jesus Christ. Its intention is the bracketing together of Jewish and Christian God-talk, not about their demarcation. It is to be understood as a theological formula of the belief in the opening of the Covenant of Israel to the Gentiles, and has its roots in the so-called *economic* Trinity.

If we look at the history of the emergence of the doctrine of the Trinity in the first four centuries of the early church, we notice that it is embedded in the search for an adequate way of talking about Jesus Christ. It served as a clarification of a particular understanding of God, as it has emerged from reflection about Jesus Christ. It is intended to give expression to, as well as the understanding of Jesus Christ, the biblical proclamation of God's salvific actions (*Heilswirken*) in Israel, in Jesus Christ and in the present life of the church. So understood, the three-membered structure of God-talk emerges first from its own history, out of the insight that the various biblically engendered experiences of God have to be seen as bracketed together, so to speak clearly of the one and the same God.[3] This means neither more nor less than this: without the doctrine of the Trinity the Old Testament would not belong to the Christian Bible. The insight that God is, in a trinitarian way, One, rests on a bracketing together of the various forms of God-talk with the one God-talk, a bracketing that is implicitly already to

---

3. Ritschl, *Logic of Theology*, 141. "It (the doctrine of the Trinity) arises out of the present worship of God and exerts pressure towards putting thoughts about the Spirit in the church in a separate compartment with the appearance and activity of Jesus and the God of Israel and creator of worlds."

be found in the Scripture. Despite all contrary interpretations in the history of Christianity, the doctrine of the Trinity rests on the implicit biblical axiom that the God of the Jews is none other than the God of the Gentiles.

Thus we could ask whether it really is plausible to contend that the doctrine of the Trinity as such represents a symptom of the distancing of Christians from the Jews. From a Christian point of view in any case, this cannot be the case. I want now to establish this point in the following excursus, with reference to the discourse about God in the Hebrew Bible.

Excursus: Biblical Theology of the Name of God as an Equivalent to Trinitarian God-Talk

A theological theory always seems especially plausible if its intention is recognizable in other theological themes. For an explanation of the trinitarian theological axiom proposed here, we can refer to another domain of theological speech about God, one that, incidentally, is significant for Karl Barth. This is the biblically grounded theology of the name of God. In what is to follow I refer to the relevant discussion by Christian Link, who explicates this theology with a constant sideways glance to Karl Barth's doctrine of the Trinity.[4] The comparison is particularly interesting because we can observe here a basic polarity that also will play a role in the doctrine of the Trinity. In his article, Link demonstrates how the biblical theology of the name of God is largely characterized by the idea that God gives up his own "selfness" in giving his name, so that it is known who God is, but that the significance of God's name is only made manifest in the concrete process of the covenant history, although the name of God is already known. And further still: insofar as God gives his name in the history of his people, God makes himself absolutely dependent upon its course, from the manner of the particular concrete calling and the interaction with God's glory—although it would be wrong to suggest that it was the people of Israel who gave God this name. The giving up of the name is the initiative of God, and this calls and draws the covenant people into the common

---

4. Link, "Die Spur des Namens," 37–66. In Christian Link I refer to a German theologian who, as an outstanding expert in the theology of Karl Barth, also emphasizes precisely the possibility of explicating a Christian dialogue with Judaism.

history in quest of the name. It remains the trace of the name of God, but it takes up the one who walks in His glory. The truth of God remains God's truth, also and exactly then, when it has "bound itself to the ways in which God walks."[5] It is a dynamic of freedom and dependence that is fundamental here, in which the freedom of God the plainly loving one is that which implies a self-chosen dependence and vulnerability and in this way creates relationship. This freedom is therefore not easy to describe, and even less to conceptualize. It is this conceptual dynamic that gives the form of expression to the vitality of God. In the words of Christian Link, in reference to Eberhard Jüngel's famous book on Karl Barth's theology: "Far removed from being absorbed in the conceptual content of an idea of God, He [the God of Israel] determines his own divine being in the journey of his people, as being 'in becoming.'"[6]

Now I would like to move from this reflective sketch on the theology of the name of God to an understanding of the concept of the Trinity that takes the trinitarian God-talk to be a different form of expression for the same living God-tension. The conceptual tension between unity and plurality and between the immanent and economic Trinity is the mould into which the doctrine of the Trinity is, as it were, poured and formed, and this confirms that it speaks of the same God. The biblical theology of the name of God contains this same tension, so I would like to develop Christian Link's explorations further by way of the combination of three governing expressions:

Self-Revelation

The stories of the Old Testament carry the imprint that God is not named by human beings on the basis of their experiences, but that God names God's own name. God himself thus shapes the relationship in which God's name may/should/can be invoked, and by which, inasmuch as we may presume to name God, God reveals his might and glory (*kabod*).

---

5. Ibid., 50.
6. Ibid., 49.

Concealment

The name by which God names Godself is at the same time distinctly "nameless."[7] "I am who I am and who I shall be" eludes a conceptual formula, and in the same breath in which Jahweh names his own name, he abandons it as a name for invocation (Exod 6:3) and warns against looking on his face (Exod 33:12–33). God refuses to let himself be "locked in" by the invocation of human beings.[8]

Actualization

Exactly what the name of God means is made known only in the history with God in which at first he involves himself, allowing himself to be invoked and named, by his correspondingly nameless name, in a concrete situation. Everything that can be said about the experience of God is anchored here, and is therefore to be seen as the outworking of the covenant activities of God. The anthropomorphic way of naming and describing God in the Hebrew Bible is thus misunderstood if taken as purely mythological speech. It is the form in which concrete, actual speech about God can be exercised, and it is enabled through the nameless naming of God as the one who both accompanies and is always coming. Through this human beings, walking in the "trace" of the self-naming God, can find and call upon the concrete name of God in their concrete human and linguistic life of relationship.

The structural triad of self-revelation, concealment, and actualization forms a complex whole in which in the Hebrew Bible the vitality of God comes to expression, and from which creaturely life may come to know itself. If any one piece of this is removed, speech about God is deprived of its dynamism, and that means either trivialized or distorted. For example, if we retain the self-revelation without the concealment, then the actualization is rendered impossible and the name of God becomes an empty cipher. God's glory would be without vitality, and companionship with God would in the truest sense become unthinkable. If we retain concealment without the possibility of the actualization of naming, then God would be something vaguely numinous, exactly comparable to the God-talk that Barth feared in his critical comments

---

7. Ibid., 48, referring to Miskotte, *Wenn die Götter schweigen*, 128.
8. Ibid., 40–42.

on mysticism. Only through the three components together can it be shown how believers in the particular experience of God name the God of self-revelation, know God personally and know of God, without being able to name and describe God in general terms. Only in the combination of the three elements can it be highlighted that the "namelessness" of God is not, in the words of Christian Link, an "absence of concreteness as we are in the habit of thinking about contents or referents which remain anonymous. It is far more the condition for applying the most diverse names and to discern, in their history, the authentic 'trace' step by step."[9] With encouragement from Franz Rosenzweig, Link develops these thoughts further into the eschatological vision, that in the redemption God could also be redeemed from God's names, from their misuse as well as finally also from his revealed name as such.[10] This can be understood as the eschatological speculation of believers which is directed to the unity of God and in which the invocation of his names are experienced as the way to that unity. The work of theological construction then becomes the contemplation of God's truth, and that will also be rediscovered in the theology of the Trinity. So in the theology of the name of God in the Hebrew Bible a tension becomes clear between a general and a concrete form of speech about God, which is rooted in God's own involvement in the history of creatureliness. It is from within this framework that Christian Link refers to an old Jewish model of the bifurcation between God's self and God's name.[11] He discerns here a structure that foreshadows the New Testament language of the incarnation:

> [I]n the gift of the name and the will in which God allows his name to dwell in Israel, that is, to represent himself in a humanly comprehensible manner, already the basic form of the incarnation is established, not only the condescension but also the adoption of human nature. The event of the incarnation as presented in the gospels moves explicitly in this already prepared form as Karl Barth had already observed in his typical attention for intra-biblical coherence: "exactly into this place—not the Jahweh of Sinai or heaven, but finally the name of the Lord who

---

9. Ibid., 50.
10. Ibid., 50–51, with reference to Rosenzweig, *Stern der Erlösung*, 426–27.
11. Ibid., 59. For further development of this argument in reference to Karl Barth, see 51–54.

dwelled in a stone temple in Jerusalem—into this place steps the human existence of Jesus of Nazareth."[12]

When, in the following reflection, the relation of the economic and immanent Trinity will be contemplated, so this will be done in this uncovered trace of the God-talk of Israel. In this perspective the triune naming of God in the history of salvation comes close to the three-fold "self-repetition"—as it must in the history of the one who allows himself to be drawn into the concrete naming in the trace of the name of God. Triune naming of God is then seen as rooted in the history of actualizations of the name of God, insofar as Jesus of Nazareth is understood as the actualization of the name of God in the uncovered trace of his self-revelation. This means Jesus brings nothing new, but manifests the old in a new actualization. In the words of Christian Link, who plays on Karl Barth's trinitarian motif of the "repetition" of God, God in revelation becomes his own repetition (*Doppelgänger*).[13] "Thus nothing new is proclaimed here, but, so to speak, the most ancient and the first, the God who as 'once again another' God wants to be known as God, is proclaimed in all the world. In Jesus a 'new book of old stories' is opened."[14]

The Trinity as a "Thick" Experience of God [cont.]

Back to the doctrine of the Trinity. It can now be understood as a concept for holding together the three names of the God of Israel and the Gentiles. I would like to suggest as a consequence of this point of departure that we understand the discourse of three trinitarian "persons" as a *thick experience of God* in the trace of the name of God, of his self-naming reference. As in a sort of time travel, believers in Christ thereby span a spectrum from before until after this rediscovery of the ancient name of God, from before until after the Christ-event, as the fixed point for their perception of the presence of God. Their experience and naming of God is anchored in the fixed point of Christ as the name of God, and they relate it back to the presence of God in Israel as well as forward to their experiences of the *Christus praesens* in their own lives. In this

---

12. Ibid., 58–59, quotation from Barth from *CD* I/1, 318.

13. *CD* I/1, 316.

14. Link, "Spur des Namens," 59, citing Marquardt, *Das christliche Bekenntnis zu Jesus dem Juden*, 116, where reference is made to *CD* I/1, 319.

"time travel," differentiated biblical naming and metaphors for God are applied in order to express different principal highlights of God's presence: God as Father, for the beginning of Israel's experience of God, and as Creator; God the Son or the Word, for his decisive manifestation in the Christ-event, as Redeemer or the one who draws near; and God the Spirit, for God's driving and renewing dynamism. We could of course debate the question as to whether these metaphors represent the only possible options for representing in language the threefold fundamental experience of God. Feminist theologians are not alone in insisting that the first two metaphors, Father and Son, have indeed contributed to a harmfully masculine overemphasis in ecclesial speech about God.[15] And it may well be regrettable that Sophia, the figure of wisdom, has not been given greater weight.[16] The Jewish speculation mentioned above concerning the redemption of God from his names could encourage us to feel also the provisional nature of trinitarian speech as an enrichment, seeing this theological conceptualization now in the framework of the complexity of self-revelation, concealment, and actualization.

Beyond these problems of the linguistic and biblical dimensions of the doctrine of the Trinity, this remains definite: talk of Father, Son, and Spirit, as it has become the basic framework of trinitarian discourse, and as it recurs in our liturgy this talk presents, so to speak, the surface structure for binding together the major themes of the experience of God's presence. Trinitarian speech can be traced back to the junction points of Christian experience of God, which understands itself in the light of the self-revelatory initiative of God as God given. It signifies "points of experience of the holy in the world."[17] When we place the emphasis of trinitarian speech on this level, so we speak of course of the so-called "economic" or "history-of-salvation" (*heilsgeschichtliche*) Trinity. This is so to say, a "Trinity from below," which hesitates to speak of further speculation about the relationships between the three modes of divine experience, Father, Son, and Holy Spirit. At most the Son and Spirit are seen here as missions of the Father, already active in creation but that in the Christ, event have occasioned a particularly effective manifestation

---

15. Janowski, "Trinität," 364–67. LaCugna, "The Baptismal Formula," 235–50.

16. See for example, Elizabeth A. Johnson's suggestion of speaking of Spirit-Sophia, Jesus-Sophia, and Mother-Sophia in *She Who Is*.

17. Wohlmuth, "Zum Verhältnis von ökonomischer und immanenter Trinität—eine These," 128.

of God and that occasion ongoing interaction between God and humanity.[18] At first, however, this trinitarian talk of God is merely implicit because purely economic speech about God hesitates absolutely to make statements about Godself, about who God shows himself to be in this threefold bracketing. In agreement with Piet Schoonenberg, I would like to speak of the three "junction points" as constellations of experience of God. This is a reversal of the older perspective, from the human experience of God to junction points in God's experience in his history of relationships with human beings. This reversal makes allowance for biblical speech about God, as it had earlier imprinted itself on the theology of the name and in which Christian Link discerns a pre-figuring of the theology of the incarnation. It takes seriously the belief that God in his truth gives himself into the world, takes its "flesh" and allows himself to be affected by it—always however under the initiative of God, on whose account Piet Schoonenberg along with Karl Rahner reflects on God's changeability "to another," which does not diminish his identity.[19] This reversal of perspective throws light on the "who" question. At the very least it allows us to say that God allows himself to be affected in his own identity by his relationships with human beings. This is a hard and fast consequence of the belief in the incarnation which can be found over and over in the history of theology, and without whose insistent assertion the dynamic of God-talk could be lost.

---

18. Schoonenberg, *Der Geist, das Wort und der Sohn*; Schoonenberg, "Trinität—der vollendete Bund," 115–17.

19. Schoonenberg, *Wort*, 140–44; ibid., "Gott ändert sich am andern," 69–81. In principle, Schoonenberg makes the suggestion, with his emphasis on the concrete level of the economic Trinity, to speak of the *a priori* of God's initiative already in the bracketing of his action in the economic level and without speaking of the ontological priority of the immanent Trinity—exactly as in the theology of the name of God. Thus the gulf between him and Karl Barth seems to me not nearly as deep as is often thought. At any rate, Barth would not say the doctrine of the immanent Trinity is to be understood noetically. Rather it designates the structure of God's essence as revealed in the incarnation, and so represents a way of knowing in the wake of revelation—*fides quaerens intellectum*. This is none other than Schoonenberg's theology, which also presents the freedom of God in his loving-changeably unchangeableness, as the driving force of the sending source—in this sense explicitly as the one who comes: "in this we know that the initiative lies with God, and our prayers are an answer to that initiative" (*Wort*, 151). On Barth, see the enlightening analysis by Grube, *Unergründbarkeit Gottes?* 123–61.

Contemplation on the Vitality of God: Speech about the Immanent Trinity

The significance of immanent-trinitarian talk of God is contemplative and not propositional. It invites us into a contemplative point of access into a confession of belief in the vitality of God. As such it establishes the Christian starting point for each inter-religious dialogue.

Our first thesis has already attempted to express the idea that speech about the economic Trinity asserts the God of Israel to be also the God of the Gentiles. This in turn suggests the following questions: Has God in this history with Israel, Jesus, and the church perhaps then also developed further, and so changed? Was God's presence to the people of Israel as effective as it was in Christ? Or does he become the merciful God only with the Jesus experience, as our pupils in confirmation classes apparently still learn? Does the acknowledged different experience of God thus also suggest a different quality of God's presence?

This, or something similar, is how we may imagine the question that led finally to the formation of speech about the "immanent" Trinity. Here we can surely discern at the very least a difference in outlook between Judaism and Christianity. For where, in the theology of the name the concealment, the "namelessness" of God is allowed to stand as such, within the knowledge of God's name, Christian theological effort proceeds, albeit with considerable caution, to operate with provisionally established names for God. Now we begin in fact to say more than the biblical text. There is a "language gain" in the contemplation of God.[20] The reason for this is the fundamental confession: as God makes his intentions known to us in Jesus Christ, and allows himself to be named by us as the God of Israel and the Gentiles, so can we most adequately speak about God. In short: as God shows himself to be in Christ, so he also is. As he gives himself in his name, and as he gives himself in Jesus Christ, so may we take this name as truly his real name. The contention in the early church about the doctrine of the Trinity has its basis in this believing confession. This concerns the essence of God: inadequate concepts are excluded, and with them any anxiety we might feel about the possibility that God may be different from what he has shown himself to be in his struggle for justice and abundant life in Jesus Christ. As God shows himself to be and allows himself to be named *ad extra*, in

---

20. Ritschl, *Logic of Theology*, 174.

the economic Trinity, so he really has to be, as, so to speak, immanent Trinity. Perhaps we feel compelled by God's coming in Jesus to say more about his being, about the name, than we did earlier, so as not to let the actualization of the Christ name simply explain itself. Considered on its own, this name would simply be the name of a "new God"—and this is exactly how Christology is (mis)understood by Jews and Muslims. In order to counteract this misunderstanding we want now to say clearly: God's *ad extra*, God's "outside," should not be thought of as a consequence of his temporal-spatial contingency, but must be traced back to his authentic original self-revealing intention in the giving of his name. The development of the doctrine of the Trinity in the early church follows the insight that behind the epistemological *a priori* of the economic, salvation-history doctrine of the Trinity, there stands an implicit ontological *a priori* of God in Godself. This finds its expression in the concept of the immanent Trinity.[21] The junction points of the experience of God are established by Godself, and are by no means arbitrary. This is what is intended by speech about the immanent Trinity.

However, the decisions regarding the Trinity at the Council of Constantinople in 381 seem far too provocatively formal and abstract: one being, three hypostases or persons, which are equally fully divine and to be distinguished through their differentiated modes of procession, either begotten or breathed out. Think about God in this way, the three great Cappadocians teach us, as if God's three differentiated hypostases were constantly dancing with one another in a perichoretic embrace. New patristic work by the Anglican scholar Sarah Coakley highlights the fact that this can only work if all the hypostases *will* the same thing, if there is just one will, in other words.[22] Therein lies the legitimacy of all trinitarian fantasies based on one divine Subject. If it were not one will, it would be no dance, but some sort of wild ruckus. Indeed we could expand this: it would be no dance at all if the one will did not nourish itself in mutuality. Be that as it may, following the lead

21. See the careful wording of Wohlmuth, *Ökonomischer und immanenter Trinität*, 135 n. 17: "Thoughtful faith must not be allowed to flatten out the points of salvation history experience into the logic of time and space, but has to come to them in their trinitarian otherness, i.e., as irreducible revelation, and become familiar with the threefold proximity of the absolute mystery as inextinguishable personal event."

22. On Gregory of Nyssa's emphasis on the unity of the trinitarian will as a counterweight to the threeness of the persons, see Coakley, "Persons in the 'Social' Doctrine of the Trinity," 123–44, esp. 131.

of the Cappadocians we can speculate about the one and the three, but nothing is said about the suffering of God, nothing of God's loving-kindness, of God's insistence on justice. In short, nothing is said about anything substantive! Have we here yet another aspect of the concealment of God, which is carried along within the theology of the name of God? Are we not sent back here to the level of actualization, exactly as in the theology of the name? In any case we can say this: speech about God's immanent trinitarian being as a consequence of the biblically testified experience of God is to be seen initially as a rule of speech, as a formula that should help us correctly to hold together the wide variety of biblically testified experiences of God. We can say further: Jewish talk hesitates at exactly this speech rule, in any case at its explication, and Christian theology takes heed of the Jewish warning against the heretical self-explanation of this actualization, at least to a limited extent, by the taste of concealment of God which can be observed in the theology of the Cappadocians. We can sense the black hole of actualization because without content from the economic level it remains abstract.

This is also the case even if we find it necessary to seek clarity from the name of Jesus Christ on the immanent level, because otherwise the economic names would be no longer discernible as names of the One God. Indeed we can also give content to the formula of the immanent Trinity insofar as it is explicitly placed in relation to the biblically testified language of the history of salvation. The rule tells us, however, that this content is always directed substantively towards the One God, who has entered into a history of relationship with human beings. Only in this context does the "speech gain" (Ritschl) of the doctrine of the Trinity become clear. It is regrettable that this connection has been greatly obscured over the course of time because theology moved directly to speaking about the immanent Trinity without creative content. This in turn meant the relational and historical dimensions were lost, and instead an isolated immanent Trinity was offered as the only content of proclamation. To speak of the difficulty of the doctrine of the Trinity then means in fact to speak of the difficulty of holding together speech about the economic and immanent Trinity.[23]

---

23. On the relationship between the economic and immanent Trinity see Rahner, "Remarks on the Dogmatic Treatise *De Trinitate*," 77–102, especially 89; see also Jüngel, "Das Verhältnis von 'ökonomischer' und 'immanenter' Trinität," 265–75. For the *a priori* of the economic Trinity see Schoonenberg, *Trinität*. For an opposing position,

The speech rule does however seem to point to something substantive. It is in the tension between unity and diversity that the bracketing function of the Trinity becomes visible. It now becomes "characteristic" of God, and both aspects recur within the history of the doctrine of the Trinity: a constant stumbling block, and yet also a constant inspiration to creative God-talk—a final repetition (*Doppelgänger*) to the inner dynamic of the theology of the name of God.

It is interesting that as much in church congregations as in the academic sphere there is the experience that people very often in the first instance have a static defensiveness to the doctrine of the Trinity. But when they get the opportunity to visualize the unity and diversity, and think through this, do they very often become filled with eagerness. They find themselves wanting to play with different models in which this tension comes to expression. It seems to me that this can itself give rise to an experience, to an event of knowing as a growing sensitivity for the perception of complexity. Experiences of complexity awaken experiences of complexity in life, in our own stories and of the complexity of God. We can also relive this experience in reading Augustine's book on the Trinity. It is even possible that our anxiety in the face of complexity can be dismantled by this thought experiment. Bound up with such God-talk comes growth in our trust in God.

We can experience these encounters with the doctrine of the Trinity when above all it is designated as a contemplative speech form, but in no way as propositional speech. The theology of Jürgen Moltmann can be drawn in for such a reconsideration.[24] As is well known, it offers a basic change in perspective: the threefold structure of the Trinity is here used expressly to speak of God as a plurality who in his missions directly "creates history." But also beyond the trinitarian missions the Trinity is three-personed as a community of subjects. Moltmann runs the risk here in being understood to be uncompromisingly tritheistic. Only slightly exaggerated, we could hear him saying that God is a subject as a plurality and relationality of subjects, and so we should also be, and God helps us in this endeavor. In Europe, in North and South America, and also in Asia concepts of the Trinity are emerging that sug-

---

moving from the immanent Trinity, see Greshake, *Der dreieine Gott: Eine trinitarische Theologie*, 317–25.

24. Moltmann, *Trinity and the Kingdom of God*.

gest a binding community.²⁵ This shift in perspectives, with differentiation and relationality at its center, promotes a picture of God as a God who is constantly dynamic, always in movement, and who insists on being in relation. I can myself well remember how stirring I found the discovery of this social dimension of the Trinity was during my own student years.

Interestingly, and contemporaneous with this development, we can find another way which also wants to emphasize the vitality of God. It recommends an almost complete dissociation from any speech about the immanent Trinity and suggests an economic Trinity as process. The triunity of God appears here as a great collective movement of Son and Spirit sent from the Father, and which makes sense only in this movement directed *ad extra*. The American Catholic theologian Catherine LaCugna is an example: in Godself we may not think of God as triune. Rather, God is, in Godself, mystery.²⁶ She can appeal here to Gregory of Nyssa, and work with his notion of the "infinite mystery" of God.²⁷ In both cases the immanent triunity is avoided, and in its place the early church dictum taken with absolute seriousness; that God's *ousia* is not to be seen. Mystery, unchangeability, and infinity here stand for discourse about the ineffability of God, which however does not lead to unknowability or further transcendence. Again we find here the element of concealment in this theology, typical of the theology of the name of God, along with dovetailing the knowledge of the self-revelation and actualization of God. In this frame of thought the immanence of God remains open from below, in that an insight is given into God's movements of sending and gathering—which for these writers alone count for God's triunity. In the reception of this theological concept a remarkable effect emerges: we are led into a movement of thought and contemplation in which we find ourselves only very fleetingly thinking about God as a three-personed Essence. It is no picture that presents itself here of three persons gathered around a table, or indeed dancing around one another. From those associations live the contemplation, on the part of Moltmann and others, of the vitality of God. They have

---

25. For background see, Link-Wieczorek, "Trinitätslehre, Protestantische Tradition und ökumenische Diskussion," 974–80; and Maurer, "Tendenzen neuerer Trinitätslehre," 3–24.

26. LaCugna, *God for Us*.

27. Ritter, "Dogma und Lehre in der Alten Kirche," 205–6.

to concede that each "person" in the doctrine of the Trinity is to be associated with an individual "subject," and thereby offers major cause for far-reaching tri-theistic misunderstanding. The movement of mission and gathering, on the other hand, draws on the image of an overflowing source, the abundance of life in which the association of the threeness of the Trinity functions as a marker of a "thick" or condensed means of access, which will finally pass away again in the flow of God's vitality. It allows us to think of God as a subject who neither disintegrates immediately into a threeness but who also is not simply a closed autonomous entity, but who pushes backward in his self-gathering, being in Godself pure dynamism and vitality. So at this point I would like to offer a proposal.

A Proposal: Trinitarian Persons as Openings to Contemplation

In the final chapter of his inspiring little 1968 book on the theology of the Holy Spirit, Hendrikus Berkhof recommends not using the term "persons" in our trinitarian talk of God any longer.[28] Despite many learned treatises and attempts at clarification in theology and philosophy, it is just too ambiguous. It is exactly here that we sense being misunderstood in inter-religious dialogue. Berkhof can be seen together with the attempts of Karl Barth and Karl Rahner precisely to avoid using the term "persons" but to talk instead about "modes of being" or "modes of subsistence." What we hear in this term "person," or rather how we evidently hear it used in our everyday communication, is clearly not the same as it was in the understanding of the ancient world. That is why Barth and Rahner thought their alternatives—"modes of being" or "modes of subsistence"—to be less misleading to our ears today. Above all they believed that their alternative terms would precisely reflect the intention of the classical doctrine of the Trinity. "Person" in the modern sense, characterized by total self-relatedness, is precisely not what was intended. Trinitarian "persons" should indeed shine a critical light onto this self-centric notion of the person. This is exactly about the vision of a different kind of personhood—intuiting a relationship to God and hoping more and more for the final perfection of the world. It is the

---

28. Berkhof, *Doctrine of the Holy Spirit*, 111.

vision of persons who constitute themselves only by relating to others in the light of God. This kind of person will become apparent in the encounter with God, because God is personal, in exactly this way. This is, as we must say, exactly what the so-called social doctrine of the Trinity wants to say with its terminology. This is what is intended by talk about the plurality of interconnected trinitarian persons.

Anyone who has studied theology knows this, and handles language more carefully. At least this is what they will have learned; that in theology some things do not mean exactly what they seem to mean. Anyone who attends Christian worship frequently may well have learned this, too. Or indeed anyone who has had the experience of prayer and understood that the Holy Spirit must make itself known, to give meaning to the words. What I want to say is this: that it takes a certain exercise to be able to understand the nature of the theological speculation to which talk about the three persons of the Trinity can invite us. It is a provocative game of varying nuances in the notion of the "person," especially if, despite every objection of Barth's, Rahner's, and Berkhof's, the plurality of three persons is to be emphasized once again by Moltmann and others in the social doctrine of the Trinity.

What is happening here is ultimately theological contemplation.[29] It seems to me that we are invited here to a never-ending and always-to-be-perfected movement of knowing. First there is the irritating suggestion of three Gods: Father, Son, and Holy Spirit—this suggestion is there and will remain, even if we do know that it is not at all meant like this. It will also remain so because we know that it can be heard like this. After the irritation follows the correction (hopefully): no, three Gods are *not* what is meant. With the correction implicitly a criticism is uttered—both ideas impinging at the same moment—the criticism of the notion, now understood as a false notion, of the person as a self-defined "a-social" individual. No, it is not about three Gods; that would be to understand God in terms of the modern understanding of persons. Ernstpeter Maurer talks of a feeling of "dizziness" with which one can

29. It is a matter of ongoing discussion as to whether the "person" concept of the so-called social Trinity is really so unambiguously to be traced back to the trinitarian thought of the Cappadocians as the Orthodox theologian John Zizioulas, among others, has suggested. See, for example, Turcescu, "Person versus Individual," 527–39; on Zizioulas' interpretation of the Cappadocians see, *Being as Communion*, 27–65, and 83–89; Gunton, *Promise of Trinitarian Theology*, 86–103; and Papanikolaou, "Is John Zizioulas an Existentialist in Disguise?" 601–7.

be seized when confronted with trinitarian concept—and that is about right.[30] I would call it a feeling of dizziness of a contemplative thought movement.[31] In the early church and the Eastern Church of today, the theology of the Trinity still has a much stronger spiritual function. There we can also seek to experience in this movement of thought a sense of being drawn into the presence of the God witnessed to in the Bible. This is understood no less as an experience of knowing God.[32]

So knowledge and contemplation appear not as contradictory categories. There is no clash of the rational and the irrational or of the "comprehensible" and the "incomprehensible." It is more about a familiarity that emerges from participation in the actions of the one known. In a similar way we "know" a good friend by taking part in his or her life. Desiring relationship is, in this understanding, an essential component in the work of human relationships. I understand it as a form of the work of relationships when, in the Catholic and Orthodox traditions, mystical practice is nurtured. Through this way of knowing, it seems to me, believers receive the invitation of God to work on relationships, and so exercise a way of thinking that cultivates participation in the life of God.[33] It might well be that this is not always clearly heard in Protestant talk of coming to know God by the gift of faith: the inten-

---

30. Maurer, "Trinitätslehre," 14.

31. See for example the "spiritual" method of reading by Aquinas by Kerr, "Tradition and Reason," 37–49. In his spiritual method of reading Thomas Aquinas the British Dominican Fergus Kerr interprets the introductory questions of *Summa Theologiae*, De Deo, as a way of training in thinking metaphysically, by which superstitious implications should be excluded. "If *this* highly abstract treatise on God is not just a set of metaphysical theorems that turns the living God of the Bible into the abstract 'God of the Philosophers,' as so many people suppose, then we might begin to see our way towards re-reading these questions as a spiritual exercise, a discipline that searches out the temptations to idolatrous conceptions of God which retain their grip even when we are deeply immersed in scripture" (45). We can think here of the scholastic doctrine of *intellectus* in Dietrich of Freiburg, which can in any case be described in terms of a contemplative movement of thought, leading to knowledge but not to resolution. See also Flasch, *Einführung in die Philosophie des Mittelalters*, 171–80.

32. Coakley, "Re-thinking Gregory of Nyssa," 441; in relation to Jewish thought, see Wohlmuth, "Trinitarische Aspekte des Gebetes," 83–101; Lesniewski, "Erkenntnis in der Gottesbegegnung," 42–54.

33. In this sense I understand the reception of the mystical tradition by Jürgen Moltmann as the completion of his endeavors on this theme. See his "Theologie der mystischen Erfahrung," 127–45; with regard to participatory knowledge, see ibid., 129f.

tion to emphasize the difference between God and the human person seems just too great. But when we think about it a little further, we have to admit: here also is the primary intention to think about faith on the basis of a habitual assurance, as a gift. And this is no different from a Spirit-motivated abiding in the covenant of God; in other words, in a participatory state of knowing.[34] Also, in a Protestant view, faith lives from the possibility of coming to the certainty of the nearness of God. In non-Protestant traditions, a sensibility for the nearness of God can emerge from the contemplative movement of thought that draws a person into the presence of God.

This means that the idea of the immanent Trinity has emerged within the Christian tradition only because one can sense the contemplative effect of this knowledge of God in terms of participating in this immanent Trinity. On this I find myself in agreement with the interpretation of Sarah Coakley and others. If one understands the doctrine of the Trinity in this way, its practical relevance also becomes clear. In spite of all talk of "immanence" and the priority given to it—and we see this many times in the history of theology—ordinary believers and highly sophisticated theologians alike have found in the vision of the trinitarian life of God a model for their own individual human and communal, ecclesial lives. It is not only Orthodox Christians who celebrate a vision of participation in God and a social ethic in the eucharistic community.[35] The language gain of trinitarian theology thus becomes less important for showing the reasons or the root of the doctrine of God, as in Karl Barth, but rather for ascertaining the contemplative culmination of the vision of the presence of God.

Summary: Consequences for Inter-religious Dialogue

So where do we stand? If it were not for reflection on the biblical testimony to a differentiated acting of God in relationship, then trinitarian God-talk would be unnecessary. From here, from the economic level, believers create a new language about the being of God. Obviously this takes the form of an immanent Trinity, which speaks of the triune being of God in a way that reflects the economic Trinity. If we think in terms of the superficial dissimilarity between the subject and its abstract reflec-

---

34. For background, see Link-Wieczorek, "Glaube," 117–19.
35. Zizioulas, "Die Eucharistie in der neuzeitlichen orthodoxen Theologie," 163–79.

tion in art, we could ask whether a structurally similar triune concept of the immanent Trinity were absolutely necessary. But without question this structure opens up creative possibilities for talking about God: it can create a tension in images between unity and diversity, individual personality and triunity, which assures believers through contemplation of the vitality of God and the promise of God's coming. To this degree it makes sense to designate, as the basic framework of the doctrine of the Trinity, this tension between unity and threeness, as a rule of language, as the content of speech about the immanent Trinity, and as an ever new and creative speech gain. The new speech seeks to lead to an established contemplation of belief in God's vitality. As such it draws us into liturgy and doxology. Indeed, the basis for this, and its content, had to emerge from the level of the economy. Here the main direction is established: the belief in the identity of the God of Israel and the God of Jesus Christ who, in the self-giving of his nameless name, invites us to call him by the names from out of the history of his works.

Let me now briefly draw out three consequences for inter-religious dialogue. The demand that the doctrine of the Trinity places upon Christian-Muslim dialogue is that Christian faith insists that the living God in Jesus Christ is none other than the Jewish God of Israel. Any Christian-Muslim monotheism is only to be recognized as a function of Jewish-Christian-Muslim monotheism.

The doctrine of the Trinity is relevant to inter-religious dialogue not as a form of speech about the being of God, but as a rule that marks out the boundaries of Christian God-talk. It marks out the constellation of connections in which concepts, metaphors, and ideas, be they similar or different, develop their significance. This significance is not to be defined once and for all, but to be discovered in the contexts of everyday life. One such context could be inter-religious dialogue. Christian participants do not arrive at the dialogue with ready-made concepts, but at most with rules to combine and interpret, in which the economic doctrine of the Trinity defines the boundaries of faith in the opening of God's covenant with Israel to the Gentiles.

Speech of the immanent Trinity as talk about Godself will cause misunderstanding if it, and not the economy, is taken to be the framework for discussion. This is the essence of the following theses with regard to the Muslim misunderstanding of the doctrine of the Trinity.

The Muslim criticism of the trinitarian speech of God, as found in the Qur'an, is mostly nourished by three specific misunderstandings, which are also to be found quite frequently even within Christianity. The three misunderstandings are as follows:

- The misunderstanding of the metaphoric trinitarian concept of "persons," which then again has its basis in
- An implicitly monophysite christological tendency to talk about the person of the Son, as well as
- A reversal of the order of perception, of the economic and immanent Trinity

All three misunderstandings have their roots in the misconception that the linguistic form of the immanent Trinity is taken as a template for the economic Trinity, so that its contemplative character is misunderstood. We are not to say that Jesus is the second person of the Trinity—that is going to create a linguistic and conceptual mix-up in which we cannot but be misunderstood.

But we could carefully and invitingly talk about the vitality of God, and about God's movements of mission and gathering, in which God draws us human beings into his history of relationship. This is the meaning of the doctrine of the Trinity and with it the simple Christian motive for inter-religious dialogue. For if there were no mission of God, there would be no reason for dialogue with others: they would mean nothing to us. In a participatory knowledge of God this, however, is not possible. A contemplative trinitarian vision places us with all, in our creatureliness, into the perspective of God and lets us look at the world and others through the eyes of God. It stands therefore very much at the end of the speech about God and not at the beginning. The form of triunity becomes itself provisional. Looked at in that light it also seems correct to say that we could talk differently about God: rather than as Trinity, we could talk about God as mystery, as unchangeableness or as infinity—as long as the economic frame of reference is not put aside. If we could succeed in explaining the contemplative character of the three-persons language, including to people outside of the Christian tradition, we could have gained a great deal for inter-religious dialogue. In my opinion it can only succeed if the process of contemplation be integrated into the common search for the adequate talk of God in inter-religious dialogue—but only if the participants enter into this conversation not as those who claim to know, but as inquiring seekers. That is why I am not so optimistic if the participants in inter-religious dialogue claim to know exactly from the very start where the inter-religious differences lie.

Bibliography

Barth, Karl. *Church Dogmatics*. 4 vols. Edinburgh: T. & T. Clark, 1956–75.
Berkhof, Hendrikus. *The Doctrine of the Holy Spirit*. Atlanta: John Knox, 1976.
Coakley, Sarah. "Persons in the 'Social' Doctrine of the Trinity: A Critique of Current Analytic Discussion." In *The Trinity: An Interdisciplinary Symposium on the Trinity*, edited by Stephen T. Davis et al., 123–44. Oxford: Oxford University Press, 1999.
———. "Re-thinking Gregory of Nyssa: Introduction—Gender, Trinitarian Analogies, and the Pedagogy of *The Song*." *Modern Theology* 18 (2002) 431–44.
Flasch, Kurt. *Einführung in die Philosophie des Mittelalters*. Darmstadt: Wissenschaftliche Buchgesellschaft, 1987.
Greshake, Gisbert. *Der dreieine Gott: Eine trinitarische Theologie*. Freiburg: Herder, 1997.
Grube, Dirk-Martin. *Unergründbarkeit Gottes? Tillichs und Barths Erkenntnistheorien im Horizont der gegenwärtigen Philosophie*. Marburg: Elwert, 1998.
Gunton, Colin. *The Promise of Trinitarian Theology*. Edinburgh: T. & T. Clark, 1991.
Janowski, J. Christine. "Trinität." In *Wörterbuch der Feministischen Theologie*, 2nd edition, edited by Elisabeth Gössmann et. al, 564–67. Gütersloh: Verlagshaus, 2002.
Johnson, Elizabeth A. *She Who Is: The Mystery of God in Feminist Theological Discourse*. New York: Crossroad, 1993.
Jüngel, Eberhard. "Das Verhältnis von 'ökonomischer' und 'immanenter' Trinität." In *Entsprechungen: Gott—Wahrheit—Mensch*, Ebehard Jüngel. München: Kaiser, 1980.
Katz, Steven T. editor. *Mysticism and Religious Traditions*. Oxford: Oxford University Press, 1983.
Kerr, Fergus. "Tradition and Reason: Two Uses of Reason, Critical and Contemplative." *International Journal of Systematic Theology* 6.1 (2004) 37–49.
LaCugna, Catherine M. "The Baptismal Formula: Feminist Objections and Trinitarian Theology." *Journal of Ecumenical Studies* 26 (1989) 235–50.
———. *God for Us: The Trinity and Christian Life*. San Francisco: HarperSanFrancisco, 1991.
Lesniewski, Krzysztof. "Erkenntnis in der Gottesbegegnung. Überlegungen zum Beitrag der apophatischen Dimension orthodoxer Theologie zur Ökumene heute." *Ökumenische Rundschau* 51 (2002) 42–54.

Link, Christian. "Die Spur des Namens: Zur Funktion und Bedeutung des biblischen Gottesnamens." In *Die Spur des Namens: Wege zur Erkenntnis Gottes und zur Erfahrung der Schöpfung. Theologische Studien*, Christian Link, 37–66. Neukirchen: Neukirchener, 1997.

Link-Wieczorek, Ulrike. "Glaube." In *Taschenlexikon Ökumene*, edited by Athanasios Basdekis et al., 117–19. Frankfurt: Lembeck, 2003.

———. "Trinitätslehre, Protestantische Tradition und ökumenische Diskussion." In *Evangelisches Kirchenlexikon*, vol. 4, edited by Erwin Fahlbusch et al., 974–80. Göttingen: Vandenhoeck & Ruprecht, 1986.

Marquardt, Friedrich-Wilhelm. *Das christliche Bekenntnis zu Jesus dem Juden: Eine Christologie.* Vol. 2. Munich: Kaiser, 1991.

Maurer, Ernstpeter. "Tendenzen neuerer Trinitätslehre." *Verkündigung und Forschung* 39 (1994) 3–24.

———. "Trinitätslehre." *Glaube und Lernen* 17 (2002) 11–23.

Miskotte, Kornelius Heiko. *Wenn die Götter schweigen. Vom Sinn des Alten Testaments.* Munich: Kaiser, 1963.

Moltmann, Jürgen. "Theologie der mystischen Erfahrung. Zur Reconstruktion der Mystik." In *Freiheit und Gelassenheit: Meister Eckhart heute*, edited by Udo Kern, 127–45. Munich: Kaiser, 1980.

———. *The Trinity and the Kingdom of God.* Translated by Margaret Kohl. London: SCM, 1986.

Papanikolaou, Aristotle. "Is John Zizioulas an Existentialist in Disguise? Response to Lucian Turscescu." *Modern Theology* 20 (2004) 601–7.

Rahner, Karl. "Remarks on the Dogmatic Treatise *De Trinitate.*" In *Theological Investigations*, vol. 4, translated by Kevin Smyth, 77–102. London: Darton, Longman and Todd, 1974.

Ritter, Adolf Martin. "Dogma und Lehre in der Alten Kirche." In *Handbook der Dogmen-und Theologiegeschichte*, vol. 1, edited by Carl Anderson et. al, 205–6. Göttingen: Vandenhoeck & Ruprecht, 1999.

Ritschl, Dietrich. *The Logic of Theology: A Brief Account of the Relationship between Basic Concepts in Theology.* London: SCM, 1986.

Rosenzweig, Franz. *Stern der Erlösung.* Frankfurt: Suhrkamp, 1988.

Schoonenberg, Piet. *Der Geist, das Wort und der Sohn: Eine Geist-Christologie.* Regensburg: Pustet, 1992.

———. "Trinität—der vollendete Bund. Thesen zur Lehre von driepersönlichen Gott." *Orientierung* 37 (1973) 115–17.

———. "Gott ändert sich am andern." In *Auf Got hin denken: Deutschsprachige Schriften zur Theologie*, edited by Wilhelm Zauner, 69–81. Freiburg: Herder, 1986.

Turcescu, Lucian. "Person Versus Individual, and Other Modern Misreading of Gregory of Nyssa." *Modern Theology* 18 (2002) 527–39.

Valkenberg, Pim. *Sharing Lights on the Way to God: Muslim-Christian Dialogue and Theology in the Context of Abrahamic Partnership.* Amsterdam: Rodopi, 2006.

Wohlmuth, Josef. "Trinitarische Aspekte des Gebetes." In *Beten: Sprache des Glaubens—Seele des Gottesdienstes*, edited by Ulrich Willers, 83–101. Tübingen: Francke, 2000.

———. "Zum Verhältnis von ökonomischer und immanenter Trinitäat—eine These." In *Im Geheimnis einander nahe: Theologische Aufsätze zum Verhältnis von*

Judentum und Christentum, Josef Wohlmuth, 115–38. Paderborn: Schöningh, 1996.

Zizioulas, John. *Being as Communion: Studies in Personhood and the Church.* Crestwood, NY: St. Vladimir's Seminary Press, 1985.

———. "Die Eucharistie in der neuzeitlichen orthodoxen Theologie." *Die Anrufung des Heiligen Geistes im Abendmahl, Beiheft zur Ökumenischen Rundschau* 31 (1977) 163–79.

13

Temporality, Triunity, and the Third Article

The Mediatorial Work of the Holy Spirit in Karl Barth's Church Dogmatics

Antony Glading

WHEN CONSIDERING KARL BARTH'S *CHURCH DOGMATICS*, MOST SCHOLars would concur that the Holy Spirit plays a subordinate role to Jesus Christ in his earthly mission, and that this renowned theologian holds no significant role for the Spirit in his own right. However, this is far from the truth, as Barth's understanding of the role of the Holy Spirit is intertwined with his understanding of the relationships of revelation to reconciliation and redemption.

For Barth revelation and reconciliation are viewed as inseparable. Revelation without reconciliation is empty and conversely reconciliation without revelation is considered to be mute.[1] Revelation imparts the "reality" of reconciliation, whereas reconciliation forms the vital truth made known by revelation, neither of which can be held without the other, as they are both identical to Jesus Christ in Barth's formulation.[2] Both revelation and reconciliation embrace and are bound within a complex temporality, as understood in Barth's detailed explanation of "space-time and eternity" within his doctrine of God.

The relationship between what happened "there and then" in the history of Jesus Christ and what continues to happen "here and now" in the life of the believer, the church, and the world, is of vital significance

---

1. Hunsinger, "Mediator of Communion," 178.
2. Ibid.

to Barth's doctrine of the Spirit's saving work, as seen from the standpoint of both (revelation and reconciliation).[3]

Redemption on the other hand, is seen very differently by Barth, as the fulfillment of reconciliation. It is in its own right the saving work of the Holy Spirit,[4] unlike revelation and reconciliation that is seen as a "cooperative" work of both the Spirit and the person of Jesus Christ.

The Spirit is seen less directly from the perspective of revelation and reconciliation, however, from the standpoint of redemption, the Holy Spirit is viewed center stage; is redescribed teleologically as a whole, and thereby amplified and enriched.[5] Duel perspective results, where reconciliation is seen as redemption's abiding ground, and redemption is understood as reconciliation's dynamic consequence and *telos*. Redemption is seen as the proper and peculiar (and mysterious) work of the Holy Spirit (as appropriate to him), representing the consummation of all things, the resurrection of the dead and the eternal communion with God.[6]

From the viewpoint of reconciliation, the work of the Spirit serves the work of Christ; whereas, in redemption, the work of Christ serves the work of the Spirit.[7] It is important to realize that Barth's work on redemption was never started because of his death and the substantial work on reconciliation, although comprehensive, was never completed.

No critique that presupposes the separation of revelation and reconciliation is of any consequence in the overall critique of the work of Barth, as this is vital in his theological formulations. For him revelation never occurred without reconciliation and vice versa.[8]

Space-Time and Eternity: Backdrop to Revelation, Reconciliation, Redemption

This may appear a strange starting point for an essay on the mediatorial role of the Holy Spirit in the life of the believer; however, it is critical for an understanding of Barth's concept of the Holy Spirit as "*historicity*."

3. Ibid.
4. Ibid.
5. Ibid.
6. Ibid.
7. Ibid.
8. Ibid.

Barth's distinctive conception of God's eternity and space-time can only be truly understood in the light of his primary concern for *actuality*. For Barth, revelation can only be such, in as much as God's eternity "takes on" time.[9] Also, if theology is to attain a true conception of God's eternity, it must have as its starting point, the event in which eternity becomes time (without which there can be no revelation); it must start with the "actuality of the Incarnation."[10] God's eternity has actually occurred within our space-time, in the event of Jesus Christ.

This event implies the prior possibility that God is able to be eternal in this way, that his eternity does not necessarily exclude, but includes this "Time of his Word"—Jesus Christ. God's being, however, is not bound by this possibility, as if it were an *a priori* necessity; yet it is clear that his eternity must include God's genuine "readiness for time" (his gracious unnecessitated readiness to become temporal in Jesus Christ).[11]

This readiness is positively understood by Barth as "God's time *for us* in Jesus Christ."[12] The statement that "God reveals himself" or "God in His hiddenness, unveils Himself" signifies that God "has time for humanity" [and all the created order].[13]

It is important to realize that God's eternity is no negation of time, but his divine readiness to create time,[14] therefore, the temporality of creation (time in *our* reality) corresponds to God's graciousness as Creator, and finds its counterpart in the time of "the history of the covenant and of salvation."[15] Resultantly, the authentic temporality of "God's eternity" becomes the ontological basis for the temporality of creation. The possibility of Christian existence ("our time for God") depends exclusively upon the prior possibility that his eternity includes "God's time for us."[16]

9. *CD* I/2, 50.

10. *CD* II/1, 616, "In Jesus Christ it comes about that God takes time to Himself, that He Himself, the Eternal One, becomes temporal, that He is present for us in the form of our own existence in our own world, not simply embracing our time and controlling it, but submitting Himself to it, and permitting created time to become and be the form of His eternity."

11. Ibid., 618.

12. Ibid., 611.

13. *CD* I/2, 45.

14. *CD* III/1, 68.

15. Ibid., 71.

16. *CD* II/1, 62. "In our creaturely time, although it is our time, and therefore the time of our sin, He [God] has given us His divine time. He allows us our time in order

God's time for us is an *ontic* reality present in the concrete actuality of the incarnate Word; this has primacy to the subjective apprehension *in nobis* by the *noetic* action of the Holy Spirit: the Spirit being the divine *Noetic* of God, with all the power of the divine *Ontic*.[17]

Barth's conception of the "authentic temporality" of God becomes more complex as he introduces two juxtaposed ideas; firstly, that God's eternity is *non-temporal*; in the sense that God cannot possibly be "possessed" or "dominated" by any beginning, succession, and end, in their separation, distinction, and contradiction. And, on the other hand, God's eternity is authentically temporal, in the sense that it possesses and controls all beginnings, successions, and ends.[18] "God's eternity is, itself beginning, succession and end."[19]

It is not that God is authentically in time but that time is authentically in him.[20] To deny the reality of this, according to Barth, would be to deny the actuality of the incarnation, the Christ event itself.[21] This tension between the two is a mystery.

His positive conception of God's eternity as authentic temporality is paralleled and confirmed by his conception of God's *omni-presence*. God's omnipresence is not conceived by Barth as an absolute non-spatiality, or a part of some abstract or mathematically defined infinity; it is rather his "authentic" spatiality; a perfection (attribute) of God's being, in which he is pre-eminently present.[22]

God's omnipresence is his freedom to "possess" space, both in himself and distinct from himself. This (in God's divine freedom) is not a mere construct; it is rather God's particular transcendent freedom to be present in his Word to man in created space-time. He himself possesses space-time in order that he can relate to humanity and that humanity might relate to him, in and through Jesus Christ: ". . . [W]hile the Incarnation does not mean that God is limited by space and time, it asserts the reality of space and time for God and

---

that we may always have time for Him—[No!], in order that in it, He may always have time for us, Revelation Time."

17. Rosato, *Spirit as Lord*, 41–42.
18. *CD* II/1, 610.
19. Ibid., 611.
20. *CD* III/1, 68.
21. *CD* II/1, 618.
22. Ibid., 468.

the actuality of His relations with us, and at the same time binds us to space and time in all our relations with him."[23] There is no other possible way for humanity to relate to God, except via his irruption into our space-time. This is the event of Jesus Christ, who is the self-revelation of God in the created order.

It is this positive (actual) temporality attributed to God's eternity, rather than its secondary character of non-temporality that is the predominant emphasis attested to in Scripture, as the Bible has no hesitation in referring to God in temporal terms, e.g., speaking of God's years and days.[24]

The issue of temporality in relation to eternity becomes more complicated when we look further at Barth's formulation, by considering a second dialectic. The juxtaposed concepts of authentic temporality (with its temporal and non-temporal components), in tension with what he (Barth) refers to as the *pure simultaneity* of God's eternity. (For the purpose of this essay I will not enter into further detailed explanation of this concept.)

Barth draws the distinction between eternity as being "God's time," and that which constitutes "man's time." For Barth time is neither a constant (invariable), nor an absolute (unlimited), existing in its own right, to which God is in any way subject.[25] Gunton is correct when he observes that the Process theologians identification of God as an event that contains all other events involves a virtual deification of time in itself and is therefore no better than a modern form of idolatry,[26] and Barth would be in full agreement with this. As Creator, God's relationship to creation (with its spatial and temporal structures) remains that of the transcendently "free" Lord. God is never dominated by beginning, succession, and end in their separation, distance, and contradiction. This therefore constitutes the non-temporality (the *simultaneity*; referred to earlier) of his eternity.[27]

23. Torrance, *Space, Time, and Incarnation*, 67.

24. *CD* II/1, 610.

25. Torrance, *Space, Time, and Incarnation*, 60.

26. Gunton, *Becoming and Being*, 178; ibid., "Transcendence, Metaphor, and the Knowability of God," 508.

27. *CD* II/1, 608; Gunton, *Yesterday and Today*, 128, "if we are to achieve a positive Christology that does not fall prey to the absolutism of time and eternity, we must hold firmly to the bipolarity of the New Testament's approach: that this life is both fully temporal *and yet* is the place where the eternal is present."

In contradistinction to authentic temporality (God's eternity), Barth understands *our* time, in its succession and division of past, present, and future, as "fallen time."[28] The time in which we live; the time between times of Jesus' first and second Parousia; the "now/not yet" of our current reality post-Pentecost.

Now, having addressed Barth's fundamental conception of space-time and eternity along with the importance of revelation to reconciliation, and redemption, it is important to look at the role of the Spirit in both the intra-trinitarian relationships and in analogy—the life of the believer and church.

Triunity and the Role of the Spirit

Barth explains the doctrine of the Trinity in terms of the dialectical concepts of "*unity* in Trinity" and "*Trinity* in unity" (oneness in threeness and threeness in oneness).[29] The term "triunity" is a merging of these two concepts into a unified whole.[30] Barth, however, argues that when either of these formulae is discussed independently, there is an inevitable one-sidedness that occurs, and our thinking cannot progress past the one-sidedness to a true grasp of the trinitarian nature of God.[31]

For him, the "unity in Trinity" is best conceptualized in terms of a doctrine of *perichoresis*, and "Trinity in unity" is best conceptualized in terms of a doctrine of appropriation. These are two aspects of Barth's trinitarian theology,[32] both major controlling factors in his doctrinal formulations, and consequently, affecting our interpretation and understanding of the role and work of the Holy Spirit in the economy of God, with respect to revelation, reconciliation, and redemption.

It has been considered that this doctrine of appropriation has been overlooked by many scholars in their criticism, highlighting his inadequate explication of the work of the Spirit in his *Church Dogmatics*.[33]

---

28. CD I/2, 47, "the time we think we know and possess, 'our' time, is by no means the time God created. Between our time and God created-time as between our existence and the existence created by God there lies the Fall."

29. McIntosh, "Doctrine of Appropriation," 279.

30. *CD* I/1, 368.

31. Ibid.

32. McIntosh, "Doctrine of Appropriation," 279.

33. Ibid., 278.

However; it can be considered that Barth uses this doctrine as a hermeneutical tool (interpretative framework, placing it firmly within his doctrine of the Trinity),[34] for "bringing into words" the persons (divine modes of, in their *particularity*) of the Godhead in their "inseparable distinctiveness."[35] For want of a better expression, Barth's doctrine of the Trinity can be considered to contain two sub-doctrines (as bulwarks): the doctrine of appropriation and the doctrine of perichoresis. Both constitute the foundation and lens by and through which we can interpret his doctrine of the Trinity and its implications for his dogmatics.

The doctrine of appropriation enables Barth to distinguish the works of the Father, Son, and Spirit, Trinity in unity, without separating these works, and not diminishing the perichoretic unity of God. Bringing God to speech in the particularity of the divine modes of being, emphasizing the different works of the persons of the Trinity, without diminishing the communal unity of the triune God.[36]

For Barth, appropriations involve the process in which descriptions of trinitarian persons follow the preceding self-talk of God in revelation.[37] This is what Barth understands to be the "intelligibility" of appropriations. For him this is merely an interpretive tool that allows him to move beyond the incomprehensible nature of God as "Trinity in unity" and "unity in Trinity," and say something accessible to human thought.[38]

This doctrine is epistemologically grounded in the principle that God's revelation is in fact the "self-interpretation" of God, to us.[39] This means that the revelation of God corresponds to the being of God. So, "When we are dealing with God's revelation, we are dealing with God himself and not (as some Modalists would think), with an entity distinct from him."[40] The Father, Son, and Holy Spirit revealed in this self-interpretation of God is the very Father, Son, and Spirit in the

---

34. Gunton, *Becoming and Being*, 150; McIntosh, "Doctrine of Appropriation," 278–79.

35. McIntosh, "Doctrine of Appropriation," 278; Jüngel, *God's Being Is in Becoming*, 49–50.

36. McIntosh, "Doctrine of Appropriation," 280; *CD* I/1, 373.

37. Hunsinger, "Mediator of Communion," 282.

38. McIntosh, "Doctrine of Appropriation," 282.

39. *CD* I/1, 311.

40. Ibid., 311–12.

"depth of eternity."[41] For Barth, there is no knowledge of God behind the revelation of God, because God's "self-interpretation" in revelation is, antecedently and eternally, the Godness of God.[42]

So, theological reflection on the works of God in the particularity of the divine modes of being (persons) of the Trinity is, for Barth, reflection on the being of God himself (ontological grounding of process).[43] There must be a harmony with the immanent relational structure of God's being when one is appropriating God's work to any *particular* mode of being.[44]

For Barth the doctrine of appropriation is the comprehensibility of the distinctions of the divine modes of being in the truth, in a way that is acceptable to human beings.[45] It is however, (Barth would acknowledge) relative and improper talk about God. It does not however, need to be discarded, but it must be recognized as improper speech with its limitations. Being held in dialectical tension with his doctrine of perichoresis.[46] It can only ever be "relative" talk in the doctrine of appropriation, as it is a part of the provisionality of any and all talk concerning the triunity of God.

Joseph Mangina[47] and Robert Jenson are critical of Barth with respect to his doctrine of the Holy Spirit, believing that "long stretches

---

41. Ibid., 479.

42. *CD* II/1, 275.

43. McIntosh, "Doctrine of Appropriation," 282.

44. *CD* 3/1, 49. By way of example: for Barth the Father is only able to be meaningfully described as the Creator because there is an analogy between the work of creation and God's eternal fatherhood. "As the Father, God procreates himself from eternity in his Son, and with his Son he is also from eternity the origin of himself in the Holy Spirit; and as the Creator he posits the reality to all the things that are distinct from himself. The two things are not identical. Neither the Son nor the Holy Spirit is the world; each is God as the Father himself is God. But between the relationship in God himself and the relationship to the world, there is an obvious proportion. In view of this it is meaningful and right to designate God the Father in particular (*per appropriationem*) as the Creator and God the Creator in particular (*per appropriationem*) as the Father."

45. McIntosh, "Doctrine of Appropriation," 284.

46. *CD* I/1, 368.

47. Mangina, "Bearing the Marks of Jesus," 300. "The Spirit illuminates with the powerful, self-involving knowledge of Jesus Christ; but does its activity take up time and space in the created order? And if the Spirit does not enter into the travail of history—history that includes the stories of Israel, the nations and that strangely ambiguous reality we call the Church—then are we justified in confessing him as 'the Lord and giver of life'?"

of Barth's thinking are binitarian rather than trinitarian,"[48] and that the works of the Holy Spirit are nothing more than a prolongation of the works of Jesus Christ, only in a different form.[49] The concern of both these scholars, as with others, is that Barth's close association of the Spirit with Jesus Christ, especially in his doctrine of reconciliation, too often reduces the distinctiveness of the Spirit's work in the economy of salvation. Hunsinger describes the doctrine of reconciliation as Barth's Christ-centered (christocentric) pneumatology.[50]

Jenson believes that Barth's doctrine of appropriation is noticeably absent from his accounts of the distinctive work of the Holy Spirit. He suggests that a two-sided fellowship is developed between the Father and the Son, and this is seen in Barth's work on the doctrine of election and creation in which Barth primarily describes the work of the Holy Spirit as ensuring the unity between the Father and the Son.[51] I believe that Barth would vehemently oppose this claim.

It is not possible for us to think simultaneously of God's Trinity in unity and unity in Trinity in a "dialectic strategy of juxtaposition."[52] Barth's doctrine of appropriation can be understood however, as acting in a similar way to this.[53] In the same way that Barth has no problem using this hermeneutical tool in his Christology, he likewise sees no problem with a one-sided discussion of one divine "mode of being" within his various doctrines (revelation, reconciliation and redemption) because of the incomprehensibility of God's Trinity in union.[54]

Traditionally, all talk of distinctive "modes" of being was incommensurable with the reality of God's essence, and Barth would not deny this. Because of it, Barth deliberately juxtaposes the works he appropriates to each of his divine "modes of being" by thinking of each *article* in relation to a specific doctrinal formulation (Father to *Revelation*; Son to *Reconciliation*, and Holy Spirit to *Redemption*). This however, creates the unfortunate impression that he has neglected to include the roles of the other "articles." This may be why, many reading Barth's work

48. Jenson, "You Wonder Where the Spirit Went," 296–304.
49. Ibid., 300.
50. Hunsinger, *Disruptive Grace*, 157–60; ibid., "Mediator of Communion," 178.
51. Jenson, *Systematic Theology*, vol. 1, 155; *CD* II/2, 101; and III/1, 56–59.
52. Hunsinger, "Karl Barth's Christology, 326.
53. McIntosh, "Doctrine of Appropriation," 288.
54. Hunsinger, "Mediator of Communion," 288.

overlook his distinctive role of the Spirit, especially where one would expect it to be emphasized. For Barth, the Holy Spirit's overt role comes to the fore in his doctrine of redemption. The particular and mysterious role *appropriate* to the Holy Spirit and underwritten by the reconciling works of Jesus Christ. The Spirit's role here represents the "consummation of all things; the resurrection of the dead and the eternal life in communion with God."[55]

The incomplete nature of Barth's *opus magnum* leaves the reader with the interpretation that the Holy Spirit's being and role is collapsed into the person and works of Jesus Christ. This perception is due to Barth's unique approach to his doctrine of the Trinity and the articulation of the triunity of God (inclusion of *appropriation* and the doctrine of *perichoresis* within the doctrine of the Trinity, to explain the one-in-threeness and three-in-oneness of God). Nevertheless, there is substantial pneumatological content within the *Church Dogmatics*.[56]

Barth's view of the Spirit is "in a sense," in the line of Augustine; that he is the bond of love (the "common element" of fellowship—*koinonia*) within the Godhead. The Spirit is "what is common to them," writes Barth, "not in so far as they are the one God, but in so far as they are the Father and the Son."[57] The Spirit exists hypostatically as the "full consubstantial fellowship" between the Father and the Son.[58] This then constitutes his intra-trinitarian functionality "appropriate" to him, and not the Father or the Son. That is, in his divine mode of being "mediatorial"[59] in the Godness of God. The Spirit is simultaneously both mediator (agential) and mediation (non-agential) of this, at the same time a primordial, concrete form or *hypostasis* of the one being or *ousia* of God. Hunsinger would say that the Holy Spirit is God insofar as God is "eternally in communion."[60]

---

55. McIntosh, "Doctrine of Appropriation," 278–79.

56. Hunsinger, "Karl Barth's Christology," 178; Hunsinger, "Mediator of Communion"; Busch, *Great Passion*, 178.

57. CD I/1, 469.

58. Ibid., 482.

59. Ibid.

60. Hunsinger, "Mediator of Communion," 180. Although Barth would say that God's being (*ousia*) is in communion (*koinonia*) he would not speak of God's being as communion. He would instead see God's *ousia* as a readiness for *koinonia*. *Koinonia*, he would say, logically presupposes the three divine "modes of being" (*hypostases*). Although there is no *ousia* with the *hypostases* and no *hypostases* without the *ousia*,

The Spirit and the Believer

Having looked at Barth's understanding of the mediatorial role of the Spirit in the intra-trinitarian relationships and his understanding of this as analogous with the Spirit's role as mediatorial in space-time, in the "now not yet" of our lives, we shift our attention to this role in the life of the believer and the church.

For Barth the Spirit's saving work is formulated as christocentric in focus. This does not mean that Barth's opponents of the time (Schleiermacher and von Harnack) were not christocentric in their formulations, but the difference was (particularly in the case of Schleiermacher) that they were more intent on expounding a *Spirit-Christology*.[61] Barth's post-liberal distinctive, in contrast to that of the liberal and modernist trend, was to develop a uniquely *Christo*-pneumatological approach. It is Jesus Christ who constitutes the saving significance of the Holy Spirit, in a way that is not true in the reverse.[62]

Spirit for Barth does not imply that salvation consists mainly in effecting something *in nobis*, e.g. ecstatic experience, renewed disposition or a new mode of being in the world.[63] The presence and power of the Holy Spirit is to attest the nature and efficacy of what the incarnate Word of God has done for our salvation apart from us (*extra nos*)[64] and to mediate our participation in it by faith.[65] The same Spirit, who enables Christ alone to accomplish our salvation as a finished work "there and then," is the same Spirit that enables us to participate in it and attest to it "here and now" in our own history "between the times." This is

---

the divine *ousia* is logically prior. Barth identifies the *ousia* itself as a single, self-identical divine subject, is free and sovereign in trinitarian self-differentiation. The one divine subject who exists in and only in the three divine *hypostases*. *Koinonia* presupposes the divine *hypostases*, just as the *hypostases* presuppose the one divine *ousia*. Therefore in the Holy Spirit and not directly in the divine *ousia* as such, that the eternal *koinonia* of the three *hypostases* is to be found. The relation between the one *ousia* and the three *hypostases* cannot be captured by a single, unifying thought. See *CD* I/1, 368; cf. 359, 332.

61. Ibid., 181.

62. Ibid. That is, the saving significance of Jesus Christ is not to impart and bear witness to the Holy Spirit so much as the saving significance of the Holy Spirit is to impart and bear witness to Jesus Christ.

63. Ibid.

64. *CD* IV/1, 211–83.

65. *CD* IV/2, 518; 526–33; 581–84.

because Jesus Christ hasn't only enacted for us in the "past," but is and remains our salvation in action "now,"[66] he is and therefore remains the enduring focus of the Spirit's work in our and all histories (our past, present and future); as the continual presence of eternity in our "now" of space-time.

The Spirit mediates Christ's presence to us. Barth argues that the operation of the Holy Spirit and the presence of Christ coincide. Christ makes himself and the salvation he effected present through the Spirit. Now, although Barth employs this thought throughout *Church Dogmatics* IV; that in no way means that he holds a purely "non-agential" view of the Spirit. Barth's chosen expression is "appropriate" to his doctrine of reconciliation, where he understands the work and fulfillment of reconciliation as thoroughly christocentric.

The Holy Spirit is considered both the presence and action of Jesus Christ himself (God), in the power of his revelation as it begins in and with the power of his resurrection and continues in its work from this point, expressed here and now.[67] It is by the Spirit that Jesus enables people to see, hear and accept him.[68] This is the noetic role of the Holy Spirit in the life of the believer and the community of believers.

For Barth, the only "content of the Holy Spirit is Jesus; His only work is His provisional revelation; His only effect is the human knowledge which has Him as the object."[69] The Spirit both initiates and mediates the spiritual union of love and knowledge between Christ and faith (analogous with same love and knowledge mediated and experienced in intra-trinitarian communion).[70]

For us, through the preaching of the gospel message, by the power of the Holy Spirit, Jesus in a very real sense becomes present to believers and believers to him. This mutual "self-presence" becomes the basis for mutual self-impartation (Jesus by the Spirit to humanity and humanity by the same Spirit to Jesus).[71] The Spirit mediates the self-impartation of

---

66. Hunsinger, "Mediator of Communion," 181.

67. *CD* IV/2, 322–33. It would be fair to say that the more "agential" expression (which does appear throughout his dogmatics) would have re-emerged more to the fore in his doctrine of redemption (had he been able to write it).

68. Ibid., 323.

69. Ibid., 654.

70. Hunsinger, "Mediator of Communion," 182.

71. Ibid.; Barth, *CD* IV/2, 654.

Jesus himself, through which believers are drawn into union with him. The saving work of the Spirit is always Christ-centered in focus because the Spirit places Jesus to the foreground of salvation history.

For Barth, revelation and reconciliation are no less the work of the Spirit, but the objective reality of salvation is manifest in the Christ event and the efficacy and salvific actuality of this event as God's self revelation. This is why the Spirit mediates and supports Christ, by drawing attention to and pushing him to the foreground of salvation history in a self-effacing way, as Jesus Christ is the "concrete actuality" of salvation for us. With God's irruption into space-time in the event of Jesus Christ, he inaugurates an intertwining of two histories (God's and ours). For us the Spirit is at the forefront of our lives, in every moment of our being, keeping real and present the "then, now and always to be" of the Christ event; the provisional knowledge of his presence to us individually and in community. The Spirit becomes the foundation and the content of "our history" (past, present, and "yet to be") *in* Christ. In the risen Christ's ongoing self-revelation and self-impartation, the Spirit creates communion between Christ and faith. This is a part of the Spirit's communal purpose in the economy of God's salvific plan, as with the incarnation, where the Spirit effects the union of "deity and humanity" in Jesus Christ (there is an analogy here). In Christ's obedience as fulfilled in his death on the cross, the Spirit operates as the bond of peace between the Father and Son. The Holy Spirit aligns himself with the plans and purposes of the Father and the Son in the one economy of salvation. In doing so, he does not in any independent or self-advancing or supplementary way draw attention to himself but instead focuses on underwriting the reconciliatory role of Jesus Christ.[72]

The Holy Spirit is the only effective "agent" by which communion with God is at all humanly possible.[73] That is, with Christ, with the Trinity and with one another. As the mediator of communion, the Holy Spirit unites all believers to Christ, through whom they participate in

---

72. Hunsinger, "Mediator of Communion," 182. A good example of a contrary view can be found in Jenson, *Triune God,* 146–61. Jenson requires a supplemental saving work of the Spirit, since he explicitly denies what Barth takes to be the very heart of the New Testament, namely, that "Christ fully accomplished our salvation at Golgotha" (ibid., 179). Most of Jenson's censure of Barth's pneumatology and be traced back to this fundamental disagreement.

73. Hunsinger, "Mediator of Communion," 182.

the eternal communion (*koinonia*) of the Trinity, while at the same time finding communion with one another.[74]

Barth suggests that it "is the work of the Holy Spirit to bring together and hold together things that are different (disparate)."[75] The Spirit is in this case the incarnation's ultimate unifying ground, holding together otherwise disparate realities (divinity and humanity) within the person of Jesus the Christ.[76] In this sense, the Spirit's work is exemplary; not only applying to the incarnation, but in any way that Christ's relationship with his community may seem necessarily and inescapably disparate.[77] It is this miraculous and mysterious work of the Spirit that joins the disparate on account of communion, where it means "love in knowledge and knowledge in love."[78]

It is through the proclamation of the gospel that the impossible is made possible (unifying of the disparate), but only in the form of an ongoing miracle of the Spirit in the heart of the believer.[79] Nothing depends on a renewing of our capacity, infusion of virtue, acquired habits or strengthened dispositions. In our history of conversion and sanctification we are always sinners, "inescapably." Yet, despite this, the miracle of grace never ceases.[80]

The Holy Spirit grounds "the unity in which Jesus Christ is the heavenly head with God and the earthly body with his community."[81] These incongruent realities are united through the mediatorial role of the Holy Spirit across the ontological divide.[82] The Spirit gathers and

---

74. Ibid., 187.
75. *CD* IV/3.2, 761.
76. *CD* IV/1, 148.
77. *CD* IV/2, 652; and IV/3.2, 761.
78. Hunsinger, "Mediator of Communion," 187–88.
79. Ibid., 183.
80. Ibid. The commendable effort by Rogers, *Thomas Aquinas and Karl Barth*, 188–92; cf. 76–79, to bring Barth and Aquinas into convergence founders at this very point, for Rogers does not take Barth's conception of the Spirit's miraculous operation adequately into account. Stated in terms of Thomistic vocabulary, supernatural operations in the soul, as Barth understands them, do not require the actuation of habits, nor do they tend toward such actuation. Barth believes that Thomistic views to the contrary cannot (logically cannot) escape the problems of synergism. When Barth states that human freedom is entirely dependent on grace, he means without the subvention of infused habits, virtues or principles in the soul.
81. *CD* IV/3.2, 760.
82. Ibid., 761.

holds together Christ and church, coordinating them, bringing harmony and forging true unity.[83]

Barth's assertion here is explicated in contrast to what he rules out in his theological formulations, rejecting the polarities of "divine determinism,"[84] and human "free will."[85] An example of the first would be "emanationism." He would state that "it is not the work of the Holy Spirit to either overpower and make our capacity simply a function of his, or take from us our capacity as human beings. Where the Holy Spirit is present there is no servitude but freedom."[86] There is no acceptable Christian love exhibited that does not in its fullness allow for genuine human agency and freedom.[87]

An example of the second would be "synergism."[88] Barth rejects the work of Brunner (in Barth's famed essay, *Nein!*) where Brunner finds "points of contact" between humanity and the divine in adopting the Augustinian position that divine and human activity are "indirectly identical," coupled with the Thomistic position that both divine and human initiatives effect salvation. This is unacceptable to him. He also rejects the concept of "the systematic coordination of nature and grace."[89] For him, grace is not a case of repairing "this or that" human capacity, but can only constitute a "contradiction" of the fallen human nature as a whole, with all its capacities or incapacities, so that it actually transcends itself despite its fallenness. The only formal relation between grace and nature is miracle.[90]

Although Barth sees grace and nature (divine and human) coexisting together in a sort of common *history*, and moving toward a common *telos*, they do not coexist in any natural or commensurable way. Grace is rather that miracle whereby human reason is so actually contradicted, disturbed and enlightened, that it only conditionally grasps a revelation of God; and human volition provisionally fulfils divine willing.[91]

83. Ibid.
84. Hunsinger, *How to Read Karl Barth*, 207–15.
85. Ibid., 215–18; and 223.
86. *CD* IV/2, 785.
87. Ibid., 752. Also see here his comments on the theology of Nygren and Luther.
88. Hunsinger, "Mediator of Communion," 183.
89. Brunner, and Barth, *Natural Theology*, 96.
90. Ibid., 101.
91. Hunsinger, "Mediator of Communion," 97; Brunner, and Barth, *Natural Theology*, 121.

What the Holy Spirit brings to play in our lives is not a healing or restoration but, nothing short of "resurrection from the dead."[92] This in no way excludes human cooperation with divine grace, but in and of itself, it has no salvific role. Grace as a gift of the Holy Spirit makes human freedom possible, but only in the sense that it leads to new modes of action (*modus agenda*) in the believer. It is always imparted to faith in the form of receiving salvation; partaking in salvation and bearing witness to salvation;[93] human freedom is always the corollary of salvation, never causative.[94]

The distinction between grace and nature in God's salvific work through Jesus by the Spirit apply both objectively and subjectively to us; that is, not only to salvation as it has taken place *extra nos* but also as it occurs *in nobis*.[95]

In the same way as the Holy Spirit mediates communion with Christ (in the disparity of grace and nature), so also he enables us to participate through Christ in the *koinonia* of the Trinity. Those joined to Christ in faith, receive a share in the eternal Godness of God in his triunity. This is the "primal" communion of love and knowledge between the Father and the Son in the Spirit, with no *a priori* necessity for it, except that God primally decided to be God in this way and be fellowship for its own sake.[96]

God thus "receives us through his Son into His fellowship with Himself."[97] We are literally, through being *in* Christ, by and through the power of the Spirit, "taken up into God's fellowship, all that he has in and of himself."[98] Therefore, God's primal decision to be God in this way;

92. Hunsinger, "Mediator of Communion," 184.

93. Ibid., 185

94. Ibid.

95. Barth, "Extra Nos—Pro Nobis—In Nobis," 510. Cf. *CD* IV/4, 13–23. What happens is this: "in nobis, in our heart, in the very center of our existence, a contradiction is lodged against our unfaithfulness. It is a contradiction that we cannot dodge but have to validate. In confronting it we cannot cling to our unfaithfulness, for through it our unfaithfulness is forbidden and cancelled; rendered impossible. Because Jesus Christ intervenes pro nobis and thus in nobis, unfaithfulness to God has been rendered basically an impossible possibility. It is a possibility disallowed and thus no longer to be realized . . . one we recognize as eliminated and taken away by the omnipotent contradiction God lodges within us" (ibid., 22).

96. *CD* II/1, 276.

97. Ibid., 275.

98. Ibid., 276.

and "making time for us" (revelation time) that we may "have time for him;" the triune God "exists, not in solitude but in eternal fellowship,"[99] in which we participate. God's "innermost self is his self-communion; and loving the created order, he gives it a share in his completeness."[100] God is therefore able (in his freedom) to be present to and with that which is other than God, communicating and uniting himself with the other, and the other with Godself. This freedom for fellowship is another name for the Holy Spirit, who mediates our unity with Christ and through him with the eternal Trinity. For Barth this divine freedom for *koinonia* is what he refers to as "God's absoluteness."

It is not possible to participate in God's eternal love without participating in the truth of God's self-knowledge. Revelation is the effecting of this participation.[101] No knowledge of God occurs without fellowship with God,[102] so both "*knowledge* of God" and "*love* of God," is indivisible.[103] In Barth's theology, knowledge of God is essentially a form of communion with God and this knowledge of God for us is through the gospel message; this is true knowledge (according to Barth), because it participates in the truth of God's self-knowledge, manifest in the person of Jesus Christ, with his irruption from eternity into space-time. The surety and strength of our knowledge of God is in the occurrence that "God knows himself; the Father knows the Son and the Son the Father in the unity of the Holy Spirit. It is through God's revelation then, that we become "participants" in this concrete actuality of occurrence,[104] receiving and participating in God's eternal self knowledge.[105]

Despite the truth and reality of our participation in God's self-knowledge, it can only ever be *indirect* participation, because it is mediated, in and through the true humanity (the only avenue of *koinonia*

99. Ibid., 275.

100. Ibid., 277.

101. *CD* I/2, 203–79. The Holy Spirit, according to Barth, is both the subjective reality and the subjective possibility of revelation. The Spirit in other words is the means by which we come to enjoy "the communion with God which is realized in the revelation of God" (*CD* I/2, 257). God's revelation in Jesus Christ cannot be known other than by our reception of it and participation in it through the miraculous operation of the Holy Spirit.

102. *CD* II/1, 182.

103. Ibid., 32.

104. Ibid., 49.

105. Ibid., 68.

by faith and participation open to fallen humanity) of Jesus Christ by the empowering presence of the Holy Spirit.[106] In him alone, has God condescended, in order to raise us to himself[107] and in him alone is the particular "first fruit" of this knowledge of God, in by and through the Spirit that mediates participation.

Between the time of Jesus Christ's earthly presence and the Parousia, the principal role of the Holy Spirit is to form and develop the community of Christ. The Spirit gathers the community in faith,[108] builds the community in love,[109] and sends it into the world in hope.[110] The Holy Spirit's work is first and foremost in the community of believers without neglecting the importance of the individual Christian. The being of the Christian is primarily as "being in relation." It is therefore in the fellowship of community, and not in the individual, that the work of the Holy Spirit is fulfilled.[111]

In Barth's pneumatology, there is a distinct precedence of the community, but of "union in freedom," where each is united to the other in their own particularity,[112] yet indivisibility. For Barth, that which proceeds from the whole (fellowship) proceeds from the individual, in the same way that one is for all, so all are for one [each is for the other], in a bond of mutual self-giving.[113] The community as a whole then reaches its consummation as the Holy Spirit works in the lives of the individual members.[114] It is not contradictory to consider the significance of the individual as the locus of the Spirit's communal work.[115]

The Spirit creates a characteristic community, as the "body of Christ," in which Christ is the head, in that the members support each other in fellowship. Sinner loves sinner though forgiveness outworked in their lives, as their sins have been taken away. Only by the Holy Spirit do believers become free for action in this way in relation with

---

106. Ibid., 59.
107. Ibid., 55.
108. *CD* IV/1, 643–739.
109. *CD* IV/2, 614–726.
110. *CD* IV/3.2, 681–901.
111. *CD* IV/1, 150–54.
112. *CD* IV/2, 635.
113. *CD* II/2, 312.
114. Ibid., 314.
115. Ibid., 311–14.

the other, in the mutuality of love.[116] The Spirit also equips the church (in this fellowship) for freedom in solidarity with the world (but not conformity).[117]

The saving activity of the Spirit is communal (mutual and shared) in nature. The presence and power of communion joins believers to Christ and through him to God and one another, in a fellowship of faith, hope, and love.

Conclusion

It is clear that there is possible scope for ongoing reappraisal of Barth's *Dogmatics* in light of a *Christo*-pneumatological interpretation.[118] Barth's contribution to twentieth century theology cannot be over-emphasized, and renewed interest in the place of pneumatology in his *Dogmatics* has opened the door for continuing dialogue amongst scholars. Barth has attempted to present a truly trinitarian theology with his *Church Dogmatics*.

However, his conception of the relationship of revelation to reconciliation, and redemption, along with his doctrine of appropriation within his doctrine of the Trinity, tends to give the appearance that the Spirit plays a subordinate role in the economy of God's salvific plan. This I believe Barth would ardently refute. However, since he died before finishing volume IV of *Church Dogmatics* and commencing his work on the doctrine of redemption, much has been left in question as to the concrete actuality of the work of the Spirit in his overall thinking.

In addition, to the aforementioned there is no indication of the more "general" role of the Holy Spirit in relation to the created order. Where is the Spirit, and what, if any, sustaining and mediating role does he play beyond the mediatorial role of Jesus Christ to humanity and the church? My thought on this is that because of Barth's polemic against any form of natural theology, (being a deliberate and necessary corrective in Barth's opinion) espoused by existentialist, neo-Protestant, and Roman Catholic theologies of the nineteenth century, any sojourn into this role of the Spirit was consciously avoided.

116. *CD* IV/2, 818.
117. *CD* IV/3.2, 762–93.
118. See Hunsinger, *Disruptive Grace*; Hunsinger, "Mediator of Communion"; Hunsinger, "Karl Barth's Christology"; and McIntosh, "Doctrine of Appropriation."

It is possible that had he been able to complete his doctrine of redemption, this may have been introduced, as redemption (for Barth) was his locus for the *consummating* work of the Holy Spirit which must include all of creation. Having made clear his grounding of theology and his formulations of the doctrines of revelation and reconciliation from his prior work on *Church Dogmatics* I-IV, he would now be able to incorporate this without fear of apparent contradiction.

The role of the Spirit as *historicity* for Barth is understood in light of his conception of the Christ event, eternity and space-time and the interdependency of revelation and reconciliation in particular, with the Spirit making subjectively present in the "here and now" of our "now but not yet" the objective reality of what Jesus Christ has done, is doing and will continue to do, and firmly securing the believer and the church *in* Christ and he *in* us.

Bibliography

Barth, Karl. *Church Dogmatics*. 4 vols. Edinburgh: T. & T. Clark, 1956–75.

———. "Extra Nos—Pro Nobis—In Nobis." *The Thomist* 50 (1986) 497–511.

Brunner, Emil, and Karl Barth. *Natural Theology*. Translated by Peter Fraenkel, with an introduction by John Baillie. London: Bles, 1946.

Busch, Eberhard. *The Great Passion: An Introduction to Karl Barth's Theology*. Grand Rapids: Eerdmans, 2004.

Gunton, Colin E. *Becoming and Being: The Doctrine of God in Charles Hartshorne and Karl Barth*. London: SCM, 2001.

———. "Transcendence, Metaphor, and the Knowability of God." *Journal of Theological Studies* 31 (1980) 501–16.

———. *Yesterday and Today: A Study of Continuities in Christology*. London: Darton, Longman & Todd, 1983.

Hunsinger, George. *Disruptive Grace: Studies in the Theology of Karl Barth*. Grand Rapids: Eerdmans, 2000.

———. *How to Read Karl Barth: The Shape of His Theology*. New York: Oxford University Press, 1993.

———. "Karl Barth's Christology: Its Basic Chalcedonian Character." In *Cambridge Companion to Karl Barth*, edited by John Webster, 127–42. Cambridge: Cambridge University Press.

———. "The Mediator of Communion: Karl Barth's Doctrine of the Holy Spirit." In *Cambridge Companion to Karl Barth*, edited by John Webster, 177–94. Cambridge: Cambridge University Press, 2000.

Jenson, Robert W. *Systematic Theology*. Vol. 1. *The Triune God*. New York: Oxford University Press, 1997.

———. "You Wonder Where the Spirit Went." *Pro Ecclesia* 2 (1993) 296–304.

Jüngel, Eberhard. *God's Being Is in Becoming: The Trinitarian Being of God in the Theology of Karl Barth: A Paraphrase.* Grand Rapids: Eerdmans, 2001.

Mangina, Joseph L. "Bearing the Marks of Jesus: The Church in the Economy of Salvation in Barth and Hauerwas." *Scottish Journal of Theology* 52 (1999) 269–305.

McIntosh, Adam. "The Doctrine of Appropriation as an Interpretative Framework for Karl Barth's Pneumatology of the Church Dogmatics." *Pacifica* 20 (2007) 278–91.

Rogers, Eugene F., Jr. *Thomas Aquinas and Karl Barth: Sacred Doctrine and the Natural Knowledge of God.* Notre Dame: University of Notre Dame, 1995.

Rosato, Philip. *Spirit as Lord: The Pneumatology of Karl Barth.* Edinburgh: T. & T. Clark, 1982.

Torrance, Thomas F. *Space, Time, and Incarnation.* Oxford: Oxford University Press, 1978.

14

The Dynamic Stillness of God
Trinitarian Conceptions of Divine Immutability and Impassibility

Haydn D. Nelson

The Profit and Peril of Trinitarian Theological Reflection

IT CAN BE ARGUED THAT ANY CAREFUL AND REVERENT APPROACH TO trinitarian theological reflection ought to be done with a due sense of both apprehension and excitement. This is so for the subject of our reflection has challenged and perplexed generations of thoughtful believers and yet has occasioned enormous spiritual, intellectual, and practical benefit. In the light of this, one can understand Augustine as he writes: "And I would make this pious and safe agreement, in the presence of our Lord God, with all who read my writings . . . which inquire into the unity of the Trinity of the Father and the Son and the Holy Spirit; because in no other subject is error more dangerous, or inquiry more laborious, or the discovery of truth more profitable."[1]

However, such Augustinian advice also leads us to observe that the early centuries of the Christian church were characterized by the actualization of both potentials. That is, both significant truth and significant error—with the latter often receiving the epithet "heresy"—can be found as Christian theology matured and developed. Although significant error—heresy—would be seen by most as an intrinsically

---

1. Augustine, *On the Trinity*, 19. What follows is developed further in my *The Problem of the Providence of God*.

negative phenomenon,[2] the existence of various early century heresies had the positive and possibly unexpected result of effecting increased clarity and precision in the church's articulation of orthodoxy. In the succinct words of Carson, "Theological reflection and precision, ripening orthodoxy, are often triggered by heresy."[3]

Although contemporary theological discourse would typically avoid the use of a word like "heresy" because it is seen as pejorative, emotive, and carrying a lot of anachronistic baggage, it is almost inevitable that orthodoxy will seek to rein in some theological creativity if it can be demonstrated to be unwise, unbiblical, unfruitful, or simply wrongheaded. Yet, the very presence of creative steps in theology brings about a context for greater precision and illumination of Christian belief. Hence, I would argue that we should approach theological proposals with an attitude of "charitable discretion"—both interpreting them in their best light whilst remaining prudent concerning their theological and biblical foundations and the implications that are being drawn.[4] Similar to Paul in Eph 4:15—"speaking the truth in love"—we should balance truth and love—discretion and charity. To borrow from my own Australian cultural context, this approach is the theological equivalent of giving someone a "fair go."

Perhaps a case in point is the contemporary proposal known as Open Theism. Although critics of Open Theism would accuse it of having significantly overstepped—and some are not shy of using the word "heresy" particularly concerning its position on divine foreknowledge[5]—others see in it some creative and positive emphases. However, of particular interest to our discussion is the debate the Open Theism

2. Etymologically, "heresy" originally carried the simple and neutral meaning of "faction" or "party" (hence, its meaning in Acts 5:17, 15:5, and 26:5). Josephus and other writers of antiquity used the word in this way—see Skarsaune, "Heresy and the Pastoral Epistles," 9. However, it later came to be used of those who had separated or who had moved away from orthodoxy (as in 1 Cor 11:19 and Gal 5:20). Heresy began to indicate more than just simple doctrinal disagreement, but "something that undercut the very basis for Christian existence" (see Brown, *Heresies: Heresy and Orthodoxy*, 2).

3. Carson, *Gagging of God*, 356.

4. This approach has great similarity with what Sanders calls the practicing of "dialogical virtues." These virtues include honesty, integrity, empathy, teachableness, persistence, precision, articulateness and foresight (Hall and Sanders, *Does God Have a Future?* 191–92).

5. See ibid., 169–75. Letham, "Is God Omniscient?" 32, believes that Open Theism "is close to heresy."

proposal has provoked concerning the theological conceptions of divine immutability and impassibility.

For the sake of clarity, divine immutability may be defined as "God's freedom from all change, understood to emphasize God's changeless perfection and divine constancy." Divine impassibility is defined as "The traditional theological view that God does not change and thus is not affected by actions that take place in the world, particularly in terms of experiences of suffering or pain."[6] The combination of both conceptions derives from the self-evident link with the idea of *change*, or more specifically the *absence of change*, in how we might conceive God. In the words of Fiddes, "Traditional theology bound together the immutability of God with his impassibility; it insisted that to suffer meant to change, and therefore God could not suffer."[7]

Trinity and Active Constancy

Open Theism has been strident in its criticism of what it perceives as an unhealthy imbalance in classical or traditional theology on these issues. For example, Clark Pinnock writes:

> The God of the gospel is not the god of philosophy, at least not of Hellenic philosophy. The God and Father of Jesus Christ is compassionate, suffering, and victorious love. The god of philosophy is immutable, timeless and apathetic. We must speak boldly for the sake of the gospel: Augustine was wrong to have said that God does not grieve over the suffering in the world; Anselm was wrong to have said that God does not experience compassion; Calvin was wrong to have said that biblical figures that convey such things are mere accommodations to finite understanding. For too long pagan assumptions about God's nature have influenced theological reflection.[8]

Elsewhere, he writes, "Some people have gotten the impression that God is an unblinking cosmic stare or a solitary metaphysical iceberg, and they naturally have difficulty relating to God as a loving, interacting Person."[9] And we need "to distance ourselves from the tendency to

---

6. McKim, *Westminster Dictionary of Theological Terms*, 116.
7. Fiddes, *Creative Suffering of God*, 48.
8. Pinnock, *Most Moved Mover*, x.
9. Pinnock in preface to Sanders, *God Who Risks*, 1.

see God too much as a solitary, narcissistic being who suffers from his own completeness."[10] Rather than describing and understanding God in ways that seem predisposed toward images of divine impassivity and inertness, Pinnock states: "This is a God who loves being in covenant partnership with the creature and longs to draw us into a community of love, both with God and among ourselves. God's perfection is not to be all-controlling or to exist in majestic solitude or to be infinitely egocentric. On the contrary, God's fair beauty according to Scripture is his own relationality as a triune community. It is God's gracious interactivity, not his hyper-transcendence and/or immobility, which makes him so glorious."[11]

Although this debate concerning the alleged Hellenic influence upon Christian theology will no doubt continue, it can be argued that there are significant reasons for predicating a theological tension in which—in relation to immutability and impassibility—there is both an existence of change and an absence of change in God. Indeed, what both sides of the debate seem desirous of avoiding is an absolutization, in either direction, of the idea of divine change—that is, that God *changes in all senses* or that God *does not change in any sense*. In the words of Vanhoozer, who writes from within the traditional view, "This is a most important analytic point: *impassibility no more means impassive than immutability means immobile*."[12]

For example, Pinnock distinguishes between God's *character* and God's *relations with others*. He argues that God is "unchangeable in character, but is not unchanging in his relations with us."[13] Ware, a critic of Open Theism, also seeks to make distinctions in that he argues that God is *ontologically* and *ethically* immutable and yet is *relationally* mutable.[14]

It is my view that a trinitarian perspective on this issue of change provides solid theological grounding for affirming what both sides of the debate appear to desire—that God changes in some sense/s and does not change in others. As Cottrell states, "A consensus seems to be

10. Pinnock, *Most Moved Mover*, 79.
11. Ibid., 5–6.
12. Vanhoozer, *First Theology*, 76, emphasis added.
13. Pinnock, *Most Moved Mover*, 6.
14. Ware, "Evangelical Reformulation of the Doctrine of the Immutability of God," 431–46.

emerging that we should say that God changes in some ways but not in others."[15] To bring this tension into clearer view, we will treat each aspect in turn.

The Absence of Divine Change

Although I recognize that, at times, some of the fathers' language can appear intemperate or inconsistent,[16] there does seem to be significant evidence to suggest that the fathers were seeking to articulate this tension. In the light of this, then, why was it perceived to be so important to predicate so strongly the absence of change in God?

Firstly, it is possible that the fathers were seeking to contrast the Christian and biblical God from changeable created beings and from the fickle gods of the Roman and Greek pantheons. Hence, apophatic language was able to denote such a distinction and preserved the notion of God's unchangeableness—that he is ontologically secure and ethically faithful. Secondly, the very apophaticism of the language utilized affirms the divine perfection. In other words, if the perfect God were to change, then it can only be from perfection to imperfection. Hence, God cannot change.

This latter line of argument is posited by Aquinas and has received a recent articulation and development in the work of Weinandy. Weinandy argues that apophatic language primarily states what God is not, rather than what he is. As such, it primarily states negatives—that God does not change in the way that creatures or the pagan gods often do; that he can neither diminish nor increase in his goodness and perfection; and is distinct from the created order and therefore from the time that marks these changes. Yet, the positive side of apophatic language is that it, by implication, makes affirmations concerning God. If God cannot change in that he cannot be more or less perfect in his love, holiness, goodness, and so on, then this affirms his comprehensive and consummate love, holiness, goodness and so on. Weinandy's argument is that immutability and impassibility were never meant to denote

---

15. Cottrell, *God the Redeemer*, 475.

16. Brown argues that although Gregory of Nazianzus sought to articulate how deity could suffer (by inseparably uniting with Jesus and so what Jesus did and experienced, God also did and experienced), Gregory of Nyssa, "by contrast, has no conception of God suffering" (Brown, *Heresies*, 171).

God as immobile or apathetic. Rather, they actually establish the fact that God is *perfectly and completely* loving, good, dynamic, and so on.

Interestingly for our discussion, Weinandy seeks to base this understanding of immutability and impassibility upon a consideration of God as triune. He argues that since the divine persons only subsist as distinct subjects in relationship with one another, they ought to be understood as *relations in act*. In other words, God's triunity is not three divine persons *in* relationship but three divine persons *as* relationships—the persons are not at each end of a relation but are the relations themselves.

As I said earlier, he is not alone in this—for Aquinas once posed a point of inquiry as to "whether relation is the same as person." He concluded, "However, since in the reality it has in God relation is identical with essence and essence with person, as is now clear, relation necessarily is the same as person." In other words, the divine persons are not in relationship but are the relations themselves. Further, it is precisely this relationality that makes the persons distinguishable—whether it be fatherhood, sonship, or procession (*paternitas, filiatio*, or *processio*).[17]

This then leads Weinandy to the heart of his thesis. Since the divine persons are subsistent relations fully in act, and as the names for each person designate a perfect or pure act (*actus purus*),[18] "they do not have any relational potential that would need to be actualized in order to make them more relational—more who they are."[19] Therefore, the divine triunity is completely and utterly dynamic, relational, and active and cannot be more so—there is no potential in that which is perfect or pure. Therefore, immutability does not mean immobile but actually denotes the complete opposite—perfection in dynamic, perichoretic relationship. Furthermore, and by following a similar line of argument, impassibility means that, "as subsistent relations fully in act, the persons of the Trinity are completely and utterly passionate in their self-giving to one another and cannot be more passionate for they are constituted, and so subsist, as who they are only because they have absolutely given

---

17. Aquinas, *Summa Theologiæ* 1a.40.1.

18. Here he draws upon Aquinas' philosophical argument that God is *actus purus* ("pure act")—that is, that God's nature is "to be" or *ipsum esse* (to-be itself) (Weinandy, *Does God Suffer?*, 120–22). Aquinas argues that "He who is" (or "I am who I am" from Exod 3:14) is the most appropriate name for God (Aquinas, *Summa Theologiæ* 1a.13.11).

19. Weinandy, *Does God Suffer?* 119.

themselves completely to one another in love."[20] Again, if God as triune is indeed perfect relationship or perfect community, it follows that there must be a sense in which God cannot change. The alternative is to allow the possibility of potential in God that would then question the perfection or purity of the divine relationality.[21]

Two extended quotations from him are instructive in relation to his conclusions. He writes:

> Thus, there is little, if any, ground for the familiar criticism that the attribute of divine immutability transformed, within the teaching of the Fathers, the living and dynamic God of the Bible into the static and inert God of Greek philosophy. The problem is that contemporary critics of the Fathers consistently give to the attribute of divine immutability the positive noetic content of being static, lifeless and inert, something which the Fathers never argued for nor even contemplated. The Fathers grasped, as the contemporary critics do not, that to say that God is immutable is to deny those aspects of his nature—changes of a diminishing or of a developmental kind—which would jeopardize or render less than perfect his dynamic vitality as the one who truly is. While the Fathers may have snatched the attribute of immutability from the Greek philosophical vocabulary and tradition, they radically altered it so as to assert, in a philosophical manner, God's unconditional goodness and unqualified love as revealed in the scriptures.[22]

Furthermore:

> As we have noted . . . the contemporary critics invariably accuse those Fathers who uphold the impassibility of God as well as his love, compassion, mercy and anger of being inconsistent. This accusation is founded upon the false premise that to be impassible is to be devoid of passion. This, again, the Fathers never argued for nor even countenanced. The Fathers denied of God those passions which, they believed, would imperil or impair those positive attributes which were constitutive of the divine nature—his goodness and love. And equally then, such a denial

---

20. Ibid., 119–20.

21. Kaiser agrees and writes, "The ideas of immutability and impassibility, far from detracting from the dynamic character of the God of the Hebrews, actually provided an eternal grounding for that character in the primordial nature of the godhead" (Kaiser, *Doctrine of God*, 54).

22. Weinandy, *Does God Suffer?* 110–11.

amplified the intensity of these same unchangeably perfect passions. The Fathers wished to preserve the wholly otherness of God, as found in scripture, and equally, also in accordance with Scripture, to profess and enrich an understanding of his passionate goodness and love that was truly in keeping with his wholly otherness.[23]

Indeed, to negatively absolutize the notion of divine unchangeability—that is, that God does not change *in any sense*—would be to posit that God is immobile. Barth, in particular, is under no illusions as to the implications of this. He writes, "For we must not make any mistake: the pure *immobile* is—death. If, then, the pure *immobile* is God, death is God."[24] Yet, Barth argues that this is not what is meant by divine immutability. Rather, immutability is God in his "eternal actuality" as God—he is not God "only potentially" or "at any point intermittently" but, "always at every place He is what He is continually and self-consistently."[25]

Hence, arguing from this trinitarian perspective, it can be said that God does not change and this lack of change in no way compromises the triune relationality but rather establishes it as *perfect* triune relationality.

The Existence of Divine Change

The cumulation of these trinitarian formulations would appear to preclude any notion of immutability conceived in terms of inactivity or immobility—as though God were an "unblinking cosmic stare."[26] Similarly, these trinitarian proposals would also preclude any notion of impassibility portraying God as radically unmoved by emotion within his own Triune life or as aloof to human pain and suffering—as though God were a "solitary metaphysical iceberg."[27] As Jüngel puts it, "God *is* active."[28]

---

23. Ibid., 111–12.
24. *CD* II/1, 494, emphasis in the original.
25. Ibid.
26. Pinnock as cited in Sanders, *God Who Risks*, 1. Hodge comments that some are "apt to confound immutability and immobility. In denying that God can change, they seem to deny that He can act" (Hodge, *Systematic Theology*, vol. 1, 391).
27. Pinnock as cited in Sanders, *God Who Risks*, 1.
28. Jüngel, *Doctrine of the Trinity*, 64, emphasis in the original.

Yet, a trinitarian perspective does provide further illumination of how and to what extent it may be appropriate to predicate the existence of change in God. In other words, if ultimate reality—that is, God—is primarily relational, is it not the nature of personal relationship that persons, to some extent, both impact and are impacted by other persons? In other words, this person-to-person connectivity and interactivity would appear to suggest the possibility—and this needs to be carefully articulated—of some sense of change. Fiddes puts it like this, "To love is to be in a relationship where what the loved one does alters one's own experience."[29] Therefore, in the context of the perfectly loving, perfectly interconnected, perfectly relational community that is the triune divine life, is it appropriate to say that the divine persons are *changed* by their *perichoretic* interaction?

It is in the light of these considerations that Jüngel advances the thesis that *God's being is in becoming*. He is concerned that his thesis not be misconstrued or misunderstood as moving us into the Process concept of the becoming God. Rather, he argues for recognition that God is a oneness of three modes of being differentiated from each other. Hence, God's being is a self-related being and, as such, "it is structured as a relationship."[30] He concludes:

> But this relational structuring of God's being constitutes God's being not in the sense of an independent impersonal structure in relation to this being; indeed, the modes of God's being which are differentiated from one another are so related to each other that each mode of God's being *becomes* what it *is* only together *with* the two other modes of being. The relational structuring in God's being is the expression of varying "original-relations" and "issues" of God's being. God's being as the being of God the Father, Son, and Holy Spirit is thus a *being in becoming*. The doctrines of *perichoresis* and appropriation within the three modes of God's being differentiated from each other and united as "threefold" defined this knowledge: God's being is in becoming.[31]

Jüngel's point is not that God becomes another, but that the being of God is constituted relationally. The divine persons *become* who they

---

29. Fiddes, *Creative Suffering of God*, 50.
30. Jüngel, *Doctrine of the Trinity*, 63.
31. Ibid., 63–64.

are—their being—only in relation to the other divine persons. God's being is defined and constructed relationally, there is constant movement in God—it is a being in becoming. Hence, in this dynamically relational sense, Jüngel argues for a sense of change, a sense of becoming, in God.

What is to be made of this proposal? Although one can note the careful distinctions that Jüngel makes to guard against his proposal being construed as affirming development or the realization of potentiality in God, I would still contend that the language of *becoming* remains problematic. The language of becoming, in my view, conjures up more than an image of dynamic relationality, but points to the idea of development or potentiality, which may, by implication, compromise the perfection of the divine relationality.

The Notion of Active Constancy

In seeking to illuminate immutability and impassibility from a trinitarian perspective, Colin Gunton has helpfully provided some ways in which this tension might be approached. He writes in relation to immutability: "An interesting test case here are those twin negatives, immutability and impassibility. As we have seen, we do need to be able to affirm that God is immutable, in the respect that his being is ontologically secure, so that his promises can be relied on. But the tradition has sometimes turned this into something more abstract and impersonal. What is immutability trinitarianly construed? Immanently speaking, God cannot but be love; economically speaking, he will not but see to it that his purposes for the perfection of the creation come to be fulfilled."[32] In relation to impassibility, he states.

> Impassibility, as we have seen, is more problematic, for at the heart of the economic action of the triune God is the Father's sending of the eternal Son to suffer and die on the cross. As we have also seen, however, it does not follow that the suffering of the cross can be used to generate a doctrine of general divine passibility. Rather, we must say that God's historical action in the Son's suffering demonstrates that he is not "passive" in the

---

32. Gunton, *Christian Faith*, 189.

face of history. Rather the cross is the Father's relentless action in shaping history to his reconciling will.[33]

Consequently, a trinitarian perspective leads us to posit a God who engages and interacts with the world in history and yet is able also to transcend and to guide history to fulfill his purposes—he is both dynamic and directional. Similarly, he is able to experience suffering and pain and yet is able to transcend and transform both. In other words, we may say that although there is activity and dynamism in God, there is also a sense of constancy and dependability in him—this is a God in whom we can trust.[34] God is both changeable and unchangeable, yet the former does not compromise his faithfulness nor the latter his dynamism.

Hence, I would argue that a trinitarian perspective points us toward a conception that can be encapsulated in the expression *active constancy*. Indeed, Dodds coined a particularly attractive expression when he writes of the "dynamic stillness" of God's immutable love.[35] His point is the same—God is active in one sense and constant in another.[36] Indeed, Erickson argues that Process philosophy fails at this point for it assumes an either/or situation—that is, God is either dynamic and therefore changeable or impassive and therefore unchanging. By contrast, he writes, "Yet there is no real proof, only an assumption, that there cannot be an intermediate condition, namely, stable dynamism,

33. Ibid.

34. Strong seeks to articulate this tension when he writes, "God's immutability itself renders it certain that his love will adapt itself to every varying mood and condition of his children, so as to guide their steps, sympathize with their sorrows, answer their prayers." Hence, unlike a stone that has no internal experience, divine immutability is like that of a "column of mercury, that rises and falls with every change in the temperature of the surrounding atmosphere" (Strong, *Systematic Theology*, 258).

35. Dodds, *The Unchanging God of Love*, 280–82, as cited by Weinandy, *Does God Suffer?* 127 n. 45.

36. In an effort to articulate this conception of active constancy, Kaiser comments that God is "both transcendent and personal. His transcendence (ineffability, immutability, impassibility) does not reduce him to a solitary, indescribable Monad like the 'One' (*to hen*) of Neoplatonism. Nor does his personality (fatherhood, love) reduce him to the level of the gods of the Greek pantheon. He is the Father Almighty. He is ineffable love" (Kaiser, *Doctrine of God*, 55). Similarly, Hodge sees the tension as best expressed as God being immutable in his being, perfections and purposes and yet perpetually active. Whatever the language utilized, Hodge believes that "activity and immutability must be compatible; and no explanation of the latter inconsistent with the former ought to be admitted" (Hodge, *Systematic Theology*, 1:391).

or dynamism that follows a regular pattern, neither diminishing nor increasing in what it is."[37]

In a similar way, when applied to the doctrine of divine impassibility, the conception of dynamic stillness—an active constancy—presents us with the tension that God is active in that he is touched by suffering, yet is constant in that he is not overwhelmed or ontologically shaped by suffering. As Gunton states, "the point of the patristic doctrine of impassibility is that it shows that God cannot be pushed about."[38] Indeed, Bloesch believes that this is the particular difficulty in Moltmann's conception of a suffering God. He writes:

> The notion of impassibility can be retained so long as it does not mean that God is impassive and unfeeling.... The impassibility of God must not be confused with imperturbability (*ataraxia*) or apathy (*apatheia*).... God remains above pain and suffering even while descending into the world of confusion and misery. He is not invulnerable to pain and suffering, but he rises above them.... Against Moltmann I contend that a theology of the cross must be completed in a theology of glory.... Suffering is not inherent in God, but God freely wills to enter into our suffering so that it can be overcome.[39]

Indeed, if we negatively absolutize the idea of impassibility—that is, that God is unaffected by suffering *in any sense*—then we are potentially left with a God who may be able to help us but cannot empathize with us. But, it must be asked, would such a God *want* to help us? Yet, if we absolutize in the opposite direction, then we are potentially left with a God who may be able to empathize with us but cannot help us.[40]

---

37. Erickson, *God in Three Persons*, 213.

38. Gunton, "The Being and Attributes of God: Eberhard Jüngel's dispute with the classical philosophical tradition," in Gunton, *Theology through the Theologians*, 73.

39. Bloesch, *God the Almighty*, 94–95. O'Collins also questions Moltmann's trinitarianism, in particular his view that the cross is an intra-trinitarian event (with a rupture in the divine life and the Father "ceasing" to be the Father). He writes, "It is one thing to uphold a strong link between the theology of the cross and the doctrine of the Trinity, and emphasize that it was the Son of God who was crucified and was raised by the Father through the power of the Holy Spirit. But it is another thing to expound the crucifixion as not only affecting but even shaping the inner life of the tripersonal God" (O'Collins, "Holy Trinity," 5).

40. Bauckham, "'Only the Suffering God Can Help,'" 12, comments, "The message of divine suffering would be no gospel without the message of the divine victory over suffering."

Lewis sees this clearly and writes: "We do indeed have to be careful here and make necessary distinctions. If God is to understand us and identify with us he must enter into our pain and sufferings. But if God is to help us, he has to be more than the God who suffers, he has to be the God who saves; and to be the Saviour God amid so many contradictory forces, he has also to be the Sovereign God."[41] In other words, if God is nothing more than a co-victim with humanity, how can we hope in him for healing and an ultimate end to suffering? Even Fiddes, who argues against the idea of impassibility, recognizes that God must have victory over suffering. He writes, "If it is essential that a God who helps us should sympathize with our suffering, it is also essential that he should not be overcome or defeated by suffering."[42]

It is my view that a trinitarian perspective points us toward this tensional conception of active constancy. Accordingly, we have a God in whom we can trust and to whom we can bring our petitions, for although he knows what it is like to experience the struggles that we experience, he is yet able, on our behalf and for our benefit, to transcend and overcome them. And, indeed, supremely in the event of the cross and resurrection, he experiences the depths of pain, suffering, and death, and yet transcends, transforms and translates each.

Consequently, it is appropriate that we now turn to look more closely at the triune economy of salvation and how it might illuminate immutability and impassibility.

Divine Change and the Economy of Salvation

As the above has demonstrated, God should not be conceived as unfeeling or unaffected—as though his relational perfection makes him inert and apathetic toward us. Yet, we must ask to what extent the birth, life, death, resurrection, and ascension of Jesus Christ in the economy of salvation informs us in relation to this notion of the active constancy of the triune God. This is so for when divinity took on humanity in Christ, there must be some sense in which change can be predicated of God.[43]

---

41. Lewis, *Message of the Living God*, 296.

42. Fiddes, *Creative Suffering of God*, 100.

43. Moltmann, *Crucified God*, 152, believes that, "To comprehend God in the crucified Jesus, abandoned by God, requires a 'revolution in the concept of God': *Nemo contra Deum nisi Deus ipse.*"

Blocher highlights the connection between Trinity, incarnation, and change when he writes, "At the center of the economic Trinity, the incarnation: God (the Son) *became* man! If ever there was an event which implied *change* for God, it must have been the incarnation."[44] Similarly, Rahner, whom Blocher quotes approvingly,[45] states, "If we face squarely the fact of the incarnation . . . we must simply say: God can become something, he who is unchangeable in himself can *himself* become subject to change *in something else*."[46] Rahner's efforts to articulate this binary affirmation lead him to a dialectical tension. He concludes:

> The mystery of the incarnation must lie in God himself: in the fact that he, though unchangeable "in himself," can become something "in another." The immutability of God is a dialectical truth like the unity of God. . . . In the same way we learn from the incarnation that immutability (which is not eliminated) is not simply and uniquely a characteristic of God but that in and in spite of his immutability *he* can truly *become* something. He himself, he, in time. And this possibility is not a sign of deficiency, but the height of his perfection, which would be less if in addition to being infinite, he could not become less than he (always) is. This we can and must affirm, without being Hegelians. And it would be a pity if Hegel had to teach Christians such things.[47]

Consequently, what we have in the central event of the economy of salvation—the birth, life, death, resurrection, and ascension of Jesus Christ—is the supreme focal point in which the unchanging God could be said to experience change. But, again, we must be careful not to absolutize in either direction—that God changes *in all senses* or that God cannot change *in any sense*. Indeed, it can be argued that some of the early christological controversies are really examples of the absolutization of God's unchangeableness. To suggest that God only *seemed* to become human in Christ (as in Docetism); or that he only became *partially* human (as in Apollinarianism); or that Christ was *not simultaneously* divine and human (as in Nestorianism) are all examples, to

---

44. Blocher, "Divine Immutability," 17, emphasis in the original.
45. Ibid., 20–21.
46. Rahner, *Theological Investigations*, vol. 4:113, emphasis in the original.
47. Ibid., 114 n. 3, emphasis in the original.

differing degrees, of absolutizing in this other direction—of attempting to protect God from the notion of change *in any sense*.

What the incarnation of Jesus Christ appears to lead us toward is a theological tension—the triune God who cannot change (in that he is perfectly relational, perfectly loving, perfectly dynamic and so on) is yet able to change (in that the perfection of his relationality, love, and dynamism overflows towards humanity in the incarnation). Hence, while perfection of triune relationality and dynamism may, in one sense, preclude change (in that there is no potential in God to be more relational and dynamic), it is perhaps also the case that, in another sense, perfection of triune relationality and dynamism actually enables change in that it overflows in love to those who are other. In essence, one could argue that the incarnation is an expression, indeed the pre-eminent expression, of the overflow of the perfect relationality of the triune God.

In other words, perfect triune relationality—which has no internal relational potential and therefore cannot change—overflows in the economy of salvation toward human beings who are other. Furthermore, this overflow finds its focal point in the incarnation—God himself became human. In this sense, then, Rahner states that God, "though unchangeable 'in himself,' can become something 'in another.'"[48]

Indeed, Torrance describes the incarnation as a divine act of freedom in which God does what he has never done—"it took place in the sovereign ontological freedom of God to be other in his external relations than he eternally was, and is, and to do what he had never done before."[49] This is not to be understood as God surrendering his transcendence, compromising his freedom, or imprisoning himself in the space-time dimensions of the world. Rather, the nature of God's triunity is that the incarnation "flowed freely, unreservedly and unconditionally from the eternal movement of Love in God."[50] The triune nature is perfectly loving, dynamic, relational, and faithful—there is no potential yet to be actualized—and, as such, it overflows toward we who are "other."

---

48. Ibid.

49. Torrance, *Christian Doctrine of God*, 108.

50. Ibid.

Divine Change and the Hypostatic Union

In many ways, the hypostatic union found in Christ provides us with both an example and focal point of the tensions implicit in immutability and impassibility. This is so for it is the point at which divine and human dimensions most directly and profoundly intersect and intertwine. Consequently, we have in Christ the nucleus—the mysterious embrace—of both divine and human experiences of change and suffering and, therefore, it has implications for how we might conceive of divine immutability and impassibility. In particular, Christ provides us with an example of how we might conceive of God being actively constant—both dynamically engaging with humanity and yet remaining faithful and true; both experiencing and being impacted by the reality of pain and suffering and yet transcending and transforming each.

As an illustration of how this might be so, Vanhoozer draws a parallel between how we might understand divine impassibility and the doctrine of the impeccability of Christ. Firstly, he argues, as I do, that impassibility "means not that God is unfeeling but that God is never *overcome* or *overwhelmed* by passion."[51] He draws a parallel with Christ's impeccability by pointing out that the writer to the Hebrews affirms both that Christ was truly tempted just as we are (Heb 2:18) and yet was sinless (Heb 4:15). Certainly, some may feel that Jesus' sinlessness means that he could not have felt the force of temptation. Alternatively, others might claim that if Jesus did feel the force of temptation, he must have sinned. However, my view is that the New Testament rules out either option—it affirms both that he felt the force of temptation and yet was sinless.

In a similar way, he concludes, we can see how God can genuinely experience the full force of sorrow or pain and yet not be overwhelmed or constrained by it. In Vanhoozer's words, "As Jesus feels the force of temptation without sinning, so God feels the force of the human experience without suffering change in his being, will or knowledge."[52] His point is that Christ, in particular his sinlessness, gives us an example of how we might conceive of divine impassibility. If Christ is able both authentically to experience temptation and yet transcend it, is it not possible that God can authentically experience other things, such as

---

51. Vanhoozer, *First Theology*, 93, emphasis in the original.
52. Ibid.

pain, sorrow, or suffering, and yet be able to transcend them? In this way, then, Christ is the prime example of how we might conceive God being both active (in that he engages with, experiences and is impacted by human experiences) and constant (in that he transcends and brings transformation to human experiences).

Perichoresis and the Economy of Salvation

The nature of intra-trinitarian *perichoresis* perhaps also gives us a window into how we might conceive of God both entering into human suffering in an authentic way (active) and yet not being constrained or ontologically shaped by suffering (constancy).

The early trinitarian dispute between Tertullian and Praxeas concerning patripassianism[53] (Praxeas—who, of course, we know only through Tertullian's writings—argued that the Son does more than just reveal the Father *but is himself the Father*) raises the question as to the appropriateness or otherwise of conceiving how the suffering of the Son might be connected with the Father and Holy Spirit. For example, Erickson argues that there is a sense in which patripassianism is actually true and he wonders whether its rejection in the early centuries

---

53. One of the earlier trinitarian heresies—in particular, Modalistic Monarchianism (also known as Sabellianism)—received arguably one of its earliest articulations through Praxeas and only later reached its high point in the teaching of Sabellius. However, what marks out Praxeas' teachings, and why they incurred the opposition of Tertullian, is his insistence that the Son does more than just reveal the Father *but is himself the Father* (Brown, *Heresies*, 101). Indeed, when Tertullian wrote his major treatise on the Trinity, *Against Praxeas*, it appears that the intention of Praxeas (who is unknown apart from Tertullian's work) was the preservation of the deity of Christ. As such, and as seems to be the case with many heresies, the intention behind Modalism would appear to have been largely honorable. However, the problem arose that, if the Son is in reality simply a form or mode of the Father, then it must mean that it was the Father who suffered in Christ during the Passion (see González, *History of Christian Thought*, vol. 1, 148). Consequently, Modalism received the alternative names of Patripassianism or Theopassianism. However, when Praxeas realizes that his conception logically entails patripassianism, which was perhaps deemed inappropriate for deity, his response is to draw a distinction between Jesus, the man, and Christ, the υ(ποστασιj or personification of the Father. Hence, only the man suffered but God did not. However, splitting the hypostatic union in such a way was ultimately found unsatisfactory by orthodoxy in general and Tertullian in particular.

was primarily on Greek philosophical grounds rather than biblical grounds.[54] He writes:

> Clearly, the Son died in a way in which the Father and the Spirit did not, for only the Son had been incarnate. Yet Scripture has numerous indications of the part of the Father in sending the Son.... Both the act of the Father in sending the Son and in receiving the sacrifice were part of the total picture of redemption. And although only the Son actually died personally and physically on the cross, any loving parent can testify that the parent is not unaffected when the child suffers. Given the closeness of the Father and the Son—they are "in" one another, and can be said to be "one"—that effect would be accentuated, if anything. This, then, is the sense in which "patripassianism" is true—not that the Father was the Son, but that he felt what the Son was feeling. It should be noted, also, that the Spirit was involved in this redemptive work; ... the Spirit came on Jesus and indwelt and empowered his ministry. Even his emotions were in the Spirit, so that we read in Luke that "in that hour he rejoiced in the Spirit." It is therefore safe to conclude it was by the Spirit within him that Jesus was able to offer his life as a sacrifice.[55]

The point that Erickson is making is that trinitarian *perichoresis*—"the permeation of each person by the other, their coinherence without confusion"[56]—points to the possibility that both the Father and Holy Spirit, in some sense, suffered along with the Son.

What is to be said of this proposal? Firstly, it is important to note that it is not suggesting, as Erickson makes clear, that the Father *is* the Son, for that would be to confound the persons. Rather, this proposal is suggesting that the Father and the Holy Spirit, as subsisting divine persons with the Son, to some extent authentically experience that which the Son experiences. In other words, if perichoresis does mean that the divine persons mutually interpenetrate each other, then there must be a sense in which the Father and the Holy Spirit experienced what the Son experienced on the cross. Of course, we are dealing with mystery here and, hence, human language will be stretched to accommodate it. Yet, though we might debate over semantics—for example, that the Father and Holy Spirit suffered *indirectly* while the Son suffered *directly*—the

54. Erickson, *Christian Theology*, 335.
55. Erickson, *God in Three Persons*, 236–37.
56. Fiddes, *Participating in God*, 71.

reality of trinitarian perichoresis appears to be strongly suggestive of the idea that the Father and Holy Spirit experienced authentically what the Son experienced on the cross.[57] Thus, Jüngel, though not arguing for patripassianism in the sense argued by Praxeas, nevertheless states, "Thus the Father, too, participates in the passion along with the Son, and the divine oneness of God's modes of being thus shows itself in the suffering of Jesus Christ."[58]

Secondly, however, although the Father and Holy Spirit may experience, to some extent, what the Son experiences, this is not to be construed as though the Son loses his particularity as the Son—as though what he experiences is somehow subsumed into some unified divine experience. Rather, the nature of perichoresis simply means that each of the divine persons experiences authentically what the other persons experience yet without compromising their own distinctiveness—their own particularity. In other words, the Son experiences suffering *as the Son*. Though he may perichoretically share that suffering with the Father and the Holy Spirit, and so there is a sense in which God suffers in his oneness, it still simultaneously remains uniquely his own, and so there is a sense in which God suffers in his threeness. In other words, although the experience of the Son is not exactly the experience of the Father and the Holy Spirit, it is equally true that the Son's experience is not other than the experience of the Father and the Holy Spirit. We must hold in tension the oneness and threeness of God—his unity and his particularity—neither dividing the substance nor confounding the persons. As Augustine argues:

> Hold fast then what you have heard. I will recapitulate it briefly, and entrust it to be stored up in your minds as a thing, to my thinking, of the greatest usefulness. The Father was not born

---

57. John of Damascus explains *perichoresis* in the following way: "The subsistences dwell and are established firmly in one another. For they are inseparable and cannot part from one another, but keep to their separate courses within one another, without coalescing or mingling, but cleaving to one another. For the Son is in the Father and the Spirit: and the Spirit in the Father and the Son: and the Father in the Son and the Spirit, but there is no coalescing or commingling or confusion" (John of Damascus, *Exposition of the Orthodox Faith*, 17).

58. Jüngel, *Doctrine of the Trinity*, 87. O'Collins states, "One could say that the crucifixion 'affected' (not shaped) the inner life of the tripersonal God inasmuch as the Son, through assuming our human condition, underwent death on the cross. In that sense one can also say that the Father (as the Father of the Son) suffered in the Son" (O'Collins, "Holy Trinity," 5 n. 12).

of the Virgin; yet this birth of the Son from the Virgin was the work both of the Father and the Son. The Father suffered not on the Cross; yet the Passion of the Son was the work both of the Father and the Son. The Father rose not again from the dead; yet the resurrection of the Son was the work both of the Father and the Son. You see then a distinction of Persons, and an inseparableness of operation. Let us not say therefore that the Father doeth any thing without the Son, or the Son any thing without the Father.[59]

In my view, this understanding of how trinitarian *perichoresis* sheds light upon the suffering of Jesus Christ gives us a paradigm for illuminating the issues of immutability and impassibility. My argument is that a trinitarian perspective points us toward positing that God authentically or genuinely experiences suffering.

But, at a deeper level, the reality of trinitarian *perichoresis* means that when the Son took upon himself humanity, and therefore experienced all that we experience, the other persons of the Trinity could be said to experience what is human experience. In this sense, then, it could be said that God is able to suffer alongside humanity and to experience authentically what is our experience. Rather than remaining aloof from human experience, in particular human experiences of suffering, a trinitarian perichoretic perspective on the hypostatic union means that God is authentically touched by human suffering and, in a mysterious sense, suffers with us. Furthermore, to say that God suffers with us is not to say that God suffers merely at the level of empathy or identification. Certainly, the fact that God became human in Christ means that his suffering with us must *at least* mean that he is empathic with us and identifies with us. Yet, I would suggest that the notion of trinitarian *perichoresis* discussed above is suggestive of a divine experience of suffering at a deeper and more profound level. Just as God *himself* suffered in the Son, for the divine persons subsist in each other, so God *himself* can be said to be authentically touched by human suffering, and in that sense suffers with us, for the Son became human in Christ.

Furthermore, to say that God suffers or that he suffers with us is not to be understood as compromising the particularity of human experience. When a human person suffers, it is uniquely their experience and no sense of personal empathy or identification undermines

---

59. Augustine, *Sermons on Selected Lessons of the New Testament*, 262.

that reality. In the same way that I might grieve with a couple over the death of their child, my grief cannot and does not somehow supplant or compromise the particularity of their grief—their experience remains uniquely theirs while it is simultaneously shared, to differing extents, with those around them. Similarly, trinitarian perichoresis suggests to us that the Father and the Holy Spirit, as subsisting persons who perichoretically intertwine with the Son, are thus able to experience what the Son experiences and yet do not compromise the particularity of his experience—it remains uniquely the Son's experience whilst being shared. In a sense, then, we might say that though their experience is not identical to the Son's, it is also not other than the Son's. In the same way, God suffering with us is not to be construed as compromising the particularity of our suffering, but it does affirm that he, though remaining distinct from us, is yet able to connect with us at a deep and profound level.

Indeed, just as the Father and the Holy Spirit are deeply and profoundly able to connect perichoretically with the suffering of the Son, the uniqueness and particularity of the Son's sufferings means that the Father and Holy Spirit are also able to stand distinct from them, not be overwhelmed or constrained by them, and bring transformation to them. Similarly, just as God is deeply and profoundly able to connect incarnationally with human sufferings, the uniqueness and particularity of human sufferings means that he is also able to stand distinct from them, not be overwhelmed or constrained by them and bring transformation to them. Again, we are brought back to the tensional truth of *active constancy*. God is active in that he both meets and engages with humanity and does so at a deep and profound level. Indeed, the incarnation in Christ is the pre-eminent example of a triune God meeting us where we are and as we are. Hence, he knows human experience, including suffering, for he became one of us. Yet, simultaneously, he remains constant for he is not ontologically shaped or constrained by such suffering and so is able to bring transformation to it.

Certainly, the proposals that I am seeking to commend here are challenging to articulate, for we are dealing with profound mystery. Yet, it is my view that a trinitarian perspective on the issues of immutability and impassibility leads us to such a position and, hence, the language we use is, by necessity, full of tension and paradox. However, this sense of mystery is perhaps acceptable when we realize that God himself lies at the center of our deliberations.

Bibliography

Augustine. *On the Trinity*. In *A Select Library of Nicene and Post-Nicene Fathers of the Christian Church*. Series 1. Vol. 3. Edited by P. Schaff. Grand Rapids: Eerdmans, 1956.

———. *Sermons on Selected Lessons of the New Testament*. In *A Select Library of Nicene and Post-Nicene Fathers of the Christian Church*. Series 1. Vol. 6. Edited by P. Schaff. Grand Rapids: Eerdmans, 1956.

Barth, Karl. *Church Dogmatics*, 4 vols. Edinburgh: T. & T. Clark, 1956–75.

Bauckham, Richard. "'Only the Suffering God Can Help': Divine Passibility in Modern Theology." *Themelios* 9 (1984) 6–12.

Blocher, Henry. "Divine Immutability." In *The Power and Weakness of God*, edited by N. M. de S. Cameron, 1–22. Edinburgh: Rutherford House, 1990.

Bloesch, Donald G. *God the Almighty: Power, Wisdom, Holiness and Love*. Downers Grove, IL: InterVarsity, 1995.

Brown, Harold O. J. *Heresies: Heresy and Orthodoxy in the History of the Church*. Grand Rapids: Baker, 1984.

Carson, Donald A. *The Gagging of God: Christianity Confronts Pluralism*. Grand Rapids: Zondervan, 1996.

Cottrell, Jack. *God the Redeemer*. What the Bible Says Series. Joplin, MO: College, 1987.

Dodds, Michael J. *The Unchanging God of Love*. Fribourg: Editions Universitaires Fribourg Suisse, 1985.

Erickson, Millard J. *Christian Theology*. Grand Rapids: Eerdmans, 1985.

———. *God in Three Persons: A Contemporary Interpretation of the Trinity*. Grand Rapids: Baker, 1995.

Fiddes, Paul S. *The Creative Suffering of God*. Oxford: Clarendon, 1988.

———. *Participating in God: A Pastoral Doctrine of the Trinity*. London: Darton, Longman & Todd, 2000.

González, Justo L. *A History of Christian Thought*. Vol. 1. Nashville: Abingdon, 1970.

Gunton, Colin E. *The Christian Faith: An Introduction to Christian Doctrine*. Oxford: Blackwell, 2002.

———. *Theology through the Theologians: Selected Essays 1972–1995*. Edinburgh: T. & T. Clark, 1996.

Hall, Christopher A., and John Sanders. *Does God Have a Future? A Debate on Divine Providence*. Grand Rapids: Baker, 2003.

Hodge, Charles. *Systematic Theology*. Vol. 1. London: James Clarke, 1960.

John of Damascus. *Exposition of the Orthodox Faith*. In *A Select Library of Nicene and Post-Nicene Fathers of the Christian Church*. Series 2. Vol. 9. Edited by P. Schaff and H. Wace. Grand Rapids: Eerdmans, 1955.

Jüngel, Eberhard. *The Doctrine of the Trinity: God's Being Is in Becoming*. Edinburgh: Scottish Academic, 1976.

Kaiser, Christopher B. *The Doctrine of God: An Historical Survey*. London: Marshall, Morgan, & Scott, 1982.

Letham, Robert. "Is God Omniscient?" *Reformation Today* 187 (2002) 25–32.

Lewis, Peter. *The Message of the Living God*. Leicester, UK: InterVarsity, 2000.

McKim, Donald K. *Westminster Dictionary of Theological Terms*. Louisville: Westminster John Knox, 1996.

Moltmann, Jürgen. *The Crucified God*. Translated by R. A. Wilson and John Bowden. London: SCM, 1974.

Nelson, Haydn D. *The Problem of the Providence of God: How Can a God outside This World also Be Present in It?* New York: Mellen, 2010.

O'Collins, Gerald "The Holy Trinity: The State of the Questions." In *The Trinity: An Interdisciplinary Symposium on the Trinity*, edited by S. T. Davis et al 1–27. Oxford: Oxford University Press, 1999.

Pinnock, Clark H. *Most Moved Mover: A Theology of God's Openness*. Carlisle: Paternoster, 2001.

Rahner, Karl. *Theological Investigations*. Vol. 4. London: Darton, Longman, & Todd, 1974.

Sanders, John. *The God Who Risks: A Theology of Providence*. Downers Grove, IL: InterVarsity, 1998.

Skarsaune, Oskar. "Heresy and the Pastoral Epistles." *Themelios* 20 (1994) 9–14.

Strong, Augustus H. *Systematic Theology*. Philadelphia: Judson, 1907.

Torrance, Thomas F. *The Christian Doctrine of God: One Being Three Persons*. Edinburgh: T. & T. Clark, 1996.

Vanhoozer, Kevin J. *First Theology: God, Scripture and Hermeneutics*. Downers Grove, IL: InterVarsity, 2002.

Ware, Bruce A. "An Evangelical Reformulation of the Doctrine of the Immutability of God." *Journal of the Evangelical Theological Society* 29 (1986) 431–46.

Weinandy, Thomas G. *Does God Suffer?* Edinburgh: T. & T. Clark, 2000.

15

Reconciling Normative Tensions in Biomedical Ethics

Constructing an Ethics of Coinherence Informed by the Trinitarian Theology of Karl Barth

Ashley Moyse

An Introduction to the Problem

> "We live and act in the company of [an] apparently endless multitude of other human beings ... whose life and actions depend on what we do and in turn influence what we do, what we can do and what we ought to do—and all this in ways we neither understand or are able to presage."[1]

THE STRUGGLES TO COMPREHEND AND FORETELL THE INTRICACIES of human life, human relations, and human being present a challenge. Such difficulties move people to search for moral clarity and guidance in a number of locations, moving some to appropriately label ethicists as "eternal dabblers."[2] But all this dabbling has proven to be neither clarifying nor guiding. People are increasingly bound by proliferating questions and debilitated by a sense that moral integrity is being lost in the name of progress. Confusion rather than clarity, procedure rather

---

1. Bauman, *Postmodern Ethics*, 16–17.

2. "To be an ethicist seems to make one the eternal dabbler—one dabbles a little in theology, in philosophy, in political science, in practical problems, and so on" (Hauerwas, "Ethicist as Theologian," 408).

than morality is surrounding the particulars of human life, social relations, and clinical practice.

In the biomedical sciences this struggle has never been more apparent than today as ethical quandaries and moral dilemmas are increasingly specialized and seem to multiply disproportionately to the number of considered actions recommended. The need for moral guidance is critical. However, the problem of ethics is set within a culture defined by the inability to make decisions and within a discipline that lacks an agreeable and unifying decision-making paradigm. Appropriately, Zygmunt Bauman writes, "We need moral knowledge and skill.... Yet, we do not know where we can get them; and when (if) they are offered, we are seldom sure we can trust them unswervingly."[3] Similarly, Tristram Engelhardt cautions: "The moral predicament of the 21st century is that humans have never had more power or less of an understanding of how to secure a justified, concrete account of the proper goals for that power or substantive moral constraints on its use. ..."[4] Truly, there are various ethical questions that professionals, caregivers, and policy-makers attempt to wrestle with in the biomedical sciences. However, this grappling is often futile and frustrating for instead of conceding on ethical judgments, great divisions are generated and no solution advanced finds universal, or at least relevant group, acceptance. That is, for many "a sense of responsibility [remains] but an inadequate account of to whom one should be responsible or how [persists]."[5]

All of these questions, old and new, are presented to an increasingly heterogeneous moral marketplace whose plurality may be characterized by religious diversity, hermeneutic relativity, and belligerent individuality. Moreover, the tools that many ethicists use to help those seeking answers are as varied and contentious as the actions recommended. That is, though many are pursuing the same objective, the moral maze that all must ambulate is not an amicable one. Rather, at each turn one advocating the use of a certain paradigm for ethical decision-making comes face-to-face with another who, advocating for a different paradigm, may not only recommend a different action but also may contend that all other paradigms are moot.

---

3. Bauman, *Postmodern Ethics*, 16.
4. Engelhardt, "Medicine and the Biomedical Sciences after God," 210.
5. Ibid.

To be exact, the problem that persists in biomedical ethics is that individuals bring with them a particular ethical decision-making process that persuades how one may justify certain actions or modes of being. An individual that adheres to a teleological perspective may (and often will) render judgment on a specific ethical dilemma differently than an individual that adheres to a deontological perspective or an existential perspective. The reason is that these normative theories tend to view the nature and apprehension of ethics differently.[6] For this reason, the problem of decision-making is exaggerated by normative conflict. This conflict is often characterized by dogmatism and/or disregard, as some will seek justification of right human action through an analysis of possible ends, while others will seek justification through an analysis of certain duties and others through contextual virtues. Such isolated justification has led to greater conflict, distracting debate, and delayed decision-making. However, despite such delays, dilemmas, and disputes, those entrenched in the biomedical marketplace are constantly berated with circumstances that call for definitive judgments and life-changing decisions—and the vast number of ethicists, at least those enclosed within the ivory tower, refuse to accept any more than the status quo.

It was in the muck and mire where professional practice, personal trial, and moral confusion meet that I found myself attempting to address many questions asked by, and provide counsel to, those I cared for. Throughout my training and practice as a clinical applied physiologist and cancer symptoms rehabilitation specialist in both public and private settings, I was challenged by my clients who, rather than asking questions about the pathology or physiological effects of their cancer treatments and ancillary therapies, asked questions about life, meaning, and ethics. In an attempt to pursue informed responses to such questions and partner with them in their journey I found myself engrossed in the intersecting discussion of biomedical ethics and moral philosophy. Here I discovered various "ethical commands" that were objectively knowable through moral education and intended to inform certain ends, duties, or virtues pertaining to the questions asked but were characteristically treated in isolation and subject to general interpretation and misunderstanding, rather than particular qualification and careful correction, leading one to categorize relevant ethical variables in such a way that often misdirected human action. Consequently, I have come

6. Beauchamp and Childress, *Principles of Biomedical Ethics*, 21.

to think these ethical theories, when used in such plastic isolation, tend to result in confined or shallow notions of moral action and existence. I thus found myself woefully dissatisfied with the philosophical "common ground" that prevails in contemporary bioethics discourse and, therefore, began challenging the related decision-making paradigms that many stubbornly protect from both supplementary and novel insight—these challenges, however, have come through an exploration of theology and theological ethics; in particular, the trinitarian theology of Karl Barth, his commentators, and his contemporaries.

I was first compelled to explore how the doctrine of the Trinity may inform ethics after reading Barth "explain the world by the Trinity in order to be able to speak about the Trinity in the world."[7] Paul Louis Metzger's writings affirmed this pursuit as he described the doctrine of the Trinity as a "deep well from which to draw fresh insights when analyzing other key doctrines—[including] theological ethics."[8] Accordingly, as I pursued the connection between trinitarian theology and ethics I became increasingly convinced that trinitarian theology may move one to perceive the ethical predicament in the biomedical sciences and direct one toward informative, leading responses such that humans may be able to act rightly and become agents of right action. Trinitarian theology, therefore, may reveal, for the ethicist, the God who commands humanity to act and to be—who encounters humanity and frees them to respond to ethical commands as a call to action and responsibility of being.

Providing further direction and support for my reading of ethics and Barth's trinitarian theology, Miroslav Volf has written: "To think consistently in trinitarian terms means to escape this dichotomy between universalization and pluralization. If the Triune God is *unum multiplex in se ipso* (as per John Scotus Erigena), if unity and multiplicity are equiprimal in him, then God is the ground of both unity and multiplicity. Indeed, only the notion of unity in multiplicity can claim

---

7. *CD* I/1, 34.

8. Metzger, "Introduction," 6. Metzger elaborates: "Trinitarian theology frames consideration of divine and human being in interpersonal, communal terms, and views this interpersonal God as first in the order of being and knowing, with all that this shift implies for human concepts, language and culture. What follows then is not a conservative, foundationalist theological project, but rather a constructive theological enterprise that recovers and extends the Trinitarian tradition in order to reshape classic systematic loci in particular ways" (ibid., 7.).

to correspond to God. . . . [Thus] Trinitarian thinking suggests that, in a successful world drama, unity and multiplicity must enjoy a complementary relationship."[9] Such a relationship may be elaborated in the following model for biomedical ethical discourse and decision-making. The goal of the proposed model is to demonstrate just how the unity and multiplicity of the commanding triune God may reveal a deeper understanding of how ethical theories, or normative principles, may be considered in medicine. This biomedical ethics model aims to reconcile secular principles through theological reflection, demonstrating that God's modes of being, his *hypostases*, and corresponding commands may illumine deeper and fresh insights into the ends, duties, and virtues of human action and being as it relates to biomedicine.

Now at this time I must admit, it is accurate to suggest that some individuals have "exploit[ed] the name of theology for personal profit in their attempt to gain the effect of relevance."[10] Some theologians, "entering the public practice of ethics have left their special insights at the door and talk about [philosophy] just like everybody else."[11] These actions have caused others to argue, "theologians still owe it to the rest of us to explain why we should not accept their discipline as we do astrology or phrenology."[12] Positively, however, these same people admit, the peculiarity and significance of what theology does say, *if it is true*, makes the task of proving theology's worth in bioethics a critical task.[13] For that reason, articulating a theological ethic that may find acceptance within the broad bioethics community will be challenging.

Others magnify this challenge as some suggest that a peculiar Christian theological ethics cannot function among outsiders. That is, some will claim that a Christian model informed by the self-revealing God, who is Trinity, can neither be knowable nor appreciated by those who have not been captured by the God who commands. Such individuals believe the "gulf opens wide between a Christian and a secular bioethics."[14] But on the contrary, I am compelled to rebut such claims, as Daryl Pullman has eloquently written, "[If] all that Christian beliefs

9. Volf, "The Trinity and the Church," 154–55.
10. Grineizakis and Symeonides, "Bioethics and Christian Theology," 8.
11. Campbell, "Religion and Moral Meaning in Bioethics," 23.
12. Ibid., 9.
13. Ibid.
14. Engelhardt, "Medicine and the Biomedical Sciences after God," 218.

and practices do is to inform Christians about elements of the moral life that apply only to those who subscribe to the Christian view of history, the claim to universal significance is trivialized.... However, if all that Christian moral theologians and philosophers can hope to contribute is a redundant affirmation of moral truths discoverable from non-Christian starting points, one must question what relevance Christianity's particular historical understanding can or should have in ethics in general and for bioethics in particular."[15] I therefore want to carefully articulate a theological model for ethical decision-making that is, and is free to become, both faithfully Christian and clinically relevant. After all, "To speak with universally binding force is an obligation from which [theological ethics] cannot possibly seek exemption. It has to take up the legitimate problems and concerns and motives and assertions of every other ethics ... and [test] them in the light of its own superior principle. It has to listen to all other ethics in so far as it has to receive from them at every point the material for its own deliberations. To that extent its attitude to every other ethics is not negative but comprehensive."[16]

So, my thoughts on a theological ethical model that attempts to show how theology may be an integral, informative, and influential voice that challenges many to consider unified and interdependent biomedical ethical discourse rather than compartmentalized and tenuous debate will be the focus of the following essay. Specifically, what follows represents an initial attempt to better understand and articulate right human action and being by disclosing an ethical model that is formulated about and functional through the commanding and sanctifying Word of the Trinity. My hope is that this model will encourage a fruitful and instructive coinherence between normative ethical theories as an analogue that is not only informed by but also matured through an understanding of the *perichoretic commands* of the three persons of the Trinity.

---

15. Pullman, "Universalism, Particularism, and the Ethics of Dignity," 332.
16. *CD* II/2, 527.

Establishing Connections: Theory as *Praxis* or Theology as Ethics

Medical sciences, of course, do not simply exist in the ivory tower—they must do more than possess theory and knowledge.[17] Medical sciences must be applied science by nature transforming theory into therapy.[18] As physicians and medical scientists move from the theoretical to the applied they begin to engage others in such a way that demands right perspective and right conduct. Medical professions are characterized by both knowing and doing. Here one may find a corollary between the medicinal sciences and theology. That is, it is here that medicine appears to have a common purpose with the church—both attempt to articulate the means by which humanity ought to act and become well. Truly, "the medical practitioner, whose life is not dedicated to the service of the neighbor, is seen as a failure. The same applies to the Church."[19]

Theology, therefore, must be more than mere moral reflection. It must also be ethics, for neither "theology nor dogmatics can be true to itself if it is not genuinely ready at the same time to be ethics."[20] The assimilation of theology as ethics is necessary, for *knowing* theology without *doing* theology is just rhetoric—simply impossible. Ethics as theology is, therefore, wholly and rightly caught up in the command of God. That is, "If theology, and therefore theological ethics, is in principle the science of the Word of God as it is attested in revelation. . . . Its subject is not the Word of God as it is claimed by man, but the Word of God as it claims man. It is not man as he is going to make something of the Word of God, but the Word of God as it is going to make something of man."[21] The task of Christian ethics is to study the created man as the ethical agent whose actions encounter and reflect the Divine as he commands. God commits us in our action by reminding us that we do not belong to ourselves but are his creatures—creatures whose actions and being realize such commitments in free response to him, by him, and for him. That is, the study of Christian ethics attempts to discern the degree we are caught up in the limits of humanity while yet still

---

17. Branson, "Secularization of American Medicine," 14.
18. Ibid.
19. Grineizakis and Symeonides, "Bioethics and Christian Theology," 8.
20. *CD* I/2, 793.
21. *CD* II/2, 546.

able to respond to the problems, pains, and moral challenges of human existence—"this commitment is what God's will wills of our will."[22] This commitment of human action may be realized in obedience to the gratuitous command of God, which comes to us by the neighborly encounter of Christ and pneumatic witness of the Holy Spirit. Therefore, the nature of this command, as Karl Barth is clear to contend, "does not hang ineffectively in the air above man. Its particular aim and concern are with him and his real activity. It is in his sanctification that its divine majesty, truth, and power are revealed. How these appear and take effect in man's real activity is thus a further problem of ethics."[23] The latter statement is important. Understanding how the majesty, truth, and power of the Divine are evidenced in the moral *ought* of human action and being must be articulated.

In Christian theology one may encounter three questions. The first question is "Who is revealed?" The second and third ask "What does this revealer do?" and "What (or whom) does this revealer effect?" As Karl Barth suggests, once one discerns the right response to the first question, the remaining two are answered, as the three questions are not sequential but rather simultaneous, not linear but reciprocal. But such reciprocity does not necessitate stopping once one has answered the first question. That is, in order to have an understanding of the second and third questions, one must understand the first, but to have a *complete* understanding of the former one must have a full understanding of the latter two.[24] Truly, such a notion of reciprocity, correspondence, and interdependence are at the center of the doctrine of God, and moreover, fundamental to the doctrine of the Trinity (and, subsequently, essential for the proposed biomedical ethical model that follows).

The doctrine of God provides a complete framework on which all of theology may rest. Of the doctrine of God, the Trinity may be considered the keystone, for it is primary in understanding the being and mission of God, as recorded in the Holy Scriptures, encountered in the life and work of Jesus Christ, and illumined through the Holy Spirit. Barth, taking his lead from John Calvin, is clear to remind the reader of his *Dogmatics* that the doctrine of the Trinity is an essential doctrine, the center, for faith and praxis:

22. Barth, *Ethics*, 214.
23. *CD* III/4, 5.
24. *CD* I/1, 297.

> If we do not know God in the way in which He reveals Himself as the One, namely *distincte in tribus personis* [distinct in three persons], the inevitable result is that *nudum et inane duntaxat Dei nomen sine vero Deo in cerebro nostro volitat* [the bare and empty name of Deity merely will flutter in our brain without any genuine knowledge] (Calvin, *Instit.*, I.13.2).... With the confession of God's triunity stands or falls the whole of Christianity, the whole of special revelation. This is the kernel of the Christian faith, the root of all dogmas, the substance of the new covenant, ... the very heart and essence of the Christian religion itself.[25]

Though central for Christian theology, the revelation of God as triune is a challenging doctrine; it "refuses to be understood as any sort of revelation alongside which there are or may be others.... [But] it insists absolutely on being understood in terms of its object, God."[26] Within the context of understanding its object one is able to discern trinitarian language and grapple with the revelation of God's own triune being. Concomitantly, Barth writes, "the God who has revealed Himself according to the witness of Scripture, is the same in unimpaired unity and yet also the same thrice in different ways in unimpaired distinction. Or, in the phraseology of the Church's dogma of the Trinity, the Father, the Son, and the Holy Spirit in the biblical witness to revelation are the one God in the unity of their essence, and the one God in the biblical witness to revelation is the Father, the Son, and the Holy Spirit in the distinction of His persons."[27]

Therefore, when speaking of the inter-trinitarian relations, when speaking of *unitas in trinitate* and *trinitas in unitate*, we ought to begin by affirming the full ontological equality and unity of the Trinity. However, this must be qualified by the subsequent affirmation that within such equality there is a differentiation in existential activity. This means that no one member is superior to another in being, yet each has a distinctive role or mode—theologically speaking, *perichoresis* allows one to speak concurrently of the singularity of God and the plurality of his being-in-action. Donald Bloesch writes, à la Karl Barth,

> In his operations the Father represents an originating source of his other modes of activity. In his essence Father, Son, and Spirit

---

25. *CD* I/1, 302, translation included.
26. Ibid., 295.
27. Ibid., 308.

are one. We can say that the Father is the initiator of action, the Son the culmination of action and the Spirit the power of action. The Father is an originating source not as a first cause in the sense of an efficient cause but as a presupposition or ground. The Father's initiation is not independent of the Son and Spirit but together with them.... There is a unity in being but an order in procession or action.... There is a relationship of interdependence in the Godhead but also of dependence.[28]

The fundamental essence of *perichoresis* is communion or intimate fellowship—it is interdependence and dependence; thus, a reciprocating and dynamic actuality of the being-and-acting among the particular persons of the Trinity. Such fellowship, then, may be understood as relational reciprocity in that the three modes of the one essence reciprocate simultaneously rather than successive action. Thus, simultaneous reciprocity means that each member of the Trinity participates in the action of the others such that the Father acts and also receives from the Son and Spirit who, concurrently yet mysteriously, also act and receive.[29]

For Barth, who insists that any knowledge of this *perichoretic* relationship is due to God's own self-giving, the unity of God's act and being "will not lead us beyond revelation and faith, but into revelation and faith, to their correct understanding."[30] He goes on to state: "This means that the unity of their work is to be understood as the communion of the three modes of being along the lines of the doctrine of 'perichoresis', according to which all three, without forfeiture or mutual dissolution of independence, reciprocally interpenetrate each other and inexist in one another.... [Such that perichoresis is] the eternal independence of the three modes of being in their eternal communion."[31] Therefore, *perichoresis* connotes the Trinity is not comprised of discrete, independent

28. Bloesch, *God the Almighty*, 187–88.

29. Volf, "'Trinity Is Our Social Programme,'" 111. Molnar agrees that a clear reciprocity persists in the being and action of God, "who *is* one *as* the Father, Son, and Holy Spirit" (Molnar, *Divine Freedom*, 245).

30. *CD* I/1, 396.

31. Ibid., 396. Eberhard Jüngel writes, "God's being in his self-relatedness is to be formulated as *concrete* being, the mastering of this problem of formulation is still extremely difficult ... [and] the doctrine of *perichoresis* ... serves to master this difficulty" (Eberhard Jüngel, *God's Being Is in Becoming*, 31). Jürgen Moltmann writes, "the Persons [of the Trinity] form their unity, by virtue of their relation to one another and in the eternal perichoresis" (Moltmann, *Trinity and the Kingdom*, 177).

members that relate to each other from a distance but is composed of interdependent, coinhering members that constitute and elucidate one another in an intimate economy. *Perichoresis*, thus, articulates the unified act and agency of the one and many—of the particularity and unity of God's being and action.

The *perichoretic* union of the divine persons may be understood as a mutual giving and receiving of the fundamentally equal members of the Trinity. In this, the Son and the Spirit proceed from the Father yet, together, return to him. It is as though the Father's initiation is simultaneous with the active response of the Son and the Spirit. Fundamentally, one must uphold the theological maxim that God is one; yet, his reality is evident as three modes of being and acting:

> The Father is not to be understood as the true God in distinction from the Son and the Spirit, and the Son and the Spirit are not, in distinction from the Father, favored and glorified creatures, vital forces aroused and set in motion by God, and as such and in the sense revealers. But it is God who reveals Himself equally as the Father in his self-veiling and holiness, as the Son in His self-unveiling and mercy, and as the Spirit in His self-impartation and love. Father, Son, and Spirit are the one, single, and equal God.[32]

The modes of being ascribed to each person of the Trinity also express the corresponding role or function of the equiprimal members. As is commonly expressed, the Father is known as Creator and the Son and Spirit are known as Reconciler and Redeemer, respectively. But, I must ask. What is meant by these roles? What does each entail? How is each role distinct and yet correlated to the others? In what way is each command connected to ethics, biomedical ethics? It is in the response to these questions, from the revelation of God as perichoretic Creator, Redeemer, and Reconciler, that my proposed model for biomedical ethi-

---

32. *CD* I/1, 381. Jüngel writes, "If the concreteness of God's self-communication to man is to be thoroughly comprehended, then the self-relatedness of God's being in the differentiation of the three modes of being must likewise be comprehended as fellowship in which the being of God takes place concretely. This fellowship is given through 'a complete participation of each mode of being in the other modes of being'. Through this reciprocal participation the three modes of being *become* concretely united. In this concrete unity they *are* God.... [Thus,] the doctrine of *perichoresis* helps us to formulate the concrete unity of the being of God in that we think of the modes of God's being as meeting one another in unrestricted participation" (Jüngel, *Being in Becoming*, 32, 33).

cal deliberation has been constructed. It is in this model that I am able to see and understand where, and how, theology and ethics coalesce.

Perichoresis and *Praxis*: A Coinherent Model for Biomedical Ethics

Considering the delimitations of what has been stated, one may be able to appreciate and/or apprehend current biomedical ethics principles as analogues of the divine command as well as in terms of a three-principled *perichoretic* union. That is, as one is able to comprehend the relationship of the three persons of the Godhead, and the commands proclaimed and encountered, she may be moved to understand a new model relationship for ethics. The following may picture this novel iteration, which intends to coinhere otherwise conflicting normative principles in and through an analogical interpretation of the *perichoretic* union of the thrice-commanding God.

As I have stated, the three modes of God's singular being are simultaneous rather than discontinuous or successive. That is, to know the full being and action of God, knowing one mode without the others renders one's knowledge of the Divine incomplete and susceptible to misunderstanding. True knowledge of God must depend upon the complete though finite and dynamic understanding of the three modes of being, which reveal the three corresponding yet simultaneous commands (life, authority, promise). Likewise, to have a comprehensive perspective regarding ethics, a complete understanding of right human action, one must not rely upon any one principle as a complete guiding principle. Such limited perspective may render one's understanding incomplete or confused and susceptible to wrongful action. As noted earlier, various normative principles have been adopted, but individuals treat them as discontinuous principles, which at times cloud rather than reveal human responsibility. Reconciling these through an open and dynamic discussion that acknowledges their interdependence, rather coinherence, may provide a more advanced and guiding perspective for ethical decision-making and discourse.

Now you may still wonder, in what way may the doctrine of the Trinity guide the discussion of ethics? The three-dimensional shape of ethics, of human action, may include consequences, commitments, and character reflecting the three normative principles of teleological, deontological, and existential ethics, respectively. That is, the guiding normative principles may morphologically and methodologically cohere analogically as the three persons of the Divine coinhere as interdependent and simultaneous persons.

Analogically, as the Son and Spirit proceed from the Father, deontological and existential ethics may proceed from teleological ethics (and return to it). Existential ethics, however, is not only returning with deontological ethics but deontological ethics is returning through existential ethics. As the Father is the Creator, and attributed with initiating action, so teleological ethics may be considered as the initiator of action, which is carried out through deontological action and existential being. Yet, as co-equal modes the action and character of each theory is shared with or enlivened by the others. So, one may understand that the three aspects of secular ethics may be enlightened, matured, and coinhered by an understanding of the *perichoretic* relationship that is the person and mission of God.

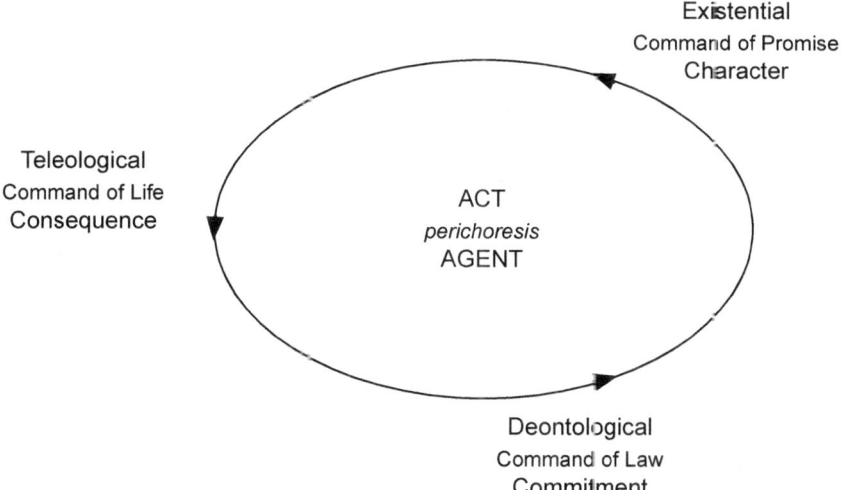

FIGURE 1. A Trinitarian Model for Biomedical Ethics

This model attempts to demonstrate the trinitarian relationship that may be applied to current theories of ethics. It is a model that emphasizes interdependent dialogue rather than independent debate between act- and agent-centered models—aiming at coherence rather than contention. Here, the figure intends to convey unity and multiplicity, a one and many, that should be revealed in thoughtful and thorough bioethical dialogue and decision-making methodologies.

Thus, by an application of trinitarian language and through an understanding of trinitarian relations, commitments and character may proceed from consequences but also return to them. Therefore, each principle may invite, direct, and receive human act and being. The model therefore urges one to understand that our being becomes virtuous as one acts as duty obliges and duty becomes right through the qualification of virtue. Each of these—duty and virtue (commitment and character)—is directed towards and accomplishes the ends of human action (consequence). Thus, the multiple variables that are typically challenged by the dialectic of act and agent are presented by and reconciled through an analogical application of the coinherent union of principles. Such a model may be considered a conceptual tool that may offer the ethicist, or human actor, a more complete and dynamic portrait of ethical engagement, such that the proposed union of ethical principles may guide one to a richer and more comprehensive understanding of right praxis. Yet, how are the multiple commands, correlated to particular normative principles, analogous to the act-in-being of the one, God?

Normative Ethics and the Commanding Trinity

Teleological Ethics and the Doctrine of God, the Creator

As it is basically construed, teleological ethics is defined by the pursuit of good acts because they do good. Therefore, according to such a notion, teleological ethics is goal oriented. Similarly, the Father's action may also be understood in terms of ends. That is, as one is able to comprehend the *missio Dei* she is brought to a theology of ends—creation as God intended (or commanded, rather). God commanded human existence and existence is good as an end for it may be regarded as a goal of *the way*—existence in relation to the Father.[33]

God the Father is attributed to act as Creator. Thus, he is Lord of creation—author of his kingdom and will.[34] But such a notion does not

---

33. *CD*, I/1, 384.

34. Ibid., 387. Barth suggests, in an attempt to root the revelation of the Father in an appropriate revelation of the Son, "The [Father] whom Jesus reveals as the Father is known absolutely on the death of man, at the *end* of his existence ... [the Way reveals] the life that His will creates will be a life that has passed through death, that is risen from death" (ibid., 377–78). Thus, life, the end of God's willed action, is a "requickening ... that is to be expected from God" (ibid., 388).

adequately reduce the complexities of God's fatherhood, for God is not only creator of humanity but also the creedal source of his other modes of being—he is Father of the Son and Spirit. As Father, the one God is the source of his oneness and creator of human being and subsequent action. This insight is rooted in God's *control* of creation. For the Father/Creator arranges nature and history so that good acts have just consequences, to himself to the ethical agent, and to other persons.[35] It is therefore appropriate to refer to God the Father as the author of existence whose action may focus on life.

Barth speaks of this Creator-teleological image when he writes, "True man is characterized by action, by good action, as the true God is also characterized by action, good action."[36] That said, the objective for human action is to aim at behaving in such a way that maximizes the "possibilities of human self-understanding . . . [within] the framework of the structure of his creatureliness."[37] So, not only is the aim of God's creation but also the action of humankind intended toward accomplishing an end—in theology, the end of God's action is the sanctification of humanity and the end of human action, as it is summarized in Bentham's impartiality criterion, is justice—in both cases, the end is aimed toward validating creaturely limitations and maximizing human life.

However, this is not an easily discernible perspective for ends are not naturally knowable. One must engage in action, having *faith* that the intended end will become an actuality. So, "Faith is the good act. . . . In faith we believe positively in the truth, validity, and goodness of the [act]."[38] That is, though one may consider certain consequences, she cannot believe in the proposed ends as objects to know or possess. Such knowledge is impossible. Rather, one must believe in and accept the proposed ends in their "invisibility, absence, and non-givenness."[39] To reiterate, humanity does not possess the natural means by which one

---

35. Frame, *Doctrine of the Christian Life*, 50. "His will stands over against our will to live, supreme, unbound, or rather in absolute control. . . . For if God is the Lord of existence in the full sense of the term, this means that our existence is sustained by Him and by Him alone above the abyss of non-existence . . . it is real in so far as He wills and posits it as real" (*CD* I/1, 388–89).

36. *CD* III/4, 3.

37. Ibid., 44.

38. Barth, *Ethics*, 265.

39. Ibid., 274.

is able to obtain a certain interpretation of future consequence—nor a natural means to obtain a certain knowledge of the Father.

Such limitation warrants the question, "How can we know to what extent we really have to do with [ends], and therefore with a valid standard for understanding the ethical event?"[40] Since humanity does not possess a clear forward perspective, one must be faithful and wait for the ethical event to be presented in history so the veracity in which the ethical event takes place may be assessed in its concreteness. As such, further deliberation is needed—assisted by an assessment of responsive duties and conscionable virtues that not only aim toward but also reflect, rather reveal, the intended end. Therefore, teleological consequences, and the Father's creation, reveal the goal of human action—the command to pursue responsible and creaturely life. But the goal is made known as one responds to the invitation to pursue life; as one responds to and embodies the subsequent, yet simultaneous variables.

Deontological Ethics and the Doctrine of God, the Reconciler

Deontological ethics is characterized by the pursuit of good actions that respond to certain authority-revealed obligations—ethics is therefore duty oriented. Theologically, the Son may be viewed as our authority and his action may be revealed as law, such that the Son, Jesus, "is Lord ... who has come to us or as the Word of God that has been spoken to us ... [who is the] authority to address and claim us."[41]

God the Son is as God the Father—equally and eternally God. God the Son, as himself the one God, is the Christ, Jesus, who is attributed to act as Reconciler. The Son's action is in response to God's teleological call to live—to live as called to live within the order (or intention) of creation. It is directed towards setting right wrongs between humanity and the Father. That is, the Son's action is an active response, which intends to restore right relations between humankind and himself, and between humankind and other humankind.

---

40. *CD* III/4, 28.

41. *CD* I/1, 411, 444. Jesus claims us as sinners who deserve the wrath of God, the Creator. The law, then, is the "law which claims man as sinner, rebel, and traitor to God and himself.... [It is] God's command [which] comes to me as superior direction by a specific fellowman commissioned by him.... [and] it claims me and I have to hear it" (Barth, *Ethics*, 272, 349).

This insight is rooted in God's *authority* over creation—meaning, as one exists as a human, such that one is called to live, we are simultaneously under obligation to obey (respond to) the Father as he informs human action through the Son. On this relationship between life and law, Karl Barth writes, "We live. In living we stand under the obligation. We live our own lives and we live in indissoluble correlation with the lives of others. As we live, this command is present. Or more accurately, this command is present as we live. It is in place. It comes to us with the event of our life-act as such. There is no avoiding it as though existence came first and the requirements were then added. No, our existence stands under requirement simply by being existence."[42]

The Reconciler-deontological command, then, comes as superior direction. It claims one and she must hear it, such that "[one] cannot break loose from the grip with which it has already gripped."[43] Moreover, the superior direction that grips one to do this or that comes to one as she encounters the other, one's neighbor, as an authority: "My neighbor is there where there is authority and ... [I] must see in him the representative, witness, and controller in matters of my conduct, where I must bend to his instruction and guidance and superior direction if what I do is to be lawful."[44]

Appropriately then, the question "What shall we to do?" is answered as one understands that beneficent action towards a neighbor (individual or societal) involves the responsibility to accept the neighbor as an authority, that counsels, corrects, and guides human action. To subordinate oneself not only to the guiding influence of considered ends but also to authority demands humility, which has the character of self-denial. Self-denial has traditionally been a key aspect of deontological ethics and corresponds to the duty to act in such a way that one's act may *benefit* life, and the life of another.

In such *loving* service to our neighbors our acts are good. That is, our acts demonstrate our commitment to responsibility—which is

---

42. Barth, *Ethics*, 263–264. Archibald Spencer, aided by the words of Karl Barth, expands on the authority of the law (Word of God): "Insofar as this Word is an act of God it 'claims man' and causes humanity to 'seek and find' the goodness of human conduct in the event of an act of God himself toward man, namely, the act of His speech and self-revelation to him. Man does good acts when he acts as a hearer of God's Word, and obedience is the good" (Spencer, *Clearing a Space for Human Action*, 200).

43. Barth, *Ethics*, 301.

44. Ibid., 355–56.

considered love. Love is required when one hears the commands to act (to law). Therefore, deontological commitments, as Christ's reconciliatory action, reveal the guide of human action—the command to love the other such that she may humbly subject herself to the authority of her neighbor.

Existential Ethics and the Doctrine of God, the Redeemer

Existential ethics is characterized by the pursuit of good acts, which come about because of good personal character—this final component of ethics is therefore character oriented. Theologically, the Holy Spirit and his action may be aimed at maturing human being and perfecting human character.

Many that support the previous two categories of ethics often dismiss this third category, and vice versa. However, existential ethics is vitally important, as are the other two—co-equals in illumining right human action. Barth addresses the tendency to reject existential ethics as mystical or illusory and asks whether or not one can rightfully reject *being* as an informative quality of a sound ethics:

> Ethicists who find a place only for a command of life or law, or one or other of the two, when they come to speak of this not wholly concealed tendency in human life, and especially in the Christian life, usually reject it with an unkindly glance.... Do we really obey [these commands] if we do not obey as children? In addition to life and the neighbor, does not our being as God's children form a third point of orientation without which we do not really perhaps see the other two.... Can all the steps that could be taken in the first two spheres be really taken meaningfully except as, in and with them, this notable step is taken beyond those spheres?[45]

The existential command expands the ethical model so that one not only addresses consequences and commitments of human action but also the character of the agent. Humanity is, in fact, claimed in such a way that cannot be fully deduced by the categories of teleology and deontology. Accordingly, we are claimed as children—as a *being* who acts in response to the creation and reconciliation of his or her *being*.

45. Ibid., 470–74.

This third action of God the Holy Spirit is that of redemption, which focuses on the restorative promise that his command will prevail and his creation will be restored. Therefore, God the Spirit, co-equal and co-eternal One, is God the Redeemer and his redemptive actions aim toward redeeming the creature's mortal being. That is, the Spirit's action is active as a command of promise, which intends to restore the character of humanity so that one may better know, grasp, or see the right response to the previous modes of human action.

Knowing this third command may come in the form of conscience, which may be embodied as virtue. Conscience is the dynamic and present message of our own hope, which orients us to appreciate who we are and who we are to become.[46] "Hope, the work of the Holy Spirit, consists in our being told . . . that our action is done in unity with the will of the Redeemer [which calls one to be as human]."[47] Thus, human action is obedient and good when it is pursued with a conscience of good character in the pursuit of creation and law.

However, the emphasis on conscience must be further delimited. Conscience quickens the character with which one has to act as it provides a relative foundation to consider duties and reflect upon proposed ends—the foundation of selfhood, or self-consciousness. It is human knowing of what only God can know: who we are.[48] Summarizing Barth's consideration of conscience, Archie Spencer writes, "Conscience is the recollection and repetition of the Word of God [and] . . . to have a conscience is to see and reach beyond the finitude that marks out my creaturely existence and, by the Holy Spirit, to 'participate in the truth itself.'"[49] Specifically, what one's conscience informs of oneself and of subsequent action is a fleeting and isolated call to listen and to speak, to become and to act. Thus: "Pressuring the conscience of others often

---

46. Ibid., 487.

47. Biggar, *Hastening That Waits*, 85.

48. Barth, *Ethics*, 475. "In conscience, our own voice is undoubtedly God's voice . . . [therefore] when my conscience speaks to me, I am *addressed*" (ibid., 480).

49. Spencer, *Clearing a Space*, 214–15. Spencer goes on to state, "Conscience 'disrupts' our existence by asking how far and in what way our actions are a step toward the eschatological determination of the human promised in the world of address" (ibid., 214–15). That is, conscience, that being virtue, provides the content of the internal response to the question "Who ought I to be?" The content of the response is the promise of an obedient response to the command of creation and reconciliation, to the Word of God. Here we discover the tangible movement of a return to true ends by way of the call of duty.

has its fatal basis in ourselves ... [and] what conscience tells us relates, strictly speaking, only to the present in the strict sense, only to the given moment.... It is thus an event and not a thing. It does not exist; it takes place. Even the most authentic pronouncement of conscience cannot be stored and then unthinkingly brought out and proclaimed as the truth the next day."[50] Therefore, the conscience informs one that she may be courageous in one instant and in fact cowardly the next or compassionate at this moment and cold a moment later. Nevertheless, one's conscience, and therefore informed character, is vital when considering which action is best suited for the situation—when considering the *hope* of the human act and being.

Conscience, and therefore existential character and the Spirit's redemptive action, reveal the goad (provocation) of human action. As the Spirit reveals our new birth as a child of God in light of creation and reconciliation, the individual embodiment of the character of good conscience may assist one to decide what act is right. Thus, Barth is correct to state, as is the intent of a trinitarian biomedical ethics, "Conscience decides whether we have to do with genuine authority, and genuine authority attests itself as such to conscience. We can also say that the child of God recognizes in the voice of genuine authority the voice of the father which he obeys spontaneously and in freedom. 'My sheep hear my voice' (John 10:27)—because they are my sheep."[51]

Moving from Theory to *Praxis*: The Need for Application

The proposed model has attempted to orient one's perspective in such a way that one may appreciate the need for dynamic and comprehensive decision-making in medicine. Traditional isolated methodologies used in ethical decision-making have not adequately addressed the complexities of the questions being asked either in biomedical sciences or of humanity. However, the coinherent model proposed may prove to be helpful in guiding human action by encouraging a dynamic and reciprocal discussion of consequences, commitments, and character. That is, through an understanding of the trinitarian relations where

---

50. Barth, *Ethics*, 494–95.
51. Ibid., 483.

three distinct persons coinhere as one, three distinct ethical theories may also coinhere for the rendering of an ethical decision or fruitful discussion—such a model and/or practice may produce a superior picture for shaping and guiding human act-and-being.

As I conclude I am compelled to recall where I began. Many have accepted the current pluralistic and secularized milieu in which biomedical science and practice must function. However, biomedical science, practice, and ethics cannot function in such ambiguity. This essay has aimed to provide a way for ethical deliberation that may contribute to the ongoing discussion in bioethics, where many ask which biomedical ethics is best to sustain growth in medicine yet protect the dignity and character of humanity in such a rapidly changing and ever progressing culture. I believe that this model, this trinitarian biomedical ethics, is able to respond to the challenges and offer the theological voice as one that is guiding and fruitful—perhaps demonstrating that the theological voice is not only a relevant voice within bioethical discourse but also a superior force for guiding ethical deliberation and informing right human action and being. In conclusion, I think it is appropriate to look to Karl Barth, whom I have relied heavily upon in this work and whose work is being honored in this volume, to offer a proper close to this theological ethics: "[This biomedical ethical model] will prove to be legitimate by making impossible any mere consideration of the ethical problem, by pointing us beyond the reflection which is, of course, necessary, by plunging us into life itself, into the responsibility which we must always carry after having reflected. . . . Precisely to the extent that that happens, [it] can and must claim and occupy its true place in life itself."[52]

---

52. Ibid., 516.

Bibliography

Barth, Karl. *Church Dogmatics*. 4 vols. Edinburgh: T. & T. Clark, 1956–75.

———. *Ethics*. Edited by Geoffrey W. Bromiley and Dietrich Braun. New York: Seabury, 1981.

Bauman, Zygmunt. *Postmodern Ethics*. Oxford: Blackwell, 1993.

Beauchamp, Tom L., and James F. Childress. *Principles of Biomedical Ethics*. Oxford: Oxford University Press, 2001.

Biggar, Nigel. *The Hastening That Waits: Karl Barth's Ethics*. Oxford: Clarendon, 1995.

Bloesch, Donald G. *God the Almighty: Power, Wisdom, Holiness, Love*. Downers Grove, IL: InterVarsity, 1995.

Branson, Roy. "The Secularization of American Medicine." In *On Moral Medicine: Theological Perspectives in Medical Ethics*, edited by Stephan Lammers and Allen Verhey, 12–22. Grand Rapids: Eerdmans, 1998.

Campbell, Courtney. "Religion and Moral Meaning in Bioethics." In *On Moral Medicine: Theological Perspectives in Medical Ethics*, edited by Stephan Lammers and Allen Verhey, 22–30. Grand Rapids: Eerdmans, 1998.

Engelhardt, H. Tristram. "Medicine and the Biomedical Sciences after God: Do Right-Worshipping Christians Know More Than Others About the Content of Morality?" *Christian Bioethics* 8 (2002) 105–17.

Frame, John M. *Doctrine of the Christian Life: A Theology of Lordship*. Vol. 3. Phillipsburg: Presbyterian & Reformed, 2008.

Grineizakis, Makarios, and Nathanael Symeonides. "Bioethics and Christian Theology." *Journal of Religion and Health* 44 (2005) 7–11.

Hauerwas, Stanley. "The Ethicist as Theologian." *The Christian Century* (1975) 408–12.

Jüngel, Eberhard. *God's Being Is in Becoming: The Trinitarian Being of God in the Theology of Karl Barth: A Paraphrase*. Grand Rapids: Eerdmans, 2001.

Metzger, Paul L. "Introduction: What Difference Does the Trinity Make?" In *Trinitarian Soundings in Systematic Theology*, edited by Paul L. Metzger, 5–8. New York: T. & T. Clark, 2005.

Molnar, Paul D. *Divine Freedom and the Doctrine of the Immanent Trinity: In Dialogue with Karl Barth and Contemporary Theology*. London: T. & T. Clark, 2002.

Moltmann, Jürgen. *The Trinity and the Kingdom*. Translated by Margaret Kohl. San Francisco: Harper & Row, 1981.

Pullman, Daryl. "Universalism, Particularism, and the Ethics of Dignity." *Christian Bioethics* 7 (2001) 333–58.

Spencer, Archibald James. *Clearing a Space for Human Action: Ethical Ontology in the Theology of Karl Barth*. New York: Lang, 2003.

Volf, Miroslav. "The Trinity and the Church." In *Trinitarian Soundings in Systematic Theology*, edited by Paul L. Metzger, 153–74. New York: T. & T. Clark, 2005.

———. "'The Trinity Is Our Social Programme': The Doctrine of the Trinity and the Shape of Social Engagement." In *The Doctrine of God and Theological Ethics*, edited by Alan J. Torrance and Michael Banner, 105–24. London: T. & T. Clark, 2006.

16

Vestiges of Trinity

Nicola Hoggard-Creegan

Introduction and Apology

IN THIS ESSAY I WILL BE EMPHASIZING THE "AFTER BARTH" IN THE title of this book, in the spirit of intentional dialogue between theology and the natural sciences which has characterized the last forty years since Barth's death. I have no desire to blend or merge the two disciplines; rather this is an exercise in what J. Wentzel van Huysssteen calls "transversal dialogue," whereby the discourse in one discipline is laid alongside that in another.[1] Transversal dialogue does not read nature to see what can be found of God therein; rather it is reading nature in light of what we know about God from revelation. This reading takes place fully cognizant of God's hiddenness and freedom, but convinced, nevertheless, that the imprint of the creator is left in the creation.

Since Karl Barth the subject of the vestiges of the Trinity in creation has not been popular in theology. Barth, of course, can be credited with the return to trinitarian theology, which had largely been neglected in the nineteenth century and post-Enlightenment period. Barth was scathing of those who might be tempted to find, or had found, vestiges of God in the natural world. He says: "[T]he original aim was to speak of God's revelation. But what really happened was talk about the world and man, and that, regarded as talk about God's revelation, must actually end by being talk against God's revelation. . . . Such a game cannot yield serious results. Taken seriously it can only signify a profanation

---

1. Huyssteen, *Alone in the World?* 69.

of what is holy."[2] Barth thought the threeness that might be manifest in creation was too distracting from the God who might otherwise be illustrated. He argues: "To illustrate revelation is to set something else at the center of attention. It is a failure in proper trust in revelation with respect to its own power of self-evidence."[3] Barth feared that analogies from nature might become a "second root" of the Trinity alongside revelation, and that natural images might become more interesting than divinity because they were closer to humanity than is God.[4] Thus he says, "People felt the foreign-ness of that which should be proved to be 'God' by means of the *vestigia*, its utter difference from the God of Abraham, Isaac, and Jacob, from Father, Son, and Holy Spirit in the New Testament with which the doctrine of the Trinity should be concerned.[5] That non-obligatory uncommissioned and perilous possibility is clearly involved in every case in which theological language claims to pass beyond the interpretation to the illustration of revelation."[6] He argued that vestiges were superficial and that they might act like a Trojan horse, smuggling in other anthropological considerations into theology.[7]

These are strong words, especially for those who would try to construct a theology from nature—which I am certainly not advocating—but in the end for anyone who would wish to see reflected in the natural world what Barth is sure could be better discerned in revelation. For who knows which God, he argues, you are discerning in the world it might not be the God of Abraham, Isaac, and Jacob. Humans do indeed walk a very narrow path between the Scylla of idolatry and Charybdis of neglecting the glory of God revealed in nature. To throw out all vestiges, however, is to my mind very puzzling. For Scripture itself, while it does guard against idolatry, does not seem to be so worried about the dangers of creation. I would argue that there are not only good reasons to reconsider the *vestigium Trinitatis,* but that Scripture itself says that the "heavens declare the glory of God, the skies the work of God's hands" (Ps 19:1).

2. *CD* I/1, 395.
3. Ibid., 396.
4. Ibid.
5. Ibid., 395.
6. Ibid., 396.
7. Ibid., 386.

The first reason why the vestiges are important, then, is that placing dogmatic theology into transversal dialogue with science gives a fuller picture of God's glory. The two ways of speaking resonate with one another. Indeed an associated reason why the vestiges are important is that if creation is not seen to reflect the trinitarian nature of God then the Trinity as opposed to the unified God is more easily neglected.

A second more apologetic reason why vestiges matter is that when theological categories are not applied to creation science alone names and defines the created order. If we cede the material world to science we cede ground to another metaphysics—the atheism of the likes of Richard Dawkins who embrace a cosmos that is the result of *only* forces acting in random or impersonal ways. Theology has in many ways abandoned nature, and seven demons have come to take up residence where one poor weak demon has been driven out. Powerful human impulses try to reconcile a theology of Word and Spirit with a scientific outlook and more often the former is trumped by the latter—or science takes over the task of natural theology and God becomes an engineer.

And it is possible that both science and religion are required to "see" nature accurately. This may well be entailed, if not directly argued in a recent interesting book by Carol Kaesuk Yoon, *The Clash between Instinct and Science*.[8] She argues that it is basic to human existence to name and observe the created world; she is bewailing the lost art of taxonomy, which is, she claims, the means by which humans have always connected with and appreciated life. "People everywhere were connected to the living world, obsessed with and fascinated by life," she says.[9] She describes how people with strokes will sometimes lose the ability to name living things, but will still be able to categorize the non-living world, perhaps proof that our brains have special areas for dealing with life. She thinks this is why we can live in the midst of a "a mass extinction that worries us hardly at all."[10] Thus, she argues, we lose the sense of life, wild life, and the power of life on its own terms.[11]

Thirdly, I tentatively argue that there is no reason why the natural world should be more of a problem than Scripture in terms of balance in interpretation. Everything depends upon the way in which we attend

---

8. Yoon, *Naming Nature*
9. Ibid., 52.
10. Ibid., 282.
11. Ibid., 284.

to revelation. The natural world is like the Word of God itself; it is veiled and partially hidden (Isa 45:15); only by means of the Spirit's impartation are we able to see it with the unity of focus that compels belief.

This too needs to be placed in context, to be modified. There is something almost miraculous about seeing nature as a window to God, or seeing nature as it is intended to be in itself, but this can't be as miraculous as both Barth and Paul Molnar present it when, for instance, Barth says that "miracle is thus an attribute of revelation,"[12] or Molnar says "this is exactly why revelation meets us as a mystery and a miracle."[13] If all revelation of God were such a miracle then Christians with this remarkable added extra would surely make much more of a difference in the world than they do. Christian seeing is very uneven, with respect to both forms of revelation. And for 50,000 to 200,000 years before Abraham, let alone Christ, humans interacted with God, and nature and imagination were presumably their primary sources. Moreover, if God has made us to interact with Godself then we have this capacity in a somewhat natural way—it is a natural instinct as Jonathan Edwards says—even if it is often denied or broken or inverted.[14] In what follows, then, I will look at three ways of finding vestigial trinities within nature.

The Naïve Physical Analogies

At one level vestiges can be somewhat arbitrary, like Anselm's analogies of the spring, the stream, and the lake all forming the greater Nile.[15] Gregory of Nyssa used the analogies of the chain and the rainbow—in the rainbow, which is one phenomenon, there are nevertheless discernible many colors. In the chain each part is ineffective except that it be a part of the whole. Nevertheless many of these analogies are not essentially analogies of three-in-oneness, but rather an illustration of the whole and the parts.

We might also think of other contenders for vestiges: the three dimensions of space, later to be expanded into four in Einsteinian physics, and now possibly into ten dimensions with string theory. There are

12. CD I/2, 63–64.
13. Molnar, *Divine Freedom*, 40.
14. Edwards, "Nature of True Virtue," 565.
15. Evans, "St Anselm's Images of the Trinity," 46–47.

certainly still only three dimensions of physical freedom but to emphasize these now appears arbitrary.[16] Nevertheless at the other end of reality from God, at the level of the smallest entities we can find, there are groups of three quarks which constitute the basic subatomic particles—the neutron and the proton. In this case, bunches or groups does not do justice to the dynamic dance of energy that models perichoresis as well as three-in-oneness—perhaps one of the best of all plain illustrations or marks of the Trinity. Even in biology there is a vestigial threeness, and a sense of anticipation. Simon Conway Morris, for instance, in describing the forward impulse of evolution describes it thus:

> In the lancelet worm the brain can only be described as a disappointment. And has no obvious sign in terms of its morphology of even the beginnings of the characteristic threefold division seen in the vertebrate brain of hind, mid and fore sections. Yet the molecular evidence ... suggests, that, cryptically, the brain of this worm has regions equivalent to the tripartite division seen in the vertebrates. The clear implication of this is that folded within the seemingly simple brain of amphioxus [the worm] is what can almost be described as a template for the equivalent organ of the vertebrates.[17]

None of these images is so compelling that there would be any temptation to build a theology or an image of a trinitarian God around these insights—nor to be confident that three-in-oneness characterized reality. Yet the parallels are interesting to believers, as is the fact that increasing knowledge in some ways brings better analogies. One begins to think that something is going on. Something threefold and interrelated is a characteristic of reality as we know it because it is made to reflect the being of God.

Trinitarian Love and Relatedness

A second category of vestige looks upon all relatedness as somehow reflecting trinitarian love and relationality, not necessarily anything particularly triune. I turn first to three theologians from the tradition:

---

16. Three is not nearly as remarkable a number as e and pi and I, and phi, which are of importance in physics and mathematics. Nevertheless 111 in base 2 is 7, which is a perfect number.

17. Morris, *Life's Solution*, 6.

Augustine, Bonaventure, and Jonathan Edwards, or to those who have used their work. These three were confident of seeing God in nature and have since been used in the interests of an ecological theology.

First, Jonathan Edwards (1703–58) had a gift of seeing "images and shadows" of divine things in nature. This is in part, of course, because his Reformed theology had a ready answer in the fall of humanity for all evil or imperfections discerned in nature. He read nature as an array of symbols and sacraments only very dimly hiding the emanating radiance of God's glory. God was evident in creation much as is "the abundant, extensive emanation and communication of the fullness of the sun to innumerable beings that partake of it."[18]

At a lower level this was evident in what Edwards called secondary beauty, in the symmetries and convergences of a petal within a flower, in the fit and proportions of architecture and machinery.[19] The virtuous person was affected by these lower level beauties—perhaps at what we would call a tacit level—sensing in them the reflection of God. "Secondary beauty affects the mind more than trivial matters do," says Edwards.[20] The godly person was able to discern the spiritual and benevolent in these symmetries and agreements. At a higher level this was exhibited by the conformities in a New England town or of a human society. He says, for instance, "So there is a beauty in the virtue called justice, which consists in the agreement of different things that have relation to one another, in nature, manner, and measure: and therefore is the very same sort of beauty with uniformity and proportion which is observable in those external and material things that are esteemed beautiful."[21] While admitting lower forms of perfection, Edwards was nevertheless willing to see the signs of God in the slightest of creatures or artefacts; the spider and its web aroused his particular curiosity. He goes on to say: "The whole material universe is preserved by gravity, or attraction, or the mutual tendency of all bodies to each other. One part of the universe is hereby made beneficial to another. The beauty, harmony and order, regular progress, life and motion, and in short, all

---

18. Edwards, "Nature of True Virtue," 530.
19. Edwards, "True Virtue," 568.
20. Ibid., 567.
21. Ibid., 569.

the well being of the whole frame, depends on it. This is a type of love or charity in the spiritual world."[22]

Indeed for Edwards it is a kind of virtue to perceive these images in nature, and to see them and the unity of their proportion and symmetry as in some sense reflecting the inner love within the Trinity itself, the Being of beings.[23] The Trinity is the epitome of love, being the perfection of consent to being within the Godhead. Edwards, says Wallace Anderson, "portrayed reality as the emanation, the 'breathing forth' of God. The word and idea were somehow unified in an epistemological, metaphysical, and even ontological sense, and conveyed the larger, underlying unity of God and creation."[24]

A second earlier example of this confidence is found in the vestiges in Saint Bonaventure (1221–1274), an Italian Franciscan, who perhaps came closer to a contemporary ecological consciousness when he saw something similar to Edwards, but in a non-hierarchical vision of all creatures perfectly in their own ways relating to God. Bonaventure was convinced that all animals reflect the wisdom of God. The fecundity and love of the Trinity is manifest also in the creation, and every creature in its own perfection bears the mark, the exemplary mark of its creator (he calls this *contuition*). Denis Edwards describes how for Bonaventure the whole creation was bound together in love, the love that belongs especially to the Holy Spirit in the Trinity.[25]

A third example comes from a discussion of vestiges in Augustine by A. N. Williams. Williams argues that if we examine the whole breadth of Augustine's work we will see that he, like Barth, was concerned lest attention to nature be idolatrous. Augustine thought it foolish also to argue to God from the natural world. Nevertheless, says Williams, "the vestigial are a tool for penetrating belief and grasping it yet more fully, not a means for establishing the content of faith independently of, or prior to, Scripture." [26]

---

22. Edwards, *Images or Shadows of Divine Things*, 79.

23. Edwards, "True Virtue," 557, 550.

24. Anderson, "Editor's Introduction," 26.

25. Denis Edwards discusses the role of Bonaventure in *Jesus the Wisdom of God*, 101–10.

26. Williams, "Contemplation: Knowledge of God in Augustine's *De Trinitate*," 123.

Indeed Williams argues that Augustine was producing ahead of his time a spiritual theology, one that was interested in the linking of knowledge and love. Augustine was arguing that contemplation of nature can be linked to love, because love is a force that binds the world together. Williams says, "If the vestigial are read together with the doctrine of God elaborated in Books I–VIII, the *De Trinitate* yields a distinctively Christian understanding of the knowledge of God rather than the generic conclusions of a natural theology. According to this model, the relation of trinitarian persons to one another, and the relation of God and humanity, are relations constituted by knowledge and love. Knowledge, like love, is a unitive force, . . . thus knower is bound to known, lover to the beloved, and knowledge and love are united to one another."[27]

Thus Augustine's theology, argues Williams, is a theology that unites the "systematic" and the "mystical" in theology,[28] it draws us to contemplation, which "forms the very substance of paradise,"[29] it connects "knowledge of this life and that of the next," and is centrally connected with truth.[30] Far from leading us astray, then, the vestiges, properly understood, can draw us to God and to the life of the Christian. This is because Augustine believed that we can participate in God, and that love is a force, uniting us to God and to other forms of life.[31]

These trinitarian relational visions of nature give us a view of creation as bearing the traces and imprint of divinity, the interconnectedness of all being gives us glimpses of God's love, especially if conformity and attractive powers and interconnection can be understood as forms of love. They require a way of seeing, which I will discuss later, a way of seeing that sees the whole and discerns the reason for the whole against the parts. This type of vestigial awareness is very far from the idolatry about which Barth is concerned. For nature becomes a means to glimpse the very glory that Scripture itself says is revealed if we have eyes to see it.

John Polkinghorne is the contemporary example of this second kind of vestigial theology. He is writing at a time when physics has be-

27. Ibid.
28. Ibid., 145.
29. Ibid., 140.
30. Ibid.
31. Ibid., 123.

come strange enough that the modernist mechanical view of nature has been eclipsed. He says that the developments "in relational and holistic thinking that are taking place within the fold of science are deeply congenial to trinitarian ways of thought. They by no means 'prove' the Trinity, but they are profoundly consonant with a theology of nature that sees the relation of perichoretic exchange between the divine Persons as lying at the heart of the Source of all created reality."[32] Polkinghorne embraces this interconnectedness, evident in both contemporary physics and in biology, and especially in phenomena like entanglement—or the ongoing linkage of one particle with another long after they have separated and are beyond causal communication—as a vestige of the love and relationality of the Trinity.[33]

Another similar example is the strangeness and connecting power of water. In a remarkable article, in April 2006 *New Scientist* Robert Matthews talks about the scientific discoveries of the effects of water that "transcend chemistry," of quantum effects in water "that make even the wackiest New Age ideas seem ho-hum."[34] These odd properties of water are necessary for life, and water is the only liquid that has them. The weak bonds between hydrogen molecules in water are responsible for water's odd and life giving properties, making it a "seething melee of order and disorder." These quantum effects are also responsible for a phenomenon known as "zero-point vibrations," which are fuelled by "energy from empty space" and result in the unusual cohesion and life-giving qualities of water. Water changes its properties around the surface of DNA, providing a communication matrix of moving protons and electrostatic charges. So water, which is so symbolically important in faith, is also mysterious and is the connective power that makes life and communication possible.[35]

This deep interconnectedness and anticipatory character rather than any particular threeness is thought to reflect the Godhead and Trinity. Polkinghorne also speaks, though, of the veiledness of reality in spite of its fruitfulness and its openness to the future.[36] This reality, always puzzling us, always requiring interpretation, always challenging

32. Polkinghorne, *Science and the Trinity*, 75.
33. Ibid., 73–74.
34. Matthews, "Water: The Quantum Elixir," 32–37.
35. Ibid.
36. Polkinghorne, *Science and the Trinity*, 76.

our intuitions, is very different from the mechanical models of the past that we could too easily claim to control and understand (though the mechanical universe was once delighted in as evidence of God). Yet fruitfulness, openness to the future, and veiledness are all are qualities of revelation in Word as well as in nature.

Semiotic Trinitarian Vestiges

A third form of vestige is least arbitrary and more connected to the interplay of threeness. The beginnings of this approach are evident in Augustine's famous triad of memory, understanding, and will in the make-up of the human being. In the mid twentieth century Dorothy Sayers saw the creative activity of humans as reflecting a trinitarian structure. She even described scalene trinities, works of art dominated by too much father, too much son, or an excess of spirit.[37]

In the nineteenth century C. S. Peirce (1839–1914) developed a deeper semiotic threeness which Andrew J. Robinson in a paper in *Zygon* has recently adapted as a trinitarian vestigial model.[38] This is of great interest because signs and interpretation are everywhere and everywhere characterize life. The most primitive cell, for instance, harbors DNA and RNA, and is a complex entity kept alive by chemical messengers and genetic and biochemical interactions carrying and relaying information from the cell interior to its cytoplasm and from the environment to the cell as a whole.

Peirce was impressed with the way in which signs pervade the universe, especially in the domain of life—in DNA and in immunology for instance. Robinson explains how Peirce developed a triadic semiotics of three elements, "a *repre-sentamen* which stands for an object and does so by means of an *interpretant*."[39] The whole universe, says Peirce, "is perfused with signs, if not composed exclusively of signs."[40] These elements form three categories: of firstness, having an underived quality; of secondness, which follows from or represents or makes visible the first; and thirdness, having a quality of mediation between the first two.[41]

37. Sayers, *Mind of the Maker*.
38. Robinson, "C. S. Peirce as a Resource for a Theology of Evolution," 111–36.
39. Ibid., 115.
40. Quoted by Robinson in ibid.
41. Ibid., 116.

Peirce himself adapted his semiotics to evolutionary theory. He was unhappy at the Darwinian description of evolution in terms of chance alone; rather this level of change was understood as unconstrained or corresponding to firstness. The constraints on the process corresponding to secondness, and thirdness, explains Robinson, is "a prerequisite for semiosis," or meaning, and hence is a maker of communication, life, freedom, and love.[42] Robinson (and Pierce) conclude that because God is love, growth comes from love, and is evident in the ubiquity of signs.[43]

For Pierce, then, creation consisted of all these elements, something unconstrained, appearing almost random, something constrained or working against the chaos, and something equivalent to life and love which is of the essence of communication. One might only see the process at the level of chaos but these other dimensions were always there if one's eyes were opened.

Robinson adapts these categories to the obvious parallels of Father, Son/Word, and Spirit. Semiosis, or the web of interconnecting signs, is perichoresis.[44] Humans are the sign-makers *par excellence* of course. We know we make signs or triads, and no sooner do we have a triadic unit of meaning than we use this triad as a building block to a further triad, and so forth until we have attempted to understand the universe. Animals are more limited but just as truly sign makers and interpreters. Life is characterized by this deep trinitarian nature, as is appropriate to a creation formed by Word and life by Spirit.

This third form of vestige is interesting because it seems to fill the universe of life. These signs are intimately associated with the possibility of life and are deeply trinitarian. In the human being, where the interpretation is conscious, they are associated with the self-reflexive nature of language that seems to touch the heart of the mystery of being and of being human. All creation speaks and yet only humans desire to interpret it all, to connect with creation and to understand it, and sometimes to possess and control it. And this reflexivity is the vestigial character most intimately connected with three-in-oneness, and with the hints of God—for the communication and the semiotic relatedness

---

42. Ibid., 118
43. Ibid.
44. Ibid., 124.

occur in animals and life forms that cannot initiate and reproduce this semiotic character as do humans.

This third type of vestige is also interesting because in evolutionary terms the secondness and thirdness are what is most controversial. Whether there is information—especially in the genome—is a category most debated in biology and cosmology today. Similarly the constraints on the evolutionary process are not universally embraced, but if they were to be so counted this would effectively mean a paradigm change in evolutionary thinking.

Are these vestiges distracting, directing our gaze away from God towards the creature as Barth feared might happen? I would argue that they do not. They help to unify our scientific and our theological knowing. We can have some sort of comfort that a trinitarian God has been present to the creatures and to humans in a trinitarian way from the beginning. All sorts of things do distract us from God, but I would nominate our highly developed tendencies to abstraction from things and our technology as more problematic than the theological discussion of traces of God in the world. In this category of distractions might be social and theological constructions that are out of touch with and in complete disagreement with biological facts as we know them—for instance deconstructive images of personhood, which deny the thick evolutionary biological givenness of persons, and the social-contract view of society, which denies the highly social character of primate communities.

I would argue that ultimately these vestiges perform a quite different function. They keep in mind a view of the world that can be seen through a number of different lenses. Vestiges may have been more of a danger within the modernist worldview, which imagined the universe as a grand machine and nothing more, encouraging us to have a sense of control and ownership. But we do not need to look far to be impressed with the revelatory nature of the natural world, sometimes its triadic arrangements, its deep interconnectedness and relationality and its semiotic character. Not only do the heavens declare the glory of God, but as Meister Eckhart says, "if you like it or not, if you know it or not: secretly, from inside, the whole of nature reaches after God."[45] Scripture, on the other hand, is often interpreted in a way that does seem to control the God of Abraham, Isaac, and Jacob, holding too heavily to

---

45. Meister Eckhart, "Into the Godhead," 168.

strictly defined dogma and not countenancing the place of culture and situation in the interpretation of Scripture.

Human Consciousness and the *Vestigium*

I want therefore, to return to human consciousness, where discernment of God begins. What is it that enables us and also hinders us in our search for God whether it is in revelation or in nature? On the one hand many theologians in the past have pointed to the particular place in which humanity stands, as priests, facing down to the world and up towards God. Yet we can choose to look in only one direction. It was Schleiermacher who described the religious consciousness as "seeing all things in and through the infinite."[46] This surely, is exactly what is required to see the vestiges of God in the natural world.

John Haught speaks to this when he says: "Likewise if you are going to be able to see any meaning in nature you would have to learn to relax your attention to its separate parts. In fact, the more you focus on atoms, molecules, cells or other entities, the less you will be able to discern any overarching meaning in their togetherness in the universe. To see the purpose of anything requires that you attend *from* the particulars *to* the overall meaning."[47]

Nevertheless, whatever God is is not to be objectified and controlled like any other object of our consciousness. Thus we might look briefly at a specific aspect of the creation as evidence of the trace of God, but it is not itself God, only a sideways look at such—like the burning bush. Otherwise, as Barth claimed, traces will be a Trojan horse, smuggling in a grammar for God that is just the human writ large. Some of what counts for "intelligent design" is doing this. These glimpses we get from the creation are just that, small snatches of an enormous, perhaps infinite symphony. We catch a tune, a harmony here and there. When we see it otherwise, as almost mapping the entirety of reality, we confuse God with the creation as Barth feared.

On the other side are examples of inability. The articulate prophets of this unreligion are Stephen J. Gould, Steven Weinberg, and Richard Dawkins. Dawkins is famous for saying: "The universe we observe has precisely the properties we should expect if there is, at bottom, no de-

---

46. Schleiermacher, *On Religion*, 36.
47. Haught, *Is Nature Enough?* 123.

sign, no purpose, no evil and no good, nothing but blind, pitiless indifference.... DNA neither cares nor knows. DNA just is. And we dance to its music."[48] And Steven Weinberg's equally famous comment: "the more the universe seems comprehensible, the more it also seems pointless."[49] It can only be remarked that vestigial theology stands in stark contrast to the very secular view we have of nature—that it has come to be by a random indifference to any purpose or direction and by the forces of survival alone.

What Edwards, Bonaventure, and C. S Peirce see of God's revelation Gould, Dawkins, and Weinberg cannot see. Evidence, for instance, Gould's famous words: "I would nominate as most worthy of pure awe the continuity of the tree of earthly life for 3.5 billion years, without a single microsecond of disruption."[50] In this case Gould's awe stands for absence, the absence of an awareness of the love that is holding all things together—or of anything acting at the level of secondness or thirdness. Gould is in awe because the universe continues in the absence of the meaning that is holding the universe together. Without this love and with only meaninglessness, he is understandably but very insightfully overwhelmed that the evolutionary process continues on, driven by randomness and by contingency.

Physics and mathematics, however, as well as giving us tantalizing glimpses of structure and beauty undergirding physical reality as we know it, also give us paradox. Whatever is going on, and however many machine-like structures and information-giving molecules there are in life and in nature these do not give us a comprehensive account of a reality that is reduced to puzzlement and paradox around the edges.

Life and wisdom as the two hands of God make sense of the truth that Jonathan Edwards and Bonaventure grasped: that love is at the center of things, that when a few created things correlate or are in harmony there is a little glimpse of love. When a unity in diverse parts is discerned, that is a hint of the love that most characterizes the trinitarian God, as Jonathan Edwards suggested. It makes sense of the experience of the mystics that when our consciousness briefly becomes attuned to the way things really are then love is not just experienced but becomes reality, albeit briefly. Vestigial theology, however, can bring the concepts

48. Dawkins, *River Out of Eden*, 133.
49. Weinberg, *First Three Minutes*, 154.
50. Gould, "I Have Landed," 46.

of wisdom and spirit from the grammar of God and into the grammar of creation in such a way that God is kept in focus when we are thinking of the created world, even while we might go to Scripture for the story and the more perfect picture of the triune God. But there remains a hiddenness to these dimensions of being. It is still possible, with Gould, to see the process as entirely random and entirely contingent and then to wonder at its continuation through three billion years without pause.

Conclusion

I have argued that we should revisit the topic of the vestiges in spite of Barth's cautions. The dangers of Barth's day are not entirely ours. We have a different problem—the abandonment of nature by theology. I have argued that seeing vestiges can strengthen faith, giving us a unity of perception that affirms faith rather than eclipsing it. Vestigial theology can be a powerful defense of a multi-layered reality that can be described and named at different emergent levels. To see the traces of the trinitarian God within the creation gives us an added sense of God's presence and glory. And vestigial theology can be an antidote to the tendency of science to distance ourselves from the creation and to control it.

Bibliography

Anderson, Wallace E. "Editor's Introduction." In *The Works of Jonathan Edwards*, vol. 11, edited by Wallace E. Anderson et al., 1–28. New Haven: Yale University Press, 1993.
Barth, Karl. *Church Dogmatics*. 4 vols. Edinburgh: T. & T. Clark, 1956–75.
Dawkins, Richard. *River Out of Eden*. New York: Basic, 1995.
Eckhart, Meister. "Into the Godhead." In *Meister Eckhart*, translated by Raymond Blakney. New York: Harper, 1941.
Edwards, Denis. *Jesus the Wisdom of God: An Ecological Theology*. Maryknoll, NY: Orbis, 1995.
Edwards, Jonathan. *Images or Shadows of Divine Things*. Edited by Perry Miller. New Haven: Yale University Press, 1948.
———. "The Nature of True Virtue." In *Jonathan Edwards' Ethical Writings*, edited by Paul Ramsey, 537–627. New Haven: Yale University Press, 1989.
Evans, Gillian R. "St Anselm's Images of the Trinity." *Journal of Theological Studies* 27 (1976) 46–57.

Gould, Stephen J. "I Have Landed." *Natural History Magazine*, January, 2001, 46–59.
Haught, John. *Is Nature Enough?* Cambridge: Cambridge University Press, 2006.
Huyssteen, J. Wentzel Van. *Alone in the World?: Human Uniqueness in Science and Theology*. Grand Rapids: Eerdmans, 2006.
Matthews, Robert. "Water: The Quantum Elixir." *New Scientist,* April 8, 2006, 32–37.
Molnar, Paul. *Divine Freedom and the Doctrine of the Immanent Trinity*. Edinburgh: T. & T. Clark, 2002.
Morris, Simon Conway. *Life's Solution: Inevitable Humans in a Lonely Universe*. Cambridge: Cambridge University Press, 2003.
Polkinghorne, John. *Science and the Trinity: The Christian Encounter with Reality*. New Haven: Yale University Press, 2004.
Robinson, Andrew J. "C. S. Peirce as a Resource for a Theology of Evolution." *Zygon* 39 (2004) 111–36.
Sayers, Dorothy. *The Mind of the Maker*. San Francisco: HarperOne, 1987.
Schleiermacher, Friedrich. *On Religion: Speeches to Its Cultured Despisers*. Translated by John Oman. New York: Harper Torchbooks, 1958.
Weinberg, Steven. *The First Three Minutes: A Modern View of the Origin of the Universe*. New York: Basic, 1993.
Williams, Anna N. "Contemplation: Knowledge of God in Augustine's *De Trinitate.*" In *Knowing the Triune God: The Work of the Spirit in the Practices of the Church*, edited by James J. Buckley and David S. Yeago, 121–46. Grand Rapids: Eerdmans, 2001.
Yoon, Carol Kaesuk. *Naming Nature: The Clash between Instinct and Science*. New York: Norton, 2009. From online excerpt in *New York Times*, August 10, 2009.

Subject Index

Apollinarianism, 14, 29, 208, 346
Apologetics, 22–26, 31, 45, 257
Appropriations, 165, 184, 211, 221–40, 316–20, 329
Arianism, 116

Cappadocians, 87–89, 95, 98–99, 112–13, 181–82, 184, 298–99, 303
Christology / Christ, xii, 13, 24, 25, 34, 49, 56–59, 87–117, 121–36, 139, 143, 152–54, 157, 159, 169, 188, 204–8, 228, 231–32, 234, 238, 246, 269, 298, 307, 315, 319–22, 329, 345
Contemplation, 289, 293–94, 297–302, 302–5, 306–7, 383–84
Creation, 36–37, 41, 53–67, 70, 75, 76, 78, 81–83, 85, 143, 145, 169, 203–8, 215–18, 224–26, 229, 233, 239, 251–52, 313, 315, 318–19, 330, 368–70, 370–72, 372–74, 377–79, 382–84, 387, 389, 391
Creator, 7–8, 24, 27, 36, 63, 74, 82, 142, 149, 169, 208, 216, 226–28, 233, 251, 313, 315, 318, 367, 368–70, 377, 383

Death, 66–67, 83–84, 104–5, 108, 112, 127, 129–30, 132, 212–14, 216, 232–34, 241–53, 339, 344–345, 350, 368

Dialogue (inter-religious), 287–89, 305–8
Docetism, 29

Ecclesiology, 59–60, 221–40, 305
Economy, 10–11, 53–54, 60–61, 71, 75–79, 85, 94–97, 101, 111, 122, 139–40, 144–45, 151–55, 157, 159, 164, 166–68, 170, 172, 175–76, 187, 190, 192, 197, 204–7, 210–13, 215, 222–24, 260, 266–67, 275, 289, 291, 294–99, 301, 305–7, 316, 319, 323, 329, 341, 344–48, 365
Election, 56–57, 60, 65, 90, 102, 110, 113–15, 121–36, 138–40, 142–47, 151–52, 155, 159, 215, 278, 319
Epistemology, 3–45, 93, 104, 122–23, 123–28, 130, 188, 227–28, 231, 261, 268, 270, 273–78, 298, 317, 383
Eschatology, 44–45, 84–85, 216–18, 247, 249, 251, 252–53, 293, 373
Ethics, 59, 221, 228–32, 239, 355–75
Experience, 4, 6, 7–11, 12–13, 35, 37, 39, 43, 45, 50, 58, 67, 79, 90–91, 99, 108, 134, 243–44, 248–49, 260, 265, 288, 289–96, 297–304, 321, 334, 340, 342, 344, 345, 347–52

Subject Index

Faith, 4, 6, 7–13, 14–15, 17–19, 20–21, 23–26, 26–32, 37–41, 43–45, 49–50, 60–61, 63, 66, 92, 134, 205, 207–8, 215, 217–18, 232, 234, 234, 255, 257, 263, 298, 304–6, 321–23, 326, 338–39, 362–64, 369–70, 383, 385, 391

Filioque, 161–200

Freedom, 11, 16, 21, 22–23, 25–26, 28–33, 36, 38, 43–44, 50–58, 61, 65, 73, 77, 80, 81–82, 93, 95, 96, 101, 104, 110, 112–13, 115–16, 123, 126–27, 129, 132–35, 145, 150, 156, 158, 164, 230, 261, 263, 273, 276, 278, 280, 291, 314–15, 321, 324–28, 334, 343, 346, 358, 360, 374, 377

Genus Majestaticum / Tapeinoticum, 105–7, 157–58

Homoousion / Ousia / Sein, 88, 94, 98, 116, 148–50, 155, 166, 169–70, 179–84, 191, 301, 320–21

Hypostases / *Seinsweisen*, 53, 59, 64, 79, 80, 95, 112, 123, 142, 157, 166, 170, 172–74, 184–87, 191, 193, 298, 320–21

Hypostatic union, 105, 231, 347–48, 351

Immanent (being of God), 54, 57, 58, 60, 71, 75, 79, 82, 94–97, 101, 111, 114, 122, 134–35, 144–45, 151, 153–55, 157, 159, 164, 167–68, 172, 175, 176, 187, 190, 192, 193, 197, 266, 291, 294, 295–301, 305–7, 318, 341

Immensity, 65–66, 72, 74, 76–77

Immutability, 104–5, 108, 114, 135, 214, 216, 332–53

Impassibility, 106, 116, 332–53

Jesus
  as light, 66
  incarnate limitations, 77
  as the intersection of divine and creaturely space, 83–84
  two natures, 104–5
  as eternally in God's being, 132–33

Judgment, 8, 44–45, 61, 127, 207, 213, 216, 232–33, 242–45, 253

Justification, 12, 17, 21, 25, 28, 38, 40–41, 232–35, 238, 245

Kenoticism, 106, 124–26, 139, 157–58

Knowledge (of God), 3–45, 49–56, 60–1, 63–64, 67, 84, 91, 94, 96, 100–2, 103–4, 114, 125, 130, 133, 135, 151, 183, 212, 221, 223, 226–28, 267, 270, 275, 277–78, 280, 290, 292–94, 296, 297, 301, 303–5, 307–8, 318, 322–24, 326–28, 359, 363–66, 369–70, 377–78, 381, 384, 388

Light, 12, 17, 40, 48–68

Logos, 35, 37, 93, 104, 106–7, 116, 135, 209, 261

Logos Asarkos / Logos Incarnandus, 132–34, 136, 144, 154–55, 157–58

Monarchy, 166–167, 180–83, 187, 189–94, 196, 198–99

Naming God, 11, 37, 55, 67, 79, 88, 97, 111, 133, 135, 141,

Subject Index   395

196, 203, 209, 289, 290–94,
   295–99, 301, 306, 327, 337
Natural theology, 4–6, 11–13, 15,
   24, 29, 37, 45, 178, 253, 257,
   276, 325, 329, 379, 334
Nestorianism, 77, 104, 116
Nicene Creed / theology, 8, 115–16,
   135, 140, 176–78, 186, 188,
   271

Omnipresence, 51, 73–76, 78, 83,
   105, 314
Open Theism, 333–35

Perfections—divine, 49–54, 63–65,
   74, 76, 209–10, 215, 216, 275,
   314, 334–37, 341–42, 344–46
Perichoresis, 34, 61, 79–80, 98–99,
   169, 171–72, 174, 180–84,
   189–90, 194, 197–98,
   222–23, 227, 229, 236, 298,
   316–18, 320, 337, 340,
   348–53, 360, 363–68, 381,
   385, 387
Prayer, 30, 203, 247, 255–81
Procession, 162–70, 171, 193–99

Reason, 5–6, 7–11, 13, 17, 36–37,
   45, 63, 305, 325
Reconciliation, xi, 7, 14, 16, 17,
   20–21, 26–27, 31, 35, 43, 50,
   52, 57–59, 61, 64–65, 83, 103,
   130, 138–39, 143, 146, 149,
   153, 156, 169, 205, 207, 208–
   10, 212–13, 215–17, 223, 225,
   227, 229–32, 233–35, 238,
   251, 275, 311–16, 319–20,
   322–23, 329–30, 342, 365,
   370–74
Redemption, 16, 18, 24, 28, 52,
   54, 64, 65, 67, 82, 84, 91,
   107, 123, 164, 206–8, 215,
   223, 225, 227, 229–31, 238,
   245–247, 293, 295, 311–16,

319–20, 322, 329–30, 349,
   365, 372–74
Revelation, xiv, 4–5, 11–18, 21–28,
   30–33, 36–42, 44, 48–62,
   65, 67, 76–79, 83, 85, 87, 89,
   90–97, 101–5, 108–9, 111,
   114, 121, 123–31, 142–43,
   147–48, 150, 153, 155–56,
   164–66, 170, 172, 175–76,
   187, 190, 191–93, 197,
   204–10, 212, 215–16, 218,
   221–22, 224, 226–28, 230,
   232, 234, 245, 264–65,
   268–79, 287–88, 291–96,
   298, 301, 311–19, 321–23,
   325, 327, 329–30, 348, 359,
   361–56, 368, 370–80, 384,
   386, 388–90
Roman Clarification (1995), 171

Soteriology / Salvation, 9–10, 30,
   50, 60, 71, 92, 109, 122–25,
   139–40, 170, 190, 192, 203–
   19, 224, 252–53, 278, 289,
   294–95, 299, 319, 321–23,
   325–26, 329, 344–46, 348–53
Space-time, 311–16, 321–23, 327,
   330
Spatiality (between creatures and
   God), 80–84
Spatiality (in God), 70–80, 84–85,
   314–15
Speech about (speaking of) God,
   8, 11–12, 14, 32, 34–35, 37,
   42, 44, 50, 57, 61–62, 71, 75,
   83, 85, 95, 114, 116, 123, 170,
   205, 208, 222–24, 226–27,
   229, 235–37, 265–66, 279,
   287, 289–90, 290–94, 294–
   96, 297–302, 305–7, 315, 318,
   358, 363, 377, 379
Spirit, 3–45, 51, 54, 58–60, 63,
   66–67, 84, 92, 96, 99, 107,
   112, 132, 161–99, 210–13,

215–16, 218, 228, 252, 302–3, 311–30, 349–50, 372–74, 380, 383
  role in our knowledge of God, 3–45
  as bringer of light, 67
  as the bringer of the presence of God, 84
  as the empowerer of Jesus' actions, 107
  in Barth's *Church Dogmatics*, 316–20
  involvement in the life of Christ, 168
Subordination, 97, 110, 138–59, 167, 170, 172, 174, 179, 184, 187, 190, 192
Suffering, 104–8, 109–10, 127, 129–32, 145–48, 150, 159, 244, 299, 334–44, 347–48, 348–53

Trinity
  Catholic influence on Barth's doctrine of, 88
  constitution of persons, 80, 194–99, 337
  Barth's derivation of, 92–97
  Barth's doctrine of, 97–102, 121–36, 141–59, 170–74, 270–78, 362–66
  use of numbers to describe, 99–100
  reconstructing Barth's doctrine of, 102–13
  Social Trinity, 264–65
  as a stumbling block to dialogue, 287–308
  vestiges of, 377–92

Universalism, 139–40

Word, 7, 11, 13, 15–17, 19, 22–32, 34, 36, 37, 39–45, 48, 61–63, 70–71, 77, 84, 87, 107–8, 111, 115, 122, 128, 132–33, 141, 143, 153, 163, 165, 169, 174, 182, 192, 196, 224, 235, 265, 275, 295, 313–14, 321, 360, 361, 370, 371, 373, 379–80

Author Index

Althaus, Paul, 241
Anderson, Wallace, 383
Anselm, xiii, 35, 40, 53, 260, 334, 380
Aquinas, Thomas, xiii, 4–6, 88, 98, 100, 197, 235, 241, 264, 304, 324, 336–37
Athanasius, xiii, 7, 11, 36, 114, 161, 171, 179, 181–83, 186
Augustine, xiii, 72, 74, 87, 162–68, 170, 171, 173–74, 176, 179, 184–86, 211, 224–25, 235, 241, 256, 271–72, 300, 320, 325, 332, 334, 350, 351, 382–84, 386
Ayres, Lewis, 88

Baddely, Mark, 141, 148–49
Baelz, Peter, 262–63
Balthazar, Hans Urs von, 97, 125–26, 256–66
Barth, Karl, xi–xii, xiii–xv, 3–4, 7, 9, 11, 12, 13–23, 23–26, 26–33, 48–62, 68, 72–73, 75, 76–80, 80–84, 87–117, 121–36, 138–59, 161–74, 185–88, 209–10, 211–12, 215, 221–35, 241–53, 255–58, 267–81, 290–94, 296, 302–3, 305, 311–30, 339, 355–75, 377–80, 388–91
Basil, 87–89, 112
Bauckham, Richard, 344
Bauman, Zygmunt, 355–56

Beauchamp, Tom, 357
Bender, Kimlyn, 231
Benson, Herbert, 259
Biggar, Nigel, 373
Blocher, Henry, 345
Bloesch, Donald, 175, 343
Boff, Lenoardo, 198
Bonaventure, 383, 390
Bray, Gerald, 175
Bromiley, Geoffrey, 150
Brown, Harold, 333, 336, 342
Brummer, Vincent, 257–81
Brunner, Emil, 325
Brunner, Peter, 253
Buckley, Michael, 262
Bultmann, Rudolf, 72, 251
Burgess, Andrew, 203–19
Burrell, David, 260, 264
Busch, Eberhard, 272, 320
Byrd, Randolf, 259

Calvin, John, xiii, 40, 130, 161, 174, 179, 183, 189, 250, 334, 362–63
Carson, Donald, 333
Chemnitz, Martin, 105
Chia, Roland, 225
Chung, Miyon, 172
Coakley, Sarah, 265, 289, 304, 305
Coffey, David, 188
Collins, Paul, 89, 97–99, 113, 114, 271, 273
Colyer, Elmer, 177
Congar, Yves, 178

Author Index

Cottrell, Jack, 336
Crisp, Oliver, 252
Cumin, Paul, 250

Dalferth, Ingolf, 205, 217, 218
Davidson, Ivor, 48–69
Dawkins, Richard, 379, 389–90
D'Costa, Gavin, 189
Deddo, Gary, 177
Dell Colle, Ralph, 185
Dodds, Michael, 342
Dorner, Isaak A., 98

Eckhart, Meister, 388
Edwards, Denis, 383
Edwards, Jonathon, 380, 382–83, 390
Erickson, Millard, 175, 342–43, 348–49
Evans, Gillian, 380

Farrow, Douglas, 189, 252–53
Fiddes, Paul, 334, 340, 344, 349
Flasch, Kurt, 304
Funkenstein, Amos, 257–58

Gallup, George, 259
Geach, Peter, 262
Giles, Kevin, 138–39, 140–51
Glading, Antony, 311–30
Gockel, Matthias, 139
Goebel, Hans Theodor, 94
Gonzalez, Justo, 348
Gould, Stephen, 390
Gregory of Nazianzus, 8, 87–88, 179, 181, 336
Gregory of Nyssa, 88, 99, 298, 301, 304, 336, 380
Grenz, Stanley, 10, 175, 268
Greshake, Gisbert, 300
Grosche, Robert, 88
Grube, Dirk-Martin, 296
Gundlach, Thiess, 94
Gunther, Anton, 100

Gunton, Colin, xiii, 54, 80, 82, 203, 209, 210, 233, 237, 303, 325, 237, 341, 343
Guretski, David, 163–77, 185–88

Habets, Myk, 161–202
Hall, Christopher, 333
Hart, David Bentley, 101
Haught, John, 389
Healy, Nicholas, 5, 231, 237–38
Hegel, Georg, 56, 87, 91–92, 100, 105, 125–27, 217, 219, 269
Heidegger, Martin, 38, 184, 250
Helm, Paul, 277
Hendry, George, 171–72
Heron, Alasdair, 171
Hodge, Charles, 339, 342
Hoggard-Creegan, Nicola, 377–91
Holmes, Christopher R. J., 55, 65
Holtmann, Stefan, 124
Hunsinger, George, 57, 62, 114, 121, 126, 139, 163, 234, 238, 272, 275, 277, 311, 317, 319–20, 322–26, 329
Huyssteen, J. Wentzel, 77

Janowski, J. Christine, 295
Jenson, Robert, 80, 98, 171, 203, 214, 241–42, 245–53, 318–19, 323
John of Damascus, 350
Johnson, Elizabeth, 9–11, 295
Johnson, William, Stacy xiv
Jones, L. Gregory, 259–60
Jones, Paul Dafydd, 139, 140, 152–53
Jowers, Dennis, 151
Jüngel, Eberhard, 236, 241, 256, 272, 278, 291, 299, 317, 340–41, 343, 350

Kaiser, Christopher, 338, 342
Kant, Immanuel, 79–80, 92
Katz, Steven, 288

Kelly, John, 99
Kerr, Fergus, 304
Kerr, Nathan, 269
Kierkegaard, Søren, 72
Kilby, Karen, 265
Krotke, Wolf, 69
Küng, Hans, 72

Laats, Alar, 151, 173-74, 274
LaCugna, Catherine, 197, 224, 257, 267, 281, 295, 301
Lash, Nicholas, 260, 266, 279
Lesniewski, Krzysztof, 304
Letham, Robert, 149-51, 172-74, 333
Lewis, Peter, 344
Link, Christian, 290-94, 296
Link-Wieczorek, Ulrike, 237-308
Lombard, Peter, 88

MacKenzie, Ian, 74-75, 77-78
Mackey, James, 265
Mangina, Joseph, 318
Marquardt, Friedrich-Wilhelm, 294
Marshall, Bruce, 259
Martyn, J. Louis, 125
Matthews, Robert, 385
Maurer, Ernstpeter, 301, 303-4
McCabe, Herbert, 265
McCormack, Bruce, 56-57, 61, 87-119, 121-28, 135, 139, 153, 157-58
McDowell, John, 255-81
McFague, Sally, 219
McGrath, Alister, 12, 277
McIntosh, Adam, 221-40, 316-20, 329
McIntyre, James, 179
McKim, Donald, 334
Menke-Peitzmeyer, Michael, 125
Migliore, Daniel, 255, 257
Miskotte, Kornelius Heiko, 292

Molnar, Paul, 3-47, 57, 121, 126, 128, 133-36, 139, 151, 185, 380
Moltmann, Jürgen, 87, 92, 98, 122-24, 130-31, 133, 135-36, 173, 182, 185, 265, 269, 272, 274-76, 300-301, 303-4
Morris, Simon, 381
Murray, John Courtney, 4-6
Myers, Benjamin, 121-37

Nelson, Haydn, 332-53
Nestorius, 77, 104, 116
Neuser, Wilhelm, 88

O'Collins, Gerald, 343, 350
O'Grady, Colin, 231
Ormerod, Neil, 188, 201, 235

Packer, J. I., xiv-xv
Pannenberg, Wolfhart, 23-26, 90-91, 175, 269, 271, 272
Papanikolaou, Aristotle, 303
Peirce, C. S., 386-87
Pester, John, 188
Pfleiderer, Georg, 122
Phillips, Dewi, 258, 260, 265
Pinnock, Clark H., 168, 334-35, 339, 340
Polkinghorne, John, 384-85
Poloma, Margaret, 259
Price, Charles, 185

Rae, Murray, 70-86
Rahner, Karl, 9, 140, 192, 241, 256-57, 262, 302, 296, 299, 302, 303, 345-46
Regnon, Theodore de, 256, 274
Rendtorff, Trutz, 124
Reymond, Robert, 175
Ritschl, Dietrich, 289, 297, 299
Ritter, Adolf, 301
Roberts, Richard, 268-69, 277, 278
Robichaux, Kerry, 188

Robinson, Andrew, 386-87
Rogers, Eugene, 324
Rosato, Philip, 314
Rosenzweig, Franz, 293

Sanders, John, 333, 335, 339, 340
Sayers, Dorothy, 386
Schleiermacher, Friedrich, 389
Schoonenberg, Piet, 296, 299
Skarsaune, Oskar, 333
Smail, Thomas, 171-72
Soskice, Janet, 256
Stackhouse, John, 175
Strong, Augustus, 342
Stump, Eleonore, 263
Swatos, William, 259
Swinburne, Richard, 264-65

Tavard, George, 171
Taylor, Iain, 24
Tillich, Paul, 265
Tolliday, Phillip, 138-60
Torrance, Alan, 15, 269, 277
Torrance, Thomas F., xiii, 3-4, 7-8, 11, 33-45, 59, 82, 87-88, 134, 161-62, 171, 176-88, 210, 273, 315, 346
Turcescu, Lucian, 303

Valkenberg, Pim, 287-88
van Driel, Edwin, 140
van Mastricht, Peter, 55
Vanhoozer, Kevin, 335, 347
Vogel, Heinrich, 131

Ware, Bruce, 335
Warfield, Benjamin, 189
Watson, Francis, 248
Webster, John, 59, 62, 72, 74-76, 77-78, 213, 278
Weinandy, Thomas, 171, 188-99, 336, 338, 342
Weinberg, Steven, 389-90
Williams, Anna, 383-84
Williams, Rowan, 109, 112, 121-28, 135, 174, 257, 275, 278
Wingren, Gustaf, 122-23, 277
Wohlmuth, Josef, 295, 298, 304

Yoon, Carol, 379

Zizioulas, John, 88, 112-13, 173, 303, 305

www.ingramcontent.com/pod-product-compliance
Lightning Source LLC
Chambersburg PA
CBHW071229290426
44108CB00013B/1338